FLIM-
FLAM!

FLIM-FLAM!

Psychics, ESP, Unicorns and other Delusions

by James Randi

Prometheus Books

Buffalo, New York

Except where otherwise noted,
illustrations and photographs are by the author.

Published 1982 by Prometheus Books

Library of Congress Card Catalog No. 82-60953
ISBN 0-87975-198-3

Author's Note

The author has had the good fortune to come under the influence of many kind and thoughtful people in the past five decades. Mr. Tovell taught more than physics—he taught curiosity. Elsie Freedman was more than a landlady—she was a second mother. Harry Blackstone, Sr., was not only the world's greatest magician—he was also a towering inspiration.

Many years ago I was introduced to a man whose name is familiar to millions, though he has never been interviewed on radio or television, does not give speeches, and has never accepted any of the many personal appearance invitations offered by his admirers. His column for *Scientific American* magazine attests to his erudition. His alter ego, Dr. Matrix, allows him to vicariously pursue delights that his real life—and his wife, Charlotte—will not allow. I'm thankful that he's on our side, I'm thrilled to call him friend, and I revel in the delight of his company. This book would not have been possible without his help and encouragement, and I take great pleasure in humbly dedicating it to journalist/mathematician/humorist and above all, rationalist, Martin Gardner.

Contents

Preface

The adventures of this book have been numerous. Contracted by one publisher with great enthusiasm, then passed on to a successor where it was received with somewhat less delight, and finally inherited by the eventual producers with no interest whatsoever in its future, the original hard-cover book was planned to have a first printing of 17,500 copies; it ended up being 5,000. Very shortly after it was officially released, it was declared out of print—with several thousand copies on back order, and some already paid for by would-be readers. Why?

A book so sought after should be a candidate for prompt reprinting in a business that has come upon hard times. But the harsh fact is that the market for books promoting belief in the paranormal is possibly the single greatest money-maker in publishing today, and this cannot be ignored by those who assign priorities in the publishing houses. *Flim-Flam!* was an albatross of sorts.

I have before me at this moment a huge file of letters from interested persons wanting to purchase the book. Some are school librarians—from the United States, England, Australia, South Africa, Canada, and other countries—who want as many as six copies for their library shelves. State and county library systems want even more. Teachers inquire about quantity prices with the intention of using the volume as a text or as a "required reading" item. I assure you, this is all very flattering to an amateur author.

Again, why? Why is this book in such demand? I think it is because there is so very little available in the way of rational, skeptical treatment of the supernatural/paranormal/occult atmosphere so much in evidence today. Dedicated academics have been forced to turn to the efforts of amateurs for the evidence they need to support their opinions.

Since this book was published, author Martin Gardner has presented us with another very welcome volume, *Science, Good, Bad and Bogus* (Prometheus Books, Buffalo, New York), which delves into many of the matters handled in this book. It proves, above all, that the parascientists make a great deal of noise about the criticisms they receive but do not come up with the evidence to support their complaints. As usual, Gardner makes a compelling case, and this book can only hope to echo it.

A modest number of footnotes and corrections have been incorporated in this edition. To do a thorough job would require an entirely new book. The facts as stated here have not changed; but in some cases new developments required the addition of certain comments to make this volume as up-to-date as possible.

I hope that interested readers will seek out more information of this kind and will support authors who dare to tell the truth about paranormal matters. Our reward is largely in knowing that our efforts have stimulated this kind of interest.

JAMES RANDI

Rumson, N.J.
May, 1982

Acknowledgments

Some small part of the material here included appeared originally under my name in *The Humanist, The Skeptical Inquirer, Technology Review, Science et Vie, La Recherche,* and other periodicals. To the editors who gave me permission to use the material again in this book, many thanks.

The staffs of the Monmouth County Library and the Red Bank Public Library were unstinting in their efforts to assist me.

Mr. Brian Coe, of the Kodak Museum, London, was exceedingly patient and generous with his time and expertise assisting with the Cottingley photos.

For assistance in many ways, I must thank Piero Angela, Dr. Isaac Asimov, Professor Persi Diaconis, Dr. Eric J. Dingwall, Ken Frazier, Michael Hutchinson, Professor Ray Hyman, Drs. Richard Kammann and David Marks, Professor Phil Morrison, James Oberg, Dennis Rawlins, Hugh Rawson, William Rodriguez, and Alexis Vallejo.

And Broomhilda . . .

Introduction

The Deadly Misinformation
— Isaac Asimov

Not very long ago, I attended a conference at which, among other things, the reliability of the news media as purveyors of scientific information was discussed.

One person at the conference table described, with considerable contempt, an item on a television news program which went into detail concerning someone who claimed he had perfected a perpetual motion device, one which got energy out of nowhere.

It was reported "straight." No effort was made by the news program to point out that according to the best scientific knowledge of the day such a device is flatly impossible; that any number of perpetual motion devices had been presented to the world in the past and that *not one* had really worked; that all the inventors, in *every* case, had either been honestly mistaken or were knowingly perpetrating hoaxes.

Whereupon, another person at the conference table (a reporter) grew amused. It was, he thought, excitement over nothing.

He said, "Oh, well, what harm does it do? The newspeople are merely reporting a claim and, if it doesn't work, so what? No one is damaged!"

Whereupon I leaned forward and said, "You really don't see the harm it does? The world has now been plunged into an energy crisis. The availability of energy is going down year by year, the price is going up year by year, and the underpinnings of civilization are growing weaker as a result, year by year.

"If civilization is to survive, humanity is going to have to make hard decisions and take strenuous action, and as soon as possible. We cannot continue to waste energy. We must develop alternate sources. We dare not continue to be heedless of the problem.

"And then some newsman tells tens of millions of people of a claim that energy can be obtained out of nowhere and feels no responsibility at all for telling them that the claim is undoubtedly mistaken. He leaves the public with the feeling that there is no energy crisis since we can get energy out of nowhere, and that therefore no hard decisions need be made and no strenuous action need be taken.

"That might just add the necessary amount of heedlessness that will keep humanity from solving this life-and-death problem and will therefore send civilization crashing. And *you* ask what harm it will do!"

I doubt that I impressed the fellow. He clearly had no idea of the power of his profession, or of its responsibilities. He had not plumbed the depth of the good it could do; or the evil, either. I presume he merely looked at his profession as a way to make a living.

It is not just this one small claim and this one small bit of sleazy stupidity on the part of a news program that assails us.

Never in history has humanity faced a crisis so deep, so intense, so pervasive, and so multi-faceted. There have never, till now, been so many people on Earth, so dependent on a complex technology, so burdened by its flaws, and so likely to witness a complete breakdown of that technology in a matter of decades.

If we are to pull through, we must thread our way carefully through the rapids that lie ahead. At every step, we will be depending on our knowledge, grasp and understanding of science, of its potentialities and of its limitations. If we are careless and over-hasty, we may destroy ourselves through the misuse of science. If we are forethoughtful and knowledgeable, we may find salvation through the wise use of science.

Under these circumstances, what crime is greater than that of deliberately misteaching the public about science, of deliberately misleading them, of defrauding them, of feeding and stimulating their ignorance?

Folly and fakery have always been with us, to be sure, but it has never before been as dangerous as it is now; never in history have we been able to afford it less.

At any other time in history, we would be grateful to any hard-headed realist who undertook to expose knaves and rascals, and would applaud his courage.* How much more must we express our gratitude and admiration to someone doing so now at this critical point in history.

Randi is one person who has the ability and the temperament for the job;—none better!

He has no academic credentials, and therefore no academic restrictions. He can call things as he sees them, and is not held back by professional politeness in discussing those scientists who not only fall for the paranormal, but promote it in their ignorance.

---

* It is sad that it *does* take courage, for trying to snatch folly from the minds of those who have been victimized by it is often rather like trying to snatch a bone from a dog. If human beings didn't find nonsense so attractive, there'd be no problem, for as someone once said, "Were there fewer fools, knaves would starve."

He does have a profession that is useful to his task. He is an accomplished professional magician and there is no trick or illusion that he is not aware of and prepared for—which is more than is true of those scientific innocents who, in dealing with fakery, are so eager to accept the surface appearance that they are easier to fool than children are (for children are, by nature, skeptical).

Randi has, at one time or another, assailed every wall and buttress of the vast Castle of Pseudoscience and has never pulled his punches. He has, for that reason, been called the "hitman" of the Committee for Scientific Investigation of Claims of the Paranormal (to which he and I both belong) and he doesn't completely deny the label.

Why should he? The practitioners of pseudoscientific fakery assail "conventional" science with every weapon of innuendo and falsehood they can think of, and demand that, in return, scientists be "open-minded." They may strike, in other words, but scientists must not return the blow, or even parry it.

Well, the hell with that! Randi strikes back and when the pseudoscientists howl, he knows he has hit the mark.

In a nutshell: Humanity has the stars in its future, and that future is too important to be lost under the burden of juvenile folly and ignorant superstition.

The unicorn is said to be a beast with the configuration of a horse and a long spiraled horn in the center of the forehead. Only a virgin, we are told, is able to approach a unicorn. For this and other reasons, no reliable reports exist to verify the reality of this animal.

So much for unicorns. Now for the other nonsense . . .

1

Flim-Flam!

And the crowd was stilled. One elderly man, wondering
at the sudden silence, turned to the Child and asked him
to repeat what he had said. Wide-eyed, the Child raised
his voice and said once again, "Why, the Emperor has
no clothes! He is naked!"
                                    —"The Emperor's New Clothes"

The last ten years have seen a great resurgence of interest in the paranormal. The recent proliferation of books, articles, and scientific papers about parapsychology (psi) and other supernatural phenomena surely must have set some sort of record, and the television and radio outlets have capitalized hugely on the general taste for the extraordinary by pandering shamelessly to that preference. Surveys have shown that many people strongly believe in such subjects as Kirlian photography, ESP, pyramid power, the Bermuda Triangle, and prophecy. The list is long.

Even a few otherwise responsible scientists have climbed aboard the flamboyant but rickety bandwagon as it careens noisily through this period of human history. Some, as we shall see, had to back away from their positions when the truth became evident; others still cling to their decisions and bolster them with feeble rationalizations. It is this turn of events which most fascinates me and impelled me to write this book.

I am not so much concerned with the perpetrators of the major hoaxes as I am with the strange and unexpected ways in which these hoaxes became accepted by this small minority of scientists. Such former wonder-workers as Uri Geller and Jean-Pierre Girard no longer seem to attract the attention of the academic world, though they are still of some small interest to a shrinking public. This book may extinguish that last spark.

It is evident to one who has spent thirty-five years, as I have, examining the purported wonders so well publicized in this decade, and the fallen wonders of previous periods, that there are certain traits and patterns characteristic of the breed. There is also a disturbing sameness to the "scientific" quackery used to support these claims of the supernatural—a sameness that is reflected in many scientific tragedies, some of which arose entirely in the minds of the self-deluded, and not as a result of some deft sleight of hand or psychological trickery practiced

1

by a performer. The reader will see, I am sure, that self-deception is an important element in these matters.

As I travel around lecturing about so-called paranormal powers and events, I am often confronted with the remark that "scientists have looked into this subject and established its validity." To this I reply by quoting Leon Jaroff, a senior editor of *Time* magazine, who has said, "There has not been a single properly designed, properly conducted experiment that has proven the existence of any paranormal power." I endorse that statement fully, and I will present in this book some excellent examples of just how evident this is to anyone familiar with claims of the paranormal and with the requirements of scientific inquiry.

In May 1976 a group of twenty-five scientists, authors, and scholars—and one lone conjurer—met at a symposium sponsored by the American Humanist Association and devoted to an examination of "The New Irrationalism: Antiscience and Pseudoscience." We were determined to do something about the unfounded claims of miracles and magical powers that were being supported by a few scientists and were alleged to be real scientific discoveries. The result of this meeting was The Committee for the Scientific Investigation of Claims of the Paranormal (CSICOP) and its journal, *The Skeptical Inquirer.* Briefly stated, the purposes of the CSICOP are:

- To establish a network of people interested in examining claims of the paranormal.
- To prepare bibliographies of published materials that carefully examine such claims.
- To encourage and commission research by objective and impartial inquirers in areas where it is needed.
- To convene conferences and meetings.
- To publish articles, monographs, and books that examine claims of the paranormal.
- To not reject on *a priori* grounds, antecedent to inquiry, any or all such claims, but rather to examine them openly, completely, objectively, and carefully.

This last objective implies an important principle which I have had to hammer home repeatedly to lecture audiences and to critics: The CSICOP does not deny that such things *may* exist, nor do I, personally. However, in light of my considerable experience in examining such matters, I will say that my assigned probability for the reality of paranormal powers approaches zero *very* closely. I cannot prove that these powers do *not* exist; I can only show that the evidence for them does not hold up under examination. Furthermore, I insist that the burden of proof be placed not on me but on those who assert that such phenomena exist. Unusual claims require unusual proof.

A related matter is the opposition's claim that I seek to prove that "psychics" use trickery by duplicating their wonders by trickery. I have never claimed—nor could I, as a logical person, claim—that my duplication of "psychic" feats shows that "psychics" use similar trickery. What it *does* show is that it is more rational to suspect trickery than to adopt the preposterous alternative.

We critics of supernaturalism are accustomed to having words put into our mouths by the opposition and by the media, and it is about time that we struck back. In this book I will hit as hard as I can, as often as I can, and sometimes quite bluntly and even rudely. Good manners will be sacrificed to honesty, and the Marquis of Queensbury be damned. Too long have many voices been unheard and unheeded. In these pages you will discover that logic and rationality are powerful forces that cannot be contradicted by the great volume of pseudoscientific and near-religious claptrap that the public has mistaken for fact. The tinkling noises you will hear as these pages are turned are the scales falling from many eyes. The groans are from the charlatans who are here exposed to the light of reason and simple truth. It is a light that pains them greatly.

It was fourteen years ago, during a heated discussion with a member of the parapsychology elite, that I was challenged to "put my money where my mouth is," and I've done just that. I am always in possession of my check in the amount of $10,000, payable to any person or group that can perform *one* paranormal feat of *any* kind under the proper observing conditions. Not one nickel has ever been forfeited; my money has never been safer, though many have tried to collect the prize. To date, more than six hundred people have offered to submit to tests, and only fifty-five have gotten by the preliminaries.

I must explain. Years of experience have taught me that I need not waste my time traveling to far places to deal with most contenders. I have established a method of preliminary testing that very quickly eliminates the weaker contenders, and I've never had any complaints from the losers, though they invariably drag in the usual silly cop-outs to explain their failures. But in these strange pursuits, that's to be expected.

As a professional magician who has performed in every part of the world for more than thirty years, I have endured long sessions with persons who claim to have psychic or magical abilities. There are only two kinds: those who really believe they have these powers, and those who think I am so dense that I will not detect their trickery. Both groups are wrong.

An example of the first type is Vince Wiberg, a "dowser"—one who uses a rod or other simple device to detect the presence of various materials, notably underground water and minerals. He also professes to be an "auragramist"—one who is able to diagnose ailments of the body by dowsing. Mr. Wiberg really believes in his powers, in spite of the episode related later, wherein he failed rather dramatically to demonstrate his powers. In the second class we can point out Miss Suzie Cottrell, who performed a series of card tricks that she represented as "psychic" demonstrations and was caught at it in a definitive manner. This you will also read of later in this book.

I have witnessed many so-called spiritualistic séances, mind-reading demonstrations, and various other apparent miracles. I have tried to be objective in my observations and subsequent conclusions. At the same time, I have also cast a healthily jaundiced eye upon any activity during these performances that tended to indicate conjuring methods or just plain chicanery. My eye has had quite a workout.

I have been introduced to soothsayers in Thailand who brazenly attempted to bamboozle me with a paper-switching trick that has been used by conjurers in the West for a century. Denmark produced a mountebank who tried to fiddle me with a glowing horoscope describing a paragon of virtue and steadfastness; the chart was, unknown to him, drawn from the birth date, birth hour, and birthplace of a convicted and hanged rapist who had to his additional credit a string of misdeeds ranging from philandering to assault. England produced some fascinating quacks, France abounded with pendulum swingers, and the United States and Canada provided their share of frauds as well.

Certainly, doubts have been cast upon the existence of paranormal powers since antiquity. Many "natural philosophers"—who would eventually be known as scientists when more organized systems of thought came into existence—disproved such claims many centuries ago. In 1692 a French dowser named Jacques Aymar was hired by authorities to discover a murderer by swinging a pendulum. Apparently, it was believed that guilt was detectable by this means. Aymar is said to have led the officials to a nineteen-year-old hunchback who subsequently was "broken on the wheel"—a particularly unpleasant death much favored as punishment for unpopular people like hunchbacks. Whether Aymar's success lay in the same tendency of police officials today to supply a list of suspects and then credit the "psychic" with the identification of the murderer, we will never know. But we do know that when Jacques Aymar submitted to tests administered in Paris by the Prince de Conde, he failed them all. Aymar could hardly have avoided the tests, since he had become a national celebrity and is still touted among the faithful as a powerful operator. One wonders what the executed youth thought of Aymar's reputed powers.

Aymar remained respectable for a time after his spectacular failure, but soon was driven from business by further scandal. If he were plying his trade today, he doubtless could survive easily, especially if certain befuddled scientists undertook to test him.

The use of "psychic powers" in a court of law is not confined to medieval France. The city of Watkins Glen, near Binghamton, New York, apparently believes in such powers and encourages their use in the courtroom. A conjurer named Philip Jordan, whose claim to fame is that he performs the table-tipping trick and several other stunts right out of the catalog, has been retained by the police force and the Public Defender's Office to work for them in that city. He actually sits at the right hand of the Public Defender and, by measuring the "aura" around each prospective juror, decides whether that person is suitable to serve on the jury. Incredible? The trial judge saw nothing wrong with it. Apparently the New York judicial system accepts supernatural powers as genuine and allows them to be used *in the courtroom process of determining the guilt or innocence of a defendant!* The Dark Ages have not quite ended in Watkins Glen.

Yes, the judge accepted this preposterous travesty of reason, and so did the New York Bar Association and the Tioga County Bar Association. Notified of this idiocy, both organizations defended the right of the defense attorney to call anyone he wished to assist him in an expert capacity. Expert? Expert in *what?* In magic tricks? In half-truths and deception? Did anyone bother to try to find out if Jordan actually had the ability he claimed to have? Well, *I* did—I offered to test Philip Jordan in front of the CSICOP, and my proposal was delivered to him by Bill McKee of radio station WENE. Jordan refused to answer our phone calls and letters.

McKee asked Bruno Colapietra, president of the Broome County Bar Association, for his opinion, and the following remarkable statement resulted. Said this worthy, "I think it is harmful to the dignity and traditions of the courts if it is allowed to be known." But, he added, it is not dangerous in itself "because experienced attorneys are not going to need psychics." He approved of using "psychics" if it is done "in an unobtrusive fashion." Does this imply that Robert Miller, the Public Defender who hit upon the brilliant idea of introducing a "psychic" into the Watkins Glen courtroom, is *not* experienced—or should it be assumed that he is merely naïve?

The local newspaper in Binghamton, the *Evening Press*, anxious not to offend Jordan's fans, ascribed the controversy that arose over this judicial stupidity to "some professional jealousy." A rather myopic commentary, but typical of Dark Ages thinking.

Lest you assume this situation is unique, consider the actions of

Judge Leodis Harris of Cleveland's juvenile court system. This learned man was written up in a national magazine, *Ebony*, which proudly acclaimed the magistrate for taking a giant step forward in logic. According to the magazine, Judge Harris's court dispenses "good, hardnosed advice . . . and an occasional dose of astrology." The judge "reads a teenager's horoscope during court session before deciding how the youth will be reprimanded for his offense." The article noted that his "use of astrology has gone over big with colleagues as well as the offenders."

Harris was instantly converted to astrology, claimed *Ebony*, when he chanced upon the horoscope of a juvenile who was before his bench and decided that the negative part of it "described the kid to a tee!" He used it in court.

All of this reminds me of the movie version of *The Hunchback of Notre Dame*, in which the accused was blindfolded and asked to reach out to two knives lying before her. She was to be judged guilty or innocent according to which she touched. Perhaps attorney Miller and Judge Harris would care to get together and perfect this technique. It certainly has as much going for it as astrology and aura-plotting. More, maybe.

Although Mr. Miller has never seen fit to answer my requests for his comments, Judge Harris wrote to me, finally, in response to my letters asking him to affirm or deny his use of astrology. He informed me that he has never used astrology in making his courtroom decisions. This certainly came as good news. Still, one wonders why *Ebony* ever said he did. More important, why did the judge refuse to answer my requests for confirmation or denial until my account was published in *The Skeptical Inquirer*, and did he not write to *Ebony*, asking the magazine to publish a retraction? No retraction ever appeared.

When I investigate so-called psychic wonders, Step One is to determine whether the actions of the performer are those of a conjurer involved in trickery. From this, a probable methodology is derived. Step Two is called Grabbing the Cheesecloth, a phrase taken from the procedure often used to expose fraudulent spirit séances: The exposer ends up clutching a handful of luminous cheesecloth—supposedly the spirit of the deceased—and the "medium" is well done. The difficulty is that the cheesecloth or other device used in the deception is not always obvious, and often not "grabbable." Sometimes the material evidence is no more than a tiny square of torn paper, a black nylon thread, or the tip of a ballpoint pen cemented into a paper tube. To the uninitiated, these articles mean nothing, but to the experienced investigator they may be everything. Then, too, there are frauds practiced by leading charlatans that do not involve a shred of physical "prop" to give them the lie; fortunately, such modern tools as the tape recorder and the infrared camera can serve the cause of sanity in many cases.

Out of perverse curiosity, I once recorded on tape the utterances of a well-known (to the police as well as to his adoring disciples) practitioner of the subtle arts of precognition and clairvoyance, Peter Hurkos. He was appearing on a popular evening TV show in one of several bookings, and he grandly "read" members of the audience, reciting intimate details about their homes, their lives, and their minds. Considerable astonishment accompanied his revelations, and when I conferred with several interested laymen the next day I was bombarded with glowing accounts of his fantastic accuracy. I carefully gave the impression that I had not seen the TV program, and let them babble on.

A few days later, I invited two of these persons to my home to put on tape their accounts of his performance. I then played for them the tape recording of the broadcast that I had made, and we discovered by *actual count* that this so-called psychic had, on the average, been correct in *one out of fourteen* of his statements! Even more damaging to this miracle-worker's reputation was the fact that the right guesses were so flimsy—for example, "There are more persons at home; I see two or three"—that any child could have done as well by picking guesses out of a hat. To the dismay of my visitors, their accounts had been far from accurate. Selective thinking had led them to dismiss all the apparent misses and the obviously wrong guesses and remember only the "hits." They were believers who *needed* this man to be the genuine article, and in spite of the results of this experiment they are still devoted fans of this charlatan.

Many "men of science" stupidly assume that because they have been trained in the physical sciences or the medical arts, they are capable of flawless judgment in the investigation of alleged psychics. Nothing could be further from the truth. In fact, the more scientifically trained a person's mind, the more he or she is apt to be duped by an enterprising performer. A scientist's test tube will not lie; another human being will. Scientists are all the more easily deceived because they think in a logical manner. All my efforts as a professional magician are based on the assumption that my audience thinks logically and can therefore be fooled by me if I work on that assumption.

We are bombarded today with wonders of "psychic photography," animals that prognosticate, and bump-in-the-night beasties that come back from Beyond. Investigation of these mummeries has been attempted mainly on the basis of wishful thinking and incompetent scientific procedure. It's about time that we woke up. *Trained* investigators should look into these matters. We must stop wasting money and labor on idiotic ideas. If there *is* something Out There, let's find out. I, for one, am willing to try.

A single book cannot possibly encompass all the idiocies that have been perpetrated upon the public in two decades. I have attempted to explain to the reader the major events in the realm of flim-flam, and I have discussed some in great detail so that they may serve as examples of what may be discovered when purported miracles are investigated thoroughly. Information has been gathered from several libraries, here and abroad, and I have maintained extensive files for many years from which items have been retrieved. A great number of correspondents contributed data in the form of clippings and affidavits, and many unhappy scientists supplied information to assist in the unmasking of fraud.

Needed is a sequel to this volume, one in which I may deal with subjects necessarily dropped from these pages. I certainly should reveal

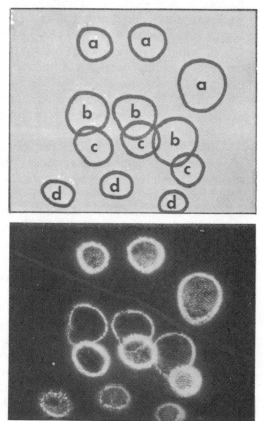

The three middle fingers of the author's left hand were placed into a Kirlian photography apparatus and four separate exposures were made. In the set marked "a," moderate pressure was applied. In "b," pressure was very heavy, and in "c" it was very light. The lower set, marked "d," was made with very light pressure but with the author's leg pressed against a metal table leg, thus grounding the subject. The "d" image on the far left shows the highly touted "streamer" effect due to this partial grounding. A great variety of images is possible merely by varying the pressure and electrical isolation of the body. Although variations of temperature, humidity, and dampness of the fingers can also affect the image drastically, these factors do not apply in this set of tests, since they were performed within a period of one minute. As is often the case with pseudosciences, the effects produced by Kirlian photography are the result of variations in conditions, and not of paranormal forces or abilities.

the facts about the 112 colleges here and overseas that are actually offering courses in ESP and other nonsense. One such, John F. Kennedy University in Orinda, California, has an "Institute of Mystical and Parapsychological Studies" under the direction of Dr. Pascal Kaplan and offers a Master of Arts degree. Perhaps this university will be the first in the world to have to call back some of its "products"—as Ford and General Motors have had to do—because of defects in processing.

The prognosticators—typified by Jeane Dixon, whose recorded predictions over the telephone are offered by the Bell System for the price of one message unit—deserve a chapter of their own. This same great seer startled us in 1977 by predicting that in 1978 actress Farrah Fawcett would get a crew cut, President Jimmy Carter would resign, and Pope Paul VI would astonish the world with his vigor and determination. Such a batting average deserves further investigation indeed.

Another bit of claptrappery, Kirlian photography, continues to fascinate the gullible. This process is said to register the human "aura," but the illustration demonstrates just how shallow this claim is. More extensive treatment of this subject will also have to await another book.

Such eminent figures as Dr. Elisabeth Kübler-Ross, a psychiatrist who presented her brand of evidence for survival after death in a best-selling book, is now discovered to have obtained her inspiration from certain questionable goings-on at the Facet of Divinity Church, an institution dedicated to séances in which the congregation enjoys extramarital relations with "spirits"—in the dark, of course. Conveniently, these spirits predicted to Dr. Kübler-Ross that she would be persecuted for her participation. "I was told three years ago that the society in which I live would try to destroy me by any means possible," she asserts. It would seem that this matter, too, needs some looking into.

In Canada I have investigated such "psychics" as Rita Burns, whose fame rests almost entirely upon the enthusiastic hyperbole of one newspaper reporter who quoted endorsements made by the Royal Ontario Museum. Officials of the museum denied the statements only when I visited and questioned them. Rita had claimed to be working with that august organization, using her supposed powers to identify odd artifacts. Her performance was much less than successful, though her press coverage indicated quite the opposite. After extracting certain sums from a few Canadian businessmen for her "psychic" advice, she declined to meet me on a television program to examine her claims. This is an unfinished investigation that also needs more attention.

There is scant satisfaction in knowing that in another, more rational age yet to come, one's words will be read and believed easily. If such an era is not imminent, the human race may not survive its own folly in accepting uncritically the declarations of the incompetents and charlatans who corrupt science in their pursuit of harebrained ideas. Only the support and encouragement of certain prominent members of the academic world, here and abroad, have enabled me to pursue the battle in which I have chosen to become involved. It has not been rewarding from a financial point of view, and in fact has cost me substantial amounts both in travel and research expenses. But there *is* a reward—the satisfaction and salutary effect of telling the truth.

To possess specific and specialized information about any aspect of human behavior or of the environment and fail to put that knowledge to valuable use is to my mind a major failure of integrity. I have had no choice. At an early age I was driven to investigate and expose the hoaxers and their disciples, seeing clearly the emotional and physical harm they wreak upon their victims. The adage "The sleep of reason brings forth monsters" has stuck in my mind for several decades now, and I have manned the claxon to arouse that sleeper.

This kind of declaration is a familiar one in human history. It smacks of every madman who ever thought that he alone possessed the ultimate truth. But the passing years have a way of sorting out madmen; I will trust to that process for my vindication.

What I have to say is directly said and easily understood. No complex reasoning or involved formulas are summoned to prove my case, and I ask only a fair hearing and a just decision from my reader. But, as many of us have discovered in courts of law, there is often a great difference between The Law and Justice. It is when these two entities are in harmony that civilization is best served. I invoke that possibility.

A few years ago it was my privilege to perform at the White House for Mrs. Betty Ford. In planning the show, I ran into a small problem with a silk handkerchief that I intended to use, and I requested Mrs. Ford to hand it to me when I asked for it from the stage. One of her aides objected, not wishing her to become involved with the performance, but this beleaguered lady reached out to accept it, bypassing the objection, and smiled broadly at me. "Mr. Randi," she said, tucking the silk into her belt, "I shall be pleased to wear your colors." I never felt better in my life.

I ask that my reader acquiesce and wear my colors for a while as we investigate the matters at hand. The colors are true, the cause is right, and though the victory may not be immediately apparent, it is nonetheless certain.

The next chapter is typical of the book: It calls things by their proper names and uses blunt language. In it I will prove two little girls were liars, I will demonstrate that a highly respected author and personality was really a rather silly, naïve man with an overdeveloped ego, and I will show that several "experts" were self-seeking incompetents who went along with a profitable gag. I will be castigated by some for this, but it is high time that such things be said boldly and directly, without fear of recrimination. I have said these things for years in my lectures; now I am putting them in print.

I offer half an apology for the exhaustive analysis of the Cottingly Fairies episode presented in the following chapter. To demonstrate so thoroughly that there are no fairies at the foot of the garden may well appear to be a case of "overkill," but I believe that this is important to an understanding of the other arguments presented in these pages. I will also bring this into focus by listing twenty points that cover nearly all the causes of misunderstanding that have arisen in discussions of so-called paranormal events, and I will refer to the Cottingly incident and present other examples to illustrate these points. As a professional conjurer, I have been accustomed to using various subtleties to deceive, but never in the way that I condemn in this book. I am fully aware of many standard and even more nonstandard ploys used to achieve these ends, and the Cottingley Fairies hoax discussed in the following chapter includes most of them. In killing the gnat with a sledgehammer, I set up the other targets. Please bear with me throughout the carnage.

2

Fairies at the Foot of the Garden

Come out, come out!
Come out upon the hill!
Up there, down there—
Fairies—*everywhere!*
—Anonymous

The Christmas 1920 issue of London's *Strand* magazine featured a piece by that eminent author and celebrity Sir Arthur Conan Doyle, the creator of Sherlock Holmes. The adventures of the great detective had brought *The Strand* large profits and enormous circulation in England and abroad, and any submission by Doyle was most welcome. The article, entitled "Fairies Photographed—An Epoch-making Event," was an account, presented as fact, of two girls of Bradford, Yorkshire, who had photographed a number of fairies and gnomes they regularly encountered in Cottingley Glen. This case features all the classic faults of such investigations. Gullibility, half-truths, hyperbole, outright lies, selective reporting, the need to believe, and generous amounts of plain stupidity are mixed with the most outrageous logic and false expertise to be found anywhere in the field.

I will outline first the case for the defense. Since such claims immediately meet with disbelief, the proponents of this tale were and are on the defensive as soon as their case is stated, and any statements they make are necessarily defenses of their position. The straightforward account, as presented by the main proponents, is in almost all respects a very convincing one. By the time my reader has reached the end of the initial presentation, the question will arise, How can he possibly refute these facts? and one must admit that the query is expected. I hasten to add that the matter must be judged without prejudice. I promise to rescue the reader eventually and provide adequate rebuttal. Now, side by side with the "experts," we will visit with two young girls who produced one of the most famous and enduring hoaxes ever perpetrated upon our species.

World War I is over, and England is recovering its wits after sacrificing the flower of its young manhood to the struggle. It is 1920, and spiritualism is in its heyday. Everywhere, hands are pressed to tables in darkened rooms in the hope that some rap or creak will signal the return of a loved one from beyond the grave. In America, the great conjurer Harry Houdini is touring the theater and lecture circuits debunking the claims of the spirit mediums, while his friend in England, Arthur Conan Doyle, is similarly engaged—in opposition to him. Doyle, convinced of many irrationalities, has taken up the cause of spiritualism and become one of its leading lights.

Doyle has been knighted for his contribution to literature. Probably there is no person better known in England or more widely respected. His alliance with the spiritists has been a great boost to their cause, and they regularly summon shades for him to witness. He has declared the evidence for survival after death to be "overwhelming," and he will believe it to be so until his last breath. He is in good company. Sir Oliver Lodge and William Crookes, prominent scientists of the age whose contributions to science are undeniable, also have declared themselves believers and are quoted to this day as authorities on the subject.

In May 1920 Sir Arthur has heard from a friend that actual photo-

Frances and the fairies ("photo number one"). Kodak Museum, U.K.

graphs have been taken of fairies and gnomes. He has investigated and has been put in touch with Edward L. Gardner. An advocate of theosophy, a mystical philosophy that accepts such beings as real, Gardner firmly believes in such matters. Upon being informed of the evidence in a letter from Gardner's sister—for whom Doyle has "considerable respect"—Sir Arthur writes that her letter "filled me with hopes." He employs Gardner to investigate the matter for him, and Gardner's first reports to Doyle assure him that the girls are undoubtedly honest, coming from a family of tradesmen and down-to-earth people incapable of guile.

Doyle is sent copies of two photographs—known as photo number one and photo number two—that are said to have been taken in July and September 1917, respectively. The first shows Frances Griffiths, age ten, in the company of four fairies, three of them winged and the

Elsie and the gnome ("photo number two"). Kodak Museum, U.K.

other playing pipes. It is said to have been taken by her cousin, Elsie Wright, sixteen years old, who is in turn represented in photo number two, snapped by Frances, seated on the lawn playing with a gnome.

Technical details are given to Doyle. The camera employed was a Midg, which used Imperial Rapid glass plates rather than flexible film. Exposure was $\frac{1}{50}$ second, and both days were sunny and bright. Mr. Wright, Elsie's father, had loaded one plate into the camera and given it to Elsie after much cajoling by the cousins. The two girls had been saying that they often played with fairies in Cottingley Glen, near their home. They took away the camera and returned within a half hour begging that the plate be developed. This was done some days later, and the result was the first picture. Two months later the girls produced the picture of the gnome with the same camera.

Sir Arthur is enthusiastic. He puts Gardner to work on the case, having been assured that he is "a solid person with a reputation for sanity and character." Gardner submits the original plates to two "first-class photographic experts," and they are "entirely satisfied" that the pictures are authentic.

The famous physicist Sir Oliver Lodge, consulted by Doyle, is only lukewarm in his reaction, but Doyle points out that the photos were taken by "two children of the artisan class," and "photographic tricks would be entirely beyond them." He also notes that it was impossible for the girls, unskilled as they were, to have produced a successful fake on the very first try.

But more convincing and authoritative proof is provided. A Mr. H. Snelling, with more than thirty years' experience in photography, and very familiar with special studio work, has declared positively, after much study of the negatives and prints, that (1) there was only one exposure (thus no double-exposure effects were possible); (2) photo number one was taken "instantaneously" (meaning at a shutter speed of $\frac{1}{50}$ or $\frac{1}{100}$ second); and (3) the fairies in photo number one *moved* during the rapid exposure. Gardner tells us that Snelling "stakes his reputation unhesitatingly" on the truth of his verdict.

Doyle himself takes the valuable negatives to the Kodak company in Kingsway, where a Mr. West and another expert cannot find "any evidence of superposition, or other trick." But, they claim, if they set to work "with all their knowledge and resources" they could produce such a photo. Doyle declares, "It was clear that at the last it was the character and surroundings of the children upon which the enquiry must turn, rather than upon the photos themselves."

Gardner makes a strong statement concerning the photos. Confronted by criticism from one Major Hall-Edwards, a medical authority, he counters that Doyle has not "taken it for granted that the photographs are real and genuine," as claimed by the major. "It would be difficult to misrepresent the case more completely," says Gardner. "The negatives and contact prints were submitted to the most searching tests known to photographic science by experts, many of whom were frankly sceptical. They emerged as being unquestionably single-exposure plates and, further, as bearing no evidence whatever in themselves of any trace of the innumerable faking devices known." He adds that such faking would be possible only "by employing highly artistic and skilled processes."

The fact that Elsie was employed in a photographer's shop is discounted by Gardner. He denies that "to be employed as an errand girl and help in a shop indicates a high degree of skill in that profession." He concludes with, "We are not quite so credulous as that."

A Mr. Maurice Hewlett adds unkind remarks to the discussion when he describes Gardner as "deficient, it would seem, in logical faculty." Hewlett goes on to say that "we have all seen photographs of beings in rapid motion. . . . the photograph does not look to be in motion at all . . . because in the instant of being photographed *it was not in motion.*" Gardner immediately counters that "Hewlett makes the astonishing statement that at the instant of being photographed *it is not in motion.* . . . Of course the moving object is in motion during exposure . . . and each of the fairy figures in the negative discloses signs of movement. This was one of the first points determined." Gardner is right about the movement statement, and Hewlett stands corrected—*if* the fairies *were* in motion.

Several critics point out an apparent fault with photo number one of Frances and the fairies. Why, they ask, is Frances looking directly at the camera rather than at the fairies? Easily explained, says Gardner. She was accustomed to the fairies but fascinated by the camera—a new experience for her. Furthermore, Gardner asks, "would a faker, clever enough to produce such a photograph, commit the elementary blunder of not posing his subject?"

In his book *The Coming of the Fairies,* Doyle refers to a final technical proof of authenticity. H. A. Staddon, "a gentleman who has made a particular hobby of fakes in photography," has submitted a report giving a dozen reasons why he is convinced that "the chances are not less than 80 percent in favor of authenticity."

Now the investigators are excited. Experts have been favorable in their opinions and the critics have been confounded. Doyle is off to Australia for some séances, and he leaves Gardner to try the Great Experiment: Can the girls produce *more* photographs? He is not hopeful, since they have not taken any in three years, but worse than that, the pangs of puberty would by now have taken hold of Elsie, and it is well known that girls aware of the birds and bees lose contact with sprites and elves. "I was well aware," he wrote, "that the processes of puberty are often fatal to psychic power." But a great surprise is announced to Doyle while he is in Australia. The girls have produced "three more wonderful prints"—a "complete success!" The new photos were taken in late August, several months after Doyle's entry into the controversy, and he is impressed: "Any doubts which had remained in my mind as to honesty were completely overcome, for . . . these pictures were altogether beyond the possibility of fake." However, expressing a note of caution, he remarks that "it is a curious co-incidence that so

Frances and the leaping fairy ("photo number three"). Kodak Museum, U.K.

Fairy offering a posy to Elsie ("photo number four"). Kodak Museum, U.K.

Fairies and their sunbath ("photo number five"). Kodak Museum, U.K.

unique an event should have happened in a family some members of which were already inclined to occult study." But he concludes this observation with, "Such suppositions . . . are, as it seems to me, far-fetched and remote."

Gardner's detailed report tells Doyle that only three photos were possible because the weather in the area had been "abominably cold" and rainy, and on only two days were the cousins able to get to the fairy glen to take photographs. According to Gardner, he supplied the girls with two Cameo cameras—a folding type using single plates, and quite different from the Midg used earlier. Doyle reports that only one camera was used. Snelling, the expert who had vouched for the authenticity of the 1917 photos, says that these bear "the same proofs of genuineness as the first two," declaring further that at any rate the photo known as number five is "utterly beyond any possibility of faking!"

One of the new photographs—called number three and featuring a leaping fairy—is particularly interesting. Frances, whose face is shown in the photo, is somewhat blurred. Elsie has explained to Gardner that the fairy leaped up at the instant the photo was snapped (at $\frac{1}{50}$ second) and that Frances "tossed her head back" in fear that the fairy was going to touch her face. Again, experts swear that the photos were not faked.

Photo number four is quite attractive. It seems to be of a fairy in very modish costume offering a flower to Elsie. Elsie, reports Gardner, is not looking directly at the fairy figure; she seems to be looking a bit sideways. Says Gardner, "The reason seems to be that the human eye is disconcerting. . . . If motionless and aware of being gazed at then the nature-spirit will usually withdraw and apparently vanish. With fairy lovers the habit of looking at first a little sideways is common."

Later, in a more extensive report to Doyle, Gardner says that on August 26, 1920, "a number of photographs were taken, and again on Saturday, August 28. The three reproduced here are the most striking and amazing of the number." Gardner now says that he had twenty-four plates supplied to the girls and that they were marked secretly at the factory so that no switching of plates would be possible.

There is a final attempt, in August 1921, to take more photos. Stereo cameras and a motion-picture camera are supplied. There are no results, but one experiment is a resounding success. It involves a Mr. Hodson, who has a reputation for seeing fairies and other "elementals," though he has never photographed them. Sitting in the fairy glen with the girls, Hodson compares his sightings with theirs. According to Gardner, "he saw all that they saw, and more, for his powers proved to be considerably greater." Gardner concludes that since the accounts of Hodson and of the girls agree, the case is proved. He so reports to Doyle.

In *The Coming of the Fairies*, Doyle, in discussing another correspondent's report of a fairy encounter, has a moment of doubt. The writer has described a sighting in New Zealand, where she was "surrounded by eight or ten tiny figures on tiny ponies like dwarf Shetlands. . . . At the sound of my voice they all rode through the rose trellis across the drive." Doyle, referring to the horses, admits that they are mentioned by several writers and decides, "I have convinced myself that there is overwhelming evidence for the fairies, but I have by no means been able to assure myself of these adjuncts [the horses]."

Sir Arthur concludes his lengthy book on fairies with the comment that "while more evidence will be welcome, there is enough already available to convince any reasonable man that the matter is not one which can readily be dismissed, but that a case actually exists which up to now has not been shaken in the least degree by any of the criticism directed against it. Far from being resented, such criticism, so long as it is earnest and honest, must be welcome to those whose only aim is the fearless search for truth."

To sum up the case for the defense: Two unsophisticated girls, unfamiliar with photographic trickery, with no motive at all, have photographed fairies and a gnome in the glen. The photographs have been examined by experts and declared unquestionably genuine and beyond any possibility of fakery. Whatever flaws the photos have are explainable; indeed, these apparent errors are further corroboration of the authenticity of the pictures. Doyle, creator of Sherlock Holmes, cannot be fooled by any fake; the man who thought like Holmes is a master detective, and exceedingly logical. Frances and Elsie, still alive and well in England (aged 73 and 79 in 1980), have never admitted to any fakery, despite having no good reason, at this late date, to maintain their innocence if they played tricks on people long deceased. Finally, the girls lacked a reason to be dishonest. They made no money from the episode and to this day are anxious to play down the whole matter. They may even have suffered because of the controversy. (In some accounts, Elsie and Frances are referred to as Iris and Alice. This was an agreement entered into at first, to protect the identities of the girls and of the Wright family, called the Carpenters.)

Does it all sound convincing? Yes, quite, if you choose to believe that the facts are as presented: that the experts were really competent, that Doyle was a logical thinker, that the photographs could not have been fabricated by the girls, and that there was no motive to do so. But let us present some of that "earnest and honest criticism" so admired by Sir Arthur. In my opinion the facts as learned by the experts reveal that Elsie Wright and Frances Griffiths were clever little girls who lied rather convincingly and were believed by some naïve and not-too-bright persons who were in a position to transform a simple hoax into a major deception that is recounted to this day.

Sir Arthur Conan Doyle, the outstanding personality in this comedy, is a good place to start our analysis of the Cottingly Fairies. He was a physician of Irish-Scotch parentage—"well born" was the expression of the day. Lack of patients inspired him, in 1887, to put pen to paper, and devotees of mystery fiction have been ecstatic about this decision ever since. Medicine was abandoned in favor of his great detective character, Sherlock Holmes, who, with the bumbling Dr. Watson, was to give Doyle a reputation as one of the great thinkers of post-Victorian England.

To understand Sir Arthur's impact in the matter under discussion, it must be recognized that he was considered an absolutely unassailable authority on any subject he chose to expound upon. Eric J. Dingwall, the tireless investigator of psychic claims who has contributed so greatly to our understanding of both the physical and psychological aspects of these investigations, knew Doyle personally and had him classified rather well. "Doyle was never wrong, and no one dared to suggest that he could have been mistaken—in *anything*," Dingwall told me. "He was not accustomed to being doubted." Knighthood did nothing to lessen his authority when the Crown decided to bestow this honor in 1902— not for his creation of Holmes but for his contributions as a historian, notably a vigorous defense of the British Army in South Africa.

England at that time was not yet ready to mature out of the mind-set that Queen Victoria had left as her hallmark: the notion that the world was a rather predictable place and that everything was secure and stable. Little girls were always innocent and frivolous. Evil men had heavy brows and wore black. People were forever classified by birth and education. And so it went. It was the tenor of the time.

Holmes himself, though apparently an intellect of huge proportions, could not have survived outside the fictional world that Doyle wove about him. For his deductions to be correct, the consistency of his world was absolutely necessary. People in particular had to conform to type; otherwise Holmes would have been hopelessly wrong. It was just this rather naïvely invented universe that Doyle imagined into existence and projected about himself, and it accounts in large measure for his fanciful interpretation of phenomena that he came upon only late in life—the wonders of spiritualism.

Doyle lost his son Kingsley in World War I, perhaps another reason for his turn toward spiritualism. In any case—and in common with others of influence—he was drawn to this latest fad, which had been started in America (by two other girls, the Fox sisters) and had taken root firmly in England. It had become a recognized religion under the general term "spiritualism," and it flourished during the war, with so many available spirits to call upon. Doyle became one of its most ardent supporters, and his heir often remarked on the sad fact that he spent some £250,000 in his pursuit of this nonsense.

An excellent and popular author, yes. A great thinker, no. Doyle was dependent on a special, manufactured world for his conclusions to be correct. Such a special world was entirely fictional, for as we shall see, little girls are *not* always truthful, experts are *not* always right, and authorities do *not* always see with unclouded vision.

Putting aside personalities for the moment, let us examine the evidence provided by the five photographs—the five we have been allowed to see, that is. Bear in mind that the data to follow are those given by Edward Gardner. As we shall discover, much of it is wrong. The photos are:

1. Frances and the fairies. Camera: the Midg Quarter. Film: Imperial Rapid. Distance: about four feet. Time of exposure: $\frac{1}{50}$ second. Lighting: bright, sunny day. Taken by Elsie in July 1917.
2. Elsie and the gnome. Camera: the Midg Quarter. Film: Imperial Rapid. Distance: about eight feet. Time of exposure: $\frac{1}{50}$ second. Lighting: fairly bright day. Taken by Frances in September 1917.
3. Frances and the leaping fairy. Camera: the Cameo. Film: not specified. Distance: three feet. Time of exposure: $\frac{1}{50}$ second. Lighting: not specified. Taken by Elsie in August 1920.
4. Fairy offering a posy to Elsie. Camera: the Cameo. Film: not specified. Distance: not specified. Time of exposure: not specified. Lighting: not specified. Taken by Frances in August 1920.
5. Fairies and their sunbath. Camera: the Cameo. Film: not specified. Distance: not specified. Time of exposure: not specified. Lighting: not specified. Taken by Elsie in August 1920.

The Midg was a common box camera. It had an offset viewer and held twelve glass plates in holders. Its widest aperture was f11, its highest shutter speed $\frac{1}{100}$ second. The Cameo camera was a smaller bellows type that accepted single glass plates and also a ground-glass viewing plate for portraits and special effects. Both cameras used plates measuring $3\frac{1}{4}$ inches by $4\frac{1}{4}$ inches, and these were mounted in metal holders, which were different in each camera. Several different models of each camera were available.

The five fairy photographs reproduced in this book were obtained from what are believed to be the original glass negatives. Brian Coe, of Kodak in London, carefully prepared several prints from each negative when the material was submitted to him by the British Broadcasting Corporation (BBC) for his opinion. Mr. Coe is no Snelling; he *objectively* examined the prints and negatives. His discoveries are quite interesting. Reproductions in Gardner's book *Fairies* and later printings of Doyle's opus are very poor, and access to the original negatives is important. In the case of photo number two, it appears that the negative is severely deteriorated, or else it is a bad copy, but certainly more puzzling than that is the fact that it was not made with the Midg camera, for the plate holder used would not fit that camera at all! However, in view of the other evidence in the case, this is of little import, as is my observation that the photos in Gardner's book are heavily retouched, though no mention is made of this in his text.

The first photo, of Frances and the four fairies, shows that the technical information given is false. The light on Frances's face in the photograph indicates subdued, indirect illumination. She was not in bright sunlight. The emulsion used on the Imperial Rapid plates could not possibly have registered such a photo if the shutter speed had been $\frac{1}{50}$ second, but would have required a 1½-second to 2-second exposure. Tables of exposure factors from Kodak show this to be an inarguable fact. To clinch the claim, we need only look at the waterfall in the background. Such a blurring effect is obtained with exposures of this length and longer, and experiments by Mr. Coe verify this. Why did Gardner claim $\frac{1}{50}$ second? Simply because he knew that even fairies in motion cannot be "frozen" in a photo unless the shutter speed is $\frac{1}{50}$ second or less! But he forgot the waterfall. . . .

Mr. Coe's analysis of the plate-holder shadow indicates that a Midg camera was probably used for photo number one. But the distance is wrong, a fact easily determined by looking through the viewfinder. It was at least seven feet, not four feet as claimed by the "experts."

The experts also declared in their reports that the fairies were in "rapid motion." Snelling told Gardner that each figure was independently in motion, and that the movement shows as a blur. Nonsense. The figures could not have been in motion, particularly since the shutter speed was 1½ seconds or longer. Unless the fairies' flying mechanism is a radical departure from that used by the butterfly, the assertion that they were moving is not acceptable here.

Frances is not looking at the fairies. Must we accept the explanation given by Gardner—that she was "accustomed to them"? Hardly. My explanation is that she had seen lots of cutouts and didn't much care about Elsie's project!

As for photo number two, the best that can be said for it is that the distance given is probably correct within two feet. Elsie's strange, elongated hand is explained by the chance juxtaposition of her two hands one behind the other, so that a cursory examination of the photo seems to show a very abnormal right hand with impossibly long fingers. Said Gardner about this, "On my very first meeting with Elsie, I asked to examine her hand. . . . I took a pencil outline of the hand and fingers . . . and they proved to be a good deal longer than average. The appearance of dislocation at the wrist . . . I cannot explain, except as a result of foreshortening and movement." Poppycock! Gardner was supposed to have examined this photo *in great detail* and with the aid of experts. His tracing did not account for the appearance of the hand, and to suggest "foreshortening and movement" is to admit incompetence! Neither even remotely serves as an explanation.

In this photograph no shadow can be seen where it would seem a shadow of the gnome should appear, but details in the enlargements

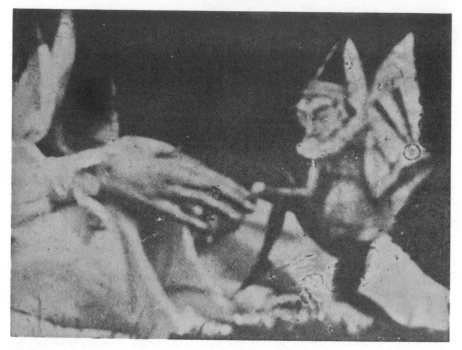

Detail of "photo number two."

Illustration of Elsie's hands as they are positioned in "photo number two."

of the original three-by-four-inch negatives are rather obscure, so not much can be determined. But a shutter speed of ⅟₅₀ second is not going to stop a gnome's pipes so sharply as this while they are "swinging in his grotesque little left hand," as claimed by Gardner.

So ends the 1917 effort. Matters that were not made clear still remain to be explained, however. Gardner admits that *other* pictures were taken in 1917 but expresses no curiosity at all about what happened to them. Doyle records that "other photographs were attempted, but proved partial failures, and plates were not kept." I'll just bet they were hurriedly discarded like so much radioactive waste. There's nothing like a set of failures around the house, waiting to be discovered!

And why were the photos ignored until three years after they were taken? Because the Wrights simply did not take them seriously, and until Mrs. Wright came under the influence of theosophy after attending a lecture by Gardner, she had no notion that anyone would take them seriously. In fact, in a recent letter Elsie writes, "My poor Dad was very much disappointed in his favorite detective writer, Conan Doyle. I heard him say to my mother, 'May, how could a brilliant man like him believe in such a thing?' " Ten points for Mr. Wright. The answer to his question is that, as chance would have it, the photos had fallen into the hands of a man who needed such evidence desperately to bolster his own delusions. It was bad seed on fertile ground, and six decades later the weeds still flourish.

Gardner, Doyle, and the experts were turning a childish prank into a *cause célèbre*. Word of the matter had gotten out, and the intelligentsia of England were atwitter. Gardner, titillated by his newfound fame, was ripe for further plucking. Instructed by Doyle to ask the girls for more photos, Gardner equipped Frances and Elsie with two Cameo cameras and twenty-four specially marked plates. It was the heyday of spirit photography, the process used by mediums to produce on photographic plates images of persons who (they told their victims) were safely in heaven and yet able to communicate by impressing their photographic images on demand. Surprisingly enough, even believers like Gardner and Doyle were dimly aware that these mediums could cheat by double-exposing the plates, and they imposed safeguards by supplying secretly marked plates to prevent the test plates from being switched with previously exposed ones. When the operators managed to produce photographic shades of the deceased in spite of these precautions, the results were declared genuine, even though the darkness of the séance room far surpassed that of the photographic darkroom. It was another case of a little expertise being useless.

Marked plates made no difference to the girls. Since their method was simply to set up cutouts of the fairy figures and snap them, they had no need to switch plates at all. But Gardner went into great detail to assure Doyle he had checked everything out to be sure that the photos the girls eventually produced were done with the supplied plates. ("Yes, Captain, we have excellent fire extinguishers on the Hindenburg.")

Three photos were produced, though Elsie admits that other photos were "attempted." No one seems to have asked the question, Whatever happened to *the other photos they took?* After all, the girls were given twenty-four plates, all carefully but uselessly marked, by Mr. Gardner.

This worthy himself remarked that "a number of photographs were taken." Did he have any interest in the others? Apparently he was not interested in the other photos, including those "only partially successful" ones that Elsie "threw . . . in the brook"! For in those other pictures, I'm sure, lies the evidence that even Snelling could not have missed.

Gardner reported that the girls were unable to produce more than three photos because the weather was wet and cold. My colleague Robert Sheaffer, of The Committee for the Scientific Investigation of Claims of the Paranormal, troubled to check the weather reports—he is accustomed to doing so during investigations of unidentified flying object (UFO) sightings and Bermuda Triangle claims—and discovered that in the Bradford area during the second half of the month of August 1920, the rainfall was *less than in any other month of that year.* Furthermore, the meteorological journal *British Rainfall* reported the weather there to have been "though cool, on the whole, dry." Thus the "almost continual rainfall" that Gardner reported did not occur. England that month had only 56 percent of the expected rainfall, and Bradford was a relative desert!

The first of this second group of photographs, photo number three, is a bit of an improvement on the 1917 pictures. The fairy figure is sharp and clear, suspended in the air before the girl's face. Frances's face and figure are somewhat blurred, and unless it is examined carefully one might accept Gardner's explanation that the girl "tossed her head back" during the $\frac{1}{50}$ second the shutter was open. The following close-up of photo number three shows an enlargement of a highlight in the girl's hair. Brian Coe of Kodak notes that this is consistent not with a continuous, rapid movement of the figure, but rather with a short movement during a long exposure. Using the same criteria as before for film speed and lighting, it is clear that this shot could only have been made with a 1½- to 2-second exposure. Frances held her head still for the opening of the shutter, then moved a bit rapidly, and held still again until the shutter closed. The leaping fairy must have been leaping *very* slowly to be frozen so still in space! Finally, the fairy figure itself is so very well done, in contrast to the others, that it must have been obtained from a magazine or book.

Photo number four is an obvious fake and is not much discussed in the fairy business. For the girls to have produced such a bad figure wearing a fully "mod" outfit suitable for *Vogue* magazine is laughable. But remember, they were not dealing with very bright critics. What is really amusing about this item, however, is Gardner's observation (accepted by Doyle) that "Elsie is not looking directly at the sprite." This is in accord with the purported shyness of the critters and is supposed to be corroborative evidence of the reality of the sad little figure. But take another look at the picture. Elsie *is* looking *directly* at the cutout. Gardner has invented another fact!

This photograph was subjected to the same "careful" scrutiny as the others and declared quite acceptable by even such an expert as Snelling, who, according to Doyle, "laughs at the idea that any expert in England could deceive him with a faked photograph." Actually, *we* should laugh, but for a different reason. This particular photo is so silly that its fraudulence can be detected by any intelligent observer, let alone a scientist with modern methods.

It is photo number five, however, that upon close examination reveals that Elsie and Frances even fooled themselves! In recent years the ladies have avoided telling outright falsehoods in response to queries about the photographs. That is why I believe, as does Brian Coe, that Elsie's statement to him that "only one exposure was made on each plate" is,

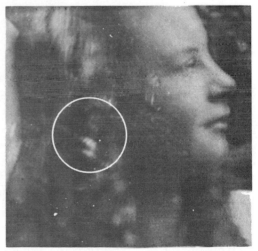

Detail of "photo number three."

to the best of her knowledge, correct. But this photo *is* a double exposure—made in error!

Mr. Coe must be credited with one of the proofs of this charge. He mentioned to me, while we were examining some of the prints, that photo number five showed a "doubling" of one margin on a contact print. A close examination of the photograph reveals two small, rounded marks at each side of the lower margin. These are the shadows of two tiny clips holding the glass plate against the metal holder. Each plate had to be held in such a holder in order to be inserted into the camera. It consisted of a sheet-metal piece as large as the plate, with retaining clips bent over at one end. The plate was tightly gripped and could not move relative to the metal clips. If the entire plate had been exposed to light, then developed, all of the plate would have shown up black, with the exception of the clip shadows where the metal protected the plate from the light. But in the camera, a regularly exposed plate was protected also at all four edges by the masking effect of the frame at the back of the camera itself—thus the "framing" effect seen here, interrupted by the clip shadows.

Shadows of the holding clips on the lower margin of "photo number five."

Now, if the plate had been inserted into the camera a second time, it would be almost impossible for it to arrive in *exactly* the same position as before, though the side-to-side alignment would have been reasonably accurate. At the *ends*, a second use of the plate would provide evidence that two exposures were made. In this case, such evidence shows clearly under strong magnification. The effect is shown in the following diagram, in which the relevant portion of photo number five is enlarged for clarity. There is no such effect visible at the top edge, because the very heavy overexposure resulting from a double shot of bright sky has "washed out" any evidence.

Unless the girls were very carefully attempting the superposition of two images, double exposure would not have been needed. A ground-glass viewing plate could have been inserted into the Cameo camera (it was equipped for such use) and wonderful effects could have been obtained. But of course, to fool such people as they were dealing with, such refinements were unnecessary.

It is my conclusion that the two girls *did* make a double exposure in the case of photo number five, and did so in error. It would have been all too easy to use the same plate twice by mistake, and further evidence proves that they did expose it a second time.

The above proof is supported by the observation that the shadows

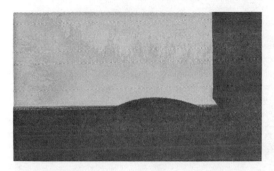

Illustration of the lower right corner of "photo number five."

at the edge of the clip are very sharp, since the clip did not move relative to the plate itself. Only the shadow of the camera back shows displacement.

As for the additional evidence, again I am amazed that the many so-called experts have for more than sixty years failed to note that there is a duplication of two of the fairy figures! The girls set up a shot with cutouts, photographed the scene, and then, when changing plates, goofed and reinserted the *used* plate. Having shot a new setup, they rushed off to develop both plates. They found one blank, and the other one a mysterious mess of seemingly translucent figures. It was a stroke of luck for them, and the dummies who examined the plates declared that a miracle had taken place!

An episode that transpired between a reporter and Elsie in January 1921 should have alerted him to the true nature of the hoax. He was sent to interview the girl for the *Westminster Gazette* and found her at Sharpe's Christmas Card Manufactory. At first she refused to see him and sent word to that effect. He persisted, and finally she met him for a very strange and forced encounter.

She began by telling him that she had nothing to say about the photographs, explaining that she was "fed up with the thing." But the reporter, determined to force a story from her, asked her where the fairies came from. Elsie said she did not know. "Did you see them come?" he asked. Yes, said Elsie, but then when asked *where* they came

Careful examination of "photo number five" reveals the partial duplication of two of the fairy cutouts, the result of a double exposure. The drawn lines show the replication.

from she laughed and told him, "I can't say." She would not say where they went after they danced for the camera, and became embarrassed when he insisted upon an answer. After a few more questions went unanswered, the reporter decided that making suggestions might loosen her up.

He asked whether the fairies might have just "vanished into the air," and Elsie mumbled, "Yes." She denied that she spoke to them, or that they spoke to her. Many more questions followed, and the duel ended with her significant comment, "You don't understand."

In this interview, aside from recent interviews conducted with Frances and Elsie, we have the crux of the whole matter: The girls created a monster and just wished it would go away. Since it apparently has become increasingly difficult over the years to tell outright fabrications about the matter, they have found it easier for all concerned if the reporters are given a few small half-facts that can be expanded into elaborate tales in print. At this date they simply will not say that the fairies were real or that the photos were genuine. Then what *do* they say?

Interviewed in 1971 by BBC-TV in England, Elsie said that she "would not swear on the Bible that the fairies were really there." In a subsequent letter to Brian Coe, she said that she would not so swear, and that if she ever had, "my friends and relatives would have stopped enjoying our family story as a big laugh." She said, further, "I admit that I may not believe in fairies. As for the photos, let's say they are figments of our imaginations, Frances's and mine."

Frances herself insisted upon being interviewed with her back to the camera. She repeatedly asked what Elsie had said in response to the same questions and merely agreed with whatever Elsie had said. Elsie's dominance over Frances, it seems, has not faded in six decades!

Elsie, fearful that her father's reputation might be impugned by certain remarks of Mr. Coe, wrote him that when she discussed the matter with her father, he said "it was nothing to lie about, and that all he wanted was that we should tell the truth of how we did it." She absolved him of any involvement, comparing his honesty with that of Abraham Lincoln (a rather strange choice for an English girl). My question to Elsie is this: Is it not time for the truth to be told? These half-admissions and evasions are *not* the truth, Elsie. They are all that stands between a final decision about the Cottingley Fairies and a stand-off.

Or are they? There is one technical advance that Elsie and Frances could hardly have been expected to foresee, and that the experts of their day could not have known. It involves a highly sophisticated system originally developed to examine satellite photos, and with this advantage we are able to put a very large nail of doubt in the already well-sealed coffin of the Cottingley Fairies.

It was the inspiration of Robert Sheaffer to apply this "computer enhancement" technology to the fairy photos. He enlisted the assistance of William Spaulding, Western Division Director of Ground Saucer Watch in Phoenix, Arizona, who had analyzed numerous UFO photographs—with very interesting results—and who agreed to put the questioned photos under the scanner. Briefly, the process consists of scanning the photo minutely by electronic means and reducing tiny picture elements to "pixels" (no relationship to pixies), each of which has a specific value. When these readings are fed into a computer with the proper instructions, it is possible for some interesting data to emerge.

Spaulding demanded two things of his enhancement process. First, he asked the computer about the fairy figures as opposed to the human figures. Were they three-dimensional? No, answered the computer. None of the fairies were "round"; they were exactly what one would expect of simple paper cutouts—with the exception of the gnome figure in photo number two, which may have been an in-depth model. Second, the machine was asked to search for the presence of any invisible-to-the-eye threads or supports, and evidence of such a support shows up in photo number four in just the position that might be needed to hold the cutout in place.

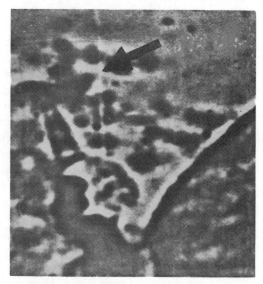

The GSW computer enhancement of "photo number four," showing what is possibly a thread support. The author believes this to be doubtful evidence; no support was necessary for the figure. The print is in negative, and shows the head of the fairy figure on the lower left between the wings of the cutout. Ground Saucer Watch

Spaulding, on behalf of the staff who performed and analyzed the tests, is quite decided about the matter on the basis of the computer enhancement. "There is absolutely no photographic evidence to substantiate these 'fairy' photographs as authentic evidence," he wrote. "In essence these photographs represent a crude hoax." Spaulding reached this conclusion despite the fact that the other information presented here was not available to him!

And where did the girls get the cutouts? While gathering material for a book on early nineteenth-century illustration, British author Fred Gettings came upon a drawing that vaguely disturbed him. An avowed believer in spiritualism and spirit photography, Gettings recognized a similarity between photographs in a Doyle book and this drawing from *Princess Mary's Gift Book*. Published in 1915 in England, this book was a very popular children's book of the day. The drawing illustrated a poem by Alfred Noyes entitled "A Spell for a Fairy," which gives explicit instructions in conjuring up fairies! Evidently Elsie found the instructions too complex and resorted to cutouts. All she did was copy the figures, making minimal changes, then added wings and cut them out. There is not the slightest chance that Elsie just happened to photograph fairies that were in positions so similar to those in a book she could have had about the house.

Except for Doyle, I have deferred until now discussion of the personalities involved in the hoax. Such considerations must be brought in, since somewhere in the personalities of the actors in this drama can be found the ingredients that allowed such a complicated piece of flimflam to develop.

Mr. H. Snelling, photographic "expert," wrote in a letter to Gardner, "In my opinion, they are . . . straight untouched pictures." He failed to see "any trace of . . . work involving card or paper models" and was entirely satisfied. Snelling was a total incompetent in this work, as the evidence proves beyond any doubt. The photos are obvious, easily exposed fakes, and he certainly did not submit them to the kind of scrutiny that any professional would have been expected to use. He was simply overpowered by the involvement of Sir Arthur Conan Doyle and ecstatic to be in on such a great moment in history. In fact, throughout the accounts of this affair, he struts about declaring that his opinion is definitive, and he "stakes his reputation" on the validity of the photos. So much for Mr. Snelling's reputation.

Mr. Wright, Elsie's father, must be discussed as well. Although several investigators have thought that he could have been the "genius" behind the plot, I think not. It is my opinion that Mr. Wright was a bystander who was drawn into the mess simply because his daughter was a convincing faker. No adult "genius" was needed to pull off this scheme. Elsie—or any other sixteen-year-old girl with her background—was quite capable of taking a number of photos of cardboard cutouts. It was a simple job; the simpletons who supported and enlarged the hoax are the most reprehensible parties. So Mr. Wright, not needed for the plot, gets good marks for honesty, but perhaps not for child rearing.

The next character to be dissected is Edward L. Gardner, who in 1945 further fleshed out the Case of the Cottingley Fairies with the publication of *Fairies—The Cottingley Photos and Their Sequel.* The book was gladly published by the Theosophical Publishing House, whose staff was anxious to prove that fairies, a mainstay of their particular brand of nuttiness, existed and flourished. It was Gardner who did most of the work for Doyle, and he polished up the account given him by the girls until it passed muster.

Gardner's business was theosophy. He was president of the Blavatsky Lodge of the Theosophical Society and was a frequent lecturer on the

Illustration for a poem in *Princess Mary's Gift Book*. Princess Mary's Gift Book

Slightly simplified versions of the fairy drawings from the book. Note their similarity to the fairy figures in the close-up of "photo number one."

subject. The choice of this man to research the Cottingley affair absolutely assured the absent Doyle that the results of the investigation would be positive. Gardner combined naïveté, commitment to the cause, and experience in handling critics—all necessary qualities for the job. He was very good at it, too. The frontispiece of Doyle's book *The Coming of the Fairies* features a portrait of the man, labeling him a "Member of the Executive Committee of the Theosophical Society" and therefore not one to be trifled with.

In his book, Gardner concentrates very heavily on the characters of the two girls and of the Wright family. Like Doyle, he felt that

Detail of "photo number one."

the actual evidence was secondary to the personalities involved, their backgrounds, and their integrity. Neither man could imagine that "common folk" were able to deceive, especially young girls. And to a man like Gardner, it was not in the least surprising that he was not allowed to be present when the girls took photos a second time in 1920. He simply accepted the conditions, however suspicious—a defect characteristic of many of those who profess to investigate such matters.

Now we come to the girls. Frances Griffiths, ten years old, was a visitor from South Africa. She arrived in Yorkshire speaking a strange variety of English and was the butt of jokes and other childish cruelties at the local school she attended. Thus her summer holidays at Bradford with her older cousin were anticipated with enthusiasm, and it may be deduced that Elsie had great influence over Frances. To ask her to pose with some cutout fairies, and then tell an innocent white lie to her parents, was surely not too complex a scheme for Elsie to work out. And how the giggling must have echoed through the glen.

Elsie was the chief plotter and culprit. A look at her background provides much food for thought. She had worked for several months at a photographer's studio nearby, retouching photographs. There was great demand for such work during World War I; every family with a boy in uniform was in the market for a portrait, in many cases taken by photographic process out of a family group and isolated. This required much clever brushwork and faking. In other cases, photos of the young men were inserted into family groups to complete them, a feat achieved through similarly delicate fakery. But Elsie did not need such technical skill to produce the Cottingley photos. It is merely of passing interest that she had experience in such matters at her job—a factor minimized in Gardner's investigation.

Elsie, at the time Gardner met her, was working at a factory where greeting cards were made. It is apparent that she was a clever artist. As this is written, Elsie Hill, as she is now known, has just seen produced a beautiful chess set that she designed. Her artistry continues—from cutouts at Cottingley to chess pieces. Her mother told investigators in 1920 that her daughter was "a most imaginative child, who has been in the habit of drawing fairies for years." The implications of all this are clear.

The Cottingley Fairies were simple fakes made by two little girls as a prank, in the beginning. Only when supposedly wiser persons discovered them were they elevated to the status of miracles, and the girls were caught up in an ever-escalating situation that they wanted out of but could not escape. When asked to repeat the performance, they did so under pressure, probably by then enjoying the hoax somewhat. Today they find it impossible to tell the same story they did some years ago, preferring to bounce the ball around a bit without committing themselves either way. That Elsie is sparing the reputation of Frances is obvious, for Frances is now employed in a position that she might well lose if the truth were known for sure.

Perhaps I have "overkilled" this matter. But the long explanation of the Cottingley Fairies controversy is excellent preparation for the presentation of twenty points that can be applied to almost every example we will discuss from here on. These are the major hallmarks of paranormal chicanery, along with examples that illustrate each point.

1. It is claimed that the subject does not seek money or fame, and thus no motive to deceive exists. Examples: The two girls had no stake in the deception that could have brought them money and, indeed, seemed to suffer more than they profited. The assumption made is that only money and notoriety are plausible motives. Ego and just plain fun are not thought to be sufficient. The Fox sisters, whose innocent fun in cracking their toe bones led to the founding of the major crackpot religion known as spiritualism, certainly had no other motive, yet what they started grew and got away from them in no time at all.

2. The subject (a child, peasant, or sweet little old lady) is said to be incapable of the techniques required; lack of sophistication precludes deception. Examples: Elsie and Frances were children and therefore not suspected of being able to use a camera with any skill or of being able to produce the fairy cutouts. Today, Russian parapsychologists are fuddled by a Mrs. Kulagina, a peasant who uses common conjurer's tricks rather clumsily to deceive them.

3. It is said that the subject has failed to pass tests designed to determine if the necessary skill is present. Examples: Gardner wrote that he "tested her [Elsie's] powers of drawing, and found that . . . the fairy figures which she had attempted in imitation of those she had seen were entirely uninspired, and bore no possible resemblance to those in the photograph." In France recently, Jean-Pierre Girard was tested for strength by his mentor, Charles Crussard, to see if he could physically bend the bars that he seemed to be bending psychically. Crussard reported that Girard was not able to do so, no matter how hard he tried! Girard and Elsie had the same advantage: They were dealing with simple folk who thought that their subjects' failure to pass a test proved them honest. It is not difficult to fail to bend a metal bar, nor is it beyond the ability of a little girl to fail to draw a decent picture.

4. Faults discovered in the story or performance tend to prove the phenomenon real, it is agreed, since a clever trickster would not make such basic errors. Examples: It was said that if Elsie had been really trying to make photo number one a good fake she would have posed Frances looking at the fairies, not at the camera. Consider the other possibility: If Frances *had* been looking at the fairies, it would have been hailed as perfectly natural! Either way, Frances wins. And when Jeane Dixon, the alleged prophet, predicts an event that does not come to pass, she is acclaimed for having been honest enough to give it a good try anyway.

5. If a phenomenon is consistent with previously reported ones, this is cited as strong evidence that it is genuine. Examples: The costumes and the size of the fairies produced on film by Elsie were in accord with storybook accounts, so verification was assumed. That the fairies were constructed to match the accounts and the expected appearance seems not to have dawned on any of the investigators. When the illusionist Uri Geller and his metal-bending tricks came along, several parapsychologists refused to accept him because "there is no precedent in the literature." The implication is obvious: If previous examples *had* been reported, they would have accepted Geller as the others did.

6. It is claimed that critics give poor or insufficient reasons for doubting reported paranormal events and are therefore not to be taken seriously. Unfortunately, this is sometimes true. Examples: Some skeptics unwisely assumed that the Cottingley photos were taken in a studio, with painted waterfall and all. Gardner demolished them by going to the actual scene and photographing it, remarking, "Another photographic company, which it would be cruel to name, declared that the background consisted of theatrical properties." Some scientists today have put their skeptical feet in their mouths by remarking that Geller could have bent or broken metals by using chemicals, magnets, or laser beams. Such claims are nonsense to anyone who knows the conditions under which the "miracles" took place. Thus, these critics, with all their good intentions, harm their own cause.

7. Prominent personalities lend their support to the claims and are considered unassailable because of prestige, academic background, and so on. Examples: Conan Doyle was almost the only reason that the Cottingley Fairies hoax was—and is—accepted by many people. Today, laser physicists, political figures, astronauts, and authors who declare upon paranormal matters are thought to have expertise that in fact they do not have.

8. Similarly, supposed experts are called in to verify the claims. Examples: Snelling, Gardner, and Hodson were "experts" carefully selected for the job by Doyle. Their acceptance of the miracle was a foregone conclusion. Metallurgist Wilbur Franklin of Kent State University was touted as an expert who could judge the validity of paranormal metal-bending by Geller, and he was widely quoted. Not so widely quoted was his reversal when he took a second look and discovered he had been wrong. Franklin was a "believer" from the beginning.

9. The findings of experts who are critical are minimized or ignored. Examples: The people at Kodak in London were called in to judge the photos and refused to authenticate them. The fact that they said there were many ways to get such faked results was played down by Doyle, who gave the impression that great technical skill was needed

for such procedures. In the same way, conjurers, whose expertise qualifies them to judge the validity of paranormal events, are largely ignored—except those among them who are found to be sympathetic to irrational notions.

10. **Those who allege paranormal events are equivocal and evasive, allowing investigators to assume facts and fill in details in support of their claims.** Examples: In interviews, conversations, and letters, Elsie has introduced half-truths and dropped hints that have led sympathetic investigators to make unjustified assumptions. Doyle, too, professed both conviction and doubt in the same volume, just in case he was proved wrong. In the case of the recent "astral trip" that "psychic" Ingo Swann made to the planet Jupiter, Swann takes little blame for contradictions in his story, allowing scientists Russell Targ and Harold Puthoff, who endorsed and sponsored the adventure, to select those aspects of this purported event that they believe to be convincing. Swann, incidentally, recently averred that he had "overshot" the planet Jupiter and landed in another solar system altogether, thus leaving Targ, Puthoff, and UFO investigator/astronomer J. Allen Hynek in need of revising their explanation of this "miracle."

11. **Conflicting versions or details of a paranormal event are ignored.** Examples: Doyle reported that one Cameo camera was given to the girls; Gardner said there were two. Doyle said that when Mr. Hodson (called Mr. Sergeant) went to the glen with the two young girls to look for fairies, "he saw all that they saw, and more," but Hodson's own account shows that they disagreed on several points. Describing a ship named *Sandra* that "vanished" in the so-called Bermuda Triangle, one author describes the craft as 350 feet in length, on a calm ocean under a "starlit sky." Records prove that the *Sandra* was 185 feet long and sank in seas buffeted by 73-mile-an-hour winds—just 2 miles an hour less than hurricane strength.

12. **A subject's ability to perform trickery is de-emphasized or ignored.** Examples: Elsie's artistic ability, job experience, and opportunity to create the fakes were circumstantial evidence of a possible hoax, but Doyle considered this a ridiculous impossibility. Jean-Pierre Girard and Uri Geller are acknowledged magicians whose abilities are unquestioned, but these qualifications are downplayed by modern-day believers.

13. **Any controls that seem scientific are used to provide authentication, whether applicable or not.** Examples: Gardner had the twenty-four photographic plates secretly marked, but this was of no value whatsoever. At the Stanford Research Institute, they put some "psychics" in a Faraday cage, a wire-mesh affair that screens out radio waves. The methods of trickery were not at all inhibited, but the experiment *sounded* just fine—on paper.

14. **It is said that the subject cannot produce phenomena on command or on a regular basis, since such abilities are ephemeral and sporadic.** Examples: The girls' inability to produce photos on all the supplied plates was excused, and they were not required to account for the missing plates. Ted Serios, who produced "thought photographs" for Dr. Jule Eisenbud a few years back, turned out hundreds upon hundreds of failures over periods of several hours, day after day, before a positive result was found.

15. **It is claimed that conditions that make deception possible are also those that allow the miracles to take place, and miracles are the more probable explanation.** Examples: Elsie and Frances got pictures only when they were alone, unobserved, and able to make several attempts. Today, Professor John Hasted of Birkbeck College in London tells us that his "psychic children" produce their best wonders when they lock themselves in their own rooms at home and are unseen. Actually, observation of the things they do reveals that they are easily done by perfectly ordinary means.

16. **Unless the critics can explain away *all* the reported details, the residue is considered an irreducible basis for validation.** Examples: Although there were many opportunities for fakery in the fairy photo matter, Doyle clung to the good character of the Wright family, the so-called expertise of the photographer Snelling, and the failure of the critics to find any cutouts. Although "prophet" Jeane Dixon has been shown to have lied about her age, to have been wrong in scores of major predictions, and to have censored uncomfortable facts from books about her, when she hits on one of her predictions—a rare event—she is acclaimed as a seer.

17. **We are told that subjects do not do well when persons with "negative vibrations" are nearby.** Examples: Adults were not allowed to be present when Elsie and Frances took the photos. The excuse was that otherwise the fairies would not appear. But when they sat with Mr. Hodson they attempted no photos, though Hodson "saw" the fairies, too! In modern parapsychology, experimenters insist that only persons with a sympathetic attitude (and who therefore believe in the paranormal) be present. The subjects, too, insist on this. Geller has gone so far as to refuse to perform when I am present.

18. **It is claimed that when money is paid for the services of a psychic, or the psychic powers are used to earn money, the powers are defeated. On the other hand—since parapsychologists like to have it both ways—money rewards, they also claim, tend to encourage performance.** Examples: Doyle agreed with Gardner that paying the girls for the photos would spoil the whole phenomenon. But Dr. J. B. Rhine, formerly associated with Duke University, said that the reward system

has great merit. Then again, we are told that psychics fail at the race track . . . and so it goes.

19. It is argued that too many controls on an experiment cause negative results. Examples: Gardner thought that trying to witness the photo-taking would "crowd" the girls. He preferred to accept the developed plates from them, even by mail, rather than to impose on them. Professors John Hasted and John Taylor in England refer to many cases in which nothing happened because they watched too closely. When controls were relaxed, lo!—there were wonderful events!

20. Any trickery detected by the investigators may be attributed to the subject's desire to please, and therefore there is a compulsion to cheat. There is no example of this factor in the Cottingley affair. Aside from present evidence, which shows that cheating *did* take place without question, there was no evidence that the girls were caught red-handed at the time of the performance, nor did the investigators find in the evidence any of the myriad clues that were there. Today, Geller, Girard, and numerous other "psychic stars" have been exposed thoroughly, but all this is forgiven by the believers.

3

All at Sea . . .

"The time has come," the Walrus said,
"To talk of many things:
Of shoes—and ships—and sealing-wax—
Of cabbages—and kings—
And why the sea is boiling hot . . ."
—Lewis Carroll
"The Walrus and the Carpenter"

It is careless of a man to fail to sufficiently research a subject on which he claims to be an authority. It is irresponsible for him to resist telling the facts when he discovers them. And it is irresponsible and callous for him to continue to misrepresent matters about which he has been informed to the contrary. *J'accuse* Charles Berlitz of these failings.

Berlitz is the author of *The Bermuda Triangle, Mysteries from Forgotten Worlds,* and *Without a Trace,* all of which contain such demonstrable errors and misstatements that the simplest investigation of the claims made easily shows that these books should have been classed as fiction rather than fact. I am told that Berlitz speaks some thirty languages, eleven of them fluently. Perhaps he is able to state his spurious claims in all thirty tongues, since he is heir to the creation of his grandfather, who founded the famous Berlitz language schools. Posterity would have been better served if he had stuck to that calling instead of becoming a very bad amateur scientist and espouser of pseudoscholarly theories.

Early in 1979 Berlitz took a group of fifteen archaeologists, explorers, and divers into the so-called Bermuda Triangle to study the "Lost Civilization of Atlantis." A brief chat with members of the Committee for the Scientific Investigation of Claims of the Paranormal (notably Larry Kusche, author of *The Bermuda Triangle Mystery—Solved*) would have saved these men the trip. But I suppose that if Berlitz was paying for his caprices, they might as well have had a holiday in the dreaded triangle. They were never safer.

The Bermuda Triangle is an expanse of ocean bounded at its three corners by Bermuda, Puerto Rico, and Miami. In 1945, when five Navy Avenger aircraft flew into the area and reportedly vanished mysteriously, the legend began to be manufactured. Within a few years the public was believing that some unknown force was snatching planes, boats, and people out of the Triangle and whisking them to some limbo or other. Berlitz was soaking up and writing down every reported incident, embellishing the tales and preparing them for publication. The result was the sale to credulous people of over 5 million copies of his first book, published in twenty languages, and more than $1 million in royalties.

When Larry Kusche set out to research the Bermuda Triangle, he had before him a formidable task. It is one thing for Berlitz to claim that something has occurred; it is another to try to prove that it did not. Meanwhile, the believers sit back smugly, hands folded, grinning widely. It is apparent that it is a matter of blind belief, rather than actual proof, where such issues are concerned. For as Kusche points out so very well, a large percentage of the so-called wonders of the Triangle were nothing but outright fabrications, with no evidence whatsoever to support them. We read about ships that are not listed in any registry, planes for which there are no records to show they ever flew, and shadowy crews and other people who in many instances were well accounted for and did not vanish into the Never-Never Land that authors like Berlitz would have us believe holds sway in the Caribbean. The Bermuda Triangle idea is nonsense, as we shall see.

I will not attempt to deal with the numerous other areas of the world that are claimed to harbor mysterious dangers. It seems that other nations, wanting to share in the silliness, have clamored to have their own Triangles recognized. Wherever anyone or anything vanishes, psychic whirlpools are invented. One author, Ivan Sanderson, even postulated twelve evenly spaced "Vile Vortexes" that spanned the globe.

Now, I admit that if there seems to be a predominance of evil forces operating in a certain locality, a cause should be sought, quite logically and properly. A particularly high incidence of traffic accidents at a certain intersection will prompt an investigation of the site by the authorities, and if indeed there seems to be more than a fair share of accidents or anomalies in the Bermuda Triangle, by all means let us look into it. But first let's get our definitions correct.

Look at the accompanying map of the area. On it you will see designated the locations of the major events that the writers would have us accept as proof of the Triangle mystery. Bear in mind that a number of these reported disappearances are represented here by the "found abandoned" markings, and that of these a good number have been explained—crews rescued and cause determined.

These "disappearances" are the ones writers such as Berlitz have listed, and therefore the truth or falsity of the mystery depends on these cases.

Excuse the rhetorical question, but how many of these alleged disappearances occurred within the Bermuda Triangle? One that is gleefully offered up by the believers actually happened in the Pacific! Others are not included here because the scale of the map would not allow me to show them—they were as far away as Ireland and the coast of Portugal.

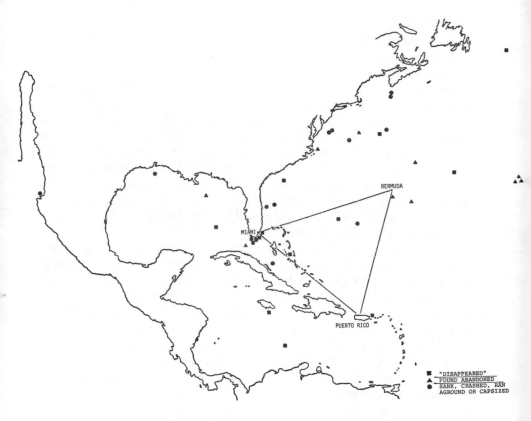

BERMUDA

MIAMI

PUERTO RICO

■ "DISAPPEARED"
▲ FOUND ABANDONED
● SANK, CRASHED, RAN AGROUND OR CAPSIZED

The "mysterious" Bermuda Triangle.

The point is that, if it exists at all, this is certainly a most diffuse phenomenon, and it appears that it only proves, as the old saw tells us, that "accidents will happen." I must mention that I refused to include on the map those alleged accidents that never took place at all or involved nonexistent craft or people. Also, you will not find here those "vanishments" that took place somewhere along a thousand- to three-thousand-mile-long plotted voyage that *might* have led the travelers through the Triangle. In some cases a ship left port and failed to show up on the other side of the world. I cannot allow the creators of the legend to include these incidents in their evidence.

One example described in Larry Kusche's book serves to illustrate how careful one has to be in accepting what is asserted as evidence. According to the claimed version of an incident discussed in *The Bermuda Triangle Mystery—Solved,* "Thirty-nine persons vanished north of the Triangle on a flight to Jamaica on February 2, 1953. An SOS, which ended abruptly without explanation, was sent by the British York Transport just before it disappeared. No trace was ever found." Now let's look at the facts.

The flight plan specified Jamaica as a destination, it's true, and this would seem to connect it with the Triangle. But the plane, when it was lost, was on a flight from the Azores to Newfoundland, in Canada, a flight that took it along a northwesterly path *away* from the dreaded area! The plan called for a stop in Newfoundland, *then* a flight to Jamaica. Since its terminal destination was Jamaica, the promulgators of the Legend called it "a flight to Jamaica" without further explanation. Moreover, the plane admittedly was lost "north of the Triangle"—nine hundred miles north of it! There is no mention of the weather, but the *New York Times* that day reported an "icy, gale-swept North Atlantic . . . strong winds and torrential rains . . . winds up to seventy-five miles an hour."

Then there is the mysterious SOS signal "which ended abruptly without explanation." This sounds logical enough. An aircraft, lashed by a severe storm in the middle of the Atlantic in winter, gets into trouble, radios the standard international distress call, and crashes without further "explanation." A tragedy, but one that has occurred *hundreds* of times around the world, and not at all strange or unexplainable. But it would have been, had not someone like Larry Kusche scrutinized the information that the promoters of this nonsense have offered the public to make their point.

The media are largely to blame for the Bermuda Triangle deception. Initially, they gave Berlitz the raw material he needed. Uncritical publishers regularly turn out books and periodicals without checking the accuracy of their contents. They call such trash "nonfiction," and the public assumes that "nonfiction" is synonymous with "truth." Some publishers even claim that the works they publish are researched thoroughly to ensure factual content, although this is not the case.

Kusche reviewed another Berlitz book, *Without a Trace,* which purports to refute Kusche's revelations in his own book but fails miserably. In the review, Kusche wrote, "His [Berlitz's] credibility is so low that it is virtually nonexistent. If Berlitz were to report that a boat were red, the chance of it being some other color is almost a certainty. He says things that simply are untrue. He leaves out material that contradicts his 'mystery.' A real estate salesman who operated that way would end up in jail." Amen.

As I sit typing this book, I wonder, as I often do, why I have to trouble with such transparent hoaxes as the Bermuda Triangle. It is the product of mass exposure, repeated lies, large profits from book sales, irresponsible publishers, a gullible public, and the current taste for the ridiculous. Men like Berlitz must be highly amused to see their pseudoscientific notions accepted so widely. There are no laws that protect the consumer from these misrepresentations as in the case of other products. That's what it boils down to: Literature about these subjects is a consumer product and should be regulated by the same laws that ensure the quality of other products. The consumer should have the right to return the product for a refund if it is faulty. The Berlitz books about the Bermuda Triangle are, in my opinion, in this category of unsatisfactory goods.

Unconvinced? Read on. The loss of Eastern Airlines Flight 401 is a good example of Berlitz's hyperbole and evasive writing. He tells us that the Eastern plane "suffered a loss by disintegration." Sounds scary, doesn't it? The image that arises in one's mind is of an aircraft peacefully humming through the sky and then suddenly beginning to break into pieces in midair for no reason at all. How strange. But not quite so strange when we discover that the crew of the plane had switched off the autopilot in the black of night over the Florida Everglades (where there are no ground lights for reference), worked on a flight problem in the cockpit, and failed to notice the loss of altitude until they *flew into the ground*—and disintegrated!

But Berlitz goes even further back into history: to 1492, and Christopher Columbus. He writes that Columbus reported "what appeared to be a fireball which circled his flagship." Really? Kusche, referring to *the same source used by Berlitz*, Columbus's own logbook, finds a reference by Columbus to a "great flame of fire" that he observed one night falling into the sea. A rational person would conclude, as would the great navigator, that the fireball was a bright meteor. There was no reported panic among the crew, as there would have been had the object "circled his flagship," a phenomenon invented by Berlitz. If it had indeed circled, and particularly if it had chosen the flagship to revolve around, there would be a mystery. But it was a perfectly explainable occurrence, noteworthy only because of its spectacular nature and the fact that it is rarely seen.

I could go on and on with more debunking of The Legend as Created by Berlitz, but I will leave you to Kusche's book after one more shot at the Triangle. I refer to the case of Flight 19, comprised of the Navy Avengers that started the controversy when they were lost at sea.

The Bermuda Triangle enthusiasts would have us believe that on December 5, 1945, five fully equipped Avenger torpedo bombers took off from Fort Lauderdale Naval Air Station in Florida on a scheduled two-hour flight into the Bermuda Triangle and back. At 3:45 that afternoon, about the time he would have called in for landing instructions, the flight leader reported that they were lost, that the crews didn't know which way was which, and that nothing seemed to be what it should be. They could not even see the sun to get their bearings, and after a final call at 4:25 they vanished, we are told, never to be seen again. A rescue plane sent to find them disappeared abruptly in the same way. Other rescue planes—three hundred of them, aided by twenty-one ships crisscrossing the area the next day—failed to find a trace of either flight. Six aircraft and twenty-seven men had disappeared in the Triangle!

Larry Kusche, after examining over four hundred pages of an official report, came to a saner conclusion. Contrary to the claims of Triangle buffs, the Navy Board of Investigation called in to examine the matter was not at all baffled by the tragedy. The Avengers had been on a training flight, a simple, common exercise to put new pilots through their paces. The bad weather conditions at the time were not dangerous unless "ditching" had to be accomplished; then the nature of the sea, described as "rough and unfavorable" in the Navy report, would be critical. The compass on the flight leader's plane failed, and the others were dependent upon his guidance. It was too late by the time he turned over leadership to another pilot, since fuel was low and they were still at sea. Strange statements attributed to the pilots by Berlitz do not appear in the report, though all information was available to the investigators. The pilots were understandably lost, flew around in confusion until out of fuel, ditched, and sank in rough seas. The search plane, known to be dangerous because of the frequent presence of gas fumes in the crew area, could easily have exploded and gone down in a perfectly explainable accident, especially in view of the conditions at the time. In fact, it *was* seen to explode by personnel on a ship in the area, and thus its real fate is known.

The Navy report listed fifty-six facts and fifty-six opinions concerning the mishap. To those who produced the report, there was no mystery. Invented radio transmissions, exaggerations, and pure fiction turned the tragedy into a supernatural event and got the entire Bermuda Triangle Mystery started off in great style. In addition, the facts were ignored by the media, and the delusion continued until Kusche, in twenty-six pages of facts and maps, demolished the "mystery" of Flight 19 in his book.

Those intrepid adventurers who set out with Berlitz to find Atlantis never issued a report. If they didn't at least dunk him in the Caribbean Sea for his presumption, they get no credit for spirit. Any red-blooded crew would do that to a captain who hung such an albatross around *their* necks.

Another idea espoused by Berlitz is his Pyramid Theory, which is based on two heavy bits of data. One is a supposed 470-foot-high pyramid under the ocean (in the *National Enquirer* tabloid it became 780 feet high!) that he says he hopes will provide proof of the existence of Atlantis and which "seems to be a repository for some strange electronic activity." The other is a 1,000-foot-long and apparently man-made mosaic resembling a road, located underwater less than half a mile off Bimini's west coast. Both, says this scholar, prove the presence of Atlantis.

Let us consider the "Bimini Road" first. To get rid of two nuisance elements that are dragged in joyfully by believers in this perfectly explainable phenomenon, I turn to the pages of *Nature*, the British science journal, where a Mr. W. Harrison reports that "columns" found two miles from the "road" site are actually cement, cast in the shape of the barrels in which the raw product was contained when it was dumped overboard during some unspecified calamity in the past. The wooden staves having rotted away, the castings were left there to be misinterpreted by the Atlantis cult. Two fluted lengths of marble found nearby are very probably of similar origin. It is not uncommon to find such junk in the area, due to the probability of groundings so close to shore and the resulting emergency measures that were needed. Shipping records show that such ballast was frequently carried by merchants for this purpose. But on such ordinary evidence are great idiocies founded.

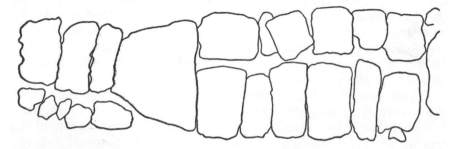

The underwater "road" one half
mile off the west coast of Bimini.

The "road" itself is quite impressive, and I can see why it would be misunderstood at first. It is a pair of semiregular strips running parallel to the shore, separated by some seventy feet and consisting of roughly rectangular blocks of highly varied sizes measuring from five to twenty feet on a side. Unless a geologist were consulted, one might easily believe them to be man-made. Actually, the "road" is made up of what is known to geology as "beach rock," and it is typical of such formations in many parts of the world. Beach rock is found as far away from Bimini as Australia and as close by as the Dry Tortugas. In fact, the south shore of Bimini itself is "paved" with such rocks.

Beach rock is formed by a cementing process of nature. Grains of sand, washed by the tides over a period of as little as a few decades, can pick up calcium carbonate from the sea, mostly from the remains of shelled inhabitants. This substance is deposited between the grains like a cement. The resulting rock mass is quite hard (limestone and marble are composed of calcium carbonate) but it fractures readily. The shore of Bimini once extended to the "road," and beach rock that bordered that shore went through a process which is happening to the fresh beach rock on the present-day shoreline. Exposed to the sun, and undermined by slipping sand that is washed away from beneath the rock slabs, the mass cracks in rather straight lines, first in one direction parallel to the shore, then at right angles. The result is long strips of bricklike rocks weighing from one to ten tons each. Later the strips are submerged as the actual shoreline changes.

But, we hear the believers saying, beach rock would have been the most readily available material to build with. True, but it would have been an inferior material, and it would be quite strange to find that it parallels the shore, but is not found inland, leading to other wonders. And why are no other artifacts but barrels made of cement found near such a structure?

But we need not pursue that line of reasoning, no matter how productive, for a geology student, John Gifford, has conducted a series of tests and observations that have proved the "Bimini Road" to be perfectly natural and not at all man-made, and subsequent tests done by E. A. Shinn at a lab in Miami have clinched the case.

If the Atlanteans had chosen to construct the "road" with beach rock, they would of course have chosen the blocks that best fit together, and thus there would be no continuous consistency in the layering of adjacent blocks. Core samples taken from adjacent blocks by Gifford and Shinn and carefully analyzed show consistent layering and grain size, much as a ballistics test shows striations to be similar on bullets from the same gun. Carbon dating was used on shell material found embedded in the rock and showed it to be 2,200 years old—much too

Beach rock on the coast of Australia. Did Atlantis extend *this* far?

young for the mythical Atlantis, even if the rocks *had* been moved by man. And perhaps worst of all, though the Bimini beach rock on the present shoreline yields scraps of glass bottles, nails, and nuts that were incorporated in its formation, nary a trace of a TV set, laser tube, or any other artifact has been found in the "road" rocks. Edgar Cayce, the reputed visionary and prophet, tells us that these things were common in Atlantis.

So the "Bimini Road" is of natural origin, formed relatively recently and in no way an artifact of any lost civilization. Who is wrong? Certainly Berlitz is, concerning this piece of evidence. And so are some *real* scientists—Dr. J. Manson Valentine and Dr. David D. Zink, a marine archaeologist and a historian respectively. Funded by the Edgar Cayce Foundation, they came to a wrong conclusion in *Explorer's Journal*. They did not do the careful, methodical work that Gifford and Shinn did, both on the site and later with samples in their lab as reported in *Sea Frontiers* (May-June 1978).

Is this information available to Berlitz? If *I* can find it, so can *he*. His consulting resources are greater, and his funds limitless. One conclusion to be drawn is that he knew the truth and ignored it, preferring the romantic legend and seeing another best-selling book on the horizon. Are there *never* any clouds on that horizon?

Then there is that giant "pyramid" under the ocean. Berlitz says he has scientific proof of it, with measurements and all. Well, we'll see. In March 1978, Larry Kusche challenged Berlitz to provide proof of the pyramid. Kusche offered to put up $10,000 against a similar amount to be wagered by Berlitz. The money would be deposited in a Massachusetts bank, the entire amount awardable to the winning party. Berlitz only had to prove that the claimed gigantic pyramid under the ocean was real to collect the money and Kusche's admission that Berlitz was right. Berlitz refused the challenge. To see why he would not attempt a proof, we must examine his "evidence."

When I consulted Bob Heinmiller, formerly of the Woods Hole Oceanographic Institution and now at the Massachusetts Institute of Technology, I was told that Captain Don Henry, who provided Berlitz with the sonar tracing that purports to show the wonderful pyramid, could have produced the tracing without any trouble. In such a representation, the vertical component is highly exaggerated for greater clarity. After all, what is needed from the chart is an idea of the depth below the boat, and this is an ideal way to portray it. In the chart shown by Berlitz, the so-called pyramid may represent a bit of underwater terrain having a gentle slope of only *2 to 3 degrees!* To get some idea of the actual incline represented, imagine a twelve-inch ruler on a tabletop with eight pennies stacked under one end. *That*, in miniature, is what

Don Henry passed over in his boat to obtain the trace he sold to Berlitz!

The tracing submitted by Henry was not "side-scanning sonar," as Berlitz claims. This detail was added to substantiate the profile obtained. The tracing is ordinary sonar, subject to the same interpretation as all other sonar traces. And the boat speed necessary to obtain such a tracing of a *real* 470-foot pyramid would have to be, at regular chart speeds, about ten inches per second! Try holding a boat at that speed to obtain such a trace. It's about half a mile per hour!

But we are assured by Dr. J. Manson Valentine of the Miami Museum of Science that "the sonar tracings clearly show a massive, symmetrical pyramid resting on a nearly flat ocean floor." I wonder when the mermaid exhibit opens at the Miami Museum of Science? Perhaps right after the exhibit of Tooth Fairy Footprints has a run.

The *National Enquirer* and *People* magazine carefully censored out a section of the sonar chart of the "pyramid" that Berlitz unwittingly left in his book *Without a Trace*. This deleted portion is obvious proof that the alleged pyramid is not what they'd like it to be. Examine the

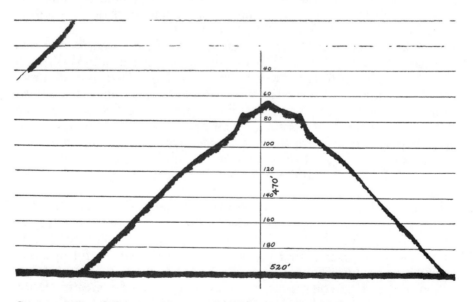

Sonar tracing of the "giant pyramid" alleged by Charles Berlitz.

illustration, and you'll see what I mean. At the upper left is a line that represents the part of the tracing that *preceded* the "pyramid" on the right. Berlitz wisely chose to ignore this, since it shows that the tracing representing the left side of the "pyramid" is actually a *continuation* of the other line. You see, a sonar tracing, on reaching the top of the chart, drops to the bottom again instead of running off the top of the paper. The "pyramid" seems to begin at the bottom; actually it began somewhere way off to the left. It's a case of the truth being evident once the entire record is seen. It's a song that is sung often throughout this book, and the tune is worth learning.

Heinmiller says that such artifacts are often found on sonar tracings. A pyramid shape can be obtained merely by encountering a small slope, then *reversing the direction of the boat* to get a reverse slope on the sonar. The effect is a pyramid—exactly what Berlitz is now trying to sell us, and for which he dragged all those experts into the Caribbean. The U.S. Navy says it's not there. Why would all those folks believe Berlitz? Because he can tell them about it in thirty languages? Or are they just a bit dense?

According to Bob Heinmiller, it is impossible to tell just what Henry passed over, or where he went, to make this tracing. We do not know the speed of the boat, the speed of the tracing paper in the chart recorder, or the vertical emphasis used. But a structure such as the one claimed by Berlitz could not possibly have escaped detection by those who have been meticulously charting the area for decades. Heinmiller is well aware of the media's attitude about the matter, for he has been called on the phone several times by people of the press who ask him to comment on the claim, and he ends up having to deal with questions about UFOs and various weird beliefs. His matter-of-fact declarations on the subject send the seekers elsewhere for more sensational opinions. Facts are just not very attractive, as usual.

There is much other evidence that contradicts this silly claim. But I tend to disagree with Larry Kusche when he says that Berlitz has perpetrated a hoax. I think Berlitz simply doesn't know any better. His accounts of other wonders give me this distinct impression. But I'll let Kusche sum up the matter himself, since it was his $10,000 that was offered in his bet with Berlitz. "Berlitz," says Kusche, "was not able to accept the challenge to prove the existence of the alleged pyramid because it is impossible to do so—since there *is* no pyramid. Had Berlitz accepted the challenge, it would have publicly emphasized the fact that he is prone to making sensational, erroneous, unprovable statements with regard to para-scientific subjects. Berlitz has once again misled the public with false information that he will not and cannot substantiate."

To Charles Berlitz, I say: Charlie, if you ever *do* find a pyramid in the ocean via sonar, it will look on your chart much like the Empire State Building because of the vertical exaggeration of the recording technique. And if you ever say you have found the Empire State Building somewhere in the Caribbean, I won't be the least bit surprised.

---4---

Into the Air, Junior Birdmen!

The sky is falling!
The sky is falling!
—Chicken Little
and other silly folks

Not unexpectedly, many of the varieties of nonsense that enchant the public are associated with the heavens. Mankind has for thousands of years looked up into the outer reaches of his world with awe and respect, envying the ability of birds to penetrate at least superficially into the sky, and peopling that region with gods. Our religions tell us that after death we may join the spirits that dwell there.

It is convenient to have one's wonders in the outer limits and beyond. That way, they may not be properly taken in hand for examination, and any surmise or assigned aspect is acceptable. It cannot be denied that the fascinating sight of a starry night gives rise to all sorts of speculation, and in this age of space travel and extraterrestrial wonders, everyone's attention has been more than ever directed upward. In most cases, we are unable to evaluate what we see.

The Sputniks and their progeny introduced a great deal of debris into the heavens, and the UFO mania was one of the results. After a considerable decline, the old notion of astrology became interesting once more, and any aspect of astronomical discovery was dragged in to support it. In anticipation of eventual planetary probes, "psychic" performers ventured to outguess the scientists by "astrally" voyaging into outer space. Primitive peoples were credited with achievements exceeding those of modern civilization and were said to have been visited by "ancient astronauts." This chapter will examine some of these fantasies.

By far, the oldest of the claptrap philosophies of mankind is astrology. In the United States alone there are more than twenty thousand practicing astrologers casting horoscopes and taking the money of literally millions of credulous believers. But there is probably no other major delusion that is more easily examined and shown to be totally without any logical basis. Thus, its hold on the public is all the more remarkable. This can only be understood when we realize just how vague and universal are the declarations it makes and notice that the average, uncritical observer resorts to the most foolish rationalizations to excuse its failure to predict and to define.

Accepting the claims of astrology is much like accepting the laws pertaining to property rights and slavery set up over three thousand years ago by the rulers of Babylon, and using their theories of medicine as well, for that is when the rules that are still used by modern astrologers today were devised. When this rigid set of regulations came up against the Christian faith, there arose a problem that was, as usual, neatly explained away by the practitioners. The one single horoscope that would seem of greatest interest to early Christians was that of Christ, but the astrologers, well aware of the opposition of the church to their art (the priests had their own methods to promote), feared casting such a horoscope because they would be accused of making God subject to the controlling forces of the heavens He had created! Such a paradox was not to be countenanced. But Roger Bacon, a devout astrologer and Christian, saved the situation with a masterpiece of rationalization. He declared, in a letter to the pope, that God had willed his son to be born at a time when the signs were auspicious and in harmony with the constellations. Bravo!

According to Evry Schatzman, president of the Union Rationaliste in France, "The actual social function of astrology is to help isolate the faithful from social and political struggles." He may be right. It certainly serves to release man from having to take the blame for his own stupidities. A bad conjunction of planets can always be blamed for unfortunate occurrences. Whatever its function, astrology is an irrationality that serves mankind poorly. Dennis Rawlins, an astronomer, perhaps said it best: "Those who believe in astrology are living in houses with foundations of Silly Putty."

I was never prouder of a member of my profession than I was when actor Tony Randall appeared on Dinah Shore's TV show on a day when astrology was being extolled. Dinah had been speaking with film star Charlton Heston and had determined that he was a Scorpio. So was another entertainer, Chevy Chase, she enthused, and remarked that she could not imagine two persons as unalike as Heston and Chase. But, she went on, the personalities of the two men *must* be similar because they shared the same birth sign! Thus was astrology reconciled with hard facts. When Randall entered and sat down, he was immediately asked to tell *his* birth sign. He snorted majestically and refused to respond, saying that to answer the query would insult the intelligence of the American people. The applause was light in the studio, but in my living room it was loud, considering it came from only one person.

It has become almost impossible to attend a social gathering without being asked your astrological sign. I always ask the questioner to guess, and the guesses are quite funny. I'm always given two or three alternatives, then asked which is correct. If I answer, "Try ——," it is immediately discovered that my outward character fits that sign. I counter by saying that I only suggested that my questioner *try* that sign, and another is chosen. And so on. Second-guessing is a popular pastime, it seems. (For some reason, I'm not very popular at these parties.)

It is one thing to argue that astrology is not a rational belief, and another to show that it does not work. The former is fairly easy to demonstrate.

For example, in the unlikely and long-sought event that the sun, moon, and all the planets lined up in a straight line to combine their gravitational pulls, the effect on the human body would be nullified if the person merely sat down from a standing position! Lowering the body a distance of twenty-five inches would bring it closer to the gravitational center of the earth and neutralize *all* effects of the other heavenly bodies that we are told have such influence!

If we consider the scale of the universe, we begin to see just how ridiculous belief in astrology can be. Astronomers measure distances in their business in terms of the speed of light. The basic unit is the light-year, or the distance light travels in one year. Since light travels some 186,000 miles in a second, a light-year's equivalent in miles is rather unwieldly. To say that the star Sirius is 51,000,000,000,000 miles away is a bit awkward; its astronomical distance of 8.7 light-years is much easier.

Similarly, light-speed units provide some idea of the distance involved within the solar system. Look up at the moon. What do you see? You see the moon as it *was* about 1.3 seconds ago. In other words, it is 1.3 light-seconds away; that's how long it took the moonlight you see to reach the earth. The sun is about 8.3 light-*minutes* away. Jupiter can be as much as 51 light-minutes away from Earth, and Pluto 5.6 light-*hours*. Some stars that we see in the night sky aren't really "there" at all; we see the light they emitted anywhere from a few years to several thousand years ago. Astrology would have us believe that if, at the moment of birth, the sun is aligned with a set of stars that aren't even "there" as we see them, one's future or character will be different from what it would be if the sun were aligned with *another* set of not-there stars. Is this not irrational?

With some 250,000,000,000 stars in our own particular galaxy that surrounds us, and about 100,000,000,000 other galaxies available to influence us, it seems that a possible 25,000,000,000,000,000,000,000 stars enter into our fortunes. For a bit of flavor, throw in a few hundred asteroids (minor planets) that are part of our solar system but not part of astrology. The possibilities are endless.

Using wishful thinking and a set of invented zodiacal signs as guides, early theorists came up with astrology—or, more correctly, astrologies, for the various races developed not only their own mythical figures but also their own rules. At this point, as in the case of so many other bogus theories, a bit of simple logic applies: If the basic idea is the same, yet more than one system arises, each giving different results in accordance with different, mutually incompatible rules, then either all the systems are false or only one is correct. The former is more likely, since astrology simply does not work, despite the believers' constant acceptance and verification of its efficiency. Ben Franklin said it well: "Quacks are the greatest liars in the world, except their patients."

We are told that the most important general astrological influence is the position of the sun in the zodiac (the set of twelve constellations girdling the sky) at the moment of birth. Thus, an examination of this claim alone should teach us something about the degree of rationality and the general quality of astrological theory.

One of the obvious questions that comes to mind concerning the influence of this "birth sign" on the character and future of each person arises when we consider those born on exactly the same day, at the same hour, and (another important consideration in astrology) in the same geographical location. Would not these persons have very similar horoscopes—indeed, identical horoscopes—and therefore the same future and personality? Not necessarily, say the astrologers. We are told that the *exact* time of birth (meaning within several minutes) can make a great difference, because the "ascendant sign" (the one rising on the horizon at the moment of birth), as well as the position of the moon in the zodiac band of twelve astrological signs, can be very important. But, we counter, what of twins, who are certainly born at nearly the same time and assuredly in the same geographical location? There is a handy explanation for any discrepancy here, too. It is said that in such cases there is a shift in the heavenly bodies during the short period of time separating the two births.

But when astrology "experts" seek to explain away any dissimilar characteristics of twins with this "change of ascendant and/or moon position" malarkey, is this not merely fitting the facts to the theory? I maintain that it is. Similarities in character and fortune are ascribed to similarities in horoscope details, and dissimilarities are attributed to even the most minor discrepancies among the charts. It is a procedure that satisfies uncritical observers but not skeptics.

The biggest rub of all, however, occurs with the all-important and most powerful of influences, the "birth-sign" designation. There are two general classes of astrology being followed today: "Sidereal" astrology and "Tropical" astrology. The first deals with the actual *constellation* in which the sun is located at the moment of birth. The second handles the *sector*, a 30-degree-wide slice of the zodiac. This division became necessary, you see, because constellations such as Virgo, which bulges beyond the confines of that allotted 30 degrees, and Libra, which occupies only half the allotted area, created a situation in which mythical figures were hanging over everywhere, and so someone had to "draw the line." Some constellations are barely within the traditional 16-degree-wide band of the zodiac, while the Man-Killing-a-Snake-or-Dragon (take your choice) is on the zodiac but not used. Ever hear of anyone born under the sign of Ophiuchus? Early Greek zodiacs were very awkward, with thirteen signs including the Pleiades, but the latter was dropped to make things neater.

In spite of the clumsy solutions to these problems in dividing the not-so-cooperative heavens, a glaring defect remains which is not generally known to the public. Were you born on August 7, for example? Astrologers tell us that this is smack dab in the middle of the sign of Leo, which extends from July 23 to August 22. Thus, one born on this happy day is certainly a classic Leo, correct? Wrong. You were actually born while the sun was in Cancer. Similarly, April 7, which is said to be a strong Aries, is actually in Pisces. Is something fishy becoming evident? Besides Pisces, that is?

As an amateur astronomer, I have long been aware that the mythological constellation figures are not really there at all. Lest this seem rather basic and evident, you should be aware that there are countless adherents of astrology with whom I have spoken over the years who believe that, given a clear night and a little instruction, they would be able to spot the main signs of the zodiac in the heavens easily. They

The constellations Leo (lion) and Cancer (crab) in the zodiac.

are wrong. Reproduced here is a pair of astrologically significant signs as sketched out by the stars. One is a lion, the other is a crab. If you can find them in there, you're a Gunga Din; if you can even draw the line separating the two, you get points.

In any case, the stars in a constellation are very unlikely to be close to one another. They are nearly always widely separated, only appearing to be close in the same way that the windshield wiper on your car might appear to be wiping the car ahead or the traffic light two blocks away.

A book somewhat facetiously titled *Astrology for Adults*, and described as "a must" by the *Fort Worth Press*, contains numerous statements that reveal much about the tactics of those who push astrology. The following passage is typical of their Catch-22 technique.

> Pisces is the sign of both the highest types and the dregs of humanity. Neptune, the deceptive planet . . . is also the planet of high ideals. Occasionally, you may find that one of your descriptions [obtained from your horoscope] does not seem to refer to you at all but may instead resemble a person or persons intimately in your life. Neptune in Gemini can give mental fantasies and confusion, or it can add the superlative qualities of genius to the mind. Pluto is the planet of crime and its opposite, that is, work for the benefit of all humanity. Saturn in Aquarius can cause accidents to the lower leg or ankles, cancer of the lymph glands or strokes . . . colds and dental troubles are the most common of Saturn's health defects.

From this and mountains of other evidence, it is apparent that, logically, astrology *should* not work. Couple this with the mathematical/ physical fact that the gravitational influence of the physician's body as he assists childbirth has far greater effect on the baby being born than the entire gravitational field of the planet Mars, and we cannot accept astrology from a philosophical point of view either. But, as with all such notions, the most important question is: *Does* it work?

Early in 1978 I had an ideal opportunity to test a pet theory of mine. The chance arose when a radio station in Winnipeg, Canada, phoned and asked me to do an interview via telephone from my home in New Jersey. I agreed, but suggested a novel approach. I instructed the host to advertise on the show that he would have an "astro-graphologist" available by phone the following week, and to tell listeners to send in samples of handwriting and their birthdates. The following week he called me while on the air and referred to three listeners he had standing by on the telephone to hear their analyses. They were asked, at the conclusion, to rate the "readings" from one to ten. My real identity was not given; I was identified by a fictitious name, sort of a nom de charlatan. I was hugely successful, getting accuracy ratings of nine, ten, and ten. This changed to straight tens when the first listener noted that I had said he "disliked hard work" when in fact, he insisted, he was a laborer and thus accustomed to hard work. "But," I countered, "I said that you *disliked* hard work." "True," he replied. "I guess you're right. I don't really *like* it." And he changed my score to ten.

The amazing thing about this episode is that I did not have the handwriting samples or the birthdates; and I read, word for word, three readings that had been given months before in Las Vegas by Sydney Omarr, one of the best-paid and most reliable astrologers in the United States, on "The Merv Griffin Show" for three members of that television program's audience. And these readings, for three *other* people, months and thousands of miles apart, were accepted and scored as 100 percent accurate! When it was revealed that I was a fake, and my real name was announced, the three listeners hung up their phones and probably had a thought or two about their powers of discrimination.

One of these Omarr readings was as follows:

> People close to you have been taking advantage of you. Your basic honesty has been getting in your way. Many opportunities that you have had offered to you in the past have had to be surrendered because you refuse to take advantage of others. You like to read books and articles that improve your mind. In fact, if you're not already in some sort of personal service business, you should be. You have an infinite capacity for understanding people's problems and you can sympathize with them. But you are firm when confronted with obstinacy or outright stupidity. Law enforcement would be another field you understand. Your sense of justice is quite strong.

Does my reader see himself/herself in that description? If so, give me ten points.

Many years ago, when two friends of mine in Montreal, Canada, started a newspaper called *Midnight,* I was asked to write an astrological column for it. Had I any notion of what that newspaper would become, I'd have run away screaming. As it was, I agreed to give it a try, seeing the chance to conduct an excellent experiment at the same time. I went out and bought an astrology magazine, clipped a few pages of daily forecasts at random, mixed them in a hat, and pasted them up in any old fashion. With the name Zo-ran at the top of the column, it went to press.

Several weeks later I watched in dismay as two office workers at the corner soda counter eagerly scanned my fake column for their individual prognostications. They squealed with delight on seeing their future so well laid out, and in response to my query said that Zo-ran had been "right smack on" last week. I did not identify myself as Zo-ran; I was only seventeen at the time, and not very scholarly-looking. Reaction in the mail to the column had been quite interesting, too, and sufficient for me to decide that many people will accept and rationalize almost any pronouncement made by someone they believe to be an authority with mystic powers. At that point, Zo-ran hung up his scissors, put away the paste pot, and went out of business.

I often wonder what would have happened had I stayed at it. Success in the occult world can lead to positions of great prestige and power. When the Nazis took over in Germany, as Dusty Sklar points out in her book *Gods and Beasts*, they were helped along by widespread belief in occult powers, symbolism, and magic, as well as astrology. Mythology became more than mere stories, and the destiny of Germany was discovered to be written in the stars. But Nazi rule needed claptrap galore to build its greatest piece of pseudoscience—the Aryan Legend. Though this myth was to be implanted in minds already prepared for it by various stupidities from astrology to hollow-earth theories, the Nazis needed to stamp out the lesser "isms" and notions that distracted the German people from this unifying doctrine. The notorious Reinhard Heydrich issued a directive aimed at removing "occultist teachings which pretend that the actions and missions of human beings are subject to mysterious magic forces." He listed astrologers, occultists, spiritualists, followers of occult theories of rays, fortune tellers, faith healers, Christian Scientists, anthroposophists, theosophists, and arisophists. They were all to be "purged." One wonders what that entailed.

But while throwing out astrology and magic, Hitler and his lackeys privately maintained their own occult advisers. One of the most powerful was an astrologer-magician named Steinschneider, who operated under the name Erik Jan Hanussen. He predicted great success for the Nazi party, at a time when it needed it, and was Hitler's darling of the moment. Indeed, Hanussen's personal charm and speaking mannerisms were studied by Der Führer carefully; he knew a good gimmick when he saw it. It mattered not at all that Hanussen was Jewish. His predictions were widely published, and they all helped the Nazi cause.

But Hanussen went a step further than was wise. No doubt he could have been court astrologer all the way to the eventual Armageddon that the stars failed to warn the Nazis about, but on the eve of the famous Reichstag fire, which is attributed to the Nazis, Hanussen had a "vision" during a séance at his home. In his inspired state, he saw a building in flames, and when the fires roared the next day it seemed to confirm his prophetic ability. A few weeks later he was grabbed in

Berlin and driven to the woods nearby, where Nazi bullets ended his career as a soothsayer.

Indeed, the belief in astrology among the Nazi hierarchy was so strong that the Allied forces employed astrologers to tell them when the Nazis would believe that the stars were right for various important undertakings. It was to little avail, however. Astrologers are accustomed to telling people what they want to hear, and tend to speak in generalities that can be interpreted in more than one way. Neither process was of any use in the war effort.

Even the scientific efforts that have been launched in an attempt to legitimize astrology have foundered. They are also prohibitively expensive and difficult to carry out. Recent attempts to test a "Mars Effect" have shown that the Red Planet is just that, and not a magic influence that reaches across space to influence our lives. The Mars Effect was supposed to have been confirmed during investigations of the claim that prominent athletes were more apt to be born when that planet was influencing their sign. Careful tests have failed to support any such claim, though fancy excuses have been plentiful. But more money will go into similar projects. There are plenty of sponsors of such idiocy waiting.

That journal of the irrational, *Psychic News*, proudly announced in April 1978 that Ingo Swann had been proved a real cosmic traveler as a result of approval by two leading lights of the paranormal firmament. According to the newspaper, "Satellites confirm his astral trip to planets," and it quoted U.S. astronaut Edgar Mitchell as saying that Swann "described things and gave details which were not known to scientists until the Mariner 10 and Pioneer 10 satellites flew by the planets and got the information." Not to be outdone, astronomer J. Allen Hynek joined the clamor. "These are matters which Swann couldn't have guessed about or read. His impressions of Mercury and Jupiter cannot be dismissed," said this learned man.

Russell Targ and Harold Puthoff of the Stanford Research Institute were the daring scientists who sponsored this exciting leap into outer space as part of their continuing quest for the unknown. It was done well in advance of the Mariner 10 spacecraft's trip past Mercury and the voyage of Pioneer 10 past Jupiter, and Targ and Puthoff found remarkable similarities between Swann's trip and another they babysat for, supposedly performed by Harold Sherman. Hynek was thrilled. Said he, "I was fascinated by the Jupiter findings of Pioneer 10 when I compared them with Mr. Swann's. His impressions of Jupiter, along with his experience with Mercury, most certainly point the way to more experimentation." That last statement deserves careful analysis. Hynek refers to Swann's drivel about Mercury as "his experience"—he apparently has no doubt that Swann actually went there. It's assumed that he did. And the "point the way" at the end is directed toward more funding of such nonsense, obviously.

But let us see just how exciting these similarities are. Here is a list of the "Jupiter findings" of both Sherman and Swann compared to what has been determined by real science.

SWANN'S CLAIMS	SCIENTIFIC DETERMINATION
Striped planet	True
80,000- to 120,000-mile hydrogen mantle	True
Yellow color	True
Glittering crystals in high atmosphere	Very likely
Stripes are bands of crystals	Wrong
Stripes are like the rings of Saturn, close in	Wrong
The crystals reflect radio waves	Probably not
Roiling gas clouds	Probable
Yellow light, rainbows	Probable
"It's liquid"	(*What's* liquid?)
Cloud cover	True
Surface has dunes of large crystals	Wrong
Tremendous winds	True
Orange or rose-colored horizon	Probable
Overhead greenish-yellow	Not known
Enormous mountain range	Wrong
Sun looks white with greenish corona	(From where?)
Sun looks smaller	Obvious
There's liquid somewhere	(?)
Sand surface is orange	Wrong
Wind blows sand crystals along surface	Wrong
It seems flat	True
A man would sink into the sand surface	Wrong
A tornado	Obvious
Surface gives high infrared count, and heat is held down	(What surface?)
Band of crystals bluish in orbit at the equator	Wrong

SWANN'S CLAIMS	SCIENTIFIC DETERMINATION
Area of liquid	Obvious
Liquid has "icebergs" in it	Wrong
Colder at equator	Wrong
Atmosphere is very thick	Obvious
Mountain chain 30,000 feet high	Wrong

SHERMAN'S CLAIMS	SCIENTIFIC DETERMINATION
Pioneer 10 on collision course with a Jovian moon	Wrong
Larger than Earth (the moon)	Wrong
Great shiny revolving ball (the moon)	True
Surrounded by a swirl of gases (the moon)	Traces, if any
Has a golden glow (the moon)	True
Emits crystal-like sparkles (the moon)	(?)
Jupiter a million or more miles away (from the moon)	Wrong
Eyes could not stand the brightness of Jupiter	Wrong
There are 17 moons around Jupiter	Perhaps
Some moons are much closer to Jupiter	(Than what?)
Moons being created by volcanic action on Jupiter	Wrong
Many asteroids between Mars and Jupiter	True
Some of these asteroids have life forms inferior or equal to ours	Very unlikely
Jupiter bulges in the middle	True
Jupiter is a gaseous mass	Wrong
Myriad colors like fireworks display	Wrong
Red mass moves across Jupiter from "right" to "left"	Wrong
Red mass is followed by a cloud	Wrong
Interior of Jupiter is liquid or gaseous	True (liquid)
Ice crystals	Very likely
Cloud cover miles deep	True
Cloud cover shines yellow, red and green	True

SHERMAN'S CLAIMS	SCIENTIFIC DETERMINATION
Reddish-brown crust on Jupiter	Wrong
Crust is red-hot molten, emits sparks	Wrong
Pioneer 10 will encounter powerful magnetic forces	True
It will encounter winds of terrific velocity	Wrong
It will encounter poisonous gases	Wrong
Atmosphere of dense and rarified layers	Obvious
Volcanic peaks	Wrong
Cones rising miles high; crystal-covered valleys	Wrong
Water	Wrong
Water in solidified form	Wrong
Water in vaporized form	Wrong
Pioneer 10 looks like a bullet with a head; objects on the side; blunt	Wrong

And this is the report with which Targ and Puthoff were "very pleased"? Puthoff said there were "remarkable similarities between the two narrations," and it never dawned on him that during the long, rambling account given by Sherman, he admitted that Swann had visited him a few weeks before this epic adventure—to compare intentions, perhaps? If so, they blew it. The "similarities" they list are: crystals, golden glow, lots of colors, cloud cover, thick atmosphere, orange color, mountain peaks, red-hot surface, cold crystals, swirls, tremendous winds, water, layered atmosphere. Remarkable, isn't it, that two men who are good, cooperative friends could be wrong on so many of their "facts"? And note that Targ and Puthoff searched not for the *truth* of the claims made by the two performers but rather for *similarities*. If they were both wrong in making the same statements, is that significant? In the wonderful world of the parapsychologist, it probably is.

When I asked the scientist and writer Isaac Asimov his opinion of the claims resulting from these flights of fancy, he was understandably annoyed—not with the effort to clear up the mess, but with the vague

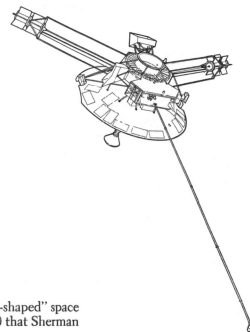

This is the "bullet-shaped" space vehicle Pioneer 10 that Sherman "saw." NASA

claims that had been made. I thank him for having had the patience to plow through much written garbage on the subject.

In summary, here is a breakdown of the revelations of "psychics" Swann and Sherman as they whirled through space to bring us the divinely divined wonders of the planet Jupiter:

Fact, but obtainable from reference books	11
Fact, but obvious	7
Fact, not obtainable from reference books	1
Probable fact	5
Unverifiable due to vagueness or lack of data	9
Probably untrue	2
Wrong	30
Total	65

Being as charitable as possible, and assuming the best concerning the paranormal powers of Swann and Sherman, we can assign them

24 out of 65, or 37 percent "hits." Their errors amount to at least 30 out of 65, or 46 percent. And this assessment deals *only* with the *number* of guesses, not with the quality of the information! Such gross errors as reporting that there are 30,000-foot-high mountain peaks on the Jovian landscape and also sandy, molten crust damn the results beyond redemption!

Or is that quite so? I don't know what Sherman has to say by way of retraction, but Swann has made himself quite clear recently. In conversation with Stewart Lamont, a producer for the BBC, Swann opined that he had not gone to Jupiter after all! Travel by astral means is so fast and giddy, said he, that he had probably shot off into *another* solar system, somewhere in another star's gravity field, and had described for the breathless Hynek, Targ, and Puthoff another planet, *not* Jupiter! Thus we have an explanation for the errors, and all is well in Wonderland once more.

But what of the scientists' acceptance of his description of the planet? According to Hynek, Swann's "impressions . . . cannot be dismissed," and the Stanford Research Institute was "very pleased." Best of all, if Swann was in another planetary system, where was poor Sherman? Does he know?

Does anyone care?

We are fortunate in the United States to have an excellent buffer against pseudoscience as well as an informative and fascinating TV entertainment: the "Nova" program. We see it in the United States on the Public Broadcasting Service (PBS) network. This program is sufficient reason for the public to support PBS efforts. In England the program is known as "Horizon" and is a joint effort of WGBS/Boston and the BBC. There is no finer, more productive alliance in the communications business.

The "Nova/Horizon" exposé of Erich von Däniken's "mysteries" was typical of the program's usual high standards, providing the viewer with ample, authoritative refutation of von Däniken's claims. But at the end of the program, when it came time to handle the "Sirius Mystery," their efforts seemed rather deficient. Although sufficient information was presented to demolish the theory, it was not definitive, and the conclusions were rather weak.

This subject was expounded by writer Robert Temple in his 1976 book *The Sirius Mystery*, which tells of the Dogon tribe in western Africa and its superior knowledge concerning the star Sirius. According to Temple, the Dogon have long known of this star's recently discovered "companion star," Sirius B (1862 is "recent" in astronomical terms), and of its orbit around the main star every fifty years. The technology used by modern astronomers to determine this obscure but scientifically exciting fact was so sophisticated that it was argued by Temple that the Dogon must have had extraterrestrial assistance to have known about it. The Dogon religion (like that of the ancient Egyptians) is very much concerned with this particular star, a bright and prominent object in this tribe's night sky.

Anthropologists have made extensive studies of the Dogon people of Mali. To begin a discussion of this tribe with the usual primitive-standing-around-naked image that is unfortunately brought to mind concerning an obscure African tribe is entirely unwarranted. The Dogon have been exposed to Western "civilization" since the late nineteenth century, and it is not at all unlikely that people living, as they do, along important avenues of travel and trade came into contact with Europeans many times. In fact, for decades their children have been attending a local French-founded school and going on to university education elsewhere. The folks at home would have no problem at all incorporating newfound facts into their religion and cosmogony.

But do the Dogon really postulate Sirius B, and do they really know about its fifty-year orbit? If they developed the idea of a small, dense "companion star," and determined the duration of its orbit, this must be attributed to superior scientific ability, psychic powers, extraterrestrial help, or sheer luck of very great magnitude.

Let us refer to Temple's book. One of his great finds is a sand picture made by the Dogon to explain their claims. The orbit, as rendered in the picture, has a roughly elliptical shape, and within that curve are two signs that are said to represent Sirius A and Sirius B. But when we consult an original source—in this case, a study by French anthropologists Griaule and Dieterlen—we find a somewhat more complex diagram containing nine signs. None of the nine rests on the circumference of the curve, as a properly drawn orbital diagram would require, but are inside the ellipse. And what of that supposed ellipse? It is more egg-shaped than not and, indeed, we are told by the two French scientists that the Dogon describe it as "the egg of the world," rather than an orbit, and that they frequently represent mythical objects within this egglike shape.

The Dogon diagram is purely and inarguably symbolic in nature; it is not meant to represent an astronomical reality at all. One symbol represents a *third* star (the "sun of women") and another the "star of women," which is supposed to orbit the third star! "Sun" and "star" refer to different entities here, since the Dogon, in spite of their alleged contact with extraterrestrials, seem not to know that the terms refer to the same thing.

The faith the Dogon had in the visitors who dropped by must be

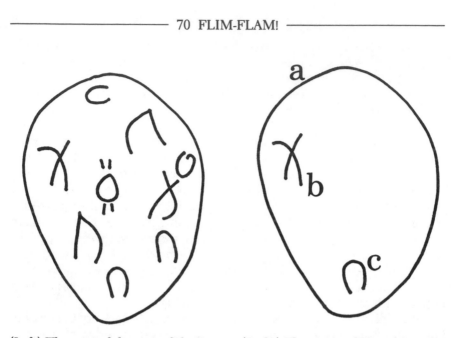

(Left) The original diagram of the Dogon. (Right) The censored Temple version of the Dogon diagram. According to Temple, "a" is the orbit/egg, "b" is the star Sirius, and "c" is its companion star, Sirius B.

somewhat dimmed by the realization that these folks just didn't know the length of their "stellar year," so to speak. You see, the Dogon say it is *sixty* years, not fifty. One would think that voyagers who have mastered astronautics and are able to travel more than 50 billion miles to a landing on Earth would be somewhat more precise.

It is extremely doubtful that the Dogon really have ancient legends that include sophisticated knowledge of stellar orbits. Even if they do, we know they did not obtain such information from visiting beings from outer space. There are many other means by which information about the Sirius double-star system could have come to them, and the rest of their cosmogony cannot be explained away except by the means Temple has used—by ignoring it as inconvenient and extraneous.

I would have liked to believe that the Dogon (as once was thought to be the case with Jonathan Swift and his guesses about Mars) knew of astronomical wonders that were beyond their means to determine. What a wonderful story to tell around the campfire. But it just isn't so.

I had the great satisfaction, many years ago, of proving to myself and to the listeners of "The Long John Nebel Show," a radio program in New York, that most people just love to get in on a good thing. Nebel and I planned in advance to perform a minor experiment, and as we settled in for a long evening of talk about the wonders of a subject very much in demand on that show—flying saucers—we made sure that the telephone lines were cleared for action. It came thick and fast.

I breathlessly described how, earlier that evening, I had been driving through the Perth Amboy area of New Jersey and had seen a V-shaped formation of triangular orange objects going overhead in a northerly direction. I said I wasn't sure whether there had been any noise, because of the traffic sounds around me. Immediately the station switchboard lit up like an electronic Christmas tree, and John's secretary began taking down reports from callers who had also been witnesses to this remarkable sighting. Some were even switched through to the studio and told their stories on the air. Within half an hour we had established the exact number of triangles and the speed, altitude, and precise direction of the formation, and had discovered that I had seen only one pass of the "saucers" when there had been several!

As I look back on it now, I think it was unfortunate that we "blew the gaff" right there on the show about an hour after going on the air. Otherwise the reported sighting would undoubtedly have gone into the vast literature about "unidentified flying objects" and would have been by now one of the unassailable cases quoted by believers. As it was, we mercifully terminated the hoax to show listeners just how easy it was to create from nothing a full-blown flim-flam that would be supported and built upon by willing conspirators.

The UFO silliness can be said to have started during World War II, when military pilots brought back stories of what they dubbed "foo-fighters," which were described as fuzzy balls of light that appeared at the wing tips and kept pace with the planes in flight. To this day, opinions about this phenomenon are varied. "Ball lightning," "St. Elmo's fire" (a static electrical display often seen on sailing ships), Venus and other bright celestial bodies viewed through haze, and various optical effects have been offered as explanations. No doubt part of the explanation lies in the willingness of some pilots to share in the experience by perpetrating small mendacities. In any case, it hardly seems to be in the same category as the more recent and familiar UFO craze.

The French and the Scandinavians reported, without too much effect, some UFO matters in the early 1940s, but until a private pilot named Kenneth Arnold came along with an account of seeing a formation of metallic-looking, "saucer-shaped" disks above Mount Rainier, Washington, in 1947, the matter was a mere curiosity, of concern only to a few journalists. The term "flying saucer" was coined, and soon photos, highly embellished reports, and interviews on the subject were in the newspapers and on the radio daily. A total of 122 sightings were reported to the U.S. Air Force in that year alone, and the annual number increased until 1952, The Year of the Great Saucer Flap, when a grand total of 1,501 UFOs were reported.

Understandably, some citizens were disturbed. It was a period of Cold War intrigue, and a nervous populace demanded explanations. The powers-that-be refused to make any comments other than to dismiss the reports as mistakes made by untrained observers. That was not enough for the curious, and when the Air Force announced in 1950 that Project Blue Book was under way to study reports of UFOs officially, there was great anticipation that revelations would follow. But the study's conclusions were not the ones expected.

In 1965, the year the Air Force issued a summary of its findings, we find this breakdown of the 887 sightings documented:

Astronomical events	245	(27.6%)
Aircraft	210	(23.7%)
Satellites	152	(17.1%)
Hoaxes, imagination, etc.	126	(14.2%)
Insufficient data supplied	85	(9.6%)
Weather balloons	36	(4.1%)
(Still being processed)	17	(1.9%)
Unidentified	16	(1.8%)

Note that less than 2 percent of the total number of sightings remain unidentified. The believers will point with great pride to this residual number and call it highly significant. But again, a lesson has been missed. In any statistical study there is a point at which "noise level" enters the picture. To use a rough analogy, your home sound system has an inherent noise level—for instance, the natural hiss of the tape player—that is always there no matter what improvements are made to suppress it. Does that mean you cannot have excellent results? Of course not. There are established minimum levels for all such "noise"—whether it be in sound, optics, radiation, or actual numbers—where the information-to-noise ratio is quite sufficient to be able to ignore the smaller amount. In the sound reproduction from a tape, one simply cannot notice the noise if it is low enough; in the flying saucer business, 1.8 percent is a very low residue indeed.

Furthermore, we must not commit the error of assuming that the 1.8 percent labeled "unidentified" are "unidentifiable." It is very possible that about 28 percent of that 1.8 percent will eventually be explained as of astronomical origin, about 24 percent will be shown to have been aircraft, and so on.

Getting into the UFO business is easy enough. A little study of the procedure for attracting the media, and adopting the style of the established UFO "experts," will serve nicely. One must be prepared to accept everything easily without any effort to check the facts, and the resulting wonderful stories will be hyperbolized and expanded by the media automatically. Indeed, bad reporting is almost the only reason belief in UFOs persists. A little research results in books that are less exciting but more factual than the one written by John Godwin about the Mantell case, to be discussed. Since the entire UFO matter has been so well and thoroughly handled by others, I will refer my reader to two books: *The World of Flying Saucers* by Donald Menzel and Lyle Boyd, and *UFOs—Explained* by Philip J. Klass. I recommend them both highly.

The NBC-TV network, with its unfailing instinct for public bad taste and its complete abandonment of integrity in two dozen programs entitled "Project UFO," concentrated on several unrelated UFO reports, representing them as related cases that substantiated one another. The series also created fully instrumented and detailed space ships in full color and roaring sound on the basis of "a bright light in the sky," and put highly colored and hyperbolized dialogue into the mouths of the featured actors—all for dramatic purposes, of course. It was stated that the series was "inspired" by Project Blue Book, and indeed only the barest "inspiration" was used. Any resemblance between the reported event and the subsequent representation on the TV screen was an accident that NBC did not permit to happen too often.

As the program closed, viewers were treated to a full-screen picture of the official seal of the U.S. Air Force. This was impressive as an official stamp of approval by the U.S. government, or so it seemed, and superimposed on this was a statement declaring the apparent conclusion of the Air Force study: "The United States Air Force, after twenty-two years of investigation, concluded that none of the unidentified flying objects reported and evaluated posed a threat to our national security."

As an experiment, I ask my reader to obtain some means of measuring seconds—an ordinary watch will do—and go back to that quoted statement. Read it as fast as possible, and time yourself. It takes me a *minimum* of four seconds to do this. But by actual measurement, NBC had that statement before its viewers, superimposed on a distracting design, for a total of just *2.4 seconds!* Why? Because it was essential to avoid criticism based on failure to state such a conclusion. Furthermore, this token concession to the truth conveyed to the viewer less than a third of the content of the conclusion reached by the U.S. Air Force!

Let us assume that some speed-reading viewer *was* able to read the concluding statement. The impression left is that the UFOs might have been extraterrestrial, but that none were dangerous. The believers could smugly relax, knowing that the truth is stated therein. But the actual conclusion, as presented in Project Blue Book (the *source* of the NBC series) is this:

> To date, the firm conclusions of Project Blue Book are:
> 1. no unidentified flying object reported, investigated and evaluated by the Air Force has ever given any indication of threat to our national security;
> 2. there has been no evidence submitted to or discovered by the Air Force that sightings categorized as UNIDENTIFIED represent technological developments or principles beyond the range of present-day scientific knowledge; and
> 3. there has been no evidence indicating that sightings categorized as UNIDENTIFIED are extraterrestrial vehicles.

There it is, directly from Blue Book, not edited and quite readable and easily understood. It is somewhat different from what NBC-TV told its audience.

But let's examine some of the sightings that the USAF studied. One of the most widely reported was the Mantell case, a case in which a life was lost, and which brought the entire matter to international attention. It happened on January 7, 1948, at Godman Air Base in Kentucky. At two thirty in the afternoon, Colonel Guy Hix, the commander of the base, was notified that a long cone-shaped object was in the sky. He asked a flight of four P-51 pursuit planes, already in the air, to investigate. Two of them soon turned back and the other continued on to the original destination, but the lead plane, piloted by Captain Thomas Mantell, reported that he was going to follow the object beyond fifteen thousand feet. Despite having no oxygen equipment in his plane to allow such a pursuit, Mantell tried to reach an altitude of 20,000 feet and blacked out. The plane went out of control and crashed. Mantell had shown signs of great excitement—almost hysteria—during the chase, and his death was reported by the press as having been caused by the UFO.

In John Godwin's *This Baffling World*, we read that "they saw a huge metallic object hovering over the field. It was shaped like a disc, its cone-like top glowing a crimson yellow." Really? Well, I don't much depend on Mr. Godwin for careful reporting. He has the date of the occurrence six months late, for one thing, and he misspells the name of the base, calling it Goodman. He also quotes Major General John

Samford, at a press conference called by the Department of Defense, as saying that the UFOs "seemed to have 'unlimited power—that means power of such fantastic higher limits that it is theoretically unlimited— it's not anything we can understand.'" This is another example of the sensational journalist's favorite ploy, the quote out of context. It fails to mention that Samford, the USAF Chief of Intelligence, was referring to the *claims made by the saucer nuts*, and that he also said that the intensive investigation had not "disclosed the existence of any material flying object, except where the report emanated from an observer's sighting of a United States plane or missile and his mistaking it for something else." *Caveat legens.*

Nit-picking? Hardly. Godwin reported that Colonel Hix dispatched a flight of three (not four) F-51 planes (not P-51s) when actually he merely asked the flight—already in the area on a mission ferrying the aircraft from Marietta Air Base in Georgia to Louisville—to investigate. The planes were not carrying oxygen equipment because the mission was a routine low-level one, and since one plane was running dangerously low on fuel it may be assumed that the others, including Mantell's, were also low. Such omissions and errors make sightings of UFOs almost impossible to research unless one consults basic sources. Godwin certainly was able to do so, but he chose not to.

What was the UFO in this case? Most books on the subject won't tell you, but the *New York Times* of January 9 told nearly the whole story. Two other pilots, Garrett and Crenshaw, "said they chased a flying object which they believed to be a balloon." Also, reported the *Times*, "Astronomers at Vanderbilt University, Nashville, Tennessee, reported that they saw some object in the sky yesterday afternoon which they believed to be a balloon, but the Weather Bureau at Nashville said it knew of no balloons in that vicinity. In southern Ohio, meanwhile, observers reported seeing a flaming red cone near the army base at Wilmington."

What none of the parties reporting knew, or were going to know for several years, was that the Navy was at that time (in fact, since 1947) experimenting with what came to be known as the Skyhook project. This was a series of experiments with high-altitude balloons that would probe the upper atmosphere and perform secret photoreconnaissance work behind the Iron Curtain. These balloons attained a diameter of as much as 170 feet at an altitude of 120,000 feet—much higher than any aircraft was able to go. At lower altitudes the balloons assumed the shape of a sphere with a long trailing cone hanging down—resembling an elongated ice-cream cone. The descriptions in the *Times* matched these characteristics of the balloons quite well.

The Air Force, through a spokesman, told the curious that Mantell

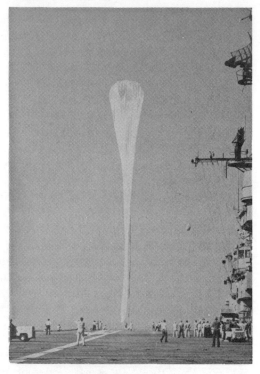

Thomas Mantell chased one of these balloons, believing it to be a UFO. Here, a Skyhook is readied aboard the USS *Valley Forge*. Note the aptness of the description of the balloon as "shaped like an ice-cream cone." U.S. Navy

had been chasing the planet Venus. Not very likely. Venus was up there, all right, but in midafternoon it would have been *very* difficult to see, and it was not in one of its brightest phases at that time. No points for the Air Force on that blunder! The UFO believers have never stopped quoting that one.

Since the weather stations in the area denied that they had any balloons up at the time, the enthusiasts have told us that we may not use that as an explanation. Checking with the Naval Research people, we cannot determine (the records simply don't exist now) whether a Skyhook balloon was up at the time. But since some pilots, the astronomers at Vanderbilt, and others saw the object and described it as a balloon, it is very likely that it was just that. Skyhooks were known to stay up as long as 180 days, wandering about widely, and the description so well fits the Skyhook that it would be amazing if the UFO was not one of the balloons. The path that we may determine for the UFO matches quite well the path that a balloon would have taken on that day, the prevailing winds being what they were. Subsequent sightings of balloons support that conclusion, since the same sequence of events took place after the Skyhook tests were made public, but when the pilots who chased these balloons returned to base, their reports were not of UFOs but of quite ordinary weather-sounding devices. And none of them died chasing will-o'-the-wisps.

To complete the misrepresentation that plagued the Mantell episode, we should look briefly at what NBC-TV's "Project UFO," produced by actor Jack Webb, did with it. It is no surprise that they exaggerated the facts of the case to create a more exciting program. As you read the breakdown that follows, remember their official statement: "This program is a dramatization inspired by official reports of Government investigations of claimed reported sightings of unidentified flying objects on file in the National Archives of the United States."

1. NBC said that Mantell was scrambled to chase the UFO. He was not.
2. NBC said Mantell reached supersonic speeds to pursue the UFO. He did not, and could not.
3. NBC showed him in a jet fighter. He was not in a jet.
4. NBC said he reached 60,000 feet. He did not.
5. NBC said he crashed at a speed of mach 1.5. He did not.
6. NBC showed Mantell using oxygen in the plane. He did not; he had none.
7. NBC said Mantell locked into the UFO with radar. He did not; he had none.
8. NBC said the wreckage of his plane was scattered over several miles. It was not. It was within a thousand yards of the central wreckage.
9. NBC showed the wreckage burning on impact. It didn't burn.
10. NBC said the Air Force finds about 30 percent of reported UFO sightings to be "unexplained." This is *more than five times* the Air Force figure.

With this program, NBC-TV maintained its reputation for distortion, misrepresentation, and exaggeration of the facts.

In the Godwin book we read of a marvelous sighting that took place the night of March 16, 1966. Deputy David Fitzpatrick photographed two "strange objects in the sky," we are told, southeast of Ann Arbor, Michigan. He used a "sub-miniature camera" to photograph the "flying objects." Well, it sounds pretty good, and the photo looks impressive, until one looks into the matter carefully, as Godwin should have done before writing about this story. When I first saw the photo I knew right away what it was. The shape of the lower object tagged it as the moon, and it was probable that the other was either Venus or a bright star. Dennis Rawlins, an astronomer whose specialty is positional astronomy, put the raw data into his computer and came up with some interesting conclusions. First, the photo was a time exposure of eleven minutes and had to have been made with a tripod. It showed the moon and Venus exactly where they should have been—not on March 16 but on March 17, the next morning. The shutter was opened at 5:42 A.M. EST and closed at 5:53. The moon was four days before New Moon phase, and the angle of the path traced is 38 degrees to the horizon. The angle of the planet Venus is 41 degrees, as predicted by the computer readout. In an hour, the sun will rise on the left of the picture. The separation of the two objects shown is 10 degrees 31 minutes, and the larger precedes the smaller by eighteen and a half minutes, again agreeing with the computer prediction. Is there any doubt that the deputy photographed the moon and Venus and sold the picture to the newspapers as a photo of two UFOs?

But John Godwin did not need the skills of Rawlins or the use of a multi-million-dollar computer to discover the true nature of the photograph. All he needed to do was visit a library and consult the good old *New York Times*. On the evening of March 25 an Associated Press story reported that (1) Fitzpatrick used a tripod; (2) the exposure was ten to twelve minutes long; (3) the photo was taken at 5:30 A.M.; and

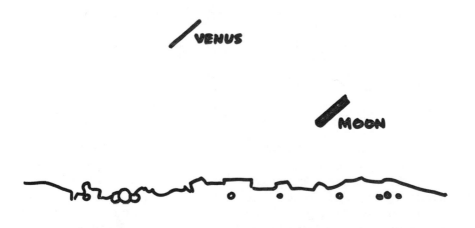

Drawing based on the photo that showed "two UFOs streaking across the night sky, March 16, 1966." Wrong on all counts. This was an eleven-minute exposure of Venus and the Moon on the morning of March 17.

(4) Fitzpatrick and Sheriff's Sergeant Schneider had been watching the objects for three hours! Can we really believe that these two men did not recognize a crescent moon in the morning sky? And the *Times* also carried the news that Dr. J. Allen Hynek himself declared that the photo was a fake! None of this information leaked into Godwin's book, however. It would have ruined a good piece of fiction.

The "contactees"—those who have experienced actual "close encounters of the third kind"—are the ones most celebrated by UFO devotees. The *National Enquirer* adores them and exaggerates their accounts with glee. One such highly touted person was Betty Hill, who said that in 1961, while driving with her husband in New Hampshire, she and Mr. Hill were abducted aboard a flying saucer and underwent various indignities that she recalled only well after she first reported the incident. Her claim has been a *cause célèbre* among UFO nuts ever since. It was immortalized in John Fuller's book *Incident at Exeter*. Fuller has brought us other thrillers of pseudoscience such as *Arigo, Surgeon of the Rusty Knife*, and the Geller epic, *My Story*. I will deal mainly with Mrs. Hill's "star map" claim, but you should know that a Dr. Simon, who hypnotized her, said afterwards, "It was a dream. The abduction did not happen." Despite this statement, the doctor was depicted by believers and the press as being highly supportive of the Hills' claim! It seems evident, based on research done by Robert Sheaffer, a prominent UFO investigator, that Mrs. Hill saw the planet Jupiter, talked her husband into believing it was a UFO, and then imagined that she had been taken aboard and made to forget the experience, which she remembered only after a dream of the supposed event kept recurring. But when she had her story in full bloom, Betty Hill was able to suddenly recall—*three years after the event*—that she had seen a navigation map in the UFO control room, and she sketched it for posterity. This map is one of several that are said to support the Hill claim.

The first thing that made the amateur astronomer in me suspicious is that her map resembles a wallpaper design more than a star chart. Stars are not so uniformly distributed in space. She has marked upon it some "trade routes" of the aliens' world, and therein lies a big reason for some of the subsequent acceptance of the map. Marjorie Fish, presently working at the Oak Ridge National Laboratory in Tennessee, tried to match the Hill map with reality and thought she had succeeded when she somewhat rearranged the viewpoint and redrew a section of the constellation known as Reticulum (the Net) to conform. At first glance there does seem to be a rough correspondence. There is also some correspondence with a third map, of the constellation Pegasus, which Betty Hill spotted in the *New York Times*. She immediately

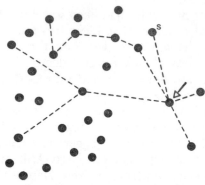

Betty Hill's drawing of the aliens' stellar navigation map with "trade routes" indicated. "S" designates the sun; the arrow points to the aliens' home star.

A section of the constellation Reticulum, reoriented and drawn by Marjorie Fish with Hill's "trade routes" added.

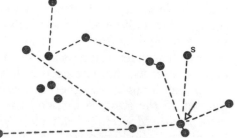

The constellation Pegasus as it appears on an ordinary star map, with Hill's "trade routes" added as she saw them.

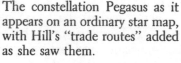

Is this star map a good match for the Hill map? If so, then *anything* can be made to fit. For convenience, I chose the Leo/Cancer map that appears on page 59, added the "trade routes," and got as good a match as any!

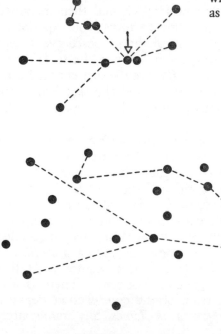

adopted it and showed the correspondence with her map. But my fine hand is in there, too, for included in the fourth map is the map of the Leo/Cancer area that appears a few pages back. On this one, too, a good match-up is possible—certainly as good as Fish's. In fact, better!

But the final blow to this terrible evidence comes when, as suggested by Carl Sagan, Robert Sheaffer, and Steven Soter, we remove all the "trade routes" and see that there is no hope of finding correspondences if the lines are not present. We have here another case of jamming facts into a theory. It is wishful thinking, and the result is the creation of another myth that is just about impossible to negate. The tabloids still publicize the story and rhapsodize about it endlessly, particularly now that Betty Hill is claiming to see flying saucers just about every night on a hillside near her home in New Hampshire. There is no shortage of admirers to accompany her to the sacred spot to ooh and aah over every meteor that flashes by and to suspiciously eye each aircraft that passes. And new Betty Hill–like stories are born every time someone looks up at the night sky and sees anything not noticed before. When such people choose to become overnight celebrities, the sensational press is glad to aid and abet them.

Are there others of greater standing in the UFO field who report wonders? Are there more convincing cases than the Mantell matter? Of course there are, and those are the cases that fill the books that promote the myth. To quote a few typical boo-boos that have enthralled the uncritical recently, I turn to such juvenile fiction as *Aliens from Space* by Donald Keyhoe, and *The Edge of Reality* by Dr. Jacques Vallee and Dr. Allen Hynek.

Keyhoe is the head of a very large UFO organization in the United States. In his book he tells of an episode that he says took place on July 1, 1954. A UFO was detected and tracked in the skies over New York State by operators at Griffiss Air Force Base, and they scrambled an F-94 "Starfire" jet plane in response. The pilot pursued the UFO, which he followed on his in-flight radar, operated by his flight companion. He saw a "gleaming disc-shaped machine" and "started to close in." Suddenly, as he approached, a "furnacelike" heat filled the cockpit, and the gasping pilot jettisoned the plane's canopy. "Stunned," he pressed the eject button, and as he floated to earth by parachute he watched the plane crash into a town below, killing four civilians and injuring five others. We are told the pilot later reported that a secondary effect was an astonishing "dazed" feeling that he could not explain.

Medical men at the air base said that the pilot was reacting to the sight of the jet crashing into the town. Keyhoe says he was told that the two flyers were "really muzzled" when they attempted to contact the families of those killed and injured in the crash. And an ominous

The same four maps with "trade route" lines omitted. Note that any similarities have vanished.

note: "Even today, the AF report on the Walesville crash remains buried, classified SECRET." How reassuring it is when Keyhoe adds, "Several investigators believe this case indicates the aliens are not hostile. No attempt was made to injure the pilots after they bailed out." All the friendly aliens do, it seems, is set fire to aircraft over a town, causing the plane to fall and leave a trail of destruction and death.

The Vallee-Hynek book discusses this case as well. Vallee, a French aficionado of UFOs, played a role in *Close Encounters of the Third Kind*, a film whose title was invented by Dr. Hynek, formerly an astronomer of high caliber who began as a nonbeliever, then fell for the stories because of their very great number. Hynek is currently the leading proponent of "UFOlogy," but has consistently refused to debate skeptic Philip J. Klass either on TV or in person to search out the truth about flying saucers. Lecturing without opposition, he is a compelling speaker. We may never discover how he would fare against an informed opponent.

And what do Vallee and Hynek say about this enthralling case in their book? They present an even more astonishing account. When Hynek tells Vallee that the crash was attributed to "mechanical malfunction," he is rebuffed for this mundane explanation and told that the malfunction was "caused by a UFO." *Two* jets, we are assured, were sent up to find the UFO, one sighted it, and then came the "heat wave" that caused the airmen to eject from the aircraft. The next day the *New York Times* ran a photo of the town in flames.

Phil Klass and Robert Sheaffer, who troubled to write a few letters and make a couple of phone calls, came up with some telling *facts* about this event. First, the date was not July 1, as Keyhoe stated, but July 2. The "unknown" was identified as a friendly aircraft—a C-47 cargo plane en route to Griffiss, not a UFO. There were two F-94C "Starfire" jets in the air on an operational training mission, a routine activity at Griffiss. The F-94 pilot reported that as he began his descent a fire-warning light came on and he discovered that the engine had caught fire. The heat was intense, and pilot and radar observer ejected because of the emergency and the critical low altitude. The plane crashed four miles away.

How do we know these facts? The U.S. Air Force issued a perfectly straightforward memorandum following the event. It is not marked SECRET, is not at all classified, and anyone may have a copy of this report simply by asking for it. A covering letter states, "There is no mention of UFO in the accident report." The reason is obvious: The Air Force treated this accident like any other. There was no mysterious alien, no unexplainable force—nothing except an aircraft that malfunctioned and crashed. And contrary to Vallee's exaggerated claim that the *New York Times* ran "a photo of the town in flames," we find instead a photo that shows a house afire and a caption explaining that two houses and a car were destroyed.

Those who espouse the UFO cause, finding nothing extraordinary about the crash, were hard-pressed to turn it into a UFO incident but perfectly able to perform under pressure. All it needed was the invention of a few details, the exaggeration of a few more, and a dedicated disregard of the pertinent facts. That's the stuff that creates UFO "incidents" and brings forth UFO "experts." It sells books, too.

Dr. J. Allen Hynek asks plaintively, "I wonder what our chances are of following up on a case like that?" They're pretty good, doctor, pretty good. Just as good as the chances of your having done *any* checking up on a contact-with-a-UFO case that your own UFO Center reported from Holland apparently based entirely on a one-page transcript of unsupported statements made by a single witness—none of which was followed up for verification! Were there any questions asked or attempts made to validate the data, or were the usual standards of UFO investigation applied?

In the book he wrote with Vallee, *The Edge of Reality*, Hynek proudly admitted the astronauts to the ranks of UFO-sighters. A total of sixteen remarkable observations were cataloged in the book, but when Hynek visited the Space Center of the National Aeronautics and Space Administration (NASA) in July 1976 he was informed of the facts behind these "sightings." Perhaps the atmosphere on the premises of a real scientific organization got through to him, for he privately (though never publicly) disavowed the reports, declaring that coauthor Vallee had insisted upon their inclusion, not he, and that the list was put in the book merely to generate interest and discussion. Readers, he told colleagues, had no right to assume that the sightings had been verified just because they were in the book! If that is so, perhaps we had better insist that all accounts be labeled "true" and "false" from now on.

Robert Sheaffer, a very active and valuable critic of these spurious claims, is rightly indignant about this matter, among many others. "The man responsible for the 'Astronaut UFO List,' George Fawcett, admitted in debate with me in 1978 that the list is '99% wrong,' " said Sheaffer. "Hynek never bothered to check it. He told a colleague or two what he'd learned at NASA, but has yet to publicly state a correction. He *still* is claiming that astronauts have seen UFOs! This kind of misrepresentation occurs again and again in UFOlogy." Any report, it seems, is enlarged, "cleaned up," published, and accepted by even the leading authorities in the field, without any serious attempt to verify the facts. Is it any wonder that real scientists throw up their hands in dismay when asked to comment on these things?

Hynek also has to answer for his claim, in *The Edge of Reality*, about a photo of two glowing oval objects hovering in the dark of space outside the U.S. spacecraft Gemini 7. These were photographed by astronauts Borman and Lovell and snapped up by the tabloids as genuine flying saucers, apparently without any attempt to discover the truth about the assertions that they were vehicles operated by extraterrestrial life. But James Oberg, a prominent UFO investigator, easily solved the mystery and exposed it in *The Skeptical Inquirer*. Oberg wrote, "This famous photograph is a blatant forgery, in which light reflections off the nose of the spacecraft are made to look like UFOs by airbrushing away the vehicle structure around them. Verdict: fraud."

Dr. Hynek, says Oberg, has accepted this analysis but, again, has never troubled to tell his readers about it. Another good story would have been dumped, and we simply can't have any cold water thrown into this crazy bathtub.

The excuse that such items were included in the book without the approval of the author simply will not wash. When an author makes declarations that are accepted because of his reputation, he has an obligation of the highest order to control whatever appears under his name.

Dr. Hynek, when his pronouncements are carefully studied, comes off as a rather dichotomous character. Philip J. Klass, examining various interviews given by Hynek, noted that he managed the following two statements in two different interviews during August 1976:

> In recent times I have come to support less and less the idea that UFOs are "nuts-and-bolts" spacecraft from other worlds. There are just too many things going against this theory.

Then he hits us with this:

> There is so much nuts-and-bolts evidence. How do you explain things you can see on radar? How do you explain imprints on the ground? How do you explain something that comes along and tears off the tops of trees? . . . How do you explain bullets ricocheting off whatever was in the sky?

He tells us that the UFOs are real, palpable, immaterial, and unsubstantial all at the same time. No wonder they evoke such wonder!

But there's much more. In the same pair of interviews Dr. Hynek both accepts the evidence for "close encounters of the third kind" (actual contact with occupants of a UFO) and strenuously denies it:

> The close encounter of the third kind . . . involves humanoid occupants. Currently we have an estimated 800 sightings of this sort on file. . . . John Fuller, the well-known writer . . . told me the fascinating story of Betty and Barney Hill. . . .

The NASA photo before retouching. The bright spots are highlights on the Gemini 7 capsule, which appears as a dark shadow here. NASA

NASA Hiding UFOs From You

The NASA photo after it was airbrushed to conceal the shadow of the Gemini 7 capsule.

My thinking was altered completely when I was called in along
with Dr. Harder of the University of California to interrogate
two Mississippi fishermen, Calvin Parker and Charles Hickson,
who insist they were literally "kidnapped" and forced to go aboard
a spacecraft, where they were subjected—just as in the case of
the Hills—to a physical examination. The tale told by these two
rugged shipyard workers held up under grueling cross-examina-
tion.

This is followed by his opinion of those who claim to have had one of
these "encounters," and bear in mind that Hynek has interviewed—
personally—not only the four persons just mentioned but others as well
who make these claims:

Frankly, I quite strenuously avoid them [those who claim
contact with humanoids from space]. I'm almost embarrassed
by the reports. None of those people have ever been able to
produce anything reliable. It's junk, just junk!

His knowledge of airline statistics needs a bit of brushing up, too.
When Dr. Arthur C. Hastings (we hear his name in connection with
some of the alleged miracles reported at the Stanford Research Institute,
so he's one of the "in" people) asked Hynek why no UFO debris—
nary a nut or bolt—has ever been produced by anyone, Hynek was
ready with a reply:

Ah, that comes up time and again! Why isn't there any
hardware left behind? Surely they must crash sometimes, surely
they must. . . . [but] Think of the thousands of commercial
planes flying daily over the U.S., yet years go by without a single
crash.

Jacques Vallee, coauthor with Hynek of *The Edge of Reality*, was present
but did not challenge this statement, which, as Klass points out, is obviously incorrect. There was an average of *five fatal airline accidents* (aside
from nonfatal crashes) in the United States during each of the five
years preceding this pronouncement. The resulting 809 fatalities were
not fictional inventions. One of these crashes even happened near Hynek's home in Chicago!

Klass sums up his observations of Dr. J. Allen Hynek with this
suggestion: "Another explanation for the lack of any artifacts of extraterrestrial origin, despite tens of thousands of reported UFO sightings, is
that there *aren't* any extraterrestrial craft in our skies."

Sounds reasonable to me . . . as reasonable as Martin Gardner's
assessment of Hynek as "the Arthur Conan Doyle of UFOlogy."

In the top photo, taken by NASA, a bit of space debris can be seen on the right. The magazine *Science Digest* retouched the picture to eliminate the debris (bottom photo). A small white speck indicated by the arrow appears in the *Science Digest* retouched photograph that did not appear in the NASA original. The magazine identified the speck as an unknown object. NASA

British newspapers were full of UFO news in January 1979, and there was great anticipation of startling revelations to be made before the august House of Lords. On January 17, the Earl of Clancarty rose to address the House on the subject of unidentified flying objects. He coupled this lecture with a motion that the House vote funds for UFO research. He admitted that he had for years been writing about them under a pen name; that name, though he did not reveal it to the House, was Brinsley Le Poer Trench. (Why, I cannot say.) He is also the founder of Contact International (which is not a worldwide matrimonial service), a coauthor of George Adamski's first UFO book, and a cousin of Winston Churchill. Some credentials!

Lord Clancarty evoked many interesting comments from many interested Lords. The preponderance of comment was very much with him and displayed an abysmal ignorance of science and logic. One noble Lord showed that he could not differentiate between a comet and a meteor, which are as unalike as candles and atom bombs. A few, we may be thankful, brought the House some sanity, and Lord Strabolgi, speaking on behalf of Her Majesty's Government, summed up the discussion nicely, pointing out that the believers accepted—and quoted, as Lord Clancarty had—dozens of totally fictitious accounts. He singled out several, acting as an excellent antidote to the biblical references that had been used in *support* of Clancarty's comments, and saying to one member of the House who stood to declare his opposition on grounds that such things were in *contradiction* to the Bible, "There really are many strange phenomena in the sky, and these are invariably reported by rational people. But there is a wide range of natural explanations to account for such phenomena. There is nothing to suggest to Her Majesty's Government that such phenomena are alien spacecraft . . . certainly Her Majesty's Government do not consider that there is any justification for the expenditure of public money on such a study." Lord Clancarty took the hint and withdrew his motion. It seems there is hope for the British, after all, at least among the nobility.

Finally, to dispel any notion that the members of the United Nations are concerned about UFOs, I must mention the 1977 proposal of Sir Eric Gairy, Prime Minister of Grenada, who asked that body to declare 1978 "The Year of the UFO." The proposal failed; it was the first and only proposal to date to obtain *no* response from the floor. Gairy printed 149 copies of his request and mentioned that Grenada had issued a three-dollar and a five-cent stamp bearing UFO pictures. It was obvious that he was very much interested in making his mark at the UN with the proposal. In a small group discussion following the submission of his proposal, he was heard by a CSICOP member to remark that he didn't "give a damn about UFOs" but was only interested in getting

This photograph was alleged to show flying saucers over the Capitol in Washington, D.C. *Omni* magazine called it the "famous UFO 'formation'" photo, and said that the white spots over the building were "thought by many to be a reflection in the camera lens." Obviously, that is just what the saucers are, despite the claims of UFOlogists. Simple observation proves the case.

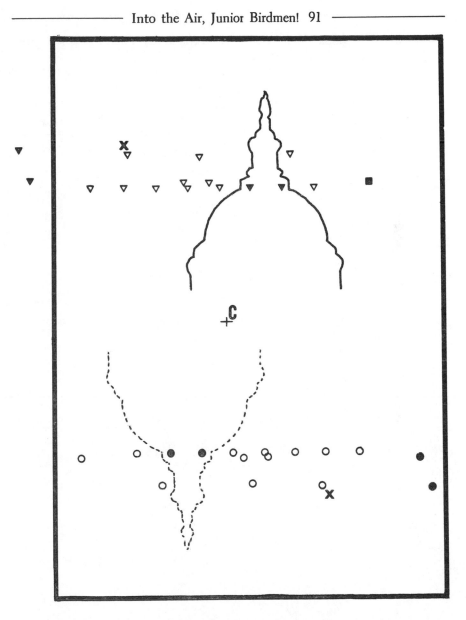

Schematic diagram of the "Capitol flying saucer" photo. The triangles represent the "saucers"; the circles are bright lights within the field. The circles and their corresponding lens flares (triangles) are located an equal distance from the optical center of the lens, marked "C." The black circles on the lower right would be flared as shown by the black triangles on the upper left, which fall outside the frame. The flares of the two black circles on the lower left are washed out by the bright image of the dome. The circle (light) on the far left has no flare, probably because it is less luminous than the others; its flare would have appeared in the position indicated by the square on the upper right. An example of an image/flare pair is marked "X."

tourists to Grenada. Very soon afterward, Gairy was deposed as prime minister.

The Flying Saucer Delusion belongs in this book as another example of wishful thinking, poor research, and outright fraud. It joins the other species of nonsense and deserves the same kind of exposure given to other irrationalities. There is no proof whatsoever that UFOs are any more exciting than the TWA flight from New York to San Francisco. And the latter phenomenon is miracle enough for me.

5

The Giggling Guru: A Matter of Levity

Muppet: It's here! It's here! My correspondence course!
Kermit: Your correspondence course?
Muppet: It's called "How to Be a Superhero"! It comes complete with a helmet, a cape, a red shirt, and an instruction book called "Invincibility Made Easy."
Kermit: I don't believe it.
Muppet: Chapter ten—"How to Fly. Flying is a simple matter of belief. Anyone can fly as long as. he believes that he can."
Kermit: I can't watch this.

—The Muppet Show
CBS Television
February 18, 1980

My friends thought I was nutty to . . . learn to levitate. It cost me a lot more than I thought, and look at me. I know now . . . it was a rip-off."
—Ruth Basilio, TM student
Consumer magazine, Wellington, N.Z.

To listen to the disciples of the Maharishi Mahesh Yogi, you'd think that "Transcendental Meditation" is something unique. In fact, speaking to any of his devotees almost always brings numerous corrections of your terminology when you fail to be precise. Because of that insistence on precision, which I greatly admire, I trust the TMers will adhere to that principle when they read the following analysis of their strange movement.

First of all, beware of using the expression "TM" to refer to anything but the genuine, approved, polished, and officially sanctioned (sanctified?) pronouncements of the Maharishi himself. The letter combination "TM" is even trademarked and patented, so watch out! You see, when you have the future of mankind in your hands, you cannot be too careful of your rights. But as we shall see, such precautions are a little like trying to get exclusive ownership of the wheel, air, or dandelions. The whole thing has been done before, using the same gimmicks. And though there is no question that it is attractive to many millions of people who need something more than they have already, its claims do not stand up under scientific investigation any more than any other mystical philosophy or notion. TMers will scream at the use of the term "mystical," but it applies.

We are told by psychologists that there are three "states of mind." One is the state of wakefulness, in which the brain and body are active. The second is the sleep state, wherein the brain and body are at rest, and the third is the dream state, wherein the body is at rest but the brain is active and productive. All of us are familiar with these three phases. But the many schools of meditation therapy would have us believe there is a fourth state, which they call the state of meditation. Use of this state, they tell us, will reduce anxiety; improve job performance, perceptual skills, and I.Q.; produce "coherent brain waves"; and bring deeper rest. In the long run, say the TMers, humanity will improve across the board—but we'll deal with that claim later. Right now, let's take a look at the miracles wrought by the TM movement, rather than the many other cults that teach some of the same lessons, the same plus variations, or somewhat different ends with similar methods. For it is the TM movement that claims many millions of followers around the globe and therefore should be subjected to the most intense investigation.

Meditation, this "fourth" state of mind, we are told, is achieved in four ways, used at the same time. The practitioner assumes a relaxed posture (the "lotus" posture is preferred) in quiet surroundings, affects a passive attitude, and endlessly repeats a "mantra." This mystical word is a specially chosen sound that can only be granted by the teacher of these mysteries and is tailored to the individual. It is the first of the Great Secrets of TM. But is it something new? Hardly. Repetition of a "holy" word is traceable to sixth-century India, where it was just as obscure and marvelous. Christian philosophers and Hebrew scholars picked up the idea and introduced it into some of the more obscure secret writings of the multitude of religious sects that came and went over the years. None of them changed the world appreciably, but it is claimed that TM will. The TM mantra is assuredly borrowed from well-established sources. So what *is* new?

The Science of Creative Intelligence is what's new. This is what's going to save us, folks, and we'd better hurry along with it. When Parsons College in Fairfield, Iowa, went broke a while back, the Maharishi snapped up the premises and renamed it (you guessed it) Maharishi International University (MIU). Here students spend long hours meditating to sharpen their minds and bodies for learning, and *everything* is slanted toward the TM philosophy. For 2.5 million dollars the Great

Guru bought the same kind of respectability that Oral Roberts purchased. It is significant that the students at Maharishi University are asked many times a day to close their eyes as they go into meditation; it gets them used to the idea.

TM is widely accepted even in the Western world, though in the United States such foreign philosophies usually take root only among a minority of cult-minded citizens. The big reason for this popularity is the apparently scientific evidence TM's devotees produce for our inspection. Okay, let's inspect it.

The TM course includes a number of "checking sessions" that follow the initial instruction in meditation techniques. Since some 50 percent of the students give it up at that point, it pays the organization to reinforce the teachings that it claims do wonders for the students. And it's a good follow-up "warranty" on the product as well. They've been through the secret initiation ceremony, and they've been given the magic word to repeat *ad nauseam;* now they need to be thoroughly convinced that the whole thing really works. During the follow-up, students are told of all the scientific support claimed by the Maharishi and given endless graphs and very carefully selected experimental results.

For starters, we are told that during meditation the body's metabolic rate drops—that, in effect, the rate of physical living is decreased. Indeed, during regular sleep the oxygen consumption of the body drops an average of 8 percent. But—now hear this—TMers claim that during meditation there is a drop of 16 percent! Yet the Royal College of Surgeons in Britain showed a drop of only 7 percent. Why the discrepancy? Simply because the RCS experimenters took care not to disturb the patient both *before* and *after* the tests, and they thus proved that the change was due to simple relaxation, nothing more. Besides, in comparison tests they conducted using TMers in "trance" and non-TM subjects listening to soft music, they found that *the oxygen consumption rates were indistinguishable.* If there is no discernable difference between the oxygen consumption of a subject listening to music and a subject practicing mystic oriental techniques, surely oxygen consumption fails as a factor in scientific confirmation of the claim.

But we are also told that the body's production of carbon dioxide decreases during TM. This is hardly a surprise, chemically speaking. Lowered oxygen intake dictates this. Is it significant? No. Although carbon dioxide production does drop, it starts dropping as soon as the subject stops moving about, continues to drop during the TM period, and then shoots up again when movement recommences. Not at all unexpected or significant. Especially when, as with the previous claim, exactly the same result is noted with subjects exposed to soft music! Furthermore, a group of fasting TMers was unable to produce any carbon dioxide changes *at all* during meditation. The relaxing effect of TM is quite real, as demonstrated. But it is neither surprising nor unique to meditation. Music can do the same thing.

Recently in California, at the Orange County Medical Center, researchers investigated hormone changes during TM. Although there are indications of decreases in some hormone production normally due to stress factors, to date no proof has been shown that such effects are unique to or due to TM techniques. One investigator, noting that blood flow goes up *in general* during TM, has said of this work, "It probably means that blood flow goes up in the brain"—but he fails to mention that this assumption is just what they are seeking to prove, and he has no right to jump to this conclusion without distinct evidence to prove it. Besides, as of this writing only five subjects have been tested, and this sample size is pitifully small. No experimenter worthy of the name would draw conclusions on the basis of such a small data sample. That has not stopped people from doing so, however.

Complicated tests involving numerous electrodes connected to the scalps of the subjects have been performed by TM scientists. Their purpose has been to prove their claim that during meditation brain waves "become coherent," though it is not clear at all just what is meant by that terminology. They assert that both alpha and theta waves (two forms of brain activity on the electrical level) seem to become synchronized during TM, but close examination of the tests pokes a few holes in that claim. When the crew of the television program "Nova" visited the TM labs, they wired up one of the crew, a nonmeditator, and his results were quite comparable to those of the TMers. The only conclusion the testers could come up with was that the man was a "ringer"—a secret meditator! Wrong. Dr. Ray Cooper of the Burden Neurological Laboratory, an experienced experimenter in this field, says that Dr. Paul Levine of the Maharishi European University at Lake Lucerne, Switzerland, who has been running these tests to prove the effects of TM, uses a system of electrode cross-connection that could easily provide, through electrical interaction, an *illusion* of coherence. Says Dr. Cooper about the interaction effect, "You can't get away from it."

Series of tests that were done to compare the effects of plain drowsiness with meditation states, using alpha and theta brain waves, showed the two states to be indistinguishable. Are we paying the TM people simply to put us to sleep? It begins to look like it. To quote authority Dr. Peter Fenwick, who has examined the TM claims of physiological changes, "Both the changes in oxygen consumption and carbon dioxide output and the EEG changes [brain-wave studies] can all be explained by accepted physiological explanations of how the brain and body work."

Okay. So far we're left with nothing but the mantra sound and the secret initiation as possible benefits of TM. But even they fail the test. Medical researchers have shown again and again that the same quality and degree of physiological change are brought on in a subject who simply relaxes completely, and that the use of the word "one"—or any other simple word—is just as effective as any mystical and secret mantra sound. Again, what are we paying for?

Concerning the alleviation of stress and anxiety, the TM experimenters have shown that meditators are better able to ignore noises—for example, the sound of a fork scraping an enamel saucepan—than are nonmeditators. Wow! But the tests have been done by highly motivated experimenters and subjects, in which often the person conducting the test is a TM advocate and therefore prone to see positive results. You don't put the accused person's family on the jury. And besides, their own tests showed that yoga students did even better in ignoring nasty noises.

A word about this experimenter's-motivation factor. Such bias and expectation fulfillment is clearly shown by a test wherein students are asked to record the results of a maze experiment involving rats. When told, for example, that white rats do better than brown rats in such tests, the noted tendency is for the students to arrive at this very conclusion by biased recording of the times the rats require to find their way from A to B in the maze, even though there is actually no real difference in the I.Q.'s of the rats. The apparent difference is the result of the experimenter's expectations. Similar results were obtained in I.Q. tests in the California school system, in which students who had been pointed out as exceptional were given higher ratings by teachers who *expected* higher performance from them and rated them accordingly. Actually, they were *not* exceptional. It's an old story.

There have been experiments designed to show this and related effects in tests of claimed TM capabilities. Told that a series of tests was something which expert TMers usually did poorly, the TM subjects accordingly did poorly. But another group of expert TMers, told that they would probably do well on the same tests, produced better results. TM testers had reported that short-term memory improved among meditators, but the tests were done without tight controls and without the use of automated recording devices to eliminate recording errors due to bias. When the tests were repeated under the supervision of scientists at Cardiff University in Wales, with tight controls and automated recording, the conclusion was that (a) meditation had no effect on short-term memory and (b) the length of time the subjects had been involved in TM had no effect on the results, either—though this had been a firm claim of the Maharishi.

Ever since the sensitive galvanometer was developed, some questionable group or other has decided to apply it to their particular craziness. The scientologists use it as a sort of electronic Ouija board; chiropractors, making no bones about it at all, simply describe it as one of their enigmatic "black box" diagnostic devices and do not claim to understand it. Actually, both groups are merely measuring the skin resistance of subjects, thus introducing—as all such groups do—a minimal amount of real science into their highly doubtful research. Skin resistance *is* an indication of emotional states, and in fact is one basis of the somewhat uncertain art of the polygraph, or "lie-detector."

TM has seized upon this gimmick as well. Michael West of Cardiff University, who compared subjects listening to soothing music against experienced TM practitioners for effects on skin resistance, has seen the TMers totally misrepresent his work in their selective reports. He disagreed categorically with their conclusions, and in his own words said of their reports, "The interpretation . . . is certainly not honest."

Proponents of TM argue that their meditation produces other changes and improvements in an individual's life, but that claim is far from proved. After all, TM students *expect* miracles that others not involved in a mystical/religious movement *don't* expect. It's natural that they will extol the wonders they believe they have discovered, and, as we have seen, they certainly read more into their supposedly scientific evidence than is warranted.

One of the most publicized claims made by the TMers is called the "Maharishi Effect." If just a tiny one percent of any population is dedicated to Transcendental Meditation, say the gurus, the quality of life will improve for all. As proof they offer the effects on certain selected communities around the world, after this one percent has been attained. TMer Professor Candy Borland, interviewed by the "Nova" television team, said, "What we found was that in the one-percent cities . . . crime rate tended to—or decrease [sic] in all cases, and the average decrease was about 8.8%; but in the control cities, crime rate increased in about 75% of them and the average increase was 7.7%. And the difference in these changes was statistically significant."

But there are other explanations. One of the cities cited for its crime decrease was Santa Barbara, California. The TM study there coincided with a major police crackdown on hard-drug users, and the noted crime rate drop was the result of a 50-percent decrease in forgery and larceny crimes—the crimes that owe their predominance in this community to the drug users, with their great need for cash. In Davis, another selected center, at the end of 1972 the police apprehended one youth who was committing some thirty burglaries a month! That, coupled with a drastic reduction in bicycle thefts owing to a police campaign, brought a drop in the overall crime rate; the serene attitudes of one out of every hundred people in the population of the town was not a factor. In Britain, too, an area is pointed out to us as an example of the one-percent effect. Derbyshire is said to have experienced a drop in crime and accidents in 1975. Really? Records consulted by the authorities there show that accidents were *up* compared with the previous year, and though crime figures did drop, they were much higher than in 1973! So it seems that the one-percent figure is only a theoretical claim— another one of many—that TM proponents had better take back to the old drawing board for reworking—or discarding.

TM headquarters has produced an expensive and elegant series of brochures printed in full color and gold, publications that try to sell the reader on the claim that science and TM are synonymous. By means of diagrams and graphs drawn from pre-1978 data, tendentious statements are squeezed out of very little evidence. I referred the whole physics/ consciousness matter to Philip Morrison, an outstanding physicist at the Massachusetts Institute of Technology. "The Pilot Projects are so audacious an example of wish fulfillment schemes that they command admiration as much as astonishment," said Professor Morrison. He was referring to the TM test areas where the Maharishi Effect was said to be so pronounced. As for TM's attempts to draw comparisons between modern physics and society, thus lending scientific stature to these ideas, Morrison declared that their fragile and weak analogies "have no force at all." They are merely amateur bits of "overstated" and "old hat" business, he said—"just puffery."

Early in October 1978, a Dr. Robert Rabinoff, bearing a Ph.D. in physics, addressed a small group at the University of Oregon. He is an assistant professor of physics at Maharishi International University, and was in Oregon to speak on the unique educational program at MIU— including the "sidhis" program. Sidhis refers to claimed miracles such as levitation and invisibility. CSICOP member Dr. Ray Hyman was there, and was determined to press Rabinoff on the subject of levitation. (Dr. Hyman is a psychologist at the University of Oregon, and an experienced conjurer as well.)

The audience perked up when Dr. Rabinoff preached the Maharishi Effect, claiming that any city in which one percent or more of the inhabitants are TMers becomes a haven from crime. This, he told the folks, was an established fact, "scientifically demonstrated." Fairfield, Iowa, home of MIU, is unique in that some 13 percent of the populace are heavy TMers! Surely that concentration of goodness and omniscience, not to mention omnipotence, should produce wonders in the immediate neighborhood? Quite so, said the professor. Since "at least two hundred people on the campus have completed the sidhis program," Fairfield is multiply blessed. The Maharishi Effect is seen everywhere. The crime rate is so low, we are told, that the chief of police has now put several officers on part-time duty. Unemployment is nonexistent. Jefferson County, where this epitomical city is located, has become bountiful as a result. In spite of comparatively poor soil in the area, crops are growing beyond the most optimistic hopes. The automobile accident rate in the state of Iowa is now the lowest in the United States! And TM is to be given total credit for all this, according to Dr. Rabinoff.

Well, being the fuddy-duddy that I am, I decided to check with the folks over there in Iowa. I fired off a few letters and made a few phone calls. The results would not have pleased the small but uncritical audience that Dr. Rabinoff spoke to. The office of Fairfield Chief of Police Miller was only amused to hear that their crime rate was so low. Indeed, not only was there no plan to dump officers, but they were hiring more, early in 1979! Mayor Rasmussen's office could not explain where such notions as those expressed by Dr. Rabinoff had come from. The Department of Agriculture was equally mystified. Figures they supplied to me show an interesting sameness in yearly fluctuations between the state average and the county average. Allan L. Seim, Production Specialist with the Agriculture Department, searched in vain for any wondrous change as claimed by Rabinoff. "Jefferson County average yields follow the same fluctuations as state average yields," said Mr. Seim, "and have not experienced any dramatic increases. . . . Neither I nor our staff member stationed in Jefferson County are aware of any 'dramatic' yield increases near Fairfield."

But there was more. Rabinoff had claimed that the low auto accident rate was to be credited to the Maharishi Effect. Really? Authorities I contacted in Fairfield told me that any possible decrease since 1973 was attributable to two factors: fewer students at the college since the Maharishi took over (about one fourth as many), and the tendency of these students to stay on campus, in contrast to the former inhabitants. There certainly has been no decrease in off-campus population involvement in accidents. In fact, the claim made by Rabinoff was that the Maharishi Effect had radiated out into the rest of the state of Iowa, resulting in the "lowest accident rate in the U.S.A." I have no idea where the man got this startling information. It was unavailable to me, and the nearest the National Safety Council could come to such data was the death rate due to auto accidents for the United States as a whole and the state of Iowa in particular. An examination of these figures provides interesting comparisons. Here are the facts:

**Percentage Change in Fatalities by Year, State of Iowa,
Compared to Annual U.S. Average**

1971	Down 4%
1972	Up 2%
1973	No change

_____Takeover by Maharishi

1974	No change
1975	Down 3%
1976	Up 18%
1977	Down 9%

The comparison with the average U.S. figures shows no dramatic changes at all, with the exception of 1976. In that year the TM movement was in full swing in Fairfield—remember, with *thirteen times the necessary 1 percent*—and there was a jump of 18 percent! And in Fairfield itself, where the Effect should be most spectacular, officials have noted no change.

As for unemployment, Job Services of Iowa supplied the following facts: 1. The amount of unemployment in the State of Iowa varied at essentially the same rate as that of the U.S. in general through this period. 2. The variances in the Fairfield area were somewhat *higher* during most of the period covered, lower only at one point—in 1977, by 0.3 percent.

The noted small decrease in unemployment seems even more inconsequential when we realize that it reflects the movement, birth, or job change of only *twenty-six persons!*

Let's hear it for the Maharishi Effect! It's obviously a roaring success . . . and all these wonderful results from only *thirteen times* the required minimum percentage of TM devotees. It seems that the Effect should be renamed "The One-Percent Non-Solution."

Dr. Hyman describes Dr. Rabinoff as a typical representative of the TM movement—well dressed in a sparkling white suit and neatly groomed. What he presented, however, was less palatable, being heavily spiced with the jargon of TM. Phrases like "the field of all possibilities," "pure intelligence," and "cosmic consciousness" abounded, serving to cover up the lack of answers to direct, simple, yes-or-no questions.

Dr. Rabinoff described the sidhis program as a system that enables one to achieve "whatever one desires"—hardly a modest claim. The mind reels just contemplating the possibilities. Visions of Sophia Loren, sacks of gold nuggets, flying carpets, and unmentionable delights crowd *my* mind immediately. But more mundanely, the professor described the MIU campus as a place where no tensions exist, everyone is eager for learning, and no learning difficulties arise. This, he told the audience, was because all students had direct access to cosmic consciousness, the source of *everything*.

But, cautioned Dr. Rabinoff, even though he himself had instant access to pure and omniscient understanding, it could not be expected that he would know all about, for example, the science of chemistry when his field was actually physics. But through TM, he explained, he now felt "an intuitive familiarity and comfort with chemistry." Okay, you figure that one out. I can't.

Reports Hyman: "As a student of physics, he [Dr. Rabinoff] says he used to have to read the text two or three times before he gained sufficient understanding to attempt the exercises. Now, through TM and the TM sidhis program, he can read textbooks in physics only once and find himself ready to do the exercises. Thank goodness for the TM program. If now, after studying physics as an undergraduate, then as a graduate student, and finally as a teacher, he could not read and understand textbooks in physics, then TM must truly be wonderful to enable him to do this!"

The general party line of TM was espoused in great detail and at great length by Rabinoff. It involves something called "pure bliss," which sounds fascinating indeed—a state during which students gain all knowledge (though not about chemistry, it seems) and are open to all possibilities. This state was compared to the state of a vacuum. This latter observation perhaps sums it all up accurately.

When we speak of the Maharishi and the TM movement of a few years back, we speak of a different organization than what we find before us today. There has been a radical step taken by the Maharishi of late, and it has been picked up by the press and highly publicized— and ridiculed—around the world, though the criticism fails to faze the believers. Anyone who has in any way followed the matter has seen the posters and brochures illustrating the latest in chic miracles—the process of levitation. Astonishingly enough, the Maharishi, seeing his enrollment figures dropping, unleashed upon the world the outrageous claim that he was offering a special course—to experienced meditators only—that would enable them to perform miracles. And no spike-through-the-tongue or asleep-on-a-bed-of-nails stuff either. *Real* miracles were promised those who came up with the required sum. Believers were told by the Great Guru that it was within their reach to soar about the skies by power of mind alone, to become invisible at will, and to walk through solid walls! For a mere pittance of about $3,000 they were offered lessons in these arts, and the guru himself announced

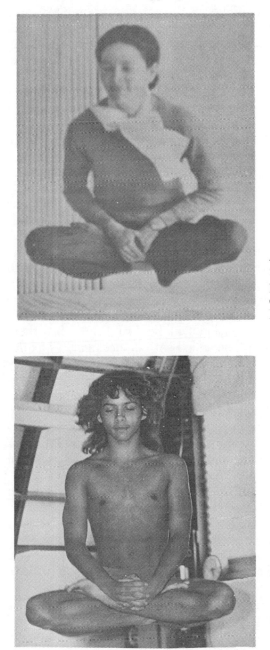

A TM student "levitating" while meditating. This is an official photo issued by the TM Ministry of Information. Transcendental Meditation

Steven Zeigler, with no TM instruction whatsoever and no gymnastic training, bounces on a mat in the lotus posture to duplicate the levitation stunt. This unretouched photo was illuminated by a strobe flash. Alt's Gymnastic School, N.J.

in 1978 on TV ("The Merv Griffin Show") that he had enrolled some forty thousand students in this course! Griffin then asked the obvious question: How many had learned to levitate? Declared the Great Guru: "Thousands!" But this great throng of soaring lotus-eaters has yet to be seen by mere mortals such as myself.

During Dr. Rabinoff's talk at the University of Oregon, a listener asked what were the actual physical requirements for levitation, invisibility, and "perfect seeing." The questioner, a physicist, did not ask *if* levitation had been done—that was assumed—but rather what force was actually used to get the body up there. Rabinoff, hard put to answer, mumbled something about a form of consciousness that was subtler than gravity. Perhaps the subtler force he was speaking of was actually the force of imagination, which seems to be the active element in these miracles-that-never-happen.

Dr. Hyman was at the end of his patience with Rabinoff. "I asked if anyone had yet actually levitated in the sense of hovering above the ground. In our ensuing interaction he displayed a skill at sleight of mouth and evasiveness that would put the combined talents of Uri Geller, Kreskin, and Russell Targ to shame. He did everything he could to avoid making a flat statement or a simple yes or no."

Asked repeatedly, Rabinoff finally said he had heard that there were cases of true levitation. And, he added with amusement, TM initiates find it quite acceptable that meditators can negate gravity. Only the most difficult person would believe otherwise, he insisted, and that Oregon audience was quite in tune with him. They and Rabinoff found it difficult to believe that Hyman was incredulous about people defying the law of gravity at will. (I must of course admit that Hyman and I are not trained professional physicists. Dr. Robert Rabinoff, Ph.D., *is* a physicist and as such can be considered qualified to come to irrational conclusions.)

When Hyman pressed the point again, Dr. Rabinoff showed a touch of impatience. Hyman was still asking troublesome questions that the professor could not answer, and he was becoming annoyed under his nice white official suit. He reminded Dr. Hyman that the sidhis were not designed as "circus stunts." The acts themselves were irrelevant. They were only ways to achieve perfect intelligence and pure bliss. (We're back to *that* again.) And the Maharishi, said the professor, would be derelict not to let us in on all that good stuff.

But, insisted Hyman, if the levitation trick was so irrelevant, and detracted from the true purpose of TM, why was it so prominently featured and hailed as a breakthrough? And wouldn't just one teensy demonstration prove the Maharishi's claims once and for all and cause the entire world to flock to his banner? Rabinoff's answer was typical cultist stuff. The Maharishi knows when and if it is appropriate to release news of such matters, he said. He has his reasons. It would be useless anyway, said Rabinoff, to release photos of the levitation taking place because they could be easily faked. But photos *were* released, professor, or don't you remember? When *Time* magazine bombed them as trivial, they were suddenly not available any longer.

The absolute dependence on the superior wisdom and "reasons" of the Maharishi, as expressed by Rabinoff, is chillingly similar to the rationalizations of other cult devotees. It is a phenomenon to think about seriously and long.

MIU president Dr. R. K. Wallace says that we must look at the "overall effect," not just any one claim made for TM, and that if we examine the somewhat cloudy aspect of an individual's personal improvement, we will see the value of TM. Okay, Dr. Wallace, but if you ask us to adopt *this* system of evaluation, you must agree to abandon your insistence on scientific proof for various aspects of TM, for these do not stand inspection. No have-your-cake-and-eat-it-too position is allowed.

Mike West of Cardiff University has seen through the fog to the central point. "I think I find it difficult to acquaint the superstructure of meditation and the organization that teaches meditation with the concept of meditation itself, which is a very simple, innocent concept. . . . I don't think that meditation needs to be sold, and I don't think a huge organization is necessary to sell it." I'll go a step further, as an individual lay observer. When I was a kid my mom used to tell me that the best way to get in tune with the world was to go into a quiet room and put my feet up for a few minutes. No mystic words, no looking into my belly button, just relaxing awhile and taking it easy. It worked then, and it works now.

The point I make—and Hyman forced this very issue when he confronted Rabinoff—is this: The TMers flood us with very complicated and tedious documents involving EEG records, hormone changes, perceptual alterations, and so on that allegedly show what is experienced by those who are said to be "undergoing the TM sidhi experience," but they offer not one shred of evidence that the guy ever gets up into the air, that a photon of light passes through his body during the invisibility trick, that he knows a single fact of any kind that wasn't previously available to him without the "all-knowing" stunt, or that he can walk through anything more substantial than a paper bag when he is doing the "walking-through-walls" idiocy. If these things *are* being done, show us! Just once. Wherever you want. Any time you want. But show us, and stop beating about with fancy evasions. Perhaps yogi Ram Daas, another strange promulgator of transcendental wonders, has the perfect cop-out that the Maharishi should adopt. In writing of miracles like astral projection, levitation, and mind reading, he answers questions with, "That's illusion, too. Forget about it. Don't think about it. Don't use it. Don't do it. Don't worry about it." Brilliant. Obviously a great thinker.

Concludes Dr. Ray Hyman, in his report, "It is all too easy to view Dr. Rabinoff as some self-deluded misfit. But, I suspect, he typifies most of us in the way we cope with the stresses of life and the search for the Answer to Big Questions about the Meaning of It All. Once an individual, especially a fairly bright one, latches onto a belief system that offers comfort and universal answers, then nature has provided him with innumerable mechanisms to avoid facing up to discomforting challenges to that belief. Rabinoff's ways of avoiding facing up to both the inconsistencies and the immoral features of the miracle aspects of the sidhis program are just more obvious than most."

For more than a year I have tried to elicit a simple answer from David Jacobs, spokesman for the International Center for Scientific Research at MIU. I have been sent endless reams of scientific papers that go on and on about supposed reactions to the wondrous feelings that subjects express. The papers are filled with hundreds of measurements and observations. They tell of fantastic instrumentation and complex metering of almost every function of the bodies of subjects who "feel" they are experiencing the levitation sidhi, but they all fail to tell us *if the guy ever got airborne!* Well, that's not *quite* correct, I must admit. One of these tedious articles says an observation was made during "a gradual lift in the air by the subject observed on the TV monitor." Lordy! Tears came to my eyes when I saw this! At last, one of the experts had declared the actual existence of the miracle I sought. I rushed to the typewriter to ask Mr. Jacobs if the great event had been videotaped, and if I might see it.

In reply, I received yet another paper from another learned man who went on at length not about the reference I made to the levitation but about the similarity between the claims of the Maharishi and observations made by the ancient Greek philosophers. And along with all this was the same paper I'd referred to, with various passages underlined in blue pencil. Nowhere in the reply was an answer to my question. Instead, I was shunted off to an obscure man in Switzerland who could perhaps "further [my] understanding." No, thanks. I have now attained a state of Complete Understanding of Transcendental Meditation. It is a pleasant state, not unlike pure bliss, in which one smiles knowingly, now fully aware that the Maharishi is a total put-on and his followers are deluded Dorothys tripping on down the Yellow Brick Road. No levitation, no walking through walls, no invisibility. Now, that's a comfort indeed. I need not fear that some nut will drift into my bathroom through the tiling, invisible and seated in a lotus position five feet off the ground.

Perhaps Jacobs grew weary of avoiding my questions, for I received a letter from one Orme-Johnson, Director of TM's International Center for Scientific Research, who informed me that now there are *four* stages to levitation. They are:

1. Shaking and Sweating (this I can manage)
2. Hopping Like a Frog (not so easy)
3. Walking on Cobwebs—Hovering
4. Flying—Complete Mastery of the Skies

Previously, it was claimed there were only *three* stages. Shaking and Sweating had been left out. Thus, instead of having accomplished only one third of their objective, the TMers have now reached the halfway mark, just by redefining their goals. Great!

But I must admit, Orme-Johnson *did* directly answer my question. "We do not claim," he said, "that anyone is hovering in the air." Oh, yeah? Dr. Rabinoff claimed it. Orme-Johnson had better check with him. TMer Doug Henning claimed it, even maintaining that he'd heard the Maharishi had trained one chap to stay up several minutes! Most important of all, in a television interview the Maharishi Mahesh Yogi said that "thousands" had learned to do it. Either the director of the International Center for Scientific Research doesn't know his subject, or there is some fibbing going on.

And what about those highly publicized photos of your people in midair, smiling vacuously, Orme-Johnson? Nowhere do I see any acknowledgment that these are phony pictures, or photos of a girl bouncing on a mattress. The text invariably describes the act of levitation and advertises that it will be taught to the customers.

Doug Henning, the brilliant young magician who astonished Broadway audiences and then moved on to further triumphs in Las Vegas and on television, has been a devoted Transcendental Meditator for years. In response to a letter from me, he promised that as soon as he had mastered the levitation sidhi I would be the first one to see him do it. But disturbing developments have taken place of late. Although Henning had honestly said that he had never actually levitated—and I appreciated his candor—he had always claimed that every time he tried he "felt lighter." His nonmeditating friends joked, "It's because you don't eat!" (Henning is known to subsist on nuts and berries and such.) Behind the scenes at one of his recent TV appearances was a sign proclaiming NO LEVITATION WITHOUT REPRESENTATION—another effort to make light of an aspect of Henning's total preoccupation with TM and associated miracles. Now, suddenly, it seems that Doug Henning has gotten carried away (so to speak) and has forgotten his previous statements. In the pages of *New Realities* (formerly *Psychic* magazine) he says, in so many words, that the first time he tried levitating *he rose three feet but fell immediately.* He continued, he says, to rise and fall quickly and was told by the Maharishi that it was not possible to stay up there until he could maintain pure consciousness at the same time.

Henning says that levitation is "stabilized pure consciousness in activity, a result of perfect mind-body coordination." Sorry, Doug; the semantics don't work as misdirection. You said you hadn't done the miracle. Then, suddenly, you say you did it the first time you tried it. Just where is the truth in all this?

World Government News, which claims that TM has achieved its goal of world peace, is an expensive, full-color magazine that tries desperately to prove the tenets of TM. Under a cartoon drawing of "Sidha Man" (representing guess who) we read a familiar quotation: "And He arose, and rebuked the wind and said unto the sea, peace, be still. And the wind ceased, and there was a great calm, and they feared exceedingly, and said one to another: What manner of man is this, that even the wind and the sea obey him?" I think I get the message.

A small, pleasant, bearded man from India, a most unlikely figure, teamed with a powerful and efficient public-relations team and supported by uncritical media stories, has turned unproved and outdated notions of Eastern mysticism into a pseudoscientific mess that has seized the imaginations of enough people to make the organization wealthy and secure.

The fact remains, however, that despite the alleged beneficial influences of TM, many people continue to die violent deaths around the world. A mass suicide occurred in Guyana in 1978, "The Year of Invincibility for Every Nation." Tears continue to be shed in every corner of the globe, and all the mantra-chanting of all those poor suckers seems only to have stirred the wind a bit. Money continues to pour into the Maharishi's coffers, and for every dollar received a child gasps its last in hunger. The Maharishi and his TM have not proved to be saviors of the world, and the thousands upon thousands who have joined the cult—with eyes tightly shut, awaiting Pure Bliss that does not come, anticipating the magical powers promised and the great surges of goodness that are not at all evident—are still waiting.

6

The Paper Chariots in Flames

Seven eighths of everything is unseen.
—The Iceberg Theorem

Erich von Däniken is a Swiss author who has become one of the most widely read writers of all time. He earned this distinction by selling some 36 million books, and he sold them because they pandered shamelessly to the public taste for nonsense. The only facts in his four books— *Chariots of the Gods?*, *Gods from Outer Space*, *The Gold of the Gods*, and *In Search of Ancient Gods*—that I depend on are the page numbers.

For fifteen years, he has perpetrated on the reading public what I characterize as a literary diddle of enormous scope. A simple examination of his work will demonstrate this. In fact, any reasonably intelligent person with access to a public library can disprove such nonsense quickly and easily.

His major claims are:

1. Beings from outer space visited earth many times in the past.
2. They mated with primitive people here.
3. Such visits are recorded in mythology and history.
4. Artifacts have been left behind that prove these visits.

Now that's a lot for an ex-hotel manager/embezzler to prove. It all depends on whether his evidence is any good.

Concerning his first point, von Däniken trots out his prize exhibit. It is a sarcophagus lid from Palenque, a site in Mexico excavated about sixty years ago that has yielded wonderful treasures indeed. The lid, from a grave discovered under a Mayan pyramid there, bears an intricate carving of a man in a somewhat fetal position which, von Däniken claims, indicates that he is an astronaut. More than that, he identifies not only a rocket-sled contraption our flyer is astride, but his oxygen tubes and other equipment as well. Flames leap from the rocket, and there is no question in the mind of von Däniken but that he has here a clear representation of a space traveler arriving on earth. Wrong.

We know the name of the inhabitant of the coffin and the date of his death. The costume of the carved figure on the lid is not at all

The carving on the sarcophagus lid from Palenque, Mexico, that, according to Erich von Däniken, includes a representation of an ancient astronaut in flight aboard a space vehicle. Actually, this figure depicts the Mayan ruler Pacal. Typically stylized figures of a quetzal bird, an earth god, and a cross form the "rocket."

unusual, but typical of a Mayan nobleman of the period. He is characteristically drawn, and with the meticulous care typical of Mayan work. The details of the artwork that von Däniken points out in an attempt to prove his point are quite common in other carvings of the era, being stylized serpent heads, earth gods, and birds, not technical wonders. All the components of the "rocket sled" can be found in other relief sculptures—highly stylized, it is true, but nonetheless there and accounted for. Ronald D. Story, in his book *The Space-Gods Revealed*, does a neat job of explaining the "astronaut" on the coffin lid.

Von Däniken next turns to the remarkable Nazca "lines," one of the most truly tantalizing mysteries of Peruvian archaeology. In the desert near the towns of Nazca and Palpa are remarkable figures drawn in the sand. Some are hundreds of yards long; there are trapezoids, rectan-

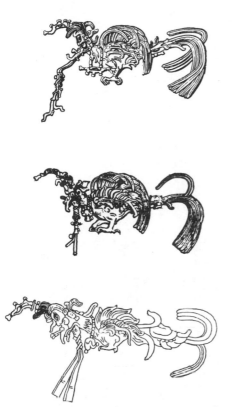

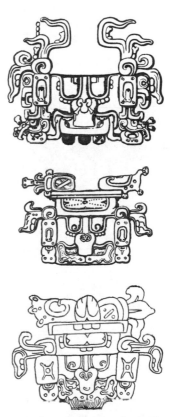

Three quetzal birds, common motifs in Mayan art. These are from the Temple of the Foliated Cross (top), the Temple of the Cross (center), and the Pacal sarcophagus (bottom). The similarity is obvious.

Three earth god figures from the same sources as the quetzal birds, respectively. The carving on the bottom represents the rear of a rocket in von Däniken's imaginative analysis.

gles, and triangles. Some are long straight lines extending a mile into the desert with great accuracy. Others—the most provocative—are drawings of such things as spiders, lizards, and birds. I will not dwell on my personal opinions and observations concerning these artifacts but will confine myself to von Däniken's distortion of their nature.

One idea he would have us accept is that they were "landing fields" for spaceships bearing astronauts from afar. Then, pray tell, why would such a craft need a long strip like this for landing? And if any did land, where are the traces? These figures are only scraped into the surface; would not the spaceships have made equally prominent markings?

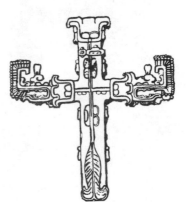

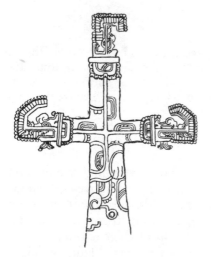

Three cross figures representing a maize "tree," from the same sources as the quetzal birds and earth gods. Von Däniken chose only the Pacal cross (bottom) as the body of a "rocket."

Gerald Hawkins, who visited the Peruvian desert some years back to apply to the lines the same technique he had successfully used on the ruins of Stonehenge, found to his satisfaction that the long lines were not astronomically oriented. So the mystery remains. But an "ancient astronaut" theory is hardly necessary.

At one point, von Däniken sticks his foot in his typewriter when he says that a section he has selected shows a "parking bay" for a UFO. It turns out, when you take a good look around, that he is actually referring to part of the leg of a giant bird drawing. He now admits that he was wrong on this point, but his *Chariots of the Gods?* still carries the error, thirty-five languages and ten years after it appeared.

Not at all loath to travel, von Däniken next makes a pilgrimage to Easter Island, where he uses another genuine item of archaeology to make his spurious point. He says that the construction of the huge statues there was impossible by ordinary folks. Really? Well, Thor Heyerdahl was interested to hear this. Apparently von Däniken never heard of the demonstration that Heyerdahl organized at Easter Island wherein an entire statue was carved, transported, and erected by the folks who now live there—and all with quite ordinary, basic tools that were available to their ancestors. But Heyerdahl takes the blame for it all: "Together with my colleagues I am to blame for not promptly having used the modern mass media for telling the public not to take his [von Däniken's] references to Easter Island seriously."

But it is with the tired old song-and-dance about the "Great Pyramid" that von Däniken really takes off on flights of invention. He has plenty of antecedents. Over a century ago, "Pyramidology" was born, when serious men actually began to imagine that they could find, expressed in the pyramid, unexplained relationships of mathematics. To these observers, as to von Däniken, mere men—especially those of darker skins—could not possibly have designed and built the structure. And whatever dark powers *did* stand behind the pyramid must have meant it as a message that only smart folks could fathom. A number of such smart people immediately announced themselves.

As prominent a person as the Astronomer-Royal of Scotland, Professor Charles Piazzi Smyth, picked up the banner in 1864, when he published his first book, *Our Inheritance in the Great Pyramid.* The claims are all-encompassing, for the Great Pyramid is not only a history of the past, said Smyth, but also a history of the future! Every major event in mankind's story is represented there, he claimed, and he labored mightily, though badly, to prove it, in an obsession that consumed the rest of his life.

Smyth was following in the steps of one John Taylor, who earlier had proclaimed that the biblical "cubit" was expressed in the pyramid.

Earth drawings near Nazca, Peru, with the modern Pan-American Highway crossing at the lower left (dotted line). The bright lines on the right side are modern tire tracks. Only ancient tracings are shown in the accompanying diagram. Instituto Geografico Militar, Peru

Taylor found that the polar radius of the earth divided by 10 million came out to about 25 inches, which he declared was a cubit. It is something he just preferred to believe.

The biblical connections of Pyramidology were further pursued. During Smyth's investigations, one of the original casing stones that long ago covered the Great Pyramid to provide a smooth and even surface was unearthed nearby. Over the ages almost all the casing stones had been taken away by locals, who obviously believed the "bread before poetry" philosophy and felt that using the big pile of stone in a practical way was permissible. It is another crime against posterity that we cannot

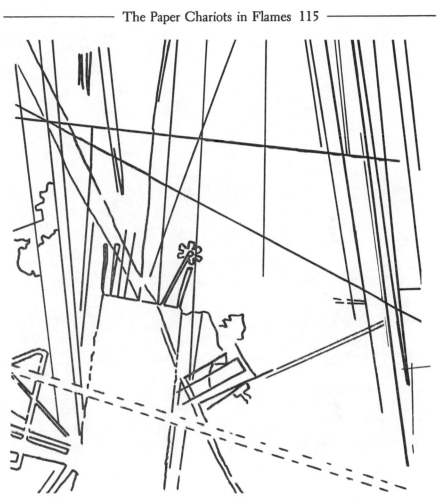

argue against. Taylor, who died before this discovery, would have been pleased to know that the stone was slightly more than 25 inches on a side, and Smyth lost no time in conclusion-jumping, his favorite sport. He declared that this new measurement was the cubit so long sought, and he also proclaimed the "Pyramid Inch," one twenty-fifth of the cubit. This is exactly one millionth of the earth's polar radius, said Smyth. But unfortunately for this stroke of inspiration, several more casing stones were then dug up, and Smyth's Pyramid Inch went out the window, for these stones had widely varying widths. As one might expect, this in no way altered the theory. Smyth pushed on, ignoring the facts.

He assigned a One Pyramid Inch/One Year ratio to distances inside the pyramid to show that the passages represented a world history and prophecy. By this means he "proved" that the world began in 4,004 B.C.—a somewhat conservative estimate of the figure, but conveniently

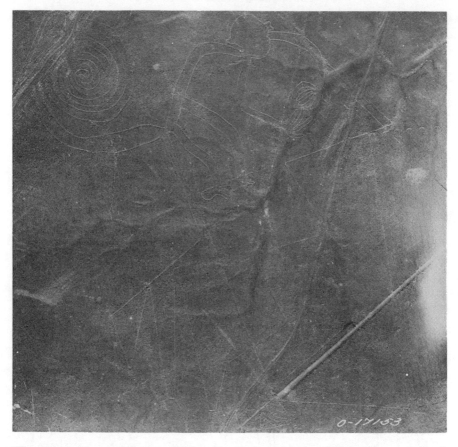

The figure of a monkey inscribed on the Peruvian desert. The scale is indicated by the width of the tire tracks on the upper left (dotted line in the accompanying diagram). Instituto Geografico Militar, Peru

in agreement with the calculations of one Bishop James Ussher, another searcher after truth who based his number on biblical calculations. Evidently, Smyth was a fan of his. Endless numbers of dates were found represented in the pyramid measurements, but as Martin Gardner has pointed out, "It is not difficult to understand how Smyth achieved these astonishing scientific and historical correspondences. If you set about measuring a complicated structure like the Pyramid, you will quickly have on hand a great abundance of lengths to play with . . . since you are bound by no rules." In fact, Gardner, in his book *Fads and Fallacies*, demonstrates that the Washington Monument proves as much

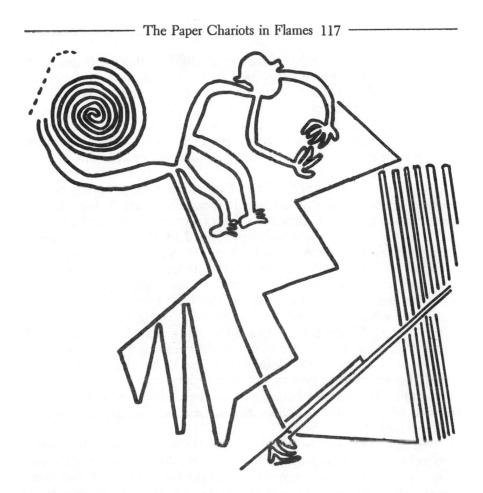

about history, astronomy, and numerology as does the Great Pyramid—if you have the patience and the time to waste on silly projects. One of Smyth's supporters, rhapsodizing over the relationship of the figure five to the pyramid, pointed out that it has five corners and five sides. The Pyramid Inch is one fifth of a cubit. There are five terminations in the human body, five senses, five books of Moses, and so on. But, Gardner shows us, there is just as much "fiveness" in the Washington Monument. Its height is 555 feet 5 inches. The base is 55 feet square, the windows are 500 feet from the base. Multiply five times the number of months in a year by the base, and you get 3,300—the number of pounds the capstone weighs. Using his "Monument Foot" (if Smyth can have a Pyramid Inch, why not a Monument Foot?) we have a base of 56.5 feet, which when multiplied by the capstone weight gives us 186,450—a figure remarkably close to the speed of light in miles per second. And so on and on.

Von Däniken can take courage from the fact that he is joined in his enthusiasm for Pyramidology by Charles T. Russell, now deceased, who founded the Jehovah's Witnesses cult. Russell announced in 1891 that before the close of 1914 the dead would all rise and again be annihilated if they chose not to accept a "second chance" to be saved. Once again, the faithful scurried into the Pyramid passageways to apply their tape measures to new predictions, seeking agreement with Russell. The year 1914 came and went.

There is one aspect of the Great Pyramid that seems to defy coincidence or wishful thinking, however. It seems fairly certain that the ancient Egyptians did not know the value of the very important constant we know as pi—often approximated as $22/7$ or 3.14. It is the ratio between the circumference of a circle and its diameter. Although both the Egyptians and the Japanese *almost* found it, they failed to recognize its importance, and its appearance in the Pyramid seems surprising. If we divide twice the length of one base side by the height of the Pyramid, we obtain pi correct within three figures. Recent investigation, as described in the "Nova" TV program, suggests that the practical Egyptians used a rolling wheel as a device to mark off distances, and the use of such a device would automatically introduce pi into the structure if the diameter of the wheel were one of the standards in use, as seems almost inescapable. But if space beings actually were there, why didn't they think to tell the Egyptians about the magical number pi? It shows up nowhere else!

Von Däniken, unable to believe that the ancients actually did the prodigious construction project themselves, tells us that no construction tools have been found in connection with the Great Pyramid. Not true. Ropes, rollers, chisels, and mallets are to be seen there and in collections all over the world. He says that we could not repeat this construction feat today, using our best technology. Again, not true. It is estimated that there are two and a half million blocks of stone in this colossal monument, and the quarries fifteen miles across the Nile River even show us some blocks partly cut out of the mass and abandoned when sufficient amounts were obtained. "Nova" discovered that today it takes two men fifteen minutes to cut a block out of the quarry. Estimates of how many blocks could be carried aboard the same size and type of vessel used in ancient times, of the labor needed for the construction of the ramps at the site, and of other logistics show that the thirty years and four-thousand-man work force estimated to have been required for the construction would seem to be adequate for the job. With more advanced technology, the labor would be a fraction of that. Again von Däniken is wrong.

The construction of the Great Pyramid of Cheops was the result of two hundred years of experiments in the art. There is even one example of a pyramid built (very early) with sides a bit too steep. It literally fell down, and the slope of another one then in the process of being built was abruptly changed to accommodate the lesson learned. It is called the Bent Pyramid. And why have the later pyramids lasted so long? Because the pyramidal shape is the most stable one for any structure. It is, in fact, the form that a structure takes when it falls down! In other words, having tumbled into a pyramid-shaped mass, it cannot collapse much further. Experience, care, dedication, skill, and hard work put the Great Pyramid where it is, not some super-beings from the stars.

We would do well to look into some of the finer points—rather than just the overall theory—asserted by von Däniken in his fascination with such wonders. It is a standard technique of miracle-mongers to present a general and faulty theory, begging for a chance to shore it up. This is done by supplying figures as fast and as forcefully as possible. The author of *Chariots of the Gods?* says that the Great Pyramid is fitted together "to the nearest thousandth of an inch." Sure. One look at the structure shows that it is literally a heap of roughly squared rocks. Variations of many inches occur on almost every block. Mind you, we would be wrong to expect anything else, and it does not detract from the skill and care of the builders to note this fact. The "core" of the pyramid was a support only. Gravity held it in place. It was the superb facing—now torn away—that polished the structure into a fine work of art. But "thousandths of an inch"? The lengths of the four sides of the Great Pyramid vary by as much as eight inches!

Even von Däniken's calculations are sloppy. He claims that the height of the Great Pyramid multiplied by one billion equals the distance to the sun. First of all, the distance of the earth from the sun varies greatly during the year. The *mean* distance is 92,900,000 miles. The height of the Great Pyramid is 480.93 feet, or .09109 miles. Given this, simple arithmetic shows that the pyramid is a shade under ten feet too short! Or did the earth move away a bit? And this is the structure that was fitted together to "thousandths of an inch"?

I could go on quoting such errors and hyperbole for many pages, but we have other best-selling fantasies by the same author to deal with.

In *The Gold of the Gods*, von Däniken abandons all pretense at truth and creates one of the most shameful and juvenile books ever to masquerade as fact. It is shocking to see it (and *Chariots of the Gods?*) classified in local libraries under 913.031—Archaeology! Of course, there is no Dewey classification for Pseudoscience, or for Outright Lies. Even the Library of Congress in Washington, D.C., lists the Castaneda books under "Yaqui History" rather than Fantasy. But then, that's Washington.

Whereas in his earlier book von Däniken is at worst revealed as rather dense, naïve, and careless, *The Gold of the Gods* gives us a totally different view of the man. In this book he tells of a visit to Ecuador in South America, where he was taken by one Juan Moricz into the legendary Caves of Gold. These caves have been spoken of by Ecuadorians for generations, though they never quite manage to take visitors into them, nor can they point out exactly where the entrances are. On one of my first trips to that country in the early 1960s, I visited the marvelous gold museum in Guayaquil, where I was accosted by an American who was there to find the caves. When I expressed doubt that they existed, he suddenly became angry and turned to an examination of the artifacts, as if to escape this unwelcome opinion. Later, speaking with the curator's assistant, I learned that the museum was plagued with *gringos* who insisted that the fabulous wealth of the Incas lay within these mysterious caverns, somewhere nearby, and would brook no argument.

But von Däniken claims he was successful, that Moricz took him into the caves. "When I first saw the pile of gold, I begged to be allowed to take just one photo," says von Däniken. "Once again I was refused. The lumps of gold had to be levered from the pile and that might make a noise and start stones falling from the roof like an avalanche." You see, he had previously been prevented from taking photos with his flash camera for fear that the cave entrance would "suddenly close." "Would my flash ignite a synchronized laser beam?" he asks. "Would we never see the light of day again? Childish ideas for men engaged in serious investigation?" That last suggestion seems the most sensible proposition in the book.

Just what the hell is von Däniken talking about? Is this his poor excuse for not giving us photos of this fabulous wealth and the interiors of the caves? No, there is a *much* better reason than that. When that excellent German magazine *Der Spiegel* became curious and went off to Ecuador to interview Juan Moricz, the man was flabbergasted. He told them that though he remembered von Däniken's visit (there are plenty of photos of the two together), *the writer never visited the caves, let alone saw the gold!* In fact, it is difficult to get Moricz to say exactly whether he *himself* has seen any treasure! I think that we are beginning to see an answer here: There are no treasure caves, and there is no gold.

True, there are caves. And true, they are most impressive. In addition, they *seem* to have artifacts inside them. It is also a fact that metal artifacts are to be seen, and these can be quite convincing to the uninformed, for they seem to imply outrageously strange events that contradict all orthodoxy. When we have examined these matters, we will begin to understand just how easily a man like Moricz can convince himself that he did not misrepresent the matter, even if von Däniken did.

Moricz, von Däniken tells us, promised him that he would be permitted "to photograph plenty of gold later, but not in such vast quantities." Then, to von Däniken's delight, Moricz took him to the Church of Maria Auxiliadora in Cuenca, where he met Father Carlo Crespi, an ancient Catholic priest who had a huge museum there in three rooms. The third room, "which he seldom shows anyone, and then unwillingly," is full of gold, we are told. Von Däniken was admitted to this holy spot and saw treasures beyond description piled to the ceiling, brought there "during past decades" by the local Indians, of whom Father Crespi is "a trustworthy friend." The collection "is indeed pure gold that has now been brought to the notice of an incredulous and astonished world."

The Gold of the Gods is filled with photos of the Crespi collection, and even the most casual student is stunned to see that on many of the metal pieces appear relief representations of elephants, hippopotami, horses, camels (not the "South American camel," as the llama is often called), and pyramids—Egyptian style! It is not at all difficult to see that if these artifacts are genuine, we have a complete revolution in the fields of archaeology, anthropology, history, and some half-dozen other disciplines, for in light of thoroughly accepted and established facts such animals and such a structure could not show up in ancient representations native to South America. True, the mammoth and the horse *were* common on that continent more than six thousand years ago—the horse was only reintroduced by the Spanish conquistadores— and I harbor a secret notion, admittedly without a grain of good evidence, that somewhere in the Mato Grosso of Brazil roams the remnants of a herd of mammoths, but along with these anachronisms we find Egyptian pyramids inscribed and rendered in relief on metal artifacts preserved by Father Crespi in his museum! Were these ideas and figures brought to those shores by "ancient astronauts," or were the ancient Ecuadorians actually Egyptians? How very exciting these ideas are! And how very salable. But true? I am perhaps somewhat better qualified than others to comment on these von Däniken tales. You see, I *have* been in a couple of the legendary Caves of Gold, and I spent much time with Carlo Crespi. Consequently, the von Däniken lies offend me immensely.

In the late 1960s, one of my trips took me through Cuzco and up into the *selva* of Peru to Tingo María, a small jungle town where there was rumored to be a "treasure cave" that previous visitors had declared to be full of man-made wonders and auriferous treasure. I was not inclined to become a full-fledged "spelunker," but I was determined to find out just what this was, so I shouldered the right gear and, with the help of local guidance, clambered up the face of an escarpment to the almost-invisible opening of the Cueva de los Leschusas. (The *leschusa* is a locally named bird similar to the *guacharo*, or oilbird, of Venezuela. A variety also lives in Mexico. It is the only bird known to live in caves, and only one of the rather terrifying critters that I was about to come upon.)

I will not detail the wonders I found in this cavern, except for the supposedly man-made artifacts; the three-inch-long white cockroaches, gigantic sowbugs, and vampire bats scurrying about like mice on crutches will have to await another effort. But these fascinating phenomena added greatly to the unreal atmosphere of this strange world.

It takes little imagination to invent giants from another world and claim that they lived in this Peruvian cave.

I do not wonder that others have allowed their imaginations to run rampant down these labyrinthine tunnels. One is suddenly out of touch with any semblance of the outside ecosphere, victim to all sorts of suggestions of dark and strange mysteries.

I came upon the giant "staircases" that had been described to me by others. They were the result of centuries of internal erosion by water, which was still at its tedious work as I observed the colossal structures. At the top of these "stairs" I discovered various seemingly bottomless holes going straight down, with scraps of rope and bits of lumber left by previous explorers still in evidence around the openings. For all I knew, the owners of these tools were moldering away at the bottom of the pits, and I was not inclined to look into them further. I had satisfied myself that the reported artifacts left there by the "giants" (you may read "Incas," "space aliens," or any other currently popular candidates) were in fact interesting but perfectly normal geological formations. And not a scrap of the elusive gold was to be seen, certainly no lumps that "had to be levered from the pile."

What appear at first glance to be giant stairs deep inside the cave are only natural geological formations.

Back in Cuzco, the ancient capital of the Inca empire and a city with which I am quite familiar, I had asked about the Caves of Gold, bearing up bravely under the exasperated sighs of the archaeologists with whom I spoke. I was sent to the Church of St. Dominic, which is constructed on and around the ruins of Coricancha ("Place of Gold"), the single holiest place in the Inca domain. It was called the greatest wonder of the hemisphere by the Spanish conquerors, who tried in vain to tear it down and settled for covering it up with modern stonework. Here, atop the wondrous Curved Wall, I was shown a barred window, beyond which lay the entrance to a series of caves allegedly chockful of Inca gold, taken there by the Indians when the Spaniards descended upon Cuzco. It was hard to believe that the invaders had sealed up such wealth and allowed such stories to get about.

It turned out that what I was peering into was a modern storeroom, inside of which excavation was going on to reveal concealed parts of the ancient ruins. The gold that had clad the andesite walls of Coricancha had long ago been stripped away and melted down by the invaders, along with the destruction of the culture that produced it. But tourists are still led to the spot and shown the provocative barred window.

We are told by the sensationalists that beyond this barred window in Cuzco is the entrance to the Caves of Gold used by the Incas. In reality, a storeroom of the Church of St. Dominic is there.

As for Moricz, he had heard tales of hidden caves full of gold and presumably had explored some caves and experienced the awe that such an investigation brings. Doubtless he had interpreted natural formations as the work of humans, if not giants. How, then, did he convince himself that caves and gold existed? Easily. He had seen and believed the Crespi material and assumed that such treasures came from the caves as claimed. But the Crespi treasure needs a bit of explanation.

When I visited the city of Cuenca high in the mountains of Ecuador to see the venerated Father Crespi, expectations of wonders were high. Various magazine articles had touted the golden objects to be seen in his museum, and I knew from research that the Cuenca area, besides producing great quantities of marble and artifacts made from the native stone, was also a major gold-producing center for the Incas. In fact, I was told that there was hardly a stream in the territory that would not produce at least a trace of gold, and I proved it to myself by panning a few flakes locally. But the value was not great enough to justify the time involved, and I abandoned all hopes of a gold rush.

Contrary to von Däniken's statement that Crespi is reluctant to show off his wares, I found that he was eager to do so. He took me through the paintings, stone carvings, and wooden items quickly, and we went finally into the Third Room. I was speechless: not for the same reason as von Däniken, however. The collection was a total, unmitigated fraud from wall to wall. Scraps of tin cans, brass sheets, and copper strips abounded, mixed with piles of rusted chain, shards of armor, and bits of miscellaneous machinery. Some of the brass sheets were embossed and scratched with everything from elephants to dinosaurs. Crude and rather poor designs were plentiful in the margins and backgrounds, and there were more representations of pyramids than I could count. The terrible truth began to dawn on me immediately.

There was one piece of gold, of a purity I could not determine. Now, I have handled a lot of Peruvian and Ecuadorian gold in my day. I have some of it in my home. There is something about its texture and particularly its weight that gives it away. And it evokes a strange flush of the body and quickness of breath that has been aptly described as "gold fever." It is intoxicating to have in your hands the one substance that has been pursued with more diligence than any other. One begins to entertain ideas of murder and flight (Father Crespi looked very vulnerable to me at that moment).

But it was shocking to see what I held in my hand. It was quite obviously a scrap of gold from a larger artifact, chopped out of the original and reworked by modern hands. I would identify it as a piece of a breastplate of some kind, now reduced to a piece about five inches square with a triangle and some crude snakes upon it, rudely embossed and fitting the irregular scrap right out to the margins. Only a few weeks before, I had been told in Guayaquil about a tragic act of vandalism involving a finely worked gold mask from the Esmeraldas area on the Ecuadorian coast. Two American gold hunters had found it, then gotten into a dispute. Their solution was like Solomon's: They sliced the mask in two, destroying its artistic, archaeological, and aesthetic value, and each departed with a certain weight of gold sheet.

I had learned that gold artifacts were often melted down—for safety reasons. It is against the law in Ecuador to possess antique gold artifacts; all such objects are the property of the government and must be surrendered. But raw or lump gold is okay. Thus the artifacts are often destroyed and sold for the value of the basic metal. What treasures are lost this way! But in questioning Father Crespi, I learned why he had so many "antediluvian" artifacts on display, in stone and metal. It developed that he provided small sums of money, clothing, and indulgences in

Father Carlo Crespi, as photographed by the author in 1966 in Cuenca, Ecuador, among some of his legitimate treasures.

return for artifacts. And he made it quite clear to all that *he preferred pieces which would prove his theory that the Egyptians and Babylonians populated South America, particularly Ecuador!* He told me that Hannibal himself had been in Ecuador with his elephants, a statement that made me doubt his sanity.

Crespi, a charming eccentric whose latest meal was evident on the front of his tattered cassock, was Italian by birth but had come to Ecuador to pursue his madness and incidentally to serve as a functionary at the Church of Maria Auxiliadora. His colleagues there treated him with respect but with a certain amusement as well. He was the local character, and tolerated as such. His museum, I was told, might be moved out at any moment to make room for more important matters. The split and rotted doors that guarded his treasures were held shut with rusted and very cheap padlocks. The pieces themselves were piled in uproarious abandon everywhere. It was evident that Father Carlo Crespi was just another deluded amateur theorist with unbounded gullibility.

There is another thing that the reader should bear in mind. Every country in South America wishes to be considered the cradle of civilization. When I spoke with a chain-smoking bishop in Sicuani, Peru, he assured me that many Peruvians harbored the belief that the Garden of Eden was right there in the Andes. Argentina has long favored the notion that the evolution of man took place right there, despite the fact that a pre-monkey type required for natural selection to produce the species *Homo sapiens* is just not found on the continent. New World monkeys split off from the prosimians very much earlier and do not enter into the evolution of humans at all, unfortunately for the many South American groups that would prefer an Andean cradle of the species. Thus, nuttiness such as Crespi's is officially encouraged.

Father Crespi had no shortage of articles to shore up his eccentric beliefs; a plethora of junk poured in at all times. Some of it doubtless came from the artifact factories that abound in Ecuador. But the nature of the entire collection was proved to me when, in looking over the piles of debris, I came upon a copper float for a toilet tank and an embossed tin can on which the words "product of Argentina" were still visible. But it was all good enough to fool von Däniken. And/or his readers. I can only conclude, based on these facts, that von Däniken is a liar and an incompetent fake.

It is astonishing what this man considers to be wonderful. At one point in *The Gold of the Gods* he shows us a photograph of a human skeleton carved in stone and asks incredulously how the stupid "heathens" could possibly have known what a human skeleton looked like! "As we know, Roentgen did not discover X rays until 1895!" he exults, having proven his stupidity once again. Then he turns to a number of photographs of hexagonal basaltic rock columns, fifteen to twenty feet long, used to construct a building in the Caroline Islands of Micronesia. "Until now," he reveals to us, "scholars have claimed that these basalt slabs were formed by lava that had cooled." Well, I have a hot news flash for him: Scholars *still* claim this. In Ireland, the Giants Causeway is quite adequate evidence that lava, cooling rapidly in water, can assume these shapes—and there the columns are up to *four hundred feet long*. But our author would prefer that we believe some space folks carved out these columns to put up a shack out in the Pacific.

We are further treated to his presumption when we see a photograph of a 10,000-year-old giant bison skull with a neat round hole in the forehead. We are not offered any evidence at all as to the size of the hole, how old the hole is relative to the skull, or whether any authorities have been questioned about it. All we get is von Däniken's typical hare-brained comment about a totally insignificant observation. "The hole in the skull could only have been made by a fire-arm," he says. "Who on earth possessed fire-arms in 8,000 B.C.?" A better question: Who on earth would believe such foolishness? Alas, 36 million people bought his silly books.

The Gold of the Gods dwells at some length on the curious Stones of Ica, on which, apparently, are prehistoric carvings showing such things as heart transplants, rocket ships, and television. There is a small "museum" in Ica, located on the coast of Peru south of Lima. The town is important as the location of genuine artifacts of pre-Inca times, as is Nazca, somewhat farther south, where von Däniken "discovered" the Nazca "lines."

The museum in Ica is an amateur affair, run by a dentist. The fakes are rather amateurish, too. I say this because my experience in Peru has acquainted me with some of the finest phony pottery and grave articles that have ever been made. Artisans there use precisely the same methods employed by the ancients in making their pottery, and since most of their product is copied directly from the fine work produced by those little-recognized masters of long ago, it is almost impossible to detect the fakery unless you know a few tricks of the trade. But the Stones of Ica have been the subject of several books, all printed in Peru and all of which take the rocks quite seriously. But those who deal in such things have known for a long time that they are utter fakes.

The "Nova" folks looked into the matter and were not long in discovering the truth. All they did was to visit the area, where they found the dentist, who was reluctant to discuss the matter when he discovered that they wanted to ask some penetrating questions rather than do the kind of careless and incomplete "investigation" von Däniken had done. Within an hour they had found out where the stones were really made and drove a few miles out of town to order a custom-made heart transplant item to be prepared while they waited and filmed the process.

The point is that *von Däniken had this procedure available to him too.* He was well equipped and financed and able to find out the truth about the stones; he simply did not want to.

Of course, merely finding a local artisan who said he was the maker of the stones, and who then made one to order that was indistinguishable from the "genuine" ones, proved only that he was a good artisan and *could* have made the whole lot. What was needed was some sort of evidence that the ones offered as genuine were actually fakes. And it was not hard to find. Great antiquity was claimed for the stones as finished items. This meant that the shallow carved grooves were bound to be weathered on the edges, a characteristic that could be seen with the use of a microscope. Careful examination by the "Nova" experts revealed that not only was there no such weathering but also that the stone custom-made on the spot was indistinguishable from the "genuine" ones.

I could have told them that there was a story going around Lima in the *huaquero* (grave-robber) hangouts that if you mentioned your profession to the doctor in Ica, then excused him for fifteen minutes, you would hear dental drills whining away in a back room until he returned from the depths of his museum with a carved stone that, by a strange and somewhat contrived coincidence, bore a picture of someone from the distant past engaged in your very profession. Also well known to *huaqueros* is an aging process used to make fake artifacts look old. It is a treatment that involves donkey dung and is best left to the imagination.

There is at least one thing for which von Däniken must be given credit. He has improved upon the crude technique of the Big Lie used by others and given us, instead, the Provocative Fact. He bombards us with interesting and in some cases quite valid bits of information and allows us to assume that what he has presented is pertinent and laden with hidden meaning and proof. The same technique was used by the Gellerites when they assured us that at no time did Uri Geller use laser beams, magnets, or chemicals to bend spoons. This was quite true. It is also quite true that he had no eggbeaters, asbestos insulation, or powdered aspirin in his pockets either. So what? To quote at random from *Chariots of the Gods?*, von Däniken gives us—with no textual connection whatsoever and each in a separate paragraph—various statements that only *seem* to support his claims: "Sumerian cuneiform tablets show fixed stars with planets." "In the British Museum the visitor can read the past and future eclipses of the moon on a Babylonian tablet." "Outline drawings of animals which simply did not exist in South America 10,000 years ago, namely camels and lions, were found on the rocks of the desert plateau of Marcahuasi 12,500 feet above sea level."

Let me explain these marvels to Mr. von Däniken. (If you are a high school student who already knows the answers, please indulge me a moment.) First: Yes, Erich, the Sumerians also had fixed stars. In fact, they had essentially the same stars we have now. And they had planets. And they had eyes to see them, so they recorded them. So what? The Babylonians knew about the *saros*, the period between eclipses, and thus they were able to predict them. And they, too, wrote down their observations. Clever, yes, but not supernatural. As for the lions and camels, you should know that the Marcahuasi drawings are of pumas and llamas, animals indigenous to South America and still found there in great numbers. What 10,000 years ago has to do with it, I cannot tell, nor can you. It *is* an impressive and nicely rounded figure, however. And rocks can be inscribed at 12,500 feet just as well as at sea level. And on and on it goes.

This man has the nerve to ask us, "How is anyone going to explain these and many other puzzles to us?" Easily, Erich, easily.

In his excellent exposé of the von Däniken fribble, Ian Ridpath says, in summing up, "It seems pointless to continue." But there is one important failing evident in all of von Däniken's writings that should be made clear: He is simply unable to admit or conceive of the fact that early man was capable of soaring visions and the technical and artistic ability to create the fortress of Sacsahuaman, the Great Pyramid of Egypt, and other wonders without assistance from outer space! But he at no point calls to our attention the miracle known as Chartres Cathedral, the Parthenon in Greece, or even Stonehenge—that most remarkable astronomical construction—*because these wonders are European*, built by people he *expects* to have the intelligence and ability to do such work. He cannot conceive of our brown and black brothers having the wit to conceive or the skill to build the great structures they *did* leave behind. Instead, to satisfy what appear to be his personal prejudices, he invents some sort of divine/extraterrestrial/supernatural intervention that he maintains was necessary to enable the inferior races to put stone upon stone or place paint upon a cave wall.

I personally feel very damaged and insulted by this attitude, and though it is an observation with which I cannot expect my reader to identify, I must mention that years ago—after having read numerous descriptions of the fortress of Sacsahuaman that guards the Inca capital city of Cuzco, with its marvelously constructed walls of stone—I finally had the opportunity to visit the site. I arose at dawn, walked the long, narrow pathway to the hill overlooking Cuzco, and saw the sun strike the cyclopean sides of this extraordinary structure. I stood in awe of the men of long ago who not only could conceive of such a project but who built it with prodigious effort and dedication. Could they have known, or even suspected, that someone from an era so far removed from theirs in time, culture, and technology would stand transfixed by their skill and audacity in giving birth to such a wonder? I literally burst into tears as I experienced a sense of reverence for those workers of miracles.

Try as he may, von Däniken cannot diminish the works created by greater men than he. For every giant, there is a little man to kick at his ankles. But the great accomplishments of long ago remain.

7

The Laurel and Hardy of Psi

With regard to Randi's new book, I guess my basic response is Ho Hum. I think that most intelligent people
now see Randi exactly as he is.
—Harold Puthoff
July 3, 1979

When a scientific paper titled "Information Transmission Under Conditions of Sensory Shielding" appeared in the British magazine *Nature* in October 1974, it had already made the rounds. As early as 1972, Russell Targ and Harold Puthoff, its authors, had submitted it to U.S. publications as a project of the Stanford Research Institute (SRI). All had rejected it. Its acceptance by *Nature* was indeed interesting, especially since it was held by the editor for an unprecedented *eight months* while he checked on what he called "a ragbag of a paper."

Nature is among the most prestigious scientific publications in the world. That its staff accepted this unusual paper seemed at first surprising, for their standards are known to be high. What is not generally known among those who have accorded the paper the imprimatur of established science as a result of this acceptance is that it had been through several submissions and revisions before it was accepted, the more harebrained material having been weeded out at the insistence of the editors. More importantly, *Nature* ran a lengthy editorial in the same issue explaining that the Targ-Puthoff paper was being published so that scientists could see the kind of material that was being turned out in the field of parapsychology. The editorial called the article "weak," "disconcertingly vague," "limited," "flawed," and "naïve." But *Nature* accepted it, and as a result it was followed by a long stream of respectful publicity. Even the *New York Times* fell into the trap, treating it as a respectable paper. If the *Times* had known what is now known about the Targ-Puthoff work, it would have been covered on the entertainment pages.

As it was, the two authors were the toast of the psi world, being asked to speak and opine on all aspects of the paranormal. They became spokesmen for what science believes to be irrational. Even before publication of the *Nature* article, they assumed this post. There was great excitement in Geneva, Switzerland, during August 1974 when Targ and Puthoff announced an earth-shaking experiment conducted in 1972 with "a gifted subject, Mr. Ingo Swann." Since this "psychic" had yet to make his daring "astral trip" to Jupiter (see chapter 4) that was to impress Targ and Puthoff so deeply, they were now only barely aware of his great powers. The two SRI scientists stood before an audience of their peers and delivered themselves of yet another Rosemary's Baby, to the admiration of all present. In fact, two of those present, Charles Panati of *Newsweek* magazine and author Arthur Koestler, gushed over the event for weeks. I tell of it here because it is an excellent example of the difference between a report and the actual event and foreshadows the later, more famous *Nature* report on Uri Geller.

Targ and Puthoff related that Swann had been taken to Stanford University, where he was confronted with a huge magnetometer, set up at that moment to register the rate of decay of a magnetic field. They told Swann, they reported, that if he were to paranormally affect the magnetic field, this would become evident on the chart recording. Swann "placed his attention on the interior of the magnetometer, at which time the frequency of the output doubled for about . . . 30 seconds." Next, they continued, Swann was asked if he could stop the field change as indicated on the chart. "He then apparently proceeded to do just that," they said. As Swann described his efforts to them, the chart recorder performed again! Then, they claimed, when they asked him *not* to think about the apparatus, the trace resumed its normal pattern, but when he again mentioned the magnetometer, it acted up again! They requested him to stop, they said, because he was by then tired from his efforts.

I ask the reader to reread the preceding paragraph carefully, to form a picture of what T&P would have us believe happened on this occasion. Then read on.

One of the people at the lecture, Gerald Feinberg of Columbia University, spoke with the man who actually built the magnetometer and who had been present at Swann's demonstration. Feinberg remarked rather wistfully that both this man and the designer of the apparatus had "apparently paid no attention at all to this report. [They] shrugged it off." Yes, they did, and had good reason to do so because they knew the report was all wet. How do I know? Because I bothered to contact Dr. Arthur F. Hebard, the builder of the device, who was present and who has excellent recollections of what took place.

Hebard was taken aback when I told him he had been quoted by Targ and Puthoff in reference to this fiasco. Not being a reader of far-out literature, he had not known of their presumption and was very irritated that he'd been made use of in this manner. This was evident in his remarks when I contacted him while investigating the Targ-Puthoff evidence.

"I find it incredible that no one bothered to check with me, as you did," he told me. "Targ and Puthoff jumped to a lot of conclusions—they were overzealous . . . and made hasty connection between the general and the specific." Puthoff never asked Hebard—*the builder of the machine*—whether he had any explanations. In fact, he had plenty of them. "There were many things which could have caused what we saw," he said. "Backup in the helium line, which was used by many different people in both buildings there, could have done it. It had happened before. The fact that Mr. Swann was not able to reproduce the effect on subsequent attempts on a later date lends credence to the view that the initial event was 'accidental.' "

But hold on here! That paragon of factual reporting, Charles Panati, had said to Targ and Puthoff that "if [Swann] does it with the frequency and repeatability—with the accuracy you say . . . it would be sort of a sledge hammer blow." You see, Panati made the mistake of believing T&P when they said that "during this and the following day when similar data with Mr. Swann were taken, the experiment was observed by numerous other scientists." The implication was that Swann *did* repeat the experiment successfully under competent observation. Wrong. According to Hebard he failed to do so, but the implication remains. Furthermore, Swann did not even repeat the test *once* during the *initial* try! Fooled you again, didn't they? The truth is that the Swann effect was *not* repeated. When I asked Hebard, "You mean it was misrepresented?" he replied, "It's a lie. You can say it any way you want, but that's what I call a lie."

Swann had stood for "ten to fifteen minutes" staring at the equipment, reported Hebard, after Targ and Puthoff told him to "do something." At no time was he asked to "stop the field change." When the curve leveled out momentarily, for whatever reason, Targ and Puthoff decided it was what they wanted. Swann was not responding to instructions; whatever happened—by perfectly normal means—was interpreted as paranormal. In fact, said Hebard, when the curve "burped," Swann asked Targ and Puthoff, "Is *that* what I'm supposed to do?" and they happily agreed that it was, without any idea what had caused the trace to waver, and without asking anyone for a rational opinion about what had caused the variance.

Then, according to Hebard, Swann went across the room and turned his attention away from the chart recorder. Others watched it to see if the irregularity would show up again. It did, which seemed to indicate that there had been another venting change somewhere in the lab complex at the university. When Targ and Puthoff saw the jump, they shouted to Swann, "Did you do *that*, too?" and Swann agreed that he had, inadvertently. In reporting this, Targ and Puthoff told Gerald Feinberg that Swann had "made several attempts and got the same effect"!

The two scientists also reported that Swann described "with great accuracy" the inside of the Stanford "quark detector." Said Dr. Hebard in response to this claim, "Mr. Swann was *not* able to describe the interior of the detector 'with great accuracy,' nor did he produce an accurate drawing of the detector. He did describe, using colors and shapes and a bit of poetic license, what he thought the detector might look like." On a hunch, I asked Dr. Hebard whether Targ and Puthoff had prompted Swann. "They gave him constant feedback," he replied. "Comments like 'That's right' or 'Tell us more about that.'" One wonders if this was typical of previous Targ and Puthoff experiments and also rehearsal for the upcoming "remote viewing" tests that proved so embarrassing to all concerned.

Note, too, that Targ and Puthoff automatically assume that when "the frequency of the output doubled" it was because the magnetic field within had undergone a change. That's a little like writing a check for one million dollars and assuming it means the money is in your account. What actually occurred was that—for one of many reasons, and as had happened before in that lab—the chart recorder showed a double trace. That's all. And it did *not* happen as Swann "placed his attention" on the task; it happened ten or fifteen minutes later. This distortion arises because when Targ and Puthoff say "at which time . . . the output doubled" we assume they mean "immediately." They don't. They credit Swann with causing a second increase in the trace while his attention was off the task, but Hebard tells us that in actual fact the change took place while Swann was across the room, and *they asked Swann if he did it!* It is a small jump from what actually happened to the eventual version manufactured by Targ and Puthoff. Small, that is, for parapsychology, but unforgivably large for any other discipline.

The biggest laugh, however, is due the last statement they make about Ingo Swann's feat. "At our request he stopped, and the observation was terminated." In other words, when the machine was operating normally, it was due to Swann's not using his terrible powers.

(This last reminds me of Gerard Croiset's most ingenious claim. Croiset, a Dutch "psychic," attended a parapsychology seminar and competed with an East German "psychic." During the encounter, the German concentrated on *withering* a flower, while Croiset concentrated on *saving* it. The flower survived, and Croiset crowed victory, saying that his powers were stronger. Of course, since they were parapsychologists, the scientists in attendance never bothered to see if the German *could* wither a flower.)

In May 1979, journalist Brian Inglis, writing in the *London Evening Standard*, provided further erroneous information in connection with Swann's non-miracle. Said he, in a gushing account, "The physicist in charge was horrified because . . . the construction of the magnetometer [quark detector] had been kept a secret, so that it could be patented, and he had got it right." Told of this, Hebard said he was anything but "horrified." The machine was an improved version of one made at Harvard, and drawings of it were posted everywhere. It was no secret at all; he had given a description of its principle and operation to Swann. There was absolutely no intention of patenting the device, and Swann was simply wrong in his attempt to describe the thing.

Inglis wrongly described the Swann episode altogether. He ended with, "They had to dig the wretched machine up at fearful expense to examine it for some fault, which might explain its unnatural behaviour; but no fault could be found." Wrong. It was never dug up at all—it wasn't even buried. And there was no reason to open it, since nothing unexpected had happened. Inglis even refers to "instructions that no more experiments of that kind would be permitted," another fabrication in an account that Hebard calls "really absurd—outright lies from a sensationalist."

Couple all this evasive and deceptive reporting with Targ and Puthoff's closing comment that tests were done the following day that were witnessed "by numerous other scientists" *and their failure to mention that Swann did nothing at all.* In a letter to *Scientific American* magazine, T&P referred to the Swann magnetometer adventure as "carefully verified and well documented" at SRI. The letter was also signed by Wilbur Franklin of Kent State University and Edgar Mitchell. The record is clear: Targ and Puthoff just cannot be trusted to produce a factual report.

Swann must have reveled in all this. He was to go on to greater victories in New York, where the American Society for Psychical Research (ASPR) tested him for out-of-body experience under what Panati called good conditions in his book *Supersenses.* According to Panati, "Swann . . . was observed by scientists, and a television camera recorded his every move." The task was to look into a small box psychically—that means without peeking—and describe the contents. He did just that, eight times out of eight! The only flaw was that he was *not* being observed. In addition, Panati was wrong about the TV camera. Don't you wish your job was as easy as Swann's? By the way, my $10,000 offer* is open to him, of course. Funny he's never taken me up on it.

Having heard the exciting news of this repeatable, flawless experiment, Panati joined Arthur Koestler in agitating for a concerted drive to raise interest in and money for a repetition of the magnetometer miracle in other labs. Panati called for "a joint or international effort,

* See chapter 13.

where several prominent scientists, from several institutes throughout the world, would get together to witness Swann influencing a magnetometer." Puthoff and Koestler thought it was a great idea. But, they were warned by another parascientist, don't forget that negative vibes may interfere! He suggested that they bring in a "psychic" disguised as a student so that contrary thoughts would not be present to inhibit the effect. I can see it now: the "psychic" in a white coat, the parascientists in caps and bells. . . .

Gordon's Law tells us: If a research project is not worth doing at all, it is not worth doing well. Hear, hear.

Targ and Puthoff have said repeatedly that in their research they do not retain successful tests and reject failures. This is not true. Not only did they do so in a series of thirteen ESP tests with Uri Geller—an experiment included in their 1974 report in *Nature*—but also in other tests as well. In fact, Geller, Swann, and another "psychic" named Pat Price were all tested at the Stanford Research Institute in a similar manner, and *many* tests were not reported on. Why? Two important long-distance tests were done with Geller, and both were failures. One was rejected—*after* it failed—because the target was deemed "unsuitable." They failed to report another Geller test in which he merely "drew pictures in the air." You can be sure it would have been trumpeted to the world, had it worked. It didn't, so no report was issued. In a desperate grab at the passing brass ring, Targ and Puthoff declared, after another simple [ten-target] test with Geller, that three of his ten guesses were "fair" even though he had "passed" on the entire set! (The subjects tested were allowed to "pass" on any test before or after it was done. That meant the test would not be counted in the final results if the subject was unsure of it. But the rule was that a test, once passed, was not reported at all.)

No report was issued on a sealed-room "remote-viewing" test of ex-policeman Pat Price that failed, nor was the total number of tests ever revealed. That number may have been in the hundreds. Price, like Swann and Puthoff a dedicated Scientologist, had been projecting his mind to far-off cities with no success. Although Targ and Puthoff had previously noted that electromagnetic shielding of the room *enhanced* results when Price was tested, this time they *blamed the shielding for the failure* and decided not to report on the tests! So, contrary to their official reports, all the Price tests were *not* included. When this same "gifted" (their term) "psychic" completely failed to guess office objects in another remote-viewing test, again no report. A simple test of his ability to detect flashing lights set off in an adjoining test area defeated Price during one of SRI psychologist Charles Rebert's EEG monitoring efforts. Targ and Puthoff never made a report on this one either.

SRI colleagues questioned the two scientists about a judging procedure in the Price tests. When three judges who had been chosen failed to come up with results good enough for Targ and Puthoff, they chose two others, who obliged with favorable findings. They chose no more. Were the announced results based upon all five judges' results? Targ and Puthoff do not tell us. A proper procedure in the remote-viewing tests with Price would have been to have him choose from among a number of photographs to identify the correct target, rather than just ramble on about his general impressions of the required answer. This would have been definitive and easily judged without ambiguity. When a psychologist at SRI suggested this, the idea was ignored. Theirs was a *good* test, according to Targ and Puthoff, and there was no need for such a process. (A 1979 remote-viewing test at Metropolitan State College in Denver, Colorado, used this more rigorous method. The results were negative.)

Of all the experiments—if I may use that term loosely—that Targ and Puthoff performed with Geller, the thirteen ESP tests are best known to students of these matters. They were the highlight of the article in *Nature*. The experimenters chose their targets from a dictionary, using a fairly acceptable random method. Geller, sealed in a test area, was supposed to guess the targets, which were drawings of the chosen words. He had the option of "passing," which was the usual arrangement in these tests. Fair enough—if that was the actual procedure.

Geller was supplied with paper and pen and asked to make a drawing that corresponded to the target. We are told that he was required to stay in the room until each test was declared terminated, at which time he would emerge and submit his effort to the experimenters before being shown the target. Again, a good procedure, *if* it was the method used.

Over a period of several days, Geller made thirteen tries at ESP guessing. Contrary to usual scientific procedure, the tests were conducted under widely varying conditions that changed every moment. Geller was able, we are told, to identify seven of the thirteen targets. That's 54 percent success, with odds of millions to one since the target pool consisted of a very great number of possibilities. Sounds impressive, until you remember the usual reporting standards of the two in charge. Actually, Geller correctly identified only *three* of the thirteen targets, and there's very little mystery about how he got two of them.

Targ and Puthoff conducted these tests and drew their conclusions in a way previously unknown to scientists but often used by bunglers. The scorecard read:

Test Number	Target	SRI Decision	Actual Result
1	Firecracker	missed	missed
2	Bunch of grapes	hit	security breakdown
3	Devil	missed	missed
4	Solar system	hit	security breakdown
5	Rabbit	passed	passed
6	Tree	passed	passed
7	Envelope	passed	passed
8	Camel	hit	passed
9	Bridge	fair	passed
10	Seagull	hit	hit
11	Kite	hit	passed
12	Church	missed	passed
13	Heart	fair	missed

The report Targ and Puthoff issued listed only three passes in the thirteen tries. Actually, in the cases of the "camel" (8), "bridge" (9), "kite" (11), and "church" (12), Geller *passed*, though this was not reported. According to the rules of Targ and Puthoff, a pass is allowed only if you miss! There were several responses to "camel," for example, and Puthoff chose the one closest to it, a horse, as the winner. They reported that "all drawings were published," but there were many that they chose to omit apparently in order to bolster the results. But, we are told, even with all this skulduggery, they did submit these results for "double-blind" decisions by people who did not know the expected findings. Yep. And in doing so, they left out numbers 5, 6, and 7, since they *were* passes, but included the *selected* responses to numbers 8, 9, 11, and 12—and *these* were passes, too! But—when carefully trimmed and weeded—they were very good evidence in favor of Geller's ESP powers! The double-blind safeguards do not take into account such careful "weeding."

At this late date, with the detailed and careful obfuscation in the reports that has been applied in the interim to conceal the needed information, it is impossible to say just how Geller fooled the experimenters during the tests done at SRI. Suffice it to say that—apart from the accommodating Targ and Puthoff—he had adequate confederates in the persons of Shipi and Hannah Shtrang, two assistants he had trained in Israel to transmit information to him in his act. Jean Mayo, a Geller devotee, was also present, underfoot all the time, and may very well have been of help to Geller as well. She was there to make the drawings for the tests. None of these people ever showed up in the "scientific" report that was published and, according to John Wilhelm's *The Search for Superman*, Targ specifically instructed Mayo never to admit she'd been there. The "security breakdown" I have listed for test numbers 2 and 4 consisted of a hole in the wall of the room in which Geller was enclosed to insulate him from the target drawing, and a discussion between Mayo and Targ about the target that not only could have been overheard but was bolstered, reports Wilhelm, by Targ's out-loud suggestion to "add a rocket ship" and Mayo's humming of the theme music of the motion picture *2001: A Space Odyssey.* Sounds like a Keystone

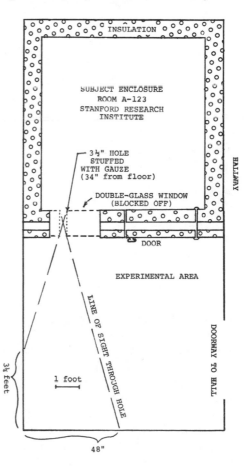

Layout of the site where Russell Targ and Harold Puthoff performed thirteen ESP tests on Uri Geller.

Kop affair, and it was. The only mystery is how Geller missed any targets at all.

But what about the three accepted passes in tests 5, 6, and 7? Why did Geller choose to pass on them, and why were these passes accepted? Because *on those three and those three only* he was up against some brains. Charles Rebert, the EEG expert and psychologist at SRI, conducted *those* three, and Geller didn't like it one bit. Nor did he have a chance to work any trickery.

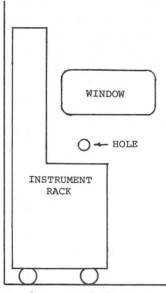

View of the subject enclosure from the experimental area.

Rebert and Dr. Leon Otis, also a psychologist, later ran a series of one hundred tests that Geller flunked grandly, falling back on the tired old "negative vibrations" alibi. The psychologists prepared one hundred targets (drawings) and sealed them in individual envelopes. Geller was asked to guess the contents of each envelope, chosen at random. The procedural rules were strict, and Geller was hooked up to the EEG electrodes to get a readout of his bodily functions while he worked. He failed to identify the targets in *every one* of the envelopes, according to the experimenters, yet Targ and Puthoff looked over the results and declared that six of the hundred guesses could be "reasonably associated" with their targets. The psychologists disagreed with this conclusion. Furthermore, *after the psychologists had terminated the tests,* conditions were relaxed at the insistence of Targ and Puthoff, and after Geller made a few trips in and out of the room—a procedure that had been forbidden in the preceding tests—he was able to identify one of a set of six *new* drawings that had been prepared. Why six new ones? Because Geller complained that the others had been produced by persons with negative feelings.

Rebert was angry when Targ and Puthoff submitted their reports to *Nature* over his objections. He directed them not to include one set of EEG experiments that he had supervised, and he informed them that their presumptuous conclusions had no basis in fact, since there was an unusual EEG pattern in only one out of six subjects tested, and even that pattern had not been properly studied. When analyzed,

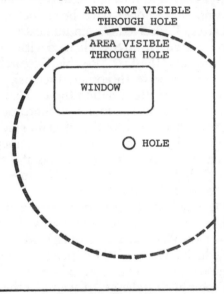

View from the subject side of the enclosure—assuming the hole can be seen through.

it proved only *different*, not *significant*. But the results were published anyway. A horrified Rebert also heard that Targ and Puthoff were going to proclaim these erroneous findings before Stanford University's psychology department, and he forbade such a blunder. The talk was canceled.

Although Targ and Puthoff claimed that Geller failed the Rebert-Otis hundred-envelope test because of the negative attitude of the experimenters, the fact remains that Geller "succeeded" only after the tight controls imposed by Rebert and Otis were purposely relaxed. Rebert published a statement saying he was convinced that Geller simply cheated.

In my book *The Magic of Uri Geller*, I complained that Stanford Research Institute scientists as well as the SRI administration had withheld important information about Targ and Puthoff and their fiasco. Of course, a major reason for that was their embarrassment. As the people at SRI felt increasingly imperiled by the news that kept leaking out, I felt it was time for a bolder approach. I sat down and wrote thirty-one letters to prominent figures there, asking if they were prepared to tell the facts about the entire situation.

Weeks went by. Then, one evening, I received a call from an individual. I was told that this person represented a group of "dozens" of scientists at SRI who were determined that the truth be told. They adopted the code name "Broomhilda," and during the next few months began giving me the information that should have been included in the SRI reports. Shortly thereafter, I received a communication from a member of a second special committee within SRI charged with looking into the Targ and Puthoff shenanigans (the first "Psychic Research Review Committee" had found everything perfectly kosher, it seems), asking me for details about my investigations of the situation there. *They* were asking *me*, and I've never even set foot on the sacred grounds of SRI. But this group seemed somewhat better organized and genuinely concerned. Regrettably, after months of correspondence with a member of the committee I was informed that their investigation was at a standstill, and that I was expressly forbidden to mention his name or to quote anything he had asked me or told me in this book.

Broomhilda verified for me much of the information I had been holding on to for years. That data now moved from the status of hearsay to documented fact. Additional facts were elicited during conversations and correspondence with individuals. Many of these persons were not aware of Broomhilda and were acting on their own. Their completely independent input supported Broomhilda's charges. Taken together, the information from all sources amounted to quite an indictment. In essence, it is this:

The psychologists at SRI had been called in to advise on the propriety of Targ and Puthoff's experimental procedures, on the validity of their report in *Nature* magazine, and on the worth of another paper later submitted to the journal of the Institute of Electrical and Electronics Engineers. They had told Targ and Puthoff they had no right to conclude, from their very ambiguous work, that any person tested had the ability to "view remotely with great clarity," as they claimed. They said that the work had absolutely no scientific validity and that Targ and Puthoff showed general inability or unwillingness to use good scientific procedures. Targ and Puthoff's assertion that Geller's powers had been established as a result of the work done at SRI, said colleagues there who were involved with the tests, was unwarranted, unscientific, and exceedingly premature. They said that the two scientists should *publish an objective and honest representation of the work.* Targ and Puthoff chose to ignore this. They published the *Nature* paper.

In advance of the submission of the paper to *Nature*, Charles Rebert, as already mentioned, made no secret of his objections. He told Targ and Puthoff that they were ethically bound to tell *Nature* that in the thirteen-target series of tests with Geller, numbers 8, 9, 11, and 12— three of them counted as "hits"—were passes. They chose not to. The *unsuccessful* Geller tests were not included in the *Nature* paper. They should have been, by any standards. Targ and Puthoff knew there had been breaches of protocol during the tests, such as the hole in the wall of the room in which Geller was confined. They did not report this. Rebert reminded them that, according to his own recollection, "hundreds of drawings were made" by Geller during the tests. Where were they? Targ and Puthoff had told the world that "all drawings are shown." Psychologist Rebert complained about Targ and Puthoff's wild rationalizations, in their attempts to account for their failures, and reminded them that though they claimed the targets were never discussed, he was there when they *were*—loudly and animatedly.

The group of scientists at SRI who worked on the tests with Targ and Puthoff objected to their use of the words "totally unambiguous" and "scrupulous" when referring to their experimental procedures. They were anything but that. Targ, told by Leon Otis that his reports were misleading, never responded to the comments. Otis concluded that Targ was willing to present unsubstantiated results to the SRI clients and feared that the scandal resulting from an exposure of such procedures could jeopardize the position of SRI as a research organization. He had underestimated the stubbornness of SRI's administration, which to this day has never publicly admitted Targ and Puthoff's manipulations of fact and of scientific method.

Hundreds of experiments that were done by SRI in testing Price, Geller, and Swann were never reported. Instead, tests with favorable results were selected, in spite of their poor control and heavily biased ambiguity, to be published as genuine scientific results despite strenuous objections from more serious and careful scientists. And it was all given the blessing of the SRI administration. After all, it brought in funding.

In all the *real* work on Geller at SRI, the *only* data ever gathered proved that (1) Geller could not perform as claimed, and (2) when they gave him the chance to use trickery, observers were convinced that he did just that, and he was successful. All the other tests lacked proper controls and were useless. When scientists within SRI issued strong statements about this situation and other aspects of experiments done by Targ and Puthoff, the two were quick to cover their tracks with further word games. A statement was issued that included a typical doubletalk term, "non-experiment." This apparently meant an experiment that is not under control but is good enough to report anyway.

Shortly after my book *The Magic of Uri Geller* appeared and helped to force the retreat of that psychic superstar, Drs. Targ and Puthoff issued a "fact sheet" in rebuttal to twenty-four of the points made in my book. This attempt was a failure, and in response to one claim that the SRI tests were done under tight controls, a scientist who was there declared flatly, "This is b.s. As far as I and my colleagues are concerned, *none* of the experiments met accepted scientific protocol." I will not burden you with the other twenty-three points; they are as easily de.nolished.

However, I must disagree with a member of the press, who described Dr. Russell Targ as "not very smart" after seeing the film that both SRI scientists had prepared to prove the wonders of parapsychology. People can change, even parapsychologists. Now Targ lets Puthoff make all the mistakes by allowing him to answer all the questions.

Targ and Puthoff prepared that highly deceptive film for SRI, advertising their efforts. It was criticized by others on the staff, and the two issued a masterpiece of evasion and license in reply. They appended to it—without his knowledge or permission—the name of Zev Pressman, the SRI photographer who had shot the film. Some of the objections that had been raised were based on Pressman's revelations about his involvement in it.

In the film, Geller was shown doing a trick wherein a die was enclosed in a box and shaken about, after which Geller identified the uppermost face on the die eight times in a row. *At no time did Geller touch the box,* said Targ. Actually, Geller not only shook the box (Targ later reported that he was like a child who liked to rattle things!) but also held it while concentrating and was even reported to have been the one to *open* it! Pressman, said Targ and Puthoff in their statement, was present during these experiments. Not so, according to Pressman, who said he had been present during a few correct throws made in other experiments, on other days—thus also contradicting Targ and Puthoff's claim that there were no other die tests done. Most damning of all, Pressman said to others at SRI that he had been told the successful throws were done *after he* (Pressman) *had gone home for the day.* So it appears the film was a reenactment of that miracle! Yet the transcript of the film includes these words: "The film portrays experiments that we performed with [Geller] just as they were carried out. Each scene has been taken from film footage made during actual experiments. Nothing has been restaged or specially created. . . . Here is another dice-box experiment. . . . This is a live experiment that you see." This section of the transcript is headed, in large capital letters, DICE BOX EXPERIMENTS.

At the close of the film, the narrator refers to what Targ and Puthoff consider to be one of the most important and convincing segments in the film—a segment that is now known to be a *restaged* and *specially created* one. He offers a recap "to remind you of those experiments we feel were best controlled . . . including the double-blind die-in-the-box experiment."

I have examined the evidence and can only come to the conclusion that this is blatant misrepresentation. There is no other way to describe it properly. Pressman did not even know that Targ and Puthoff were issuing a statement, he did not sign it, and he did not give them permission to use his name. He knew nothing about most of what appeared under his name, and he disagreed with the part that he did know about.

We are told by SRI that some thirty thousand feet of movie film about the Geller experiments was prepared. That's approximately fourteen hours of research data on film! May we see this film, gentlemen? Surely it must be astonishing stuff, and valuable as well. But no, we are offered instead only that which was released by Targ and Puthoff as the *best* of their data; not only is this amateur night at the movies but most of what is shown is admittedly not done under proper control!

The SRI film, shown to audiences all over the world, starts off with a typical blooper. As anyone with any experience in the field now knows, Geller used the art of "pencil reading" whenever he could. This consists of watching the top of a pencil as someone is using it and determining what is being written by the motion of the pencil. When the selection is rather narrow—ten digits for example—such a feat is not difficult. And in the SRI film, the first trick is just that. Geller pretends to think of something, then "transmits" it to a member of his audience. He pretends to write, but writes nothing. He retains the pencil and paper, however. He asks the victim to guess his number and write it. It can be clearly seen in the film that the victim writes a "3," and sure enough, when Geller reveals the number he has now written it is exactly the same one! If Geller fooled them all with such a simple trick, he certainly could fool them with other material. In this case, the evidence was right there for them to see. But you know how it is leading horses to water.

Following their adventures with Uri Geller, Targ and Puthoff tried a new approach to their exciting work. In a book entitled *Mind Reach*, and in a paper printed in the journal of the Institute of Electrical and Electronics Engineers (IEEE) on the subject of "remote viewing," they attempted to prove that humans can project their consciousness out of their bodies to far places. In the hands of the occultists, this has been known as "astral projection." When the parapsychologists latched on to it they called it "out-of-body experience," and it finally matured when physics adopted the illegitimate child as "remote viewing." Under any name, it is a silly notion. But it will go on and on, like the fifth act of *Othello*.

Targ and Puthoff made up a list of one hundred "target" locations in and around the Stanford University area. From these, nine were selected at random and visited singly by one of the researchers, while the "psychic" of the moment was watched at the lab. When the "sender" arrived at the location, he began transmitting his impressions of the place, and the "psychic" would talk into a tape recorder and make drawings. The results, as published, looked marvelous. Judges were used to decide, double-blind, how well the "psychic" had done. The world thrilled to another coup by Targ and Puthoff.

Leon D. Harmon, who works with the Department of Biomedical Engineering of Case Western University in Ohio, was notified by a colleague at Bell Laboratories of the submission of the "remote-viewing" paper to the IEEE. The Bell employee invited him to be a referee of the paper. Time went by, and when Harmon again checked the situation he was informed that other referees had been selected, and that the paper was well on its way to publication. He was given an advance copy and exploded with anger. He was not alone. Barney Oliver, a member of the board of IEEE, threatened to resign if it was published. There was consternation among the IEEE associates, and finally the decision to publish was upheld, because it was just too late to cancel and because the general feeling was that such controversial research should not be suppressed *just because it was unlikely to be correct*. Harmon was given the right to reply to Targ and Puthoff's claims and did so.

Harmon's brief critique was very much to the point. He made the perceptive observation that *less than 3 percent* of the entire twenty-six page article dealt with the most important part of the subject—the experimental procedures and controls. There was, of course, good reason for this, though Harmon had no way of knowing this; it would be two years before the damning evidence came to light, and then only after careful and difficult probing. Harmon demolished the paper solely by pointing out that on the basis of the information available to the reader, there were countless ways that trickery could have been used to fool the experimenters. True, these methods were possible in view of the protocol used and the performance record of Targ and Puthoff in the Geller nonsense, but in this case the flaw lay not in the experiment itself but in the unbelievable judging procedure.

Two psychologists from New Zealand, Dick Kammann and David Marks, visited the Stanford Research Institute shortly thereafter and looked at the data a little harder than others had. They had already provoked Targ and Puthoff by criticizing the Geller tests, showing that standard magician's tricks could account for Geller's success. But Targ and Puthoff were anxious to bring them into the fold. It was T&P's undoing. (Dr. Kammann even had to place a phone call to Boyce Rensberger of the *New York Times*—while Harold Puthoff stood by as a witness—and retract a statement about the Targ and Puthoff work in order to keep their confidence.) Kammann and Marks's findings, submitted to *Nature* magazine, were published in August 1978. The "mind-reach" experiment collapsed into shambles.

Even before Kammann and Marks delivered the death blow, it was evident that the usual Targ and Puthoff methods had been applied to this research too. There were photographs accompanying the drawings that had been made. The reader might easily have assumed that these photographs were part of the test, since the represented angles corresponded closely to the drawings. It was quite obvious, from the excerpts published, that the "psychics" had intended some descriptions to match places other than those actually visited, but the judges had decided, and that was that. It was all swallowed whole after being lubricated with hindsight and hyperbole.

The judging procedure had been well designed—on paper, that is. Judges were given a list of the nine locations and a package of transcripts. Their job was to match the locations with the correct transcripts. It was done with great accuracy, and the case seemed proved. But when we find that three judges appointed by other officials at SRI failed to get good results with this matching procedure, we begin to get suspicious. Targ and Puthoff, however, found two who were sympathetic, and these two did just fine. Kammann and Marks, wondering about this difference in judging ability, reached one of the judges—a successful one—named Arthur Hastings and from him obtained the original list of locations and the transcripts. They told the whole story.

A word about Hastings. He had been associated with Targ and Puthoff for years and was even called in to design the Geller tests. But Targ and Puthoff not only ignored his suggestions for controls in those tests but also excluded him from the *experiments* with Geller. You see, Hastings is a magician as well as a parapsychologist (a bizarre combination—something like a Baptist minister who is also a cardsharp!), and he was uncomfortably knowledgeable about the whole matter.

First, Kammann and Marks discovered, the judges had been given the locations *in chronological order*, and they knew it. The barest trace of experimental care would have demanded that this list be "scrambled." But it was not. Even so, it was of course not very useful unless there were clues within the transcripts themselves that would enable a careful observer to rank them in order. Plenty of those clues were available, Kammann and Marks found. The transcripts contained such goodies as Targ saying "Nothing like having three successes behind you" (making that one the fourth target), and he speaks of the target visited the day before, thus identifying the third target as well.

The next procedure was to test the theory that these boo-boos, whether intentional or not, could have allowed all locations to be matched to the targets. Indeed they could have. Kammann and Marks performed a number of such experiments and proved that when individuals were provided with the list of locations, in order and with the *unedited* transcripts, they invariably could pair them correctly. The Targ and Puthoff miracle was out the window. One test remained to be done. Using proper scientific procedure, Kammann and Marks also tested the ability of people to identify the pairings *without* the clues left in. They failed to do so. The case was complete.

In a desperate attempt to rescue themselves, T&P commissioned parapsychologist Charles Tart to re-evaluate their data. Tart edited the clues from the transcripts, and gave them to *one*—unnamed—judge who properly ranked them. *Nature* obligingly published the results, and the scientific world yawned.

But Targ and Puthoff were nowhere near through. Even before the Kammann-Marks paper appeared in *Nature*, they suspected that something was up. When I lectured at Sandia Laboratories in Albuquerque, I mentioned that the transcripts had been faulty since they contained clues. Shortly after that visit I was sent a mysterious letter that had shown up there bearing Puthoff's name and entitled "SRI REPLIES TO RANDI." I wrote to Puthoff, asking if he had indeed written the letter and if he would stand by the statements made in it. He admitted, after several months, that he wrote it but he has steadfastly refused to answer, with a simple yes or no, whether it is factual. I know why, too. Now you will know.

I quote from this letter:

> . . . according to Randi our transcripts are liberally sprinkled with remarks about other experiments, other targets, etc., which helps the judge along in his matching efforts. Could this possibly be true? Of course not! The raw data transcripts are carefully edited before being turned over to the judges; all references to targets, dates, other experiments—in short, anything that would help a judge determine actual targets, or even the chronological order of the transcripts—are removed.

Kammann and Marks say this is untrue. Hastings gave them the same transcripts he worked with, and *they are not edited.* In fact, Targ and Puthoff went to great lengths, in writing about their tests, to say that the transcripts were not in any way edited, that every word was included. The letter sent to Sandia is a lame attempt to perpetuate the story, but it doesn't work. In it, Puthoff also denies the facts about the judges being tossed out and refers to the matter of walkie-talkies being used as well. We'll handle *that* gem in a moment. But what is really outrageous is the fact that though Puthoff has now admitted authorship of this paper, he will not say whether he will stand by the statements in it! Furthermore, though *Nature* magazine invited Targ and Puthoff to respond to the Kammann and Marks piece, they chose to ignore it.* Even requests from Kammann and Marks directly to them met with silence. And when a colleague of mine finally got to them and mentioned it, Puthoff replied that he was "too busy" to answer. In view of what Kammann and Marks proved, is it possible that Targ and Puthoff merely bungled it?

Finally, in the "Summary of Experiments" section of a paper that Targ and Puthoff presented at a prestigious conference in Geneva, this time on quantum physics and parapsychology, one startling episode involving a "remote-viewing" test is described. It is referred to as "the first experiment" in a "series of experiments," and Harold Puthoff is described as "the experimenter" who also conducted the "pre-experimental" process with the subjects. I quote these words and phrases to emphasize that *it is an experiment*, and it was important enough to be a feature of their talk at this meeting. But nowhere in the description is there any mention of the fact that *walkie-talkies were used on both ends of the experiment!* If the experiment employed the same techniques that Targ and Puthoff have used in the past—cueing and prompting the subjects as in a child's game of "hot-and-cold"—it is easy to see why it was a success. But why did Puthoff not mention the walkie-talkies? Surely that should have been part of a scientific paper. When Puthoff was asked about this, he *denied* the use of the walkie-talkies! He wrote:

> Preposterous! If we used walkie-talkies during experiments, it would be easy to cue a subject into a correct response—and that's as obvious to us as to anyone else! Although we have used walkie-talkies occasionally in training, we have never, never, never—not even once—used a walkie-talkie during an experiment . . . not even to say "we're at our site." . . . Not even an unused walkie-talkie is carried by members of the outbound team. What more can I say?

But Puthoff has forgotten, perhaps, that he specifically wrote later, in the book *Mind Reach*, that *he did use walkie-talkies during this important experiment*, and he even used the same illustration for the account

---

* Charles Tart eventually answered for them, as seen two paragraphs back.

in that book as he used in the Geneva paper! But by the time the episode was printed in *Mind Reach*, it was treated as an almost-experiment—a mere whim of the moment. Previously it had been touted as a major and highly significant scientific breakthrough!

What more can you say, Dr. Puthoff? Well, you could begin by apologizing to your colleagues at SRI, who have been embarrassed by your unscientific behavior. You could apologize to the editors of the scientific journals and to the journalists who believed you when you delivered all that poppycock to them. And you might think of how to apologize to a generation that, largely because of your highly colored and hyperbolized accounts of the "non-experiments" you sold to them as miracles of the avant garde, got so screwed up in their heads that they may never be able to deal with a rational thought again.

Father Damian Fandal of the University of Dallas recommends these two rules for academics in trouble: (1) Hide, and (2) If they find you, lie!

In closing the discussion of Targ and Puthoff, I must note that they have made use of an affiliation with another parapsychologist, Charles Tart of the University of California at Davis. He has been brought into several of their projects to add a certain gloss to the proceedings, since he has a reputation as one of the most honest and dedicated workers in parapsychology. I cannot find any indication that Tart has ever misreported data or denied honest criticism. But, as we shall see, he is susceptible to the usual pitfalls. One of his most widely known books, a work that has been through many printings and is used in colleges around the world as a textbook, is *Learning to Use Extrasensory Perception.* It deals with extensive experiments Tart carried out in 1972 to prove that subjects could actually learn, during a period of testing, to improve their ESP scores. Tart had been impressed with work done by Targ and Puthoff in a similar project but had accepted their *post hoc* explanations when the experiment failed rather grandly. T&P had discovered—no great surprise—that as the controls on the tests were improved, the results approached zero. But they had decided that an automatic recorder, used to ensure that there would be no recording errors, inhibited the testees, who had obtained good results when they were allowed to test themselves (and the possibility existed of their either including or rejecting any run they tried) but did badly using the automatic recorder. Since Targ and Puthoff referred to these testees as "employees, relatives, and friends" (one was Targ's daughter), it is not difficult to sense that there just might have been an incentive to get good results for the big chiefs. After all, little Indians like to please. . . .

The T&P tests—which made no news at all, since they only demonstrated the inverse relationship between good experimental procedure and good results in ESP research—were discontinued. The National Aeronautics and Space Administration and the Jet Propulsion Laboratory of the California Institute of Technology had already put $80,000 into the tests, and their purse puckered up tight when they saw the report. But Tart had a new approach. He looked pretty good, for a while.

His idea was to set up two isolated units, a "sender booth" and a "receiver booth." In the sender booth was a TV screen and a random-number generator with a "dial" consisting of ten playing cards arranged

The "sender booth" in Charles Tart's experimental setup. Copley News Service

in a circle. There were buttons and lights beside each card. The generator presented a number and the sender concentrated on that number, pressing a signal button when he or she was ready for the receiver in the other booth to make a choice. The TV screen was connected to a camera in the receiver booth, revealing the movements of the receiver to the sender and allowing the sender to "will" the receiver to touch the correct card. The results were good, and Tart wrote his book on these experiments.

Tart inserted his foot directly into his mouth with these words in *Psychic* magazine after his research had been completed: "Strong criticism has been leveled at ESP research over the years because the phenomena could not be repeated regularly. . . . Now, a research breakthrough soon may shelve such criticism. A study carried out under my direction . . . has taken a big step toward repeatability of ESP." But hold that laurel wreath, chaps.

Careful examination by the skeptics undid the pretty picture. Tart hadn't thought of some simple methods by which this demonstration *could* have been faked, and there were several. (As it turned out, such fakery was not needed, since there was a built-in error here that would later become obvious.) In passing, let me give you just two possible deceptive methods allowed by this setup. The two testees could have had wristwatches with synchronized second hands. The minute could be divided into ten six-second segments, one for each card. For example, the sender in the photo has a 4 to transmit. He looks at his watch, knowing the receiver is doing the same. When the second hand enters the area between eighteen and twenty-four seconds, he presses the signal button. The receiver now has the information and, after an appropriate pause, indicates the number 4. A hit! Another method would be for the sender to wait until the receiver's hand—as seen on his TV monitor— was directly opposite the correct number, then press the button. Again, after an appropriate pause, another hit is scored. An even better way to camouflage the trickery would be to establish a system in which, for example, the correct number is *added* to whatever number is buzzed next to determine the correct answer. In any case, a clever receiver, once having the information, would stall before calling it to avoid suspicion. And of course there are a number of other effective cheating methods, some independent of the TV monitor or buzzer.

But Sherman Stein, a mathematician at the University of California at Los Angeles where the tests were done, in examining the raw data on which the book was based, came upon an anomaly. It seems that though Tart had checked out his random-number generator and found it gave a good *distribution* of digits, it did not *repeat* digits as it should. In 5,000 digits produced by the machine, there should have been close to 500 "twins." If, for example, a 3 comes up, there is exactly 1 chance in 10 that another 3 will be produced next. There were only 193 twins— 39 percent of the number expected. Since a subject in such tests has a tendency not to repeat a digit just used, this bias of the machine fits in nicely with the results observed. *

---

* It has now been discovered that the randomizer was defeatable. The sender could literally choose *any digit desired* so that the subject mentioned on the next page had ample means to cheat! There is no mystery at all about the phenomenal results obtained by this subject (known as PSI) now that we have this evidence.

Stein suggested to Tart that he repeat the tests using a proper randomizer, and offered to assist. Tart agreed, and they parted. Months later Stein and Tart met again. Stein asked when the tests would be redone, and Tart brightly replied that he had already repeated the tests. What were the results? Negative, but that was understandable, answered Tart. He had not had the same gifted subjects as before. Catch-22 again.

Speaking of gifted subjects, it is well to note that in Tart's first set of tests one subject had scored *very* high. Her score was *two and a half times* what could be expected by chance. But she took much longer to make her decisions, said Tart, and she often started the run *with her hand already on the correct number!* Who was she? Who was her partner? May we speak with her? Well, that's a problem. He can't give out the names, and besides, she has moved away. Too bad.

Adding an outrageous comment to all this, Tart says, "The level of scoring in the first test was so high, it would be absurd to argue that . . . the results . . . were a mere statistical fluke." *No one ever claimed that!* The results were due to bad design and implementation!

But what about the book *Learning to Use Extrasensory Perception?* Since it is based on improper experimental procedures and a repetition of those experiments proved negative, shouldn't the book be recalled? Apparently not. It is still printed, still sold, and still tells its fairy story.

Charles Tart, asked by a reporter whether my criticisms of parapsychology are valid, replied, "No, of course not. Randi just makes it up as he goes along." Even I, with my vivid imagination, could not invent the Never-Never Land that parapsychologists so comfortably inhabit. Tart has also said, in a letter to a journal that had carried one of my articles, "Randi never sees the other side of the coin." Not so, Charles. I have seen the other side of your coin. It is blank—and the coin itself is a counterfeit.

As with all schemes that depend on individuals keeping quiet, the Uri Geller myth had to eventually collapse. Although Geller managed to survive an exposé in Israel when Hannah Shtrang, the sister of his main accomplice, Shipi, revealed what she knew to the press, the publication of my book and *Confessions of a Psychic* (by Uriah Fuller—a thinly disguised Martin Gardner) seemed to write the last chapter of his meteoric career. But Geller's habit of using up people and discarding them really caught up with him when Yasha Katz, his former manager now in Israel, decided to tell all. Such other "used-up" people as Puharich, Targ, Puthoff, Mitchell, and Franklin, no matter how much they suspected that Geller had taken advantage of them, were not in a position to admit it. Katz was different.

He had tried to reach me through my publisher, and his letters had been sitting around for months before I finally received them. In my book, I had referred to Katz as a victim rather than a victimizer.

All the evidence I had at hand indicated that he was a true believer who had been swept up into the Geller entourage willy-nilly, leaving everything behind in Israel and joining Geller in his conquest of the Western world. I had only met him face to face once, and under strange circumstances.

Just before my book about Geller was published in 1975, I had appeared on a TV news show and had duplicated the Geller tricks. The next day I received a phone call from a young lady who asked to meet with me to discuss the Geller matter. I met her in New York for lunch, and she told me of her close friend, Katz, who was, as she put it, "mesmerized" by the wonder-worker. On one occasion she had called on Katz at his apartment and found that he was still asleep. A maid was there, and she was let into the apartment. She went to the kitchen and placed in the cutlery drawer a joke item that she had bought in a novelty store—a hinged knife that "breaks" when slight pressure is put on it. She left without waking Yasha, after also planting a package of tricked matches in his ashtray. It was all a gag, she said.

Later that day Katz called her in great excitement. Since she had constantly expressed doubt about Geller's powers, Katz was continually trying to convince her, and he now reported that as he lit his morning cigarette a strange column of ash had grown out of the match! Examining the packet, Katz had discovered that somehow a tricked book of paper matches had been "apported" into his locked apartment. And, declared he, there was no way that anyone could have gotten in. The door had been locked, and Geller was out of town! The girl hastened to assure him that it was all a joke, but Katz was carried away with the miracle and would not listen.

She begged me to meet with Katz, assuring me that he was willing to do so but that he did not want Geller to know. I agreed, and we decided on the China Bowl Restaurant as a rendezvous. Later that day I showed up and was met by the girl, who ushered me into the back room, where I was left alone with Katz. By the time I got there he had already filled an ashtray with cigarette butts and was very nervous indeed. His big fear was that Geller would find out he had contacted me. I assured him that the matter was between the two of us (though that condition no longer holds, of course).

Katz did everything he could to convince me. At one point, he groped around for his lighter, and I produced it from my jacket pocket. He just smiled. His coffee spoon was discovered to be bent rather acutely. Again a tolerant smile. Keys were bent without any reaction from Katz but a sigh, in despair of getting the truth through to me. And then he began telling me stories. I sat and listened, thunderstruck. He related how, on one occasion, Geller had performed a psychokinetic marvel for him. Katz had left the apartment to buy a newspaper on the street. Geller was left inside, asleep on the couch before the TV. When Katz stepped out of the elevator on his return he was stunned to find that one of the apartment furnishings—a heavy decorative planter—was resting against the wall in the hall beside the apartment door. Excitedly, he dashed inside and summoned Geller from a sound sleep, and together they wrestled the planter back inside. "Realize that the door had been *locked* when I left," explained Katz. "The planter had *dematerialized* and passed through a *locked* door into the hall, *while Uri was asleep!* And that planter is so heavy that Uri *strained his back* helping me get it back inside. Therefore *he could not have moved it himself,* even if he *hadn't* been asleep!" (I wondered just when Geller *had* strained his back, and I think I know.)

I pointed out that Geller, known to work out with weights, was probably quite capable of such a feat and that he found no impediment in a locked door which could be opened from the inside. Katz was adamant. Why, he asked, would Geller bother to fake such a thing with Yasha Katz? I think it is obvious that Geller's object was to keep people like Katz on the hook. As long as they believed in him they were his slaves, and under control. No amount of effort was too much to keep the peasants in line. But Katz had another miracle to relate.

On returning from the theater one night, Katz had seen a vinyl plastic armrest suddenly materialize before him in the rain and drop into a puddle beside him and Geller. He recalled that while looking for seats in the theater Geller had complained that there was no armrest on the seat he chose and had moved over to another seat. And, exulted Katz, that armrest matched the others in the theater! How could I explain *that?* I will not trouble my reader with the explanation I gave to Katz.

The letter that I now had from Katz was quite a surprise. He had read my book and had decided it was time to tell of how Geller had used him. He wanted me to go to Israel to get the story, and since I was about to visit Italy to work on the Italian RAI-TV network with journalist Piero Angela, I agreed to stop over in Tel Aviv. A few days after a quick phone conversation with Yasha, I was in his apartment awaiting his revelations. I was in for an earful, and filled eight long tape cassettes with Katz's account.

His main concern was a very large sum of money that Geller still owed him. An agreement he had had with Geller entitled him to a percentage of all income that Geller earned outside the United States, and he had been strung along for many months as he traveled all over the globe with the Israeli wonder. Finally, Geller had dumped him and Yasha knew he was of no further value to his employer. But another facet of all this was obviously a much more important reason for the parting. It developed that Katz had been pressed into service as an accomplice when the usually ubiquitous Shipi Shtrang was unavailable. In other words, Katz was admitting to me that he was not the innocent lackey I'd thought but instead a full-fledged trickster!

It had come about gradually, said Katz. There had been several serious talks with Geller and Shipi during which they tried to convince him of certain personality differences that he denied vehemently. There were hints that he would be taken into the Inner Circle if he would see reason, and he was not too willing to listen. Shortly thereafter, just before a performance, he was suddenly told about the "gesture code" that they were using to signal audience-selected colors and numbers to Geller onstage during the show, and Katz was shocked that evening to find himself sitting in the front row, in place of Shipi, with a cigarette in his mouth tilted upward to signal "green" to a not-so-psychic Geller.

After that, things accelerated, with Katz going along—rather unwillingly, by his account. At a meeting in London with a book publisher, a plan to convince the victim of the miraculous powers was put into effect. Geller stood up, yawned, and went off to his own room, far down the hall. Katz continued talking with the publisher, answering the phone when it rang and replacing it beside the bed with the receiver still "off" so that Geller, who had been the caller, could hear the subsequent conversation in his room. Shortly afterward they were startled when Geller burst into the room to announce that he had just "astrally projected himself" while asleep, and that his "spirit" had been in that very room and had heard every word! He repeated parts of the conversation, to the astonishment of the credulous publisher.

At a planned performance in Birmingham, England, Katz was *really* left holding the bag. Minutes before the show, with the house packed full, Shipi rushed backstage to tell Geller that the front row was full of local magicians, who were sitting with the press ready to expose the tricks that Geller claimed were genuine psychic demonstrations. Geller turned white and refused to give his performance. The show was held up while Geller and Katz conferred with Werner Schmid, the promoter. Geller insisted that the management tell the audience that there had been a bomb scare and that the show was canceled. Poor Katz had to appear before the irate audience, who were in no mood to buy such a feeble story, and tell them their money would be refunded. Then he learned that Geller, talking backstage with the reporters as he ran for the car that was to whisk him away to safety, had told them he really *wanted* to perform but that Katz would not let him do so! Katz never returned to Birmingham.

As the former messiah-disciple relationship deteriorated and the role of outright faker was assigned to Katz, he found himself doing outrageous things to make Geller's tricks possible. In San Francisco, before a TV program in which Geller was required to divine the contents of a sealed envelope, Katz was told to simply go into the producer's desk and peek at it. A nervous wreck because of fear that he might get caught, Katz did so, and reported that it was a drawing of a white flag on a flagpole. Sure enough, as Geller labored to "telepathically" determine what the target was, he went through the same histrionics as he always had in the days when Katz had believed Geller really was using psychic powers. Katz had nothing but admiration for Geller's acting ability but was dismayed by having been exploited.

By then, Geller probably thought he had Katz pulled into the picture entirely. He directed him to stand by the door of the theater as people came in and report to him backstage who had what in their purses or pockets as they paid for their tickets. Katz watched Geller take down the license numbers of various cars in the parking lot outside and note details about the people who got out of them—all for later use onstage. He was disturbed, during a visit with Danny Kaye's wife, Sylvia Fine, to see Geller take a valuable family heirloom and break it while no one—except Katz—was watching. After pretending to fracture it "psychically," Geller apologized for the unpredictable psychic forces. In Paris, Katz said he was directed to walk along behind Geller and a reporter from L'Express and toss a spoon in the air so that it appeared to be a "teleportation" from nowhere. He had seen Geller do the same thing many times before, tossing objects over his own head, from behind his back.

Katz even solved some of the methods Geller used to "read minds." Sometimes, he noted, Geller only pretended to write down something; then, when he saw the target drawing for the first time, he would quickly and surreptitiously draw an approximation of it. It was then gleefully displayed as a success. In fact, said Katz, Geller always made a great show of excitement and satisfaction on these occasions and praised the victim for having great psychic powers in being able to transmit so effectively.

The miracles of Geller's "psychic photography" were also solved by Katz. In Palm Beach he saw him simply sneak the lens cap off a photographer's camera, snap a photo of himself, and replace the cap again. It was only the first of many times Geller did this.

But it was in Italy that Katz came very close to quitting the whole operation. With Geller he visited a jewelry store, where they looked over a number of expensive watches and left without buying anything. As they rounded the corner a block away, Geller exclaimed with great excitement that a "teleportation" had taken place. He showed his wrist with a brand-new watch on it. Katz knew beyond any doubt that Geller had simply stolen it. It was no miracle at all.

Why, then, did he stick with Geller? Simply because he believed—as he still does today in spite of the evidence against Geller—that he was associated with a genuine psychic. For Katz, anything that he cannot explain assumes the status of a real miracle.

Remember the "teleported" planter in New York City and the armrest from the theater? While I was in Tel Aviv with Yasha, and he was retelling the story to me (it was, I must add, a much-embellished version of the original), he casually remarked that the planter was the one sitting beside me in the apartment! I turned to see a large affair of cemented glass blocks with plants perched on it. I remembered that Katz had told me Geller could not have lifted it. It certainly did not look too heavy for me to lift, and I offered to do so. If I could, then a man twenty years my junior certainly could. Katz objected, saying it was not necessary for me to prove anything. In fact, he did not want me to prove this fact at all, for fear of losing one of the thin threads that supported his belief in Geller. But I stood, quickly placed the potted plants on the floor, and heaved the planter up in the air, setting it down some distance away. It was heavy, but certainly not too heavy for the Great Geller to have lifted. Thus evaporated another myth. Katz smiled somewhat distractedly and immediately changed the subject. He never mentioned the planter episode again.

But he *did* speak of the theater chair armrest, made of vinyl plastic. That, too, had been retained by Katz as a sort of holy relic. As I listened once more to the story of the rainy evening when the miracle occurred, I heard details that had not been in the original and somewhat thin story. Now, it seemed, Katz was able to remember a further, very startling fact that upped the fantastic nature of the event. The armrest, when he picked it up from the puddle into which it had fallen, was *bone dry!* Wow! Remember, the credibility of the story was weakened by Katz's admission to me that he himself had accomplished several "teleportations" for Geller by tossing objects, unnoticed, into the air. Now here was the big clincher on *this* miracle—a bone-dry armrest! Without a word, I placed the object on a saucer, poured a glass of water over it, and picked it up to show Katz. It was bone dry. The vinyl had shed water quite easily. This subject was also quickly dropped.

I was fascinated to learn that Katz had been visited by a reporter from the *National Enquirer*, Donna Rosenthal. During her several hours with him in Tel Aviv she had not taken any notes, and when Katz asked her why, she replied that what he was telling her—very *negative* information about Geller—was not the kind of thing her editor had sent her to get. In the *Journal of Occult Studies,* Winter–Spring 1977–78, we read the following:

> Donna Rosenthal, a writer from the *National Enquirer* . . . and a group of people went to lunch later and heard an interesting story of her investigations of Geller's Israeli background. She had interviewed close relatives and friends of Geller and concluded quite straightforwardly that there was no doubt as to the validity of his experiences, which were easily verified by many occurrences that dated back to high school and before.

I told Katz of a story I'd heard (perhaps apocryphal) concerning the *Enquirer.* It seems that they had to fire their top reporter. He'd allowed a fact to creep into one of his stories.

But the question arises, Why did Katz go along with Geller's cheating despite his feeling that it was wrong? Easily answered. As Katz himself said, he believes in Geller's powers in spite of everything—and just because it's not *all* real doesn't mean the rest isn't. It's that simple. He has chosen to believe in a chimera, and he accepts whatever he cannot explain as the real thing and as proof of his preferred belief. This was thoroughly demonstrated to me while I was in Tel Aviv, when Yasha revealed to me that he had discovered a *genuine* one-hundred-percent psychic young fellow who was obviously the real thing, since he denied that he wanted to become another Geller. Katz offered to put me in touch with him and warned me that now I was in real danger of losing my $10,000 to this chap. I was willing, as usual, to take that chance.

The next day I got a call at my hotel. It was from a young man named Yoram Nachman, and he was most anxious to see me, not to take my prize money but to explain a few things to me. I taxied off to his home, and to a most refreshing surprise. Yoram (The Great Yorini) turned out to be a master of spoon-bending and "telepathy." Katz had given me a long description of his performance, and of course it was all wrong. Katz had specified conditions that just did not exist, and was convinced by his faulty interpretation of the performance that Yoram had real powers. But, explained the young man, he didn't want Katz to believe these things, he didn't want to become another Geller, and he didn't want to go on the world tour that Katz saw in store for him. He just wanted to graduate, serve his stint in the Israeli army, and go into business like any other fellow his age. Magic was a great interest of his, and he was sure it would always be, but *he was claiming no psychic powers,* and Katz was inventing miracles he had done! The

Great Yorini was good—very good—and he was honest as well. I felt like Diogenes at the end of the quest.

So Katz has not yet learned from his bad burn that fire is a dangerous plaything, attractive but deadly. To this day, Geller still owes him money and has accused Katz of stealing from him as a countermeasure. I am not surprised. Just a little sad.

Presently, the press officer at the Stanford Research Institute tells the curious that SRI's work with Uri Geller constituted "only 3 percent" of its output in parapsychological research. The majority of the rest is fathered by Drs. Targ and Puthoff, without whose naïveté SRI would never have become involved in the useless subject. And to the dismay of the majority of scientists—who have seen through the flummery—parapsychology continues to be paraded as a legitimate science.

8

The Great Fliess Fleece

There is a time in the tides of men,
Which, taken at its flood, leads on to success.
On the other hand, don't count on it.
—T. K. Lawson

In earlier, simpler times, theories were drummed into existence on almost any premise, and in Austria during the last century the Teutonic fascination (if not preoccupation) with numbers and measurements prompted many strange concepts, some of which persist today. One such is known as biorhythm.

Dr. Hermann Swoboda, a professor of psychology at the University of Vienna, aided by Dr. Wilhelm Fliess, an ardent numerologist and physician specializing in ailments of the nose, came up with a number of observations which indicated to them that two cycles occur in the human life-span, both beginning at the moment of birth and continuing on a remarkably accurate schedule throughout life. The first was a 23-day cycle, associated with masculine aspects, and the other was the 28-day "feminine" cycle. Later, in the 1920s, an engineer named Teltscher added an "intellectual" cycle of 33 days to the theory, and the credulous were off on another pursuit of order and meaning in the life of Man.

The new "science" was ideal for the Viennese temperament. It supported the idea that life was predictable, cyclic, ordered, and numerical. Most important of all, failures of the theory were easily explained away by suitable rationalizations dressed in scientific language. The Freudians, suddenly so popular and fashionable, were benefiting from this advantage as well. Formulating and measuring were at last to be had by simple and easily understood means, and pseudointellectuals of the day were ecstatic.

Along with Freudian psychiatry, this madness has persisted to the present day. Indeed, the rage for biorhythm and allied claptrap has hit a new high in recent years. But examination of the claims brings us down to earth once more.

The literature about biorhythm is extensive, and most of it tends to repeat the errors of earlier publications on the subject. Research done decades ago is highly regarded, being out of reach for close examination at the present time. Magazines are spiced up with biorhythm pieces quite frequently, and some newspapers run columns that purport to reveal to readers their situation for the day at a glance. Airports around the world feature biorhythm computers that trace out a series of graphs for twenty-five cents, and ads tout biorhythm services for two dollars and up.

To understand biorhythm claims, a short primer in this "science" is necessary. But first it should be pointed out that biorhythm must not be confused with real biological cycles, which scientists have long recognized and studied. It is in such confusion that pseudoscientists seek to borrow corroboration for their claims.

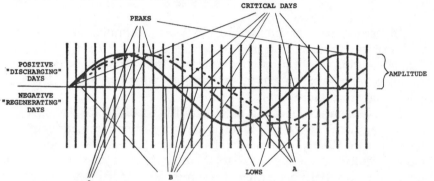

The biorhythm cycles at the beginning of a person's life, assuming a midnight birth. Each vertical bar represents midnight following a 24-hour period. The solid line is the 23-day "physical" curve, the dashed line is the 28-day "emotional" curve, and the dotted line is the 33-day "intellectual" curve. "A" points are "potentially dangerous," according to some experts, and "B" points represent "half-critical" days. In this initial 31-day month, there are 5 "half-critical" days, 5 "critical" days, one "triple-critical" day, 3 "low points," and 6 "potentially dangerous" days! There are only 4 "peaks."

Expressed on a graph that plots time (in days) against amplitude of the cycle curves, all three cycles are shown to begin at the moment of birth at zero, ascending in the positive direction, then descending to the zero line and below it into the negative area. This is repeated exactly, the three curves weaving closer and then farther apart, not to come together at the zero line exactly as at birth for more than half a century. We are told by the experts that when any curve crosses the zero line, a "critical day" has occurred, one in which there is a tendency to fail or to be susceptible to certain weaknesses. The masculine cycle is often called the "physical" curve, the feminine cycle the "emotional" one, and the third cycle the "mind" curve. There are refinements of these basic rules, as we shall see, but this is the basis for all claims made by biorhythm advocates.

As might be expected, *two* of these lines coming close together at the zero line portends a particularly dangerous "double-critical" day. A critical 23-day (masculine/physical) intersection means that one's health is in danger. Similarly, emotional criticals occur in the 28-day cycle, and mental crises are due every 33 days. Of course, *all* cycles are critical halfway through the designated full-cycle periods, since the curve crosses the line twice in a cycle. For biorhythm believers, it would seem that life is simply fraught with danger. One hardly dares to step outside one's house during most of the month. . . .

Biorhythm has become such a popular fad that some businesses have used it as an amusing diversion or advertising gimmick. The Bell System recently programmed one of its highly sophisticated computers to produce biorhythm readouts for passersby at an Air Force Association convention in Washington, D.C. Not to be outdone, Sanders Associates got into the act by putting its "Graphic 7" system to work on the same job. But Bell goofed and got one cycle two days ahead and another three days behind. When a theory is useless at best, its boosters should at least try to get the resulting misinformation right!

Bell's biorhythm ploy was astonishing, and not only because it generated "claptrap" for a sophisticated clientele. The telephone company also insisted on having the computer quote totally untrue and hyperbolic claims made in some of the madder biorhythm books. Under the heading "What is a Biorhythm?" the computer innocently pecked out the nonsense that United Airlines used 6,000 to 8,000 biorhythm charts for its employees, that 90 percent of a sample 1,000 accidents happened on "critical" days, and all the usual about the "firmly established" cycles. Mind you, it also called biorhythm a "pseudoscience" and suggested that "maybe there is nothing more to biorhythms than there is to some old wives' tales," but the impression given was that the Bell System believed enough in biorhythm to program a computer for the project, thus giving a measure of respectability to this notion. The biorhythmists can be depended upon to publicize the Bell System's use of the theory as further evidence that their quaint notion is a legitimate science.

If one looks closely enough at any popular delusion, one often discovers damning evidence that is seemingly so tidy and convincing that very little further argument is needed. While watching a self-proclaimed biorhythm expert perform his wonders on paper not long ago, I was impressed with the fact that he invariably accepted "critical" intersections of the curves when they fell a day ahead or behind. To those who are experienced observers of the operations of pseudoscience and interpretations thereof, this occasions no surprise. What's a day between friends? The excuse given for such laxity seems logical enough, however. The proponents argue that since the grand cycles start at the moment of birth and continue inexorably and precisely throughout life, there only *seems* to be an inaccuracy; that if, for example, such an apparent error occurs in the case of a person whose birth date is given as the seventh of the month, it is because birth occurred just after midnight (*almost* on the sixth, don't you see) or perhaps just *before* midnight of the seventh (therefore *almost* on the eighth).

But here is where the biorhythmists have killed, cooked, and eaten their own goose. The literature claims that though only 20 percent of all calendar days are "critical" ones, 60 percent of researched accidents fell on what were found to be critical days! If this is so, it appears that biorhythm techniques have shown that three times as many accidents occur on predicted days as chance would dictate. But as biorhythm proponent Bernard Gittelson writes in his book *Biorhythm—A Personal Science*, we must also consider "half-critical" days (those just before and just after an actual "critical" day), as my expert was doing when I observed him. And $3 \times 20 = 60$, an inarguable fact. The biorhythm theorists have simply demonstrated that mathematics works as it always has. Biorhythm accounts for no more accidents than chance would indicate. (Incidentally, *my* calculations indicate that 22 percent—not 20 percent—of all calendar days are "criticals," but I'll forgive the "experts" the minor 2 percent, since the theory doesn't work anyway. . . . But with 66 percent of the days in a year predicted as dangerous days— counting "half-criticals"—things begin to look pretty ominous in the perilous world of biorhythm.)

The "definitive" book on biorhythm theory is George Thommen's *Is This Your Day?*, and well over 100,000 copies have been sold to the unsuspecting. It is loaded with case histories—very carefully selected—presented in an attempt to prove the theory by showing that deaths and other calamities, as well as great victories and accomplishments, happen at biorhythmically determined times. These examples benefit from bearing the names of personalities such as Clark Gable, Marilyn Monroe, Pope John XXIII, and General Douglas MacArthur. Those unfamiliar with the techniques of selective sampling and unaware of proper statistical methods tend to believe that such case histories confirm the point to be proved.

The Thommen book refers to a mass of data ("eight trunks of research documentation") that, according to psychology professor Dr. Hermann Swoboda, fell into the hands of the Russians in Vienna during World War II and is thus unavailable. What a pity! (One wonders what the Russians did with it.) Since the theory at that time featured only two of the marvelous cycles, Thommen also has to account for the lack of data to support the third (intellectual/33-day) cycle introduced by Teltscher, and he claims that he has had to rely on secondhand information for that purpose. Hence, no significant documentation, including the "massive" original data so highly valued and touted by the "experts," is presented.

A book frequently referred to by biorhythm fans is *Biorhythm— A Personal Science* by Bernard Gittelson. In the introduction to this book we are told that George Thommen (to whom the book is dedicated) appeared on "The Long John Nebel Show" on radio station WOR in New York in November 1960 to warn of a possible critical day for actor Clark Gable on the sixteenth of that month. Gable had suffered a heart attack six days earlier and was hospitalized. On the sixteenth, Gable succumbed to a second heart attack. Thommen had created a sensation; the prediction was said to have been made by the "science" of biorhythm.

My personal experience with Thommen a few years later was somewhat less sensational. I had inherited Nebel's interview show when he moved to another station, and Thommen was among my first guests. I took the opportunity to ask him for a personal biorhythm chart, and one for my secretary as well. He obliged, and they arrived with our names on the neat covers. Since I'd already investigated this "science" and had read Martin Gardner's discussion of Wilhelm Fliess and his numerology nonsense, I was less interested in how well it worked for me than I was in an experiment I was planning.

Sure enough, several listeners called in asking for information about how to obtain a personal chart. I selected one woman who was willing to cooperate in a test, and who agreed to accept a free chart in return for a report at the end of two months stating how successful the chart seemed to be. She promised to keep a day-by-day diary and to rate the chart for accuracy.

The results were quite interesting. At the end of the two months, she telephoned to tell me that I should take this matter very seriously, since the chart had been "at least ninety percent accurate" in her case. I expressed interest in these results and told her I wanted to check the identification on the folder to be sure that she had received the correct chart. To our "mutual" astonishment, we discovered that she had been sent *my* chart, not the one intended for her. I blamed the whole thing on my secretary. Actually, I knew very well that she had been given my chart, but I didn't let on, and promised to send her the correct chart to check against her diary. The very next day she called to report that this one was *even more accurate*, if that was possible! We were thrilled, until we checked further, and I announced that— by mistake, of course—she had received *my secretary's* chart. There was a short pause, then a snort, and the woman hung up the phone. I could hardly blame her. She had been taken in by after-the-fact rationalization of the data, as have so many thousands who have followed the undulating curves and erratic reasoning necessary to make the facts fit this theory. So much for Thommen and his charts.

As for Dr. Wilhelm Fliess and his preoccupation with numbers and cycles, I will leave an analysis of the mathematics of his assertions to mathematicians such as Mr. Gardner. It is interesting that Gittelson fails to mention in his book a curious practice of this nose doctor. Dr. Fliess often administered cocaine, and the marvelous effect it had on his patients made this physician one of the most popular in town. He had discovered that there were "cyclic changes" in the mucous membrane lining the nose, and he related these variations to sexual problems. He also isolated areas inside the nose where he believed "genital cells" abounded, and he stimulated these areas by dabbing cocaine on them. The results were hailed with great enthusiasm by his patients, who returned often for treatment. Fliess prospered. This rather odd medical procedure cannot help but color one's opinion of the worth of the biorhythm theory cofounded by the doctor.

Fortunately, a great deal of careful work has been done recently that provides reliable material upon which to base a decision concerning biorhythm theory. It is buried in scientific periodicals and obscure journals to a large extent, but occasionally it surfaces, as it has several times in *The Skeptical Inquirer*, the publication of the Committee for the Scientific Investigation of Claims of the Paranormal.

Is there any proof that biorhythm actually works? Gittelson, in the "Notes" section of his book, writes, "Biorhythm does not always work, but very few things do." True. The point is, does it work at all, and if so, does it work any better than random charting?

His book provides many answers to this question. Although it is one of the best-selling books currently available on the subject, it adds little to the other volumes about biorhythm that have crowded bookshelves since Thommen introduced biorhythm to this country. For one thing, Gittelson devotes much space to discussions of such long-studied phenomena as "circadian rhythm." (Such a natural cyclic rhythm occurs in plants and animals every twenty-four hours, whether or not the subject is in a position to "know" of the rising and setting of the sun. Thus, a plant contained in a completely artificial environment nevertheless tends to react to the natural world outside and its diurnal rhythm.) Like other pseudosciences, biorhythm seeks respectability by adopting recognized and demonstrable phenomena.

Gittelson also uses many of the rationalizations that astrologers use, and in much the same way. For example, it seems that biorhythm does not compel, it only impels, a point astrologers make about their own "science." Thus, any discrepancy between fact and theory is forgivable. But Gittelson is quite aware of this weakness and says so. The author presents his case in such a way that *any* analysis can be interpreted as consistent with the theory. The following passages in his book are notable for the many qualifications and excuses that may be employed to fit the facts to the theory and vice versa:

> Regarding the first requirement—the ability of biorhythm to predict behavior—there is a real problem of interpretation. The three great rhythms are interdependent. None of them is so strong that it overwhelms the other two; they always act in concert to affect us. True, on critical days there is a good chance that the rhythm or rhythms showing temporary instability will dominate, but never completely. On an emotionally critical day, for example, it sometimes happens that the strength of the physical and intellectual rhythms neutralizes any threat. This is even more likely on non-critical, or mixed, days which are the ones which occur most often. If all three rhythms are in the low (or recharging) phase, you are not likely to perform at your peak. But exactly how far below your best you will in fact perform remains an area of controversy and uncertain interpretation.

There are other loopholes in the biorhythm theory as explained in this book. Regarding forecasts of performance in sports, Gittelson writes, "Benthaus [a biorhythm "authority"] . . . believes that a player's class will always show—that a first class player at a biorhythmic low point will always prevail over a second class player at a biorhythmic peak." This provides an excellent excuse for the failure of an athlete to perform in accordance with a prediction of his chart.

"If biorhythm does *not* seem to work for you," writes Gittelson, "you may be one of those rare individuals who are arhythmic and do not respond fully to internal cycles." In addition, the reader is informed that people who are "arhythmic" may pop back into rhythm at any time!

The author refers to the claim made by Gunthard, another biorhythm proponent, that

> some people are "rhythmists" and some are "non-rhythmists"; or, to put it another way, some people appear to be more sensitive to biorhythms than others . . . is it simply that some people develop different ways of dealing with biorhythms, and that some of these methods effectively mask biorhythmic effects? Or is it that the strength of biorhythms—the amplitude of the sine-waves used to represent the curves—varies in different individuals, and also for the same individual at different times?

Again: "Wallerstein and Roberts . . . found that the *direction* in which a rhythm was moving could be as important—and perhaps more important—than whether the rhythm was above or below the zero line."

Refer to the biorhythm chart for the latitude *this* allows in interpretation! A final example: "Several researchers who have dealt with accidents and biorhythm have suspected that days when two rhythms cross each other while going in opposite directions—regardless of whether they cross in the positive or negative phases—are potentially dangerous days." Refer again to the chart, and the points labeled "A."

On the basis of these passages in Gittelson's book, it is obvious that the biorhythm theory can be made to fit *any* situation.

The author devotes several pages to a claim that major industries in the United States have used biorhythm, or at least have investigated the phenomenon. He writes that Procter & Gamble experimented with it but adds that they deny both the experiment and its successful results. He tells us that United Airlines, U.S. Air, Continental, Pan American, and Trans World Airlines have explored the biorhythm theory, and that they all disavow their experiments or interest. But United has done much more than that. In its October 1977 edition of *Executive Air Travel Report* (published well before the quoted edition of Gittelson's book), United says officially that *researchers found no correlation between the negative phases of any or all biorhythm cycles and an increase in the number of aircraft accidents. Furthermore, no cycle—physical, emotional, or mental—could be assigned a role in causing accidents.* The Gittelson book tells us that "United . . . pilots have not yet received charts." Actually, some 4,000 pilots received charts in this study!

Gittelson himself quotes some opinions that are critical of the biorhythm concept. Says Dr. Franz Halberg, of the University of Minnesota Medical School, who has written about genuine biological rhythms, "[George Thommen] is talking of immutable, fixed rhythms. . . . As to any similarity with my own work, it's like Smith and Schmidt. We have only the name in common." Says Dr. John Hastings of Harvard: "This is not a serious subject being studied by serious scientists." Professor Colon Pittendrigh, who looked into the subject at Stanford University: "I consider this stuff an utter, unadulterated fraud." The National Institute of Mental Health describes biorhythm as "a mythology." However, Douglas Kelley, of the National Safety Council, says, "When chemistry was at the state where biorhythm is today, it was called alchemy. But alchemy became chemistry, and within fifty years research may do the same for biorhythm." Nonsense. Alchemy was dedicated to a search for the Philosopher's Stone, which would change base metals into gold. The Stone was never found, and peripheral facts discovered during the search were later incorporated into the true science of chemistry. The only future for biorhythm is to become an abandoned quest, and the case histories of poor logic and research that remain from its wreckage eventually may well be incorporated into the study of abnormal psychology.

Gittelson also quotes Robert W. Bailey, of Bell Labs in Piscataway, New Jersey, as saying, "If there's something to it, I haven't found it yet." The author then points out that Bailey's work is "still in its early stages" and has "covered fewer than 300 employees." When interviewed by phone, Bailey was aghast at the reference.

Bailey, who works with the Human Technology Division of Bell Labs, told me that "many thousands of individuals" were charted on the basis of biorhythm theory and that "an intensive investigation" was carried out four years ago—well before Gittelson's book was published. "It became very clear to us," he said, "that after having translations made of the original Fliess/Swoboda writings on the subject, it turned out to be a system of pure guesswork based on numerology. We looked at it as carefully as anyone has, and we found not one reliable fact in it."

Surely advocates of biorhythm cannot summon up the old excuse that parapsychologists often use—that scientists are unwilling to look at the evidence they present. Bailey and his colleagues carried out a definitive, proper, and well-documented investigation into not only the roots of this so-called science, but its performance as well.

It simply does not work.

Currently available are some very precise and reliable methods of applying computer technology, not for the purpose of generating biorhythm charts—which any mathematical dub can do—but to determine whether there is any real basis for this "science." Terry Hines, in a review of such studies, published in *The Skeptical Inquirer*, lists some damning evidence.

Concerning accident predictions, 13,285 cases were examined in British Columbia, 4,346 aircraft mishaps were studied using naval aircraft figures, 4,063 general aviation accidents were looked into, and 400 accidents at army installations were investigated. Biorhythm failed all tests. In 181 auto accidents wherein the driver was at fault, and in 205 general highway accidents, no hint of biorhythm activity appeared. In addition, 150 "work-related" vehicular accidents and 506 fatal driving accidents were investigated. No biorhythm effects were found. At the Oak Ridge National Laboratory, 112 accidents were analyzed, including a selected group of 67 in which the victim was at fault; and 400 coal mining accidents, along with 210 other on-the-job industrial accidents, were examined. No biorhythm influences were noted.*

A simpler study can be made of athletic performance, which the biorhythmists tell us is greatly affected by the wondrous curves. The facts and figures needed are easily available to the investigator. Two

---

* In the UK, the Accident Investigation division of the Department of Transport issued an official report after extensive investigation of biorhythm influence. No evidence at all was discovered.

investigators of the theory studied the performances of the University of Florida swimming and bowling teams; they also analyzed 100 no-hit baseball games, the batting performances of 70 major-league players, and golfers' records. No significant biorhythm effects were discovered.

If they were valid, biorhythm charts would make it possible to predict likely death days for humans, and such claims are widely made. But recently the death dates of 274 baseball pitchers were examined for such an influence. No correlation was found. Another study of 105 miscellaneous deaths again produced negative results. Is it any wonder that legitimate scientists have no interest in the claims of the biorhythm advocates?

The biorhythm "experts" and the countless books and articles on the subject have paid little attention to certain inevitable "super-critical" days that (their theory implies) must arrive in the life of every mortal more than 29 years old. An examination of the literature reveals that these crucial days are given no special importance, a fact that is most surprising.

The theory tells us that whenever one of the cycles (23 days, 28 days, or 33 days) reaches the zero line, a critical day is upon us. Thus, the 23-day cycle brings a critical day every eleven and a half days, and so on. But, as already mentioned, worse dangers are in store when a double-critical day arrives with *two* of the curves intersecting the line. And we can only shudder with apprehension at the prospect of that most terrifying moment of all, the legendary "triple-critical" day. But all is not as perilous as it seems, for triple-criticals are rather rare. I put my rudimentary mathematical skills to work and discovered that the entire three-cycle phenomenon returns to the starting point only after 58 years and 68 days (plus or minus one day), when the curves are just as they were at the moment of birth. (The one-day variable is due to an unequal number of leap years. If the subject is born in the last 10 months of a leap year or at any time during the year following a leap year, the number of days is 68. If the subject is born in any other part of any other year, the number is 67. In the case of any birth date in the nineteenth century, an extra day must be added to the figure obtained by the above rules because the leap day was dropped in the leap year 1900. This figure is given imprecisely in at least one book, *Biorhythm*, by Hans. J. Wernli, as "58 years plus approximately 66 days.")

Of course, since critical days also arrive halfway through each cycle, there is another triple-critical day when 29 years and 34 (or 35) days is reached, and another at 87 years and about 102 days—if we are fortunate enough to reach that advanced age, when things are rather critical anyway, biorhythms or no. But at these points, the 23- and 33-day cycles are ascending, as at birth, while the 28-day curve is dropping. Still, biorythm tells us that these are the *most critical* days in our lives. (There could be a fourth triple-critical day at age 116-plus, but at present we may ignore this unlikely situation.)

This leads to an interesting possibility. Would it not seem that many more deaths occur at these points in the human life-span? With physical, emotional, and intellectual levels at zero simultaneously, surely the individual is extremely vulnerable to these conditions. I see, in the books, numerous charts showing the deadly influences on the lives of the famous deceased—but not one of them falls on one of these triple-criticals!

Biorhythm "science" manages to overlook one important possibility: that the interpretation of the charts is entirely dependent on preknowledge of the events and their placement in time. Reading significance into the charts is easy when we know the time of some deadly event and see the curves before us. Or is this only a naïve and prejudiced opinion of mine? I have before me the biorhythm charts of several persons who died within the month shown. Yet when I show these to the "experts," they can only point out *a number* of dangerous positions in that period, and seldom do they come close to the actual death position. Or do I expect too much?

For those who delight in complexity, some of the more devoted students of this wonderful pursuit have, in their wisdom, ascertained still more cycles in the human life-span that they say we would do well to heed. I cannot certify that the conventional biorhythm promoters agree with these newcomers, but feel that I should point out the latest claims so that not one nuance of the art will be neglected. There are, we are told, many additional aspects, such as a "compassion" cycle (38 days), "aesthetic" cycle (43 days), "self-awareness" cycle (48 days), and finally a "spiritual" cycle of 53 days. Thus we must look for criticals (not to mention double-criticals or worse!) at intervals of 11½, 14, 16½, 19, 21½, 23, 24, 26½, 28, 33, 38, 43, 48, and 53 days! How fraught with critical days we now find our lives! A simple calculation demonstrates the possibility of 37% to 59% single critical days. *

I can imagine hitting a 23/33/43/48-day critical conjunction, at which point one would be likely absentmindedly to step off a ladder while painting the house puce and suffer a broken leg.

George Thommen once appeared on a well-known radio show to startle me with the declaration that in 95 percent of all births he had studied the sex of the child had been predictable based on a knowledge of the mother's biorhythm data! He said that when the physical/mascu-

---

* Multiply by 3, if you accept "½-critical" days as well!

line cycle was at a high point during the period of conception, a boy was likely, and that the opposite was true when the emotional/female cycle was high. Such a percentage seemed remarkable and easily provable, but at the time the means for such a determination were not at my disposal. Happily, W. S. Bainbridge, Professor of Sociology at the University of Washington in Seattle, troubled to check this claim. His results were just as interesting as Thommen's assertion: the biorhythm theory flunked again. Bainbridge eliminated cesarean births, difficult labors, and induced births from a sample of over 300 subjects. He was left, after random rounding off, with births of 100 males and 100 girls. Of these cases there were 104 in which there was no definite "high" or "low" that could, in all fairness to the theory, be used. Of the 96 remaining, in 48 of the cases the biorhythm prediction was right, and in 48 it was wrong. But the wife of a biorhythm "expert" whom Bainbridge was dealing with had an ingenious solution to the failures. Perhaps, she said, these kids grow up to become homosexuals with an indeterminate sex identity! And when Professor Bainbridge asked the "expert" (who actually teaches classes in this pseudoscience) to calculate the sexes of the children based on his data, his associate was unable to do so during the *three months* he was allowed. This is a familiar situation. Faced with producing simple, direct proof, the proponents fail and often retreat into obfuscation.

The so-called science of biorhythm is nothing more than glorified numerology that, on the basis of a simple birth date and some supposed research, generates infantile notions about predetermined cycles that govern human existence. It is one of the purest—and simplest—forms of idiocy to assume the mantle of logic and science.

9

The Medical Humbugs

To follow foolish precedents, and wink
With both our eyes, is easier than to think.
—William Cowper

Homo vult decipi; decipiatur.
"Man wishes to be deceived; deceive him."

There is certainly no aspect of the whole parapsychology-occult-pseudoscience-spiritualism matter that more deserves condemnation than the widely publicized racket of Psychic Surgery. In Brazil, the Philippines, and now all over the world, sleight-of-hand artists have used the simplest of deceptions and the flimsiest of rationales to manufacture the notion that they can actually place their hands within the human body without making an incision and remove from it offending "tumors" and other materials that they claim cause various malfunctions. All this is done in the name of religion and psychic powers.

During two visits to the Philippines back in the 1950s, I heard of these wonders being performed some distance from Manila. When it was discovered that I wanted to visit these places and look into the claims, I was suddenly summoned to the Immigration Office, where my passport was "inspected" by being confiscated for several days. This was an effective warning that my inquiry was not welcome. The official who questioned me asked me repeatedly whether I was there representing any press service or media outlet and kept referring to "causing trouble" for "religious people." In the end I was not only refused information but told that it could be dangerous to travel in certain remote areas of the islands. I took the hint, and when my passport was returned to me after the Canadian consulate there insisted upon it, I left without ever seeing the performance of these backwoods charlatans.

In Brazil, too, I found it difficult to contact the operators, though I made it quite clear that I was willing to pay for a demonstration. There, it was necessary to have the approval of the local spiritualists before an invitation could be issued. It was no surprise to discover that such validation was not obtainable.

But the more incautious of the "psychic surgeons" have left us a record on film that effectively damns them as fakes. The experienced eye is able to determine conclusively that simple trickery is used to perform these miracles. Hoping that the camera would not reveal their flummery, the so-called surgeons tossed "tumors" and other debris about amid copious flows of blood and alcohol, showing us exactly how it was done. It was simple sleight of hand. Several times I have duplicated the effects on film to be used on television in Italy, England, Canada, and the United States.

With all the information available to them, one would suppose that prominent medical associations would have prepared statements concerning these practices. To find out if any of the British organizations were either interested in knowing the methods of the "psychic surgeons" or had any statements to make, I contacted their offices. The British Medical Association, the Royal College of Surgeons, and the Royal College of Physicians all were queried. None was in the least interested in knowing more about the subject, and only one answered with the lame pronouncement that "those who depend upon such treatment may be disappointed." How true. Death is the ultimate disappointment.

The American Medical Association has never responded to my requests for a statement. Their concern is for the doctors, not the patients. Perhaps the philosophy is to let the patients learn from their errors.

I recall that some years back, when the book *Arigo: Surgeon of the Rusty Knife* by John Fuller was released in Britian, Dr. Chris Evans and I attended the soirée thrown by the publishers. As it turned out, we were the only rational people there. We watched a film, produced by Dr. A. Puharich (before his involvement with Uri Geller), about the miracle surgery performed by one José Pedro de Feitas, who took the stage name of Arigo in the jungles of Brazil and became one of the saints of the paranormal by doing primitive surgery and writing useless prescriptions. He was praised by Dr. Puharich and by Fuller, who gave us such priceless documents as *Incident at Exeter* and *The Interrupted Journey*, both classics of claptrap about UFOs. Fuller used to write for the TV show "Candid Camera" and has lost none of his inventiveness since.

At one point during the film, which was narrated in person by another dedicated believer, Dr. Ted Bastin of Cambridge, we saw a subcutaneous cyst being removed from a patient's scalp by Arigo. This is an operation I have seen performed several times by a missionary in Peru without any anesthetic at all. In fact, I performed the same operation on myself when I developed a cyst on my forehead that threatened to become a third eye. Such an affliction is simply a bit of harmless fatty substance under the skin that forms a lump. It often goes away without treatment, being absorbed into the system harmlessly.

Bastin referred to the thing as a cyst, and I agreed that it looked just like one. But when I pointed out to him that the very book we were discussing featured a frame from that same section of the motion picture and described the cyst as "a scalp tumor," my objection was met with dismissal as an overemphasis on detail. Again, hyperbole had been liberally applied to bolster the case. There is a *vast* difference between a scalp tumor and what was shown in the film. Later during the showing of the film Dr. Evans and I were in hysterics, to the dismay of the others there, when, as Bastin droned on about the "absence of any pain or discomfort" and "little or no bleeding," the screen showed a patient being treated for a dreadful boil on his back. At the moment that Arigo's scalpel hit the boil, a terrifying gush of blood and pus burst forth, and the patient was grabbed by attendants who held him on the operating table in his agony. Blood was everywhere, and the pain was quite evident.

Arigo was an amateur doctor, like hundreds of "healers" in remote parts of the world where medical care is difficult to come by except at their hands. He had picked up—as had my missionary friend in Peru, Joe Hocking—the rudiments of elementary surgery, basic dentistry, and good psychological manipulation. Often, the presence of someone who cares is more important to a patient than a man in a white coat. Arigo dressed up his act with some mumbo jumbo about a dead German doctor—Dr. Fritz—who whispered prescriptions into his left ear. The scribblings that resulted were filled by the local pharmacy. It is interesting and revealing to note that no one but his assistant could read these scribbles, which he reduced to typewritten prescriptions for useless and inapplicable combinations of drugs that nonetheless seemed to give relief in some cases. Arigo obviously knew of the placebo effect, too. And the only pharmacy in town was run by his brother.

Arigo was given his greatest support by just such books as Fuller's. As an example of this author's total disregard for fact, we may examine his description of an operation he saw in the Puharich film. Most of the rest of his book is based on data given him by Puharich, since Fuller never saw Arigo at all, except on film. The operation is the boil-lancing already mentioned, and Fuller's description of it is a total misrepresentation of the action as shown in the film. "As usual," writes Fuller, "he plunged the knife in brutally, cut deeply into the flesh of the small of the back—a sector heavily served with blood vessels and therefore inclined to bleed profusely. Very little blood flowed out, but the abscess was drained . . . the patient was totally calm and without pain." Nonsense. Arigo merely lanced a boil. It hurt, and it bled. That's all.

Arigo operated on Dr. Puharich himself. He had a simple lipoma, a lump of fatty tissue growing under the skin of his arm. Technically, it is a tumor of fat growing harmlessly and easily excised, since it is not attached in any way to the body but moves about beneath the skin loosely. Arigo told him to look away, made a small cut over the lump, popped it out, and stanched the blood. But Fuller says, "Two wildly improbable medical events had taken place: the removal of the tumor and total absence of infection." Wildly improbable? Hardly. The assumption is that all cuts not made in the operating room become infected, and that removal of lipomas is a dangerous process. It is not; in fact, it is among the very simplest of surgical procedures. Arigo did something that was quite ordinary, with expected results, and Puharich and Fuller would make it a miracle *because it is one of Arigo's very few documentable performances.*

One of the "impossibilities" that Puharich marveled at was Arigo's frequent stunt of pushing a knife blade up under the eyelid. It seems that Arigo did this to impress patients with his powers, for it was performed regardless of what the claimed ailment was. Now, when I was a kid in Toronto, Canada, there was a young chap named Grey who lived just down the street. Every year that the traveling carnival came to town, they would hire him as "The Popeyed Boy" and he would stand before gawking crowds pushing a table knife up under his eyelid. As he pulled the eyelid up and away from the eyeball, the very strong illusion was given that his eyeball was protruding, though it was merely being exposed to the audience. It's an easy stunt, and of course Puharich snapped it up and put it into his bag of documented Arigo miracles.

To prove the impossibility of the stunt, Puharich immobilized a rat by clamping its head down, then shoved various things into its eye. The rat, he reported, didn't like it at all. Thus the scientist triumphs again: Since rats resist having things pushed into their eyes, Arigo is a saint. But Puharich went a step further. He chose a volunteer lab worker and told her what he was going to do, warning her that at "the first sign of discomfort" she should signal him. (Arigo never gave any such warning. He simply pushed the knife in, always with the patient backed against the wall.) Then a "small, smooth" knife was selected (suggesting that Arigo's knives were large and rough) and inserted under the lid "a fraction of an inch." The girl signaled discomfort, and it was withdrawn. Scientific proof, of course. Then how come I can push a knife under my eyelid and endure the experience?

There seems to be little evidence that Arigo used blatant sleight of hand. (An exception is one instance mentioned by Fuller when he reports that Arigo removed a man's liver with his bare hands. Fuller spends no time at all trying to convince the reader of this feat, as if he were embarrassed by it all.) The Filipino "surgeons," however, cannot perform without it. Their trickery consists of two or three basic gimmicks coupled with the most transparent playacting. There is always much laying on of hands, "balancing of magnetic forces," and massaging with

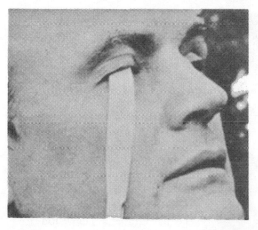

In the photo on the left, Arigo startles witnesses by placing a knife blade under a patient's eyelid. But the stunt is easily done, and painless, as the author shows in the photo on the right. It simply does not hurt, and anyone can do it. Piero Angela, Italy

oil and holy water. Patients are preached to and prepared for days before any actual "surgery" takes place. One of the best documentaries on the subject was the Granada TV production "World in Action." This British program actually followed the victims from their boarding of the aircraft for the trip to the Philippines through the treatment and then back home. Mike Scott was narrator and host of the show.

The film showed the "surgeons" at work kneading the flesh vigorously, usually that of the abdomens of fat persons. (Thin people have to be content with lesser treatment, for reasons that will become clear.) Much water and oil was applied, and then the miracle began. From beneath the hands a stream of blood spurted, and an incision seemed to appear. José Mercado, the performer, was suddenly awash in a pool of blood and reached for a wad of cotton, which was pressed into his

José Mercado, a "psychic surgeon." Granada Television

Mercado's assistant. Granada Television

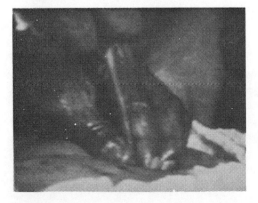

Mercado's hands as he pulls a "tumor" from the victim, withholding some of the material for a repetition of the trick a few moments later. Granada Television

hand by an assistant. This wad was dabbed about, the two hands coming together in the process. The left hand was pressed to the body, the right fingers went under it, and after a bit of poking about a fresh gush of blood was seen. Then a scrap of whitish tissue began to be pulled up from the body. It snapped loose and was discarded. Another piece was produced from beneath the left hand and treated the same way. The area was mopped up and no incision was seen to remain. The operation was over.

After trying unsuccessfully for days to obtain some of the tissue and/or blood that resulted from the fake operations, Scott finally snatched a "tumor." His account is revealing. "I grabbed what appeared to be a large growth which came out of the body. Two thirds of it proved to be cotton wool. One-third of it was a long stringy piece of tissue . . . a long stringy piece of meat which could be anything from a piece of lamb chop to . . . a piece of human body, I suppose. If you want my guess, lamb chop. And it's not very funny. It's very distressing."

Scott would be interested to learn of Dr. P. J. Lincoln's discoveries concerning a bloodstain and a "tumor" brought back by another group of patients from the Philippines also treated by psychic surgeons. Lincoln

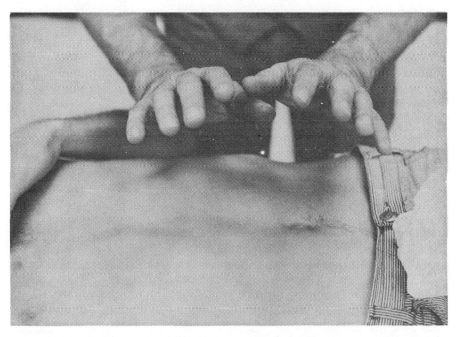

Photo 1. The author's hands approach the patient at the beginning of "psychic surgery." Note the false thumb on the right hand. Technology Review

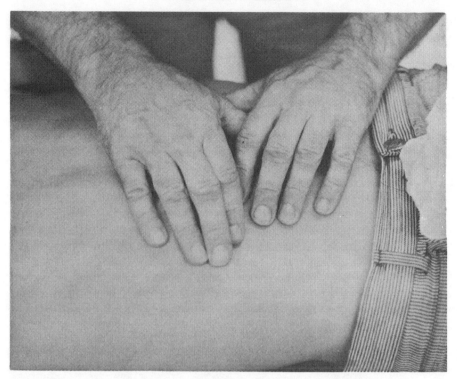

Photo 2. The hands are placed upon the site. Technology Review

is a specialist in blood group serology and forensic medicine at London Hospital Medical College. He found that the blood sample was from a cow, and that the "tumor" was a piece of chicken intestine. But, incredibly, the spiritualists have a rationalization for all this, claiming that the miracle has now been proved all the greater! Supernatural forces, they tell us, have converted the deadly tumors into innocuous substances that cannot infect human beings.

How is it all done? Certainly there is lots of blood, and the chicken guts don't just come from nowhere, do they? No, no more than the magician's rabbit comes from nowhere. I recall the remark of one magician who was asked how he pulled a rabbit from a hat. "Well," he said, "the first thing is to get the rabbit *into* the hat." True, true.

There are two gimmicks. One is a simple device that can be purchased in any magic trick shop. Examine Photo 1. It is visible there, purposely, if you look hard. It's a false thumb—sort of a large thimble that looks like a thumb—and it's filled with blood before the operation. The body is wet down and the maneuvers shown in the following photos are performed. In Photo 2 the false thumb is being pulled off the real

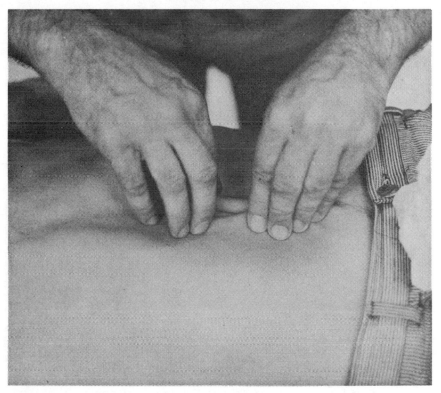

Photo 3. The flesh is kneaded and creased. Technology Review

thumb to cause the blood to flow, along with the bits of tissue concealed with it. In Photo 6 the fake is being put back on the thumb, and in Photo 7 it is being picked up in the cotton wadding to be discarded.

But José was getting much more blood from another source. When he reached for more cotton, something else was handed him too. It was a small piece of a balloon, red in color and loaded with blood. His fingers went under his hand to puncture that balloon, and then pulled forth the piece of red rubber as if it were some elastic tissue from inside the body. It was immediately discarded. Other fragments of chicken parts were then produced as additional "tumors."

The "psychic surgeons" also appear to reach *inside* the body, their fingers penetrating the abdomen. This is done with fat people, with the fingers curled up and the knuckles pressed into the flesh, giving the impression that the fingers are inside. That's all there is to it, but it fools many people.

And the "surgeons" themselves? What do they do when *they* need

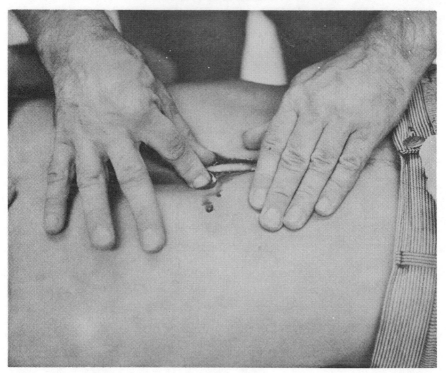

Photo 4. Blood suddenly appears as an "incision" is made. Technology Review

a doctor? Tony Agpaoa, one of the wealthiest men in the Philippines as a result of his quackery, had his own appendix removed—in San Francisco, in a *real* hospital. When his young son fell ill, Tony took no chances. He could afford a regular hospital, and used it. Why? Because, we are told, the healers cannot use their powers on themselves. But Tony, there are dozens of available "psychic healers" there whom you taught yourself! Surely, if planeloads of dying people fly all the way to the Philippines for treatment, won't you avail yourself of these wonders?

The promoters of these charlatans advertise that there is no charge for their services. And there isn't. But how do the patients get there? They fly there (though the Federal Trade Commission forbids advertising for the tours in the United States) at about $1,300 a head, stay at the hotels, buy meals at astronomical prices, then pay registration fees and operating room charges. When they are ready to leave—just as sick as when they arrived, but much poorer—they are given a set of envelopes bearing the names of each person with whom they came in contact

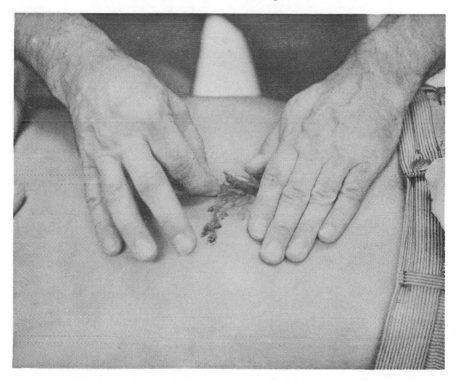

Photo 5. Fibrous material begins to appear and is pulled out. Technology Review

during the stay, and they are expected to donate freely. Says the brochure provided by the Christian Travel Centre:

> Patients are reminded that the Philippine Healers are extremely religious, and at all times say that they are "Instruments" for this healing work, and as such, can promise nothing other than to give of themselves in healing the sick. It should also be remembered that they are extremely poor, and are specially brought to Manila from their various Sanctuaries to help you. Will you therefore please be as generous as you can when giving your donation on the final day of your treatment.

This quotation is a statement by Tom Williams, whose carefully edited and hyperbolized film showing the "surgeons" at work has been shown all over the world and has lured countless people into the hands of these fakes. They ignore or discontinue legitimate treatment in order to take advantage of the latest in fashionable miracles. And they die.

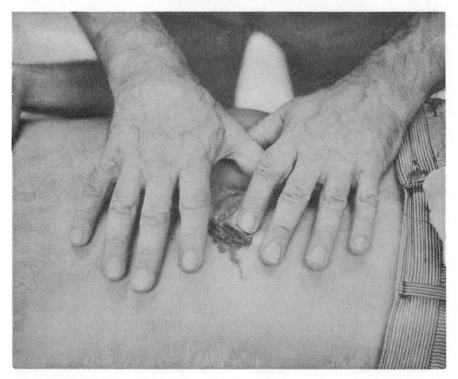

Photo 6. The "incision" appears to close as the "tumor" is removed. Technology Review

The Granada film showed that very grimly, giving the results in the cases of all the patients who could be tracked down. Some declared that they had been healed, then suffered a relapse. Others just "felt a little better." Some were dead before the film was shown; others died subsequently from their ills.

"People have been helped—and cured; when I say helped, you see, I mean cured. And you can check with your people in England. If it will not stand the test, I challenge you." So said the man in charge of the "psychic surgeons" in the Philippines to Mike Scott before Scott returned home with the Granada film team. Scott took him up on this challenge, submitting to the Department of Forensic Medicine at Guy's Hospital, London, the samples that he and his associates were able to snatch from the fakers. Blood samples turned out to be the blood of cows and pigs. A growth removed from a little girl's neck proved to be a biopsy sample from a mature woman's breast. There were *no* cures

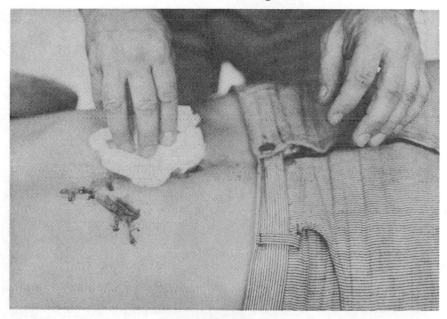

Photo 7. The area is cleaned up. There is no sign of an incision; only the stringy "tumor" material remains. Technology Review

among the large group of patients who made the long and expensive trip. The tumors were still there.

Said one "cured" patient when interviewed, "I think it's fantastic . . . marvelous. . . . Oh, I'm very confident because I myself have had some—well, several growths taken out. . . . I just think they couldn't possibly have been there . . . they were quite large growths." Yes, they were large, and they were pieces of chicken, lady; they were not part of your body. Your doctor told you, when you returned to England, that your tumors were still there.

Ironically, the Christian Travel Centre insists in its brochure that "participants must have an International certificate of vaccination against smallpox . . . inoculation against cholera and a course of anti-malaria tablets are strongly recommended." Sure. So you can have a grubby faker rub chicken guts and cow blood on your tummy and take your money while singing hymns. Sounds logical.

One incident sums up the deceit involved in this cruel business. After Mike Scott grabbed the fake tumor, the camera crew was excluded from the operating room at the hotel, and when the camera was later

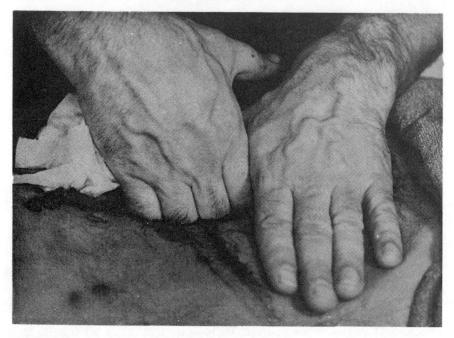

The author's hands apparently enter the body of the subject. The fingers of the right hand are merely folded under to create the illusion that the body is being penetrated. This time, the copious flow of blood was obtained from a piece of balloon (seen on the left), which was extracted from the liquid as if it were a tumor. GONG, Hamburg

allowed to "peek," the patients had been positioned in such a way that nothing could be seen. Granada had their number, and they knew it.

When I visited England in 1978 to expose the fakery of David and Helen Elizalde, two "healers" who were working through the Spiritualists' National Union, it was a simple matter to show, in one film shot, that the performers' fingers were not inside the patient's body but merely curled up. But the funniest part came at the close of the film—a segment not used on TV—when the two were shown in their kitchen after a long day of healing and sleight of hand: David was cutting up a chicken for supper.

In the spiritualist press it was claimed that the Elizaldes made not a penny from their labors. But it was admitted that there was a £10 registration fee for each patient, and some ninety patients were seen *each day*. Also, a donation could be left if the patient wished. Most wished. Now, $1,640 a day is pretty fair money. The Elizaldes

Tom Williams, who leads the afflicted into the hands of the so-called Filipino healers "on behalf of the Christian Travel Centre" in Manila. The organization is not affiliated with any Christian church. Granada Television

stayed ten days. Not bad, for a racket that requires little more than a couple of chickens, a plastic thumb, and a dozen balloons. Perhaps these items are even deducted in computing their income tax—oops, I almost forgot! These are religious folks, remember? They are free of such encumbrances, of course!

In 1979 I again went to England, and the Elizaldes were further exposed on a BBC program. The BBC host branded them as "fakes, hoaxers, and frauds." Forensic tests of their "tumors" and blood proved them to have come from a pig. The Elizaldes looked a tad disturbed by the exposure, but Mr. Gordon Higginson, the sponsor of the tour they had undertaken in England, simply refused to believe the evidence. Standard procedure.

I repeat my offer, tailored this time to the "psychic healers." If they can show me a case in which a doctor has diagnosed a disease that is not self-terminating or subject to periodic remission, and then prove that the patient underwent psychic healing and without medication was healed as a result of that ministration, I will pay them my $10,000.

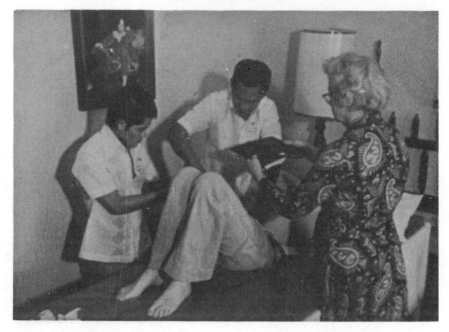

After Mike Scott's television crew became suspicious, the patient was put in this position to block camera angles. Note the opened bible to aid concealment. Granada Television

Surely that is an offer worth accepting. Or maybe they would like to extract a tumor while I watch. I think not. . . .

When all else fails to convince the skeptic, promoters of the paranormal fall back on the Sleeping Prophet, Edgar Cayce (pronounced kay-see), who is credited with having made accurate diagnoses and having prescribed cures for distant patients who sent him letters—and this despite having little or no information about them. Cayce is also famous for his "life readings"—descriptions of former and present lives of people derived from their names alone. He claimed that it was all done while he slept, and that he never remembered a word of what he said while entranced. The Association for Research and Enlightenment is the result of all this, and its library of thirty thousand case histories is great material with which to regale the credulous. Moreover, the rationalizations that Cayce and his supporters used to explain his numerous and notable failures are prime examples of the art of evasion.

Cayce was a gentle man who looked like a schoolteacher, with rimless glasses and a receding chin. When he died in 1945 he was already well on the road to psychic stardom, and thereafter his reputation took off in earnest. The current rebirth of interest in the irrational has brought forth more than a dozen books—and reprints of old ones—that tout his wonders. Bookstands are full of Cayce items, and at my lectures he is frequently cited by believers in the audience as one of the invincibles of the trade.

Of course, Cayce is remembered for his apparent successes, not his failures. Disciples claim many thousands of verified instances in which this "master psychic" correctly diagnosed illnesses and prescribed cures. But *did* he? I recommend that my readers perform some research by carefully studying any of the many books on the Sleeping Prophet. It must be said of Cayce's followers that they are quite unashamed of the myriad half-truths, the evasive and garbled language, and the multiple "outs" that Cayce used in his readings. In some cases these crutches were clearly stated, without any attempt to disguise them. But such is the nature of the zealot that no matter how damning the evidence of the documents, faith marches on undaunted.

Cayce was fond of expressions like "I feel that . . ." and "perhaps"—qualifying words used to avoid positive declarations. It is a common tool in the psychic trade. Many of the letters he received—in fact, most—contained specific details about the illnesses for which readings were required, and there was nothing to stop Cayce from knowing the contents of the letters and presenting that information as if it were a divine revelation. To one who has been through dozens of similar diagnoses, as I have, the methods are obvious. It is merely a specialized version of the "generalization" technique of fortune-tellers.

Cayce's "cures" were pretty funny. He just loved to have his patients boiling the most obscure roots and bark to make nasty syrups. Perhaps the therapy was based on nauseating the victim so much that the original illness was forgotten. And it is no secret that his cures were quite similar to the "home remedies" described in the handy medical encyclopedias that were bedside reading in many rural homes in the late 1800s. Beef broth was one of Cayce's favorite remedies for such diverse diseases as gout and leukemia. Who can fault a nice man who prescribes a cup of hot soup?

But did cures actually result from all this? The matter is hard to prove, either way. The testimony of some of his patients hardly represents the whole. Dead patients cannot complain, and those who were not cured would benefit little by writing a letter of complaint. After all, this good man had tried to help them, and just because it hadn't worked in some cases was no reason to knock the process. As for those who wrote to affirm that they had been cured, there is an important factor to consider. I'm sure you've heard the joke about the man who is found yelling at the top of his lungs in the park. Asked why, he replies that such a procedure keeps rogue elephants away. But, counters his questioner, there are no elephants around here for a thousand miles! See how well it works? is the triumphant reply. The point is that just because Cayce prescribed a boiled root drink does not mean that that nostrum achieved the cure reported. Nor should we forget that many of the illnesses reported to physicians are totally imaginary or self-terminating.

But can the skeptics prove that Cayce's cures are attributable to ordinary causes? It would require a huge expenditure of money to do the necessary research for such a job, and in most cases the information would not be available anyway. Frankly, the vague, very evasive, simplistic diagnoses and cures attributed to Edgar Cayce hardly need such research. Examination of the record at hand is quite sufficient to deny him sainthood. The large and well-funded organization that he founded survives today as a result of preferred belief, not because of adequate proof.

In a revealing book entitled *The Outer Limits of Edgar Cayce's Power*, by E. V. and H. L. Cayce, his notable failures are excused in typical fashion. The authors assure us very strongly that the book, though it admits the failures, explains all of them quite satisfactorily. But I'll let you judge for yourself. Here, with the Cayce verbiage stripped away to the essentials, is what they tell us he divined about the Hauptmann/ Lindbergh kidnapping case while in a trance:

1. The baby was removed at 8:30 (A.M. or P.M. not specified) from the Lindbergh home by one man. Another man took it and there was a third person in the car.
2. The baby was taken to a small, brown, two-story house in a mill section called Cardova near New Haven. The house used to be green.
3. Schartest Street is mentioned; also Adams Street, which has had its numbers and name changed.
4. The house is shingled. Three men and one woman are with the child. The woman and one man were actually named.
5. The child's hair has been cut and dyed.
6. Cardova is related to the manufacture of leather goods.
7. Red shale and a new macadam road on a "half-street" and "half a mile" are mentioned.
8. The boy has been moved to Jersey City and is not well.
9. Hauptmann is "only partly guilty." Cayce asks for "no publicity on this case."

Well, that's quite a lot of information is it not? Unfortunately, most of it is wrong. True, Adams Street was found, and it had been named only a few weeks earlier. But this information was available to

Cayce during one of his rare waking periods. Besides, Adams Street proved a dud. "I've always had my doubts about anything very authentic in such matters," said Cayce when confronted with the facts. Well, so have I, Ed, more now than ever before after examining your record. But we should give the disciples (and Cayce) a chance to rationalize this one, so here goes with a list of their excuses:

1. The readings picked up the mental plans of *others* who had *also* planned a kidnapping of the Lindbergh baby. (Poor psychic aim.)
2. The thought patterns of others involved distorted the readings.
3. Mental static was very heavy.

No wonder Cayce asked for no publicity! It was a great fiasco, and he had psychic egg on his face. But these excuses are accepted by the believers as quite legitimate—to this day.

There are more surprises for us. Cayce even gave diagnoses when the "patients" were *dead!* How could that be! Surely death is a very serious symptom and should be detectable. But we have failed to take into account the ingenuity of the breed, apparent in the following examples.

Cayce gave a reading on a Monday for a little girl who had died of leukemia on Sunday, the day before. The letter had been written while the child was alive. He gave a long and typical diagnosis and a long and complicated dietary cure. An excerpt from the reading will suffice to show just how lucid and informative it is: "And this depends upon whether one of the things as intended to be done today is done or isn't done, see?"

No, Eddie baby, I'm afraid I don't see at all. The defendants deserve a chance to present their alibis, however, so we'll take a look at those given in this case. The girl, Theodoria Alosio, was diagnosed by Cayce with a lady aide recording the details in a session "conducted" by the aide's cousin. Here are the rationalizations:

1. The person who sought the reading was not related to the child.
2. Only the child's mother had "an open mind."
3. The doctor in charge was not told about the reading. (How about the coroner? On the other hand, what could either of them have done for the child even if they had known? The child was *dead.*)
4. There was "conflict between the recorder and her cousin at the time of the reading."
5. The steno recording the details was thinking about *another* little girl at the time.

6. The reading was given in reverse order, the physical check preceding the prescription. (Then why didn't the great psychic detect *death* and skip the prescription?)
7. Cayce had been given a newspaper clipping from the preceding week, and had given a reading for *that* date.
8. The reading was given *on the condition*, not on the child herself.
9. The reading was given on "the period of seeking," not on the moment at hand.
10. (This one must be stated in Cayce's own deathless words) ". . . if the proper consideration is given all facts and factors concerning each character of information sought, as has been given oft, the information answers that which is sought at the time in relationships to the conditions that exist in those forms through which the impressions are made for tangibility or for observation in the minds of others." (So there!)
11. The reading given can be useful "for the next case."
12. Nothing can be done except as God wills it. (Poor God, left holding the bag again!)
13. The desire of the party was for a spectacular cure.
14. Leukemia is the focus of the subconscious rather than the child.
15. The attitudes, desires, purposes, and motives of the patient and the person conducting the reading had a bad influence.

Is that enough rationalization for one big boo-boo? Apparently it is, for the Cayce folks have accepted it. But let me regale you with one more example of Cayce's medical prowess. For another *dead patient,* Cayce prescribed the following noxious mixture: Boil together some wild cherry bark, sarsaparilla root, wild ginger, Indian turnip, wild ginseng, prickly ash bark, buchu leaves, and mandrake root. Add grain alcohol and tolu balsam to the mess, and give it to the patient—during waking periods is specified—for ten days. I consulted my own (nonpsychic) physician about this remedy and he commented that such a mixture just *might* raise the dead! And note the preponderance of "wild" ingredients. How basic and natural it all sounds.

Rationalization time again. Say Cayce's disciples about this case:

1. No definite appointment was made for this reading.
2. The conductor of the reading held the letter—written while the patient was alive—in her hand during the reading.
3. The patient herself did not request the reading; thus there was a lack of strong need on her part.
4. Cayce was emotionally upset that day.

I am reminded of the old story wherein the lady at the funeral calls out, "Give him some chicken soup!" Told that such a remedy would not help at this late stage, she correctly replies, "Well, it couldn't *hurt!*" More grist for the believer's mill.

In a valiant attempt to prove that Cayce had a good batting average in his readings, the authors of *The Outer Limits of Edgar Cayce's Power* did a jolly bit of research at the Association library in Virginia Beach, Virginia. They selected 150 cases at random from the files and tabulated them. Their findings, they reported, showed *more than 85 percent success* for Cayce, verified by actual reports of the cured patients! Quite impressive, if true, and certainly indicative of marvelous psychic powers. But again, as one might suspect, close examination leads to a somewhat different conclusion.

They listed their findings thusly:

No reports made	74 —	50%	(actually 49.3%)
Negative reports	11 —	7%	(actually 7.3%)
Positive reports	65 —	43%	(actually 43.3%)
	150		

Then they reasoned that since the "no reports" portion was impossible to judge, this could be discarded. The final table looks like this:

Negative reports	$^{11}/_{76}$ — 14.4%	(actually 14.5%)
Positive reports	$^{65}/_{76}$ — 85.5%	

Thus the results are rather remarkable, by *their* figuring. If I hear cries of "Unfair!" at this point, I fully concur. And I object, as well, to the specialized terminology the authors use to describe the 11 negative reports. They are not called "failures" or even "errors." They are referred to as "considered inadequate."

But we need to examine these figures even further, as the two authors apparently did. They tell us that 46 of these 150 persons *were present* at the readings, and that of those absent, 35 did not give any information in their letters appealing for help. Thus 69 persons among the 150 *did* give information to Cayce. Now, you and I would agree, I'm sure, that prophet Edgar Cayce, with the patient present, has a much greater chance than otherwise of finding out something about the illness involved, and a greater opportunity to discover many other facts that can surely be worked into the reading as evidential information. So in a total of 115 (46 + 69) of the 150 cases it was possible to make accurate statements about them and probably get a "positive" report from the patient thereby. That's a big 76.6 percent, friends.

Another point: Why did the 74 patients *make no report?* Remember, they almost *had* to be believers in Cayce to ask for a reading. It was their lives they were dealing with. Do you seriously think they would respond with a negative report, *or fail to send in grateful thanks and affirmation for a success?* Not very likely. Thus we may safely assume that the majority of the 74 cases were *not* successes—pardon me, were "considered inadequate."

Even if we are exceedingly liberal with these folks, and give them 50 percent of the 74 no-reports as "positives," their 85.5 percent suddenly shrinks to 68 percent. But I refuse to do that, because I maintain that my argument as to the probable reasons behind the no-reports is correct. The authors are stuck with a bad analysis, and to make matters worse they proceed in their book to elaborate on this sample of just 0.5 *percent* of the available data to arrive at totally misleading figures. Statisticians are prone to murder and maim for much less provocation.

My own (admittedly amateur) analysis concludes that only 23.3 percent of the sample has any hope of being demonstrably positive at all, and knowing the criteria and the quality of the data, that small percentage of the one-half-of-one-percent sample shrinks even further.

Before we leave the Sleeping Prophet to his permanent nap, it would be well to deal with another of his supposed powers, one which is always trotted out in discussions as "heavy" proof of his abilities. Locating buried treasures is one field that would seem to be safe from most fraud or second-guessing. After all, if a "psychic" can locate long-lost or secreted treasure, fakery seems impossible. In his attempts at this miracle, Cayce took no chances. He called in Henry Gross, the famous "dowser," who put his forked stick to work along with Cayce's powers to find purported millions in jewels and coins buried along the seashore. Gross joining with Cayce was a little like setting out to sea in a leaky boat, then at the last minute throwing in some cast-iron life jackets.

Presumably, Edgar Cayce dozed while Henry Gross dowsed, wearing out several sticks in the process. They dug up tons of mud, sand, and gravel, looked under rocks, and in general disturbed the landscape something awful. No treasure. Weeks of work gave them only blisters. How could such a powerful team of psychic-plus-dowser fail to locate the prize? Rely on the alibi manufacturers to come up with something suitable:

1. The psychic impressions were picked up from the spirits of departed Indians and pirates, and such undependable shades are known to want to play jokes on the living.
2. Maybe the treasure *was* there but had been removed. Cayce was reading in the past again.
3. There were doubts, fears, and cross-purposes at work among the seekers.

4. Were the directions Cayce gave based on headings from true north or compass north?
5. Was the information given to Cayce meant for digging *now* or for another time, perhaps in the *future?*

Well, there it is. The matter of Edgar Cayce boils down to a vague mass of garbled data, interpreted by true believers who have a very heavy stake in the acceptance of the claims. Put to the test, Cayce is found to be bereft of real powers. His reputation today rests on poor and deceptive reporting of the claims made by him and his followers, and such claims do not stand up to examination. Read the literature, with these comments in mind, and the conclusion is inescapable. It just ain't so.

10

The Will to Believe

Man's capacity for self-delusion is infinite.
—Dr. Elie A. Shneour
Biosystems Research Institute

The desire to see favorable results where none exist is obviously the source of much of the "evidence" presented by parapsychologists. This failing is not limited to those who seek to prove paranormal phenomena; there are also examples of such wishful thinking in the annals of orthodox science. One such case occurred not so long ago as to have faded from memory and serves to show how far even an accomplished scientist can go in pursuit of the nonexistent.

René Blondlot was a renowned French physicist from the city of Nancy who was hailed as a careful and inspired observer after he determined the speed of electricity traveling through a conductor, a very difficult measurement. It proved to be somewhat less than the speed of light in a vacuum (186,000 miles per second). The method he used in the experiment was brilliant. But while trying to polarize X rays, which had been recently discovered by Roentgen, he claimed in 1903 to have found a new invisible radiation which he called (in honor of his home city) "N Rays." He used prisms and lenses made of aluminum to refract these rays (much as a glass prism or lens refracts light rays), thus, he said, producing an invisible spectrum. He claimed to be able to detect the bands of this unseen spectrum by passing a fine thread, coated with fluorescent material, through its supposed area. As the thread varied in brightness under the N Rays, he would read off the positions to an assistant. To him, and to at least fourteen of his close friends in science, these positions were definitely determined and could be seen at any time. Scientists in other parts of the world thought they saw these wonders, too, and reported on them.

But where did these rays come from? X rays were produced by high voltage in an evacuated tube. Light rays came from heated substances and other sources. But N Rays were, frankly, too strange to be true. It was claimed that every substance emitted the radiation, with the exception of dead wood; all experimenters agreed on this point.

196

Jean Becquerel, the son of a very famous scientist father (the discoverer of nuclear radiation), and himself an accomplished and gifted scientist, said that N Rays were not emitted from "anesthetized metals"—metals exposed to ether or chloroform—but that they could be conducted along wires, like electricity!

The French Academy, hearing of this discovery, prepared to award Blondlot its highest prize. But before they could do so, an American scientist aroused suspicions when he visited Blondlot's laboratory and reported his findings to *Nature*, the British science journal.

Dr. Robert Wood, the visitor, had tried to duplicate Blondlot's experiments and had failed. During his visit, he proved beyond doubt that N Rays had an entirely subjective existence. He did this by secretly lifting the aluminum prism from its place in the viewing apparatus, after which Blondlot continued to read off the expected positions of luminosity as the thread moved across the imaginary spectrum. The procedure could not possibly have worked without the prism, but Blondlot was still seeing the spectrum! An assistant, suspicious of Wood, offered to read off the positions. Believing that Wood still had the prism removed from the apparatus, though Wood had by then replaced it, the assistant announced that he could see nothing, and that the American had probably interfered with the equipment. He examined it, found it complete, and just glared. But the case was proved: N Rays did not exist. The contentions of assistants and colleagues who had done all they could to keep Blondlot's delusion alive were discredited.

The situation is not much different today. Associates of those who have similar misconceptions either refuse to speak up or support the insanity by trying to save the perpetrators from exposure.

N Rays having been debunked, the findings were published in *Nature*, picked up by *La Revue Scientifique*, and expanded in the latter journal. The French Academy had published more than one hundred papers about N Rays by then. After the exposure, it published only two more. Blondlot, scheduled to receive the LaLande prize, was not censured by the Academy but rather was given the prize and a gold medal as planned, though the award was presented "for his life work, taken as a whole." N Rays were not mentioned.

During my visit to France in 1978 to deliver a series of lectures about claims of paranormal events, I addressed an audience of some 140 conjurers, scientists, and reporters in the city of Nancy. Two of those present were physicists from the University of Nancy where René Blondlot had done his work, and where he was a professor of physics for six years after the exposure. I had found references to N Rays previously in almost every encyclopedia and science reference book I had consulted. But in that audience in Nancy, the *home* of N Rays, not one person had ever heard of them! Even the Larousse Encyclopedia had been washed clean of the embarrassing episode, mentioning only Blondlot's other work.

Without getting too technical for the average reader, I will try to explain a very important point concerning the N Ray case. In a standard spectroscope—an instrument that directs light through a prism to disperse it into its component colors (spectrum)—light enters through a slit. Certain kinds of light (that resulting from heating common salt—sodium chloride—in a flame, for example) breaks up not into a continuous spectrum from violet to red, as in a rainbow, but into a series of bands, each of which is as wide as the width of the slit. (In the case of heated salt, a prominent feature of the spectrum of sodium—two close bright yellow lines—shows up strongly.) Dr. Wood was astonished to find that, though the slit in Blondlot's N Ray apparatus was two millimeters wide, the scientist claimed to be making measurements as small as one tenth of a millimeter! This was a little like expecting to separate sand from birdseed by using chicken wire as a sieve. When questioned about this, Blondlot told Wood that it was one of the inexplicable properties of N Rays!

Here we have the catch. A scientist has come up with what he insists are proper observations, and upon being shown that they are not possible he falls back on the conclusion that this is a unique phenomenon that does not obey the rules governing all other phenomena, instead of concluding that there is nothing there in the first place.

It might be argued that X rays are also extraordinary, and that scientists would have failed to discover them if they had not been willing to examine the possibility that certain rays penetrate otherwise opaque objects and register on a photographic plate, and even reveal the shadows of bones in the human hand. Nothing like this had been expected, the argument continues, and, as in the case of N Rays, it was in opposition to everything that scientists of the day considered possible.

Well, not quite. Researchers had been plotting the spectrum and filling it in nicely. When they discovered that photographic plates accidentally became exposed when certain equipment was present nearby, they investigated and determined the cause. They could repeat the effect—they *all* could—and they had firm evidence to prove it. The question that Blondlot asked was, *Do you see the lines at these determined positions?* instead of, *Do you see any lines, and if so, in what positions?* If the latter question had been asked, N Rays would have been the delusion of *one* mind, not many.

Determining the truth about N Rays would have required a double-blind experiment. In such a test, the experimenter is unaware of the expected outcome, and those who control the test and judge the results are also not told what is expected, or what proportion of the samples are expected to be different, and so on. In this way, no presumed result (and therefore bias) is possible. Parapsychology needs many more experiments of this nature, and until the tendency to refuse such tests is overcome it will remain, at best, an unproved idea.

Three examples of my recent investigations of "miracles" that fail to pass double-blind testing illustrate the point. The first involved one Stanley L. Wojcik, whose card advertises, among other specialties, "Ghost Hunting" and "Séances." Stanley appeared with me on "The Candy Jones Show" on WMCA radio recently. He brought with him his "dowsing rods," which were one of the two general varieties used by dowsers. His rods consisted of two coat hangers straightened out to form long L-shaped pieces. These are held, one in each hand, so that it is exceedingly difficult to maintain them parallel to one another and horizontal. The slightest tipping of the hand causes a rod to swing about wildly. Deluxe versions of these rods have lubricated bearings in special handles. The idea is that the dowser advances with the rods held parallel and extending straight out in front until some object or substance is "sensed," at which point the rods either come together or diverge. Of course, it is simple for the operator to unintentionally (or quite consciously!) tilt the hand slightly, causing the rod to behave in a manner quite out of proportion to the small impetus given it.

Wojcik allowed himself to fall into a rather neat trap on the program. First, I innocently asked him if he would demonstrate how the rods behaved when detecting a small pile of coins. He produced coins from his pocket (I would not have supplied the coins, lest he claim that mine were "special" ones!) and put them on a small table in the WMCA studio. The dowsing rods obediently crossed precisely over the coins as he approached. Next, I asked if it would still work when the coins were covered with a piece of paper. Of course it would, and this was demonstrated. In an envelope? Naturally! This test, too, was a success. Now I was ready. I produced nine other envelopes, each with a bit of paper inside to simulate the lump made by the coins. Wojcik and the host of the show, Miss Jones, looked away as I selected at random a single card from among ten numbered cards I had in my pocket. The target envelope containing the coins was then placed among the other nine envelopes in the position indicated by the number on the selected card, and the ten envelopes were placed in a row on the floor. Wojcik was invited to find the target.

We did the test several times. Wojcik failed every time. At one point, after identifying the wrong envelope, he blamed it on a metal pipe he said was below the floor. I was ready for that, and we simply did not place an envelope in that spot for the other tests. The dowser,

Dowsing rods: two stiff wires, each bent at a right angle at one end and held loosely and parallel in the neutral position.

A *very* slight tilt of the right hand has caused the rod to veer to the left. This supposedly indicates the presence of oil, water, metal, or other underground material.

A slight tilt of each hand causes a dramatic spreading of the rods. This, too, is said to indicate the presence of the material that is sought.

who had claimed fantastic percentages previously, scored zero. During the tests he had entered into conversation with me and had learned that I had no belief in an afterlife. When the tests were finished, I hit him with a fact that demolished his objection that there had been other metal masses in the room that "threw me off." He had averred that metal in the area was fatal to results, yet he had unerringly located the pile of coins under the paper while they lay (unknown to him) on *a solid cast-iron table weighing over thirty pounds!* If *that* was not sufficient to affect the dowsing rods, what was? An ounce or so of coins? But Wojcik had a ready answer. Said he, "There's no sense talking to you, Mr. Randi. You don't even believe in a life after death. What a *sad* life you must have!" There was something very sad there that night, but it was not I. . . .

The astute reader will note that there is an apparent defect in the experiment. Remember, conditions were not ideal, and I frankly was taking a bit of a chance under these circumstances. In a double-blind test, it is essential that the experimenter not know the expected result, but in this case I was quite aware of which envelope contained the sought-after target. Because I had no one to assist me in the studio, I had to be the one to watch the operator to make sure he did not violate the protocol, and I noted that on two occasions he actually nudged the envelopes with his foot as he walked along. I had to restart the test at that point, since the target envelope would be apt to make a noise, while the others would not. Either result could give Wojcik information he should not have. I stood to one side as I watched him walk about, taking every precaution I could to avoid giving any clue.

Magicians are adept at this. On stage, the performer is well aware of what is *really* taking place, and part of one's art consists of not giving oneself away by involuntary reactions at crucial moments. If I had become too talkative as Wojcik approached the target envelope, for example, it could have obviously or subliminally alerted him. The test was flawed in this respect, but necessarily so under the circumstances. It is obvious that the flaw was not prejudicial to the results, however, though I do not deny this deficiency in the design of the experiment. I had offered my $10,000 to Wojcik that evening, and the offer was also made to the parties involved in the following examples.

A gentleman came from California all the way to Albuquerque, New Mexico, to see me and have his powers tested. He was a huge man, Vince Wiberg by name, affable, enthusiastic, and quite honest, in my opinion. He really believed he had the abilities he claimed. His specialty was dowsing for "auragrams," and in several letters sent to me at my home in New Jersey he had outlined in detail just what he could demonstrate—in contrast to many others, who like to appear for testing without having said anything in advance.

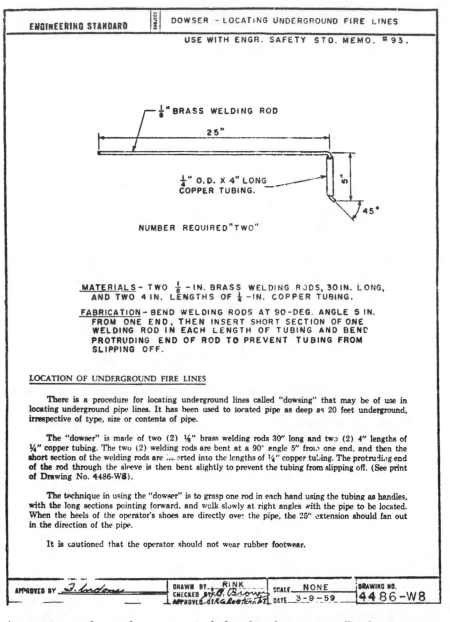

ENGINEERING STANDARD	SUBJECT	DOWSER – LOCATING UNDERGROUND FIRE LINES

USE WITH ENGR. SAFETY STD. MEMO. #93.

$\frac{1}{8}$" BRASS WELDING ROD

25"

$\frac{1}{4}$" O.D. X 4" LONG COPPER TUBING.

5"

45°

NUMBER REQUIRED "TWO"

MATERIALS – TWO $\frac{1}{8}$ –IN. BRASS WELDING RODS, 30 IN. LONG, AND TWO 4 IN. LENGTHS OF $\frac{1}{4}$ –IN. COPPER TUBING.

FABRICATION – BEND WELDING RODS AT 90-DEG. ANGLE 5 IN. FROM ONE END, THEN INSERT SHORT SECTION OF ONE WELDING ROD IN EACH LENGTH OF TUBING AND BEND PROTRUDING END OF ROD TO PREVENT TUBING FROM SLIPPING OFF.

LOCATION OF UNDERGROUND FIRE LINES

There is a procedure for locating underground lines called "dowsing" that may be of use in locating underground pipe lines. It has been used to located pipe as deep as 20 feet underground, irrespective of type, size or contents of pipe.

The "dowser" is made of two (2) ⅛" brass welding rods 30" long and two (2) 4" lengths of ¼" copper tubing. The two (2) welding rods are bent at a 90° angle 5" from one end, and then the short section of the welding rods are inserted into the lengths of ¼" copper tubing. The protruding end of the rod through the sleeve is then bent slightly to prevent the tubing from slipping off. (See print of Drawing No. 4486-W8).

The technique in using the "dowser" is to grasp one rod in each hand using the tubing as handles, with the long sections pointing forward, and walk slowly at right angles with the pipe to be located. When the heels of the operator's shoes are directly over the pipe, the 25" extension should fan out in the direction of the pipe.

It is cautioned that the operator should not wear rubber footwear.

APPROVED BY *J. Anderson*	DRAWN BY RINK	SCALE NONE	DRAWING NO.
	CHECKED BY *O. Brown*		4486-W8
	APPROVED *D.R. Rooten* DATE 3-9-59		

A prominent chemical company includes this data in its official engineering files. Curiously, the admonition to "not wear rubber footwear" disagrees with what the big-time dowsers say. No wonder they can't find those underground fire lines!

I was in Albuquerque to lecture at Sandia Labs, where two scientists had fallen for a deception perpetrated by a pair of teenagers who were simply picking up reflections of large letter cards in the experimenters' eyeglasses. I was there to meet and inform these chaps, and I had also invited several local "psychics" to show up, including the teenagers. Vince Wiberg was the only one who materialized.

At my hotel room I had two Sandia people as witnesses. First, Vince showed us that his dowsing rods would cross when held over a large metal film can that I had placed on the floor. We tested this at many locations around the room. It worked every time—when the dowser knew where the can was. (In all fairness, it should be mentioned that Vince did not care for this test, since it was not his specialty.)When the can was covered with a blanket after being placed according to a randomizing procedure while he *and* I were out of the room (to prevent feedback from me), Mr. Wiberg was not able to score. At this point we gave him the test he preferred.

He had made claims concerning an ability to diagnose illness in the body, and we were ready to test him on this point. I'd seen many such attempts before, and I was not expecting very much success. Usually, these "readings" were general, concentrating on back pains and head-aches—pretty safe guesses—followed by a lot of second-guessing. To get around this, Mr. Wiberg agreed in advance that the testees would write down their ailments and seal them in envelopes before the divining rods began swinging. This was to ensure that none of those tested changed their minds about what ailed them after the reading, and that Wiberg had proof of this. We started with me, since I had a clearly definable ailment, one that in fact was known to several people at Sandia.

Mr. Wiberg asked me to stand and assume several different postures while he waved his rods about. He read off to a witness a series of numbers, said to represent the strength of the "aura" about my body. This is a supposed, normally invisible envelope of energy that surrounds the body, and which is said to show up via Kirlian photography (discussed in chapter 1).

When it was all over, he gave his diagnosis. The problem, he told me, was in my right ear, or thereabouts. I did not react in any way but asked him if there were any other indications. He had gently probed me with questions during the dowsing process, and had made several suggestions, but I had not reacted at all. Now I asked if the diagnosis was complete and told him that he would not be allowed to add anything after the envelope was opened. He agreed.

The actual ailment was an almost-healed fracture in my left wrist. It was still quite painful and had given me much trouble that day. Zero for this diagnosis, but Vince did mention that it was difficult to find almost-healed problems. I did not allow him this rationalization.

One of the Sandia gentlemen, who had expressed deep convictions about paranormal matters, had brought with him a young woman I'd not met before. We were told that she had an ailment (which was known to her companion), and, unseen by me, she wrote it down and sealed it up. Vince went to work on her. It was all I could do to prevent her and the Sandia man from answering queries and suggesting areas to be tested. I'd have liked to have the man out of the room, but the woman preferred to have him there. The reason soon became obvious.

Wiberg told us that the young woman was in good health and that there was only "perhaps some trouble here in the lower back." Nothing could have been further from the facts: She was in an advanced stage of lung cancer. Vince Wiberg rationalized that this type of illness is not localized and is thus hard to find. This I would not allow him either, and besides that it is quite untrue.

The dowser left, having failed to earn either my reward or the validation of the Committee for the Scientific Investigation of Claims of the Paranormal. He was quite subdued, and his parting remark was that he was seeking funds to "perfect" his methods. I suggested that he find a phenomenon first, *then* work on perfecting the study of it. This fell, I expect, on deaf ears. He seemed not to be dissuaded at all but merely set back momentarily and eager to correct his methods. The test was definitive, though only two test subjects were used. I'm willing to test a hundred, if need be. But Vince Wiberg will go on believing, changing his beliefs only to the extent necessary to accommodate the failures. When faced with facts, throw out the evidence but never the theory—that's the philosophy of the players in this game.*

The Metromedia news department, to its considerable credit, decided to do an in-depth study of the paranormal in the spring of 1978. I was called in as a consultant, and since some "psychics" were visiting me at the time for testing, I asked them if they would mind being filmed. They agreed, and we met at my New York office with a film crew. Here I will relate only one of the test procedures with one of the performers; the rest belong in another section.

The subject was a statuesque blond ex-dancer whose calling card advertised her as *Sue Wallace, Doctor of Magneto-Therapy.* I had encountered Miss Wallace at a "Psychic Fair" in Bricktown, New Jersey, the week before; she'd been the only person to respond to my offer to test (for the $10,000 reward and the validation of the CSICOP), even though I'd handed out forty-four such offers at the gathering. I had observed

---

* As of this writing, Wiberg has decided that he *was* correct on both the film-can attempt and the diagnoses. Such a version is a total invention.

her methods and had spoken with several "patients" after they had been diagnosed. The conversations had been quite interesting indeed.

One woman, told that she had goiter trouble, was amazed that Sue had been able to discover that fact. And when I asked her if she was impressed, she said that she was even more struck by the diagnosis of her back trouble "right here [gesturing] where she said it was!" and of several other minor ailments she'd not even suspected. Now, I'd been right there making notes, though I hadn't told the patient this, and I let her rave on, then recapped the whole episode for her. First, I asked her how long she'd had goiter trouble. She had no idea. In fact, she had no proof at all, or any previous suspicion, that she *had* goiter trouble. Her vigorous nodding had been in response to the repeated question from Sue, "Do you understand?"—*not* in response to the correctness of the diagnosis! As for the back problem, Miss Wallace had suggested to her that there was "maybe a problem in the back?" In response, the patient had pointed to her upper left back and asked, "Here?" whereupon Miss Wallace agreed. Thus, the *patient* had pointed out the location, not the operator!

At this point, a woman standing nearby chimed in. She told us that she'd recovered from open-heart surgery and was out of bed for the first time. Miss Wallace had failed to detect her problem and, when told about it, had explained that since the surgery had been a success there was no longer any illness! But that was inconsistent with a diagnosis she had given earlier that day in the case of a man who had undergone exactly the same test. She had mentioned heart trouble to him, and he had replied in an astonished voice that he'd undergone open-heart surgery. There had been oohs and ahhs left and right, of course.

One other "diagnosis" deserves mention. It became obvious to me that Sue Wallace very frequently referred to "problems with the reproductive organs" when confronted with any female more than forty years of age. She scored frequent "hits" with this ploy, augmented by one of the common "outs" used when the patient would deny any trouble in that area: "I often call problems well before they develop," Sue would caution. "Sometimes the illness doesn't show up for several months— or years. But it's there, believe me."

Her escape from one particularly glaring boo-boo shows her versatility in the face of defeat and illustrates her cool approach. It happened with a rather proper-looking middle-aged woman who seemed determined not to listen to any nonsense. I recorded the conversation verbatim.

SUE: There is a problem with your right ovary.
PATIENT: Impossible. Impossible. My right ovary was removed about—

SUE: Don't tell *me!* [smiles] I'm telling *you.* There's a problem there. No mistake.

PATIENT: But it's *removed!*

SUE: Listen to me. These doctors take your money—you know?—and they do these operations, but they don't *need* to—you know?—and just because they cut out your ovary, I mean, the trouble is still there. I'm getting it. . . .

PATIENT: Still there?

SUE: Let me try again. [She does the diagnostic procedure again.] Yes, the trouble is there. A bit below the ovary. But I get it very strong.

PATIENT: Well, I don't know. I haven't had any problem. Not now.

SUE: Well, I get it very strong.

Note what has been done. Miss Wallace, faced with a decided contradiction, has to back up a bit and make some fast qualifications. She has a difficult subject, one who is not about to ignore mistakes and just go her way. This one wants results. Sue throws up the money-hungry doctor image—which she did several times during the long period I observed her at work—and then suddenly the problem is *in the area of* the right ovary rather than the ovary itself. She would not back down on her decision; she simply shifted the affliction's location a bit.

Almost invariably, Sue Wallace announced impending problems when the patient denied presently existing ones. "You'll see" was her frequent phrase just before dismissal. Twice she came up with another clever hedge. It occurred when she got absolute denials of anemia in one case and liver trouble in another. She fixed the patient with a glare and asked, "But you've had headaches, haven't you?" The answer, not unsurprisingly, was yes. "That's the first sign," said Miss Wallace ominously. "You'll see."

Just how many people did "see" after they were out of Sue's hands, we will of course never know. We were not in a position to follow up a selected number of cases, as was Dr. William Nolen when he researched his wonderful book *Healing.* Nor will we know how many of Sue's patients railed against their doctors for failing to find the illnesses diagnosed by magnetic power.

I must mention that Sue Wallace was not charging for these services; she took donations instead, sold pyramids and magnets, and gave out literature extolling her health-food store and her ideas about "disease-free living." If her personal appearance reflects her methods, she is a winner. She is physically impressive, to say the least.

This *Doctor of Magneto-Therapy, Lecturer, Researcher and Para-Psychologist* would stand out in any crowd. Perched on her head was a wire pyramid—to concentrate her powers, of course—and she was selling small, powerful composition magnets wrapped in prismatic mylar plastic and labeled both "North" and "South." Prices ranged up to thirty-five dollars for a piece of magnet that can be purchased for one dollar in surplus stores—but without the colorful wrapping and the labels. She claimed that application of the correct pole of the magnet to the

Sue Wallace, "Doctor of Magneto-Therapy," as she was tested with the $10,000 prize at stake. The wire contraption on her head is a "magic pyramid." Metromedia TV

right place brought about cures, and they were selling well. I was very glad to have a shot at her and perhaps expose her practices to public view. As you will see, she failed the tests in our filmed Metromedia-sponsored meeting, but though this was seen on television in a widely watched program, she still carries on in Stratford, New Jersey.

Miss Wallace had a bizarre method of diagnosis. The patient stood beside her with one arm extended straight out to the side. Sue would *think* of a part of the body, then pull down on the arm. If the arm went down easily, there was trouble in that area. Do you follow that? Of course, a little experimentation will convince my reader that an arm held in that position can offer very little resistance when pulled down. It all depends on how much force is placed on it.

Sue Wallace used this arm-pulling method in another demonstration that she said she could depend on, which involved cigarettes. In fact, she said, she was trying to sell the discovery to the tobacco companies. She claims she can remove the toxicity of a cigarette by "magnetizing" it. I must not tell you the exact procedure, since she believes she has a million-dollar idea here, but the proof was in a demonstration she performed many times—without a single failure—at the Psychic Fair. A patient was asked to hold a "magnetized" cigarette in his hand, arm outstretched as described. Sue could not force his arm down. But when he held a regular, untreated cigarette, he was affected by the toxins, she said, and therefore his arm sank under her effort. Of course, it was Sue Wallace who was applying the pressure, so the method is obvious.

Lest you think that such a nutty procedure is limited to "doctors of magneto-therapy," witness a recent popular book about "kinesthetics" that actually claimed a subject's arm was more easily depressed after sugar was ingested than before. A New Jersey dentist actually tried to convince me of this, to the amusement of my colleague Alexis Vallejo, who showed me the sugar lump that he had palmed off instead of placing it under his tongue as instructed when the doctor tested him. It was obvious to Vallejo that the dentist merely pressed harder when he thought the sugar was there.

The cigarette stunt was the one we decided to test in a double-blind experiment at my New York office. Convinced that it worked, Sue agreed to be tested. Our method was simple and direct and would show whether the power existed. It was always possible that Miss Wallace might be sensing the presence of a magnetized or nonmagnetized cigarette through some other means and subconsciously applying more or less pressure in the test.

She gave us ten cigarettes. I labeled each one from A to J, and one was selected at random. A young woman in the TV crew wrote down the letter (unknown to anyone else) and then left the room for the rest of the experiment. The chosen cigarette was "magnetized" by Sue without anyone's knowing its identifying letter, and then it was mixed with the others. She was not allowed to touch or see any cigarette again. She chose a member of the office staff, and he held each of the cigarettes in turn. Sue had been asked to tell us which cigarette was the magnetized one, but she chose to eliminate them instead, telling us which ones were *not* the ones she sought. I went along with this request, since it did not change the result and gave her no advantage except a more dramatic presentation.

She pressed the subject's arm until his eyes popped out. The first session resulted in a win for her. But I had been careful to say, before the tests commenced, that a series of at least ten runs would be required. I was not about to allow one win to decide the matter, or neglect to delineate the rules in advance. Sue Wallace failed from then on.

It was interesting to me to note that while we were testing the others who had come along that day prior to Sue's test, she was out in the hall charming some of the young men from my office. It was not very difficult to do; they are notoriously susceptible to such influence. One of them, Jay Raskin, was the eventual subject chosen for the experiment.

In the first run just described—which resulted in a win for Miss Wallace—the cigarettes had been mixed together. As she began to lose in the other runs, she asked that we modify our procedure by *not* mixing the cigarettes, so that the "magnetic" power would not "rub off" on the control cigarettes. Yet this problem had not arisen when she had her win, and the mixing had been thorough. This kind of unreason is common in the history of these wonders.

In summary, these three tests were excellent examples of how genuine double-blind experiments expose spurious claims in which experimenter expectation is active. Stanley Wojcik, though he may believe that he has the powers he claims, was not only unable to perform under proper experimental conditions but also gave no adequate reason for his failure to do so. His fans will continue to worship him in spite of the evidence. Vince Wiberg is still seeking to "perfect" what I did not find to exist. Sue Wallace will still convince the unwary, though she failed to produce when tested properly. All these persons are welcome to return to be tested, but I think they will resist the invitation.

Remember, too, that Blondlot, the scientist who subjectively "saw" the nonexistent N Rays, was not in his dotage when he did so; he was only fifty-four years old, and an accomplished researcher. No one is immune to wishful thinking and to stubborn adherence to error in the face of facts. As it happened, Blondlot went insane as a result of his delusions and the subsequent exposure.

Thus we see that scientists are prone to the same faults as the rest of us. They can be blinded by their expectation of new discoveries and can read into their observations much more than is warranted. But proper experimental design, particularly double-blind design, can prevent such errors. We do not expect such procedures from the amateurs, but we must demand them from the professionals. Otherwise, purported scientific discoveries become fanaticism, nothing more.

11

Off the Deep End

One may be able to quibble about the quality of a single experiment, or about the veracity of a given experimenter, but, taking all the supportive experiments together, the weight of evidence is so strong as readily to merit a wise man's reflection.

> —Professor William Tiller,
> parapsychologist, Stanford
> University, commenting on
> psi research

It is the quality rather than the quantity that matters.
> —Lucius Annaeus Seneca
> (4 B.C.–A.D. 65)

Belief in the paranormal is not restricted to persons of lesser intellect. One would think that only children believe in Santa Claus, that witches are the delusions of rural bumpkins, and that astrology is the delight of the senile. Not so. Well-read, educated, intelligent people around the world desert common sense and learning to pursue such matters. What surprised me in the extreme was to find that an organization comprised of the intelligentsia seems overly committed to this brand of nonsense! The group is known as Mensa, and membership is limited to those who possess IQs in the upper 2 percent of the population.

I am not much deceived by the outward trappings of such an organization. Possession of a "high IQ" often has little to do with one's ability to function as a rational human being. It merely means that some admittedly imperfect tests indicate one has a better-than-average potential for good thinking. Like a scalpel that is never put to use by a skilled hand in a good cause, brainpower is often not put to work.

One unhappy Mensa member has kept me notified of current trends in the group. The lead article in the April 1978 *Mensa Bulletin* was entitled "Psi-Q Connection" and asked the pregnant question, "Is there a psychic component to IQ?" The author, Richard A. Strong, is Coordinator of the Psychic Science Special Interest Group and editor of its newsletter. His article wondered if high IQ scores could be due to ESP rather than intelligence—a disturbing thought indeed for Mensa, which may be composed of ordinary folks who cheat and pick up their smarts from others, a sort of cerebral shoplifting!

Some "M's" claim healing powers; many claim to see auras. One Dan Conroy was said to be learning the "sidhis" of Transcendental Meditation so that he could levitate his intelligent body in the air. If he is as successful as the other 39,999 people taught by TM's Maharishi Mahesh Yogi, he's still grounded.

The Special Interest Groups are listed regularly. The July-August 1978 listing contains—besides the "Psychic Science" bunch—Astrology, Dianetics/Scientology, Fortean Mysteries, Graphology, Transcendental Meditation, UFOs, and Witchcraft-Occult. The last group invites us to "Visit the realm of fairies; re-link with the ancient powers." Sure.

At a gathering in Norfolk, Virginia, "IQ Level and TM" and "The Paranormal" were subjects worthy of deep thought. In Rochester, New York, Mensa featured a graphologist and "Psychic Readings." In San Diego, intellects were recharged with "Parapsychology" and "Criswell Predicts"! But the New York City group topped them all with a double-header: "Astrology PLUS Biorhythms" followed by "Pornographic Peruvian Pottery"! And buried in the back pages of the *Mensa Bulletin* we find a seven-line notice from "M" Bob Steiner offering $1,000 to anyone who can perform a wonder of parapsychology that he can't explain or duplicate. There were no takers.

So, if you have in the past fallen for the hucksters of psi, and if you are embarrassed by it all, take hope. The smartest folks in the world are no smarter than you are when it comes to belief in the ridiculous.

The public has been badly served by scientists who lean upon their considerable reputations in other fields to give weight to their declarations on the subject of parapsychology. I have noted that possession of a driver's license permits one to drive an automobile only if the privilege is not abused; perhaps Ph.D.s should similarly be withdrawable in science.

The Computer Age came to parapsychology long ago. Back in the early 1960s, the technology was applied to ESP testing by the United States Air Force Research Laboratories. A specially designed computer setup dubbed VERITAC was used to test thirty-seven subjects with 55,000 randomly generated numbers to determine once and for all whether psi powers existed. Psychologist C.E.M. Hansel, in closing his book *ESP: A Scientific Evaluation*, remarked, about the then-just-started series of tests, "If twelve months' research on VERITAC can establish the existence of ESP, the past research will not have been in vain. If ESP is not established, much further effort could be spared and the energies of many young scientists could be directed to more worthwhile research." When VERITAC tests, supervised by an electronics engineer, a psychologist, a mathematician, and a physicist, were completed, they proved—once again—that subjects do not have the ability to guess or to influence events any better than chance would have it. The team of scientists involved carefully pointed out a fact that in the decade to follow became blatantly evident: Parapsychologists tend to throw out "nonsignificant" data and report the "positive" material.

The "energies of many young scientists" that Hansel hoped could be directed more usefully are still being squandered on the pursuit of nonsense. VERITAC was thrown out as "nonsignificant."

Dr. Thelma Moss has got to be awarded some kind of medal for sheer nerve. The evidence that she is eligible is quite obvious in the discussion of "levitation" in one of her books, *The Probability of the Impossible*. The instructions on how to achieve this miracle are explicit. We are told to seat a person in a chair and have four others stand at the corners of the chair, and then the magic ceremony begins. We need a mystic chant, we're told, and Dr. Moss, in her scientific study of this process, has discovered that the words "hot fudge sundae" are just fine, as is the term "chocolate cake." Her attempts to use "abracadabra," however, have shown that expression to be unsatisfactory.

Each standee holds his or her index fingers together, side by side. Then those standing at the shoulders of the levitee insert these fingers under the armpits, from the rear, and the other two insert their fingers under the knees of the seated person. All chant the magic words of choice and then heave. Lo, the seated person wafts upward and is said to be "levitated"!

If it sounds just like the stunt you used to do at summer camp or at birthday parties, I wouldn't be surprised at all. That's just what it is. Mind you, there are all kinds of variations—placing the hands over the head while chanting, counting backwards from ten, and so on— but it's the same old trick. Did I say "trick"? Not according to Thelma, who goes on in her book to describe other miracles of like nature, calling such things "feats for which science has as yet no explanation." She says the levitation trick "may be a variant of the extraordinary feat performed by 123-pound Mrs. Maxwell Rogers, who, in 1960, lifted one end of a 3,600-pound automobile." Right on, Dr. Moss! May we have further details about this feat, or should we merely choose to believe, as you have done?

And just how mysterious is the "levitation" she describes? Really, if science has no explanation, I fear for that discipline. Any high school student could tell Dr. Moss that a person is easily lifted when the individual's weight is divided equally among four others, all lifting together on cue and having enormous advantages of position to obtain great leverage.

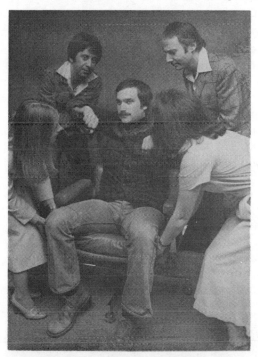

The forefingers are placed in position beneath the "levitee."

Lifting straight upward simultaneously, four people easily levitate a fifth.

But Dr. Moss is not alone in her delusion concerning the stunt. Colin Wilson, in his book *The Geller Phenomenon*—which has the distinction of being liberally strewn with errors—relates an account of the former superstar attempting a "levitation" with Colin himself. Says Wilson, "Uri, Shipi, Trini and another woman tried to lift me. . . . Naturally, it was impossible." But when Uri directs a concerted effort, says the caption under a photo, "immediately the author begins to rise in the air." Here is the assumption that the four could not lift the author, and the suggestion that he then just sails up and away by mysterious powers. This is patently false, and thus is rationality slain by the jawbone of an ass.

Finally, if we really look into the history of this parlor stunt we discover just how old a piece of claptrap it is. Samuel Pepys, in his famous diary, recorded that this trick was being performed by French schoolgirls as an entertainment back in 1665, and it was old even then! The French used a quaint poem to expedite the trick, and one assumes that they did not attain success by using "abracadabra," since modern science has shown that word to be ineffective. We know that, because

Don LePoer, a "levitator," explains how "the power" is given to those of his calling as they raise the victim. Not only is his explanation nonsense; he dropped a man in his attempt to levitate him. Metromedia TV

it has been researched—by a leading parapsychologist, no less. To assist parapsychology in its search for the Secret of Levitation, here is the poem:

> Voyci un Corps mort
> Royde come un Baston,
> Froid comme marbre,
> Leger come un esprit.
> Levons te au nom de Jesus Christ.

My translation of the old French:

> Here is a corpse
> Stiff as a stick,
> Cold as marble,
> Light as a ghost.
> Let us lift you in the name of Jesus Christ.

Pepys had been told of the performance by a friend who witnessed it in France, prompting him to remark that "this is one of the strangest things I ever heard, but he tells it me of his owne knowledge, and I do heartily believe it to be true."

The May 1978 issue of the British publication *Psychic News* head-lined a great "breakthrough" in paranormal research when Brian Inglis, author of a great deal of other nonsense along the same line, penned "An Historic Bending Experience." It soon became clear just what had really been bent. Drawing on an account in the September 1977 issue of the *Journal of the Society for Psychical Research (JSPR)*, Inglis gave his carefully omissive version of an experiment conducted by John Hasted, Professor of Physics at Birkbeck College, London. It was *supposed* to be a report of a major advance in parapsychology but a number of qualifying truths were cunningly dropped among the codswallop: "Psychics do not as a rule perform well in laboratories, or indeed in exacting test conditions of any kind" and "parascience has been pursuing two elusive quarries, quantifiability and repeatability." So much for the "breakthrough."

Hasted had performed many experiments to prove that children have powers enabling them to bend together masses of paper clips inside glass globes. The December 1976 *JSPR* issue described such tests, admitting that it was found necessary to leave holes in the globes and stating that the "scrunch" of paper clips obtained "cannot be produced physically inside a glass globe containing a small hole, but it can be produced paranormally by child subjects under these circumstances." Then, in a follow-up letter to the *JSPR* in June 1977, Hasted admitted that two experimenters (one of them Denys Parsons of the British branch of CSICOP) were able to show that "scrunches" were easily made by perfectly ordinary means in glass globes with an orifice as small as 2.5 millimeters. Exit the experiment.

Another test consisted of hanging ordinary latchkeys from electrical leads terminating in embedded strain gauges to test for bending by paranormal influence. Inglis said these tests were conducted in the homes of the psychics, at their leisure. Children were the subjects, "tests were deliberately kept as informal as possible . . . and the subject was encouraged to do his own thing (making aircraft models) to pass the time."

Rather detailed accounts given by Hasted of the conditions of some experiments led me to suspect that the sharp "spike" tracings he got on his chart recorder connected to the electronic circuitry might be due to static electricity, not paranormal influence. He said the subject squirmed about and held his hands out to the dangling key occasionally, whereupon a result was recorded on the chart. But the very sharp spike is typical of a static discharge registration, so I sent off the circuit diagrams, which were kindly supplied by Professor Hasted, to Dr. Paul Horowitz of Harvard University for comments.

Dr. Horowitz replied, "You are, of course, right in your interpretation. . . . If that 'experiment' convinces anyone of anything, then they typify the utmost in gullibility. What's happening is that common-mode [extraneous] signals, not being rejected owing to a disastrous choice of amplifier configurations, are driving the subsequent amplifiers into nonlinearities. This is a classic problem with strain gauges, since the genuine (normal-mode) signal is typically very small. . . . [It would be] better for Hasted to do the thing right, which means, among other things, to use one of those channels to display the *common-mode* signal, while the rest are busy displaying normal-mode signals. The absence of such a channel shows that he hasn't been careful, and effectively nullifies any result he claims. . . . All data that emerge from that apparatus are worthless, and will continue to be, until the amplifiers are replaced with [proper] instrumentation amplifiers with satisfactory, common-mode rejection. . . . [Hasted] has plenty to do before anyone even mildly critical will believe him."

Dr. Horowitz has just completed a book on electronics. The book discusses the considerable problems inherent in the use of strain gauges, and the specific sensitivity of the Hasted circuit to extraneous signals—such as static charges generated by squirming little boys—is documented.

Brian Inglis commented on the Hasted experiments, saying that the skeptics could now fall back on the "last resort argument, collusion." Collusion? Who needs collusion when the experimenter follows weak methodology and the kid is allowed to do things his way? "Hasted has evolved an experiment which physicists can replicate anywhere," Inglis continues, "given the co-operation of a psychic, with whatever protocol they consider necessary." According to this reporter (he was charmed by the Swann magnetometer report too), the Millennium has arrived. But don't slip into the white robes just yet, folks.

As a conjurer, I must comment on Inglis's closing points. He says that conjurers look upon laboratories as "positive havens for deception." Hardly. Only laboratories run by incompetents would offer a conjurer conditions to his liking. Finally, Inglis writes, "Hasted's work will give stage magicians something to practice in the long winter evenings." Wrong. We conjurers (and other rational people) are too busy trying to figure out how men like Hasted and Inglis are still believed as spokesmen for parascience when the record is so damning. Hasted himself has said, "Validation without high credibility of the validators is inadequate. The credibility of a validator is his own responsibility." Very true. . . .

Hasted's work on this subject is *typical* of the entire field. He is a respected and supposedly competent researcher, revered by the believing public as one of the outstanding scientists at work today in parapsychology. The problem is that the public never gets to know the truth about the misleading experiments and discoveries that are reported by parapsychologists.

Briefly, I will touch upon some of the reports that demonstrate the sloppy thinking and procedures often employed by these people. Again, I will borrow Professor John Hasted's reasoning powers to illustrate the case. In December 1977 I wrote to the *JSPR* expressing my amazement that scientists were having such a hard time designing a simple test to determine the validity of ESP. I referred to the tests of spoonbender Julie Knowles and others, provoking a reply from Hasted. I will enumerate and comment on a few of the points he used in rebuttal.

Referring to my intentions, he said that I was claiming I could "disprove the existence of a phenomenon without even beginning to understand what it is." Wrong. I have never claimed to be able to prove a negative—an impossibility. The burden of proof is on Hasted, who must prove there *is* a phenomenon, not on me to show there is none. The "historic experience" described above is not sufficient. Hasted also charges that "Mr. Randi . . . *demands* that metal be bent in sealed perspex [acrylic plastic] tubes." Wrong again. I have never demanded any such thing. It is the wide-eyed nincompoops (nincompoop: a corruption of the Latin *non compos*—"not of sound mind") who investigate spoon-bending children, who claim the kids can do this. Hasted himself claimed, at the Royal Institution, that his kids could do it! All I'm asking is that they do it for me—and receive my $10,000 and an apology.

Says Hasted, "Dr. Wolkowski [says], 'Girard has bent a nail, a metal strip and a spring inside identified laboratory-sealed glass tubes without orifice.' " Are you sure, John? Wolkowski has also said that Professor John Taylor of King's College was a witness to such a miracle performed by Girard, but Taylor told me, "I am absolutely sure that at no time did [Girard] achieve or even attempt to do anything in my presence. . . . I . . . hope that Wolkowski's memories of that situation become a little more precise." And Wolkowski refuses to answer a simple question I have repeatedly asked him: Where are these sealed tubes?

Julie Knowles was a young English girl who worked with John Hasted as a spoon-bender. According to Hasted she was a good worker, very strong and dependable. His description made her seem like just the

Julie Knowles seated before the clock-mirror-candle setup and holding the spoon. The blackened bowl of the spoon can be seen in the mirror.

one to walk away with my $10,000. Upon my arrival in England on other business, I received urgent phone calls and letters from Mrs. Hasted, begging me to come to Bath to watch tests of Julie in the lab there. I set aside time to do this and showed up in Bath in the company of colleagues to witness this wonder. We sat Julie in the lab and retreated behind a one-way mirror so as not to disturb her. Her mother, looking very fierce, stayed in a remote office, refusing to come anywhere near me except to collect the check. The girl sat there for two hours holding a spoon, the upper bowl of which was blackened with carbon to prevent her touching it without leaving evidence both on her hands and on the spoon that she had done so. Hasted sat nearby, saying constantly that he was seeing the spoon bend and nodding and smiling encouragingly. He had signed an agreement saying that our protocol was satisfactory, and he expected success. I knew damn well that as soon as Julie was discovered not to have any psychic powers working, he would rationalize like mad. I was right.

Hasted later complained that the protocol was complicated (it was not), that I had said Julie was "highly touted" (she was, by both Hasted and his wife), and that I had failed to test the unbent spoon for such changes as "nominal strain, residual stress, dislocation loop density, micro-hardness, grain structure, electrical resistance, specimen dimensions, etc." He ignores the fact that, unlike certain poor experimenters, we who designed the protocol for testing Julie Knowles *specified in advance* that we were testing for gross bending of a simple teaspoon, a feat the girl was said to be able to do. We did not intend to search for obscure peripheral effects and decide after the fact that *any* discovery was signifi-

Professor John Hasted at the Knowles test at Bath University. Hasted remained aloof from the procedure, refusing to have anything to do with the controls and observations.

cant. When Hasted goes to the races he is not allowed to collect at the betting window if a horse he bet on to win comes in sixth and sideways. He simply does not recognize an adequate and proper experiment when he sees one!

Hasted called my conditions for the experiment "crude." No, John, they were simple and direct. Hasted said the spoons used were unlabeled. They *were* labeled, quite adequately and permanently. He complained that only one side of the bowl was blackened. That's quite true. Since we had decided that a downward bend was to be attempted (there's that damned insistence on announcing in advance what we intended to do, in very clear terms!), it was necessary only to blacken one side, where pressure would have to be applied. Blackening both sides would have allowed the possibility that Julie would disturb the blacking on the underside of the spoon in setting it down, which would have invali-

The spoons were easily bendable by this means.

dated the experiment. *We knew what we were doing.* In his rebuttal to my letter in the *JSPR*, Hasted says that he points out these things "in order to deflate Mr. Randi's claims that he is a better witness than scientists." This is a statement I have never made. But I will say that I am a better witness than *some* scientists.

Hasted ended his denunciations with the comment that "experimental design had better be left to professional experimenters and not to professional deceivers." No, Professor Hasted, let us say that experimental design had better be left to *competent* professional experimenters. Then we professional deceivers can get back to the entertainment business.

I hope that my reader has recognized in these retorts to my *JSPR* letter the techniques of misquoting, inventing claims, overlooking the facts, exaggeration, and implying the inferiority of the opponent. They are cheap shots, ineffective at best. I will admit that I cannot manage calculus as I'm sure he can, and I cannot claim his education, but I sure as hell can catch a kid bending a spoon! In fact, any moderately intelligent person can do just that, unless he has a compulsion to play dim-witted.

When Steven North, a wonder-child metal-bender whom Hasted declared genuine, was undergoing tests at Birkbeck College that were attended by Granada TV, a young woman who was with the crew peeked in at Steven during one of the tests in which he was—as usual—left unattended and unobserved except by recorders hooked up to the metal samples. This is a favorite Hasted method of testing children. She distinctly saw him bending a sample with his bare hands and hastened to tell Hasted. But the scientist shrugged it off as an error on her part. Smiling, he said, "Steven may cheat in the *next* world, but not in *this!*" I have no interpretation at all of this comment. It is typically Hastedian.

These methods of experimentation pioneered so bravely by John Hasted have been adopted by Professor Ferdinando Bersari, who teaches physics at the University of Bologna. This researcher tested Italian children, who found that some adults in Italy were just as silly as their counterparts in England. Again, sealed plastic tubes held samples of metals to be bent. "These children cannot be capable of sleight of hand or tricks," Bersari confidently declared in a speech. "If they succeed in producing a paranormal phenomenon, then it must be genuine. . . . I set out Plexiglas containers with the objects to be bent inside. Then I hermetically closed the containers with stoppers made of sealing wax. . . . Sometimes the stoppers were made of acrylic resin, so that the containers were actually welded and had to be broken to be opened. . . . Even under these conditions, a wide range of objects were bent: spoons, screwdrivers, rods of iron, steel, aluminum and plastic."

But again the facts damn the claims. In the description just quoted, the impression is given that the kids could and did bend samples in tubes with *welded* seals. Pressed, Bersari tells us that he cannot produce *one* of the "welded" tubes with a bent sample inside. The others were easily opened surreptitiously, as John Taylor found out in England, but the welded tubes were unsolvable. Later in the same speech, Bersari reveals that he also "observed" his subjects by merely watching a chart recorder in the next room, as Hasted did. But this fact is carefully concealed in the language used.

Bersari's kids were to have met me to try for my $10,000 when I visited Italy, but Bersari suddenly became very shy and decided against it. Funny, but I never met any of Hasted's kids either, except Knowles, and she scored a big zero. Bersari, defending his methods, says that "present research, in spite of the difficulties and absurd prejudices encountered, continues to add valid contributions." Sure.

Another *cause célèbre* that has faded away but made a big splash while it lasted was the "thoughtography" feat of Ted Serios, ex-bellboy turned "psychic," who discovered that by using a simple little device and gathering a few simple minds about him, he could work magic. Serios showed Dr. Jule Eisenbud, a Denver psychiatrist, that he could cause images to appear on the film of a borrowed and controlled Polaroid camera. For two years Eisenbud supported the Polaroid Corporation by purchasing vast quantities of film and having Serios make silly pictures. It was all described in a book by Eisenbud, *The World of Ted Serios*, which documents just how easily a psychiatrist can miss discovering his own delusions. In one episode Serios was asked to produce a picture of the *Thresher*, a nuclear submarine that had just been reported missing. Serios obliged, providing an image Eisenbud claimed actually *was* the *Thresher*, though in metaphorical form. To the untrained mind it *seemed* to be a photo of Queen Elizabeth II of England in her coronation robes, but that just shows how we ordinary folks can miss the great truths of science, not having the extensive training that would enable us to see beyond that mere superficiality. For, as Dr. Eisenbud shows, Queen Elizabeth is easily translated into the submarine.

Now it will be admitted that Liz has put on a few pounds in recent years, but her outline in no way resembles an atomic submarine. The doctor's proof is even more esoteric, as behooves a parapsychologist. Eisenbud explains that the Queen's name in Latin is Elizabeth Regina, and there we have half of it! What? You didn't see it? You'll *never* be a parapsychologist at this rate! Let's look at it again, shall we? ElizabeTH REgina. Is that better? Eisenbud's keen mind discovered the initial four letters of THRESHER in the middle of the Queen's Latin name! How clever of him. Being a Freudian psychiatrist, he might be expected to drag Mom in here somewhere—and he does. Queen Elizabeth is a mother figure to millions. And the sea is the mother of all life, it is said. The *Thresher* is in the sea. The French for "mother" is *mère*. The French for "sea" is *mer*. Note that these two words are similar. Ted Serios is attached to his mother, and her name is—Esther! Isn't parapsychology just grand, folks? For in the name Esther we have the SHER we sought to complete THRESHER!

Serios has faded from the scene, though he was the darling of the psi nuts for quite some time. *Fate* magazine tried to give him a comeback a while ago, running an article with two very fuzzy photos that it said were "psychically" produced by Serios and that were supposed to show the then-fugitive Patty Hearst with short-cropped hair. I have looked at those photos and I cannot see a person, let alone Patty. A few days after *Fate* hit the stands, Patty Hearst was apprehended. She had long hair. A miss? No, of course not. The explanation given for

Serios's boo-boo was that his photos showed her as she *wanted* to be. Or did I lose you somewhere?

Serios accomplished his wonders with a simple device that is easily made. You will need a small, positive (magnifying) lens, preferably about half an inch in diameter and with a focal length of about one and a half inches. The latter can be ascertained by measuring the distance between the lens and the image of a distant object cast upon a piece of paper. You'll need a small tube—as long as the focal length—to hold the lens. From any color transparency (a thirty-five-millimeter slide or a sixteen-millimeter motion picture frame, for example) cut a circle

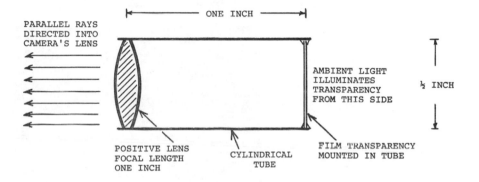

Diagram of a typical Serios gimmick. The left end is held close to the lens of a Polaroid camera focused to infinity and the image on the transparency is thrown onto the Polaroid film.

that will fit onto one end of the tube and attach it with glue. The lens is fitted to the other end.

You use the Serios gimmick by holding it in the hand with the lens end toward the palm. The victim—holding the Polaroid camera, which has been focused to infinity (distant)—is to snap the shutter when your hand is held before the lens. Keep the tube pointing straight into the camera. If it is off-center it will produce smeary pictures, as Serios did on many occasions. The photo that results is usually of poor but interesting quality. The pictures are often in the middle of a Polaroid frame, with a circular shape surrounded by black, as would be expected. If you like, you can be sure your device is not detected by placing a loose tube of paper around it. The device will slide out easily, and you can offer the paper tube for examination, though any parapsychologist will hesitate to look too carefully.

In 1967, writer Paul Welch had a piece on Serios in *Life* magazine that was totally supportive. The paper tube, which Serios called his "gismo" and which was used to conceal his optical device, was never mentioned. Although it was prominent in all of Serios's work, and showed up in most photos, *Life* chose to censor all reference to it to make a better story, for once the "gismo" was made known it would not be hard to figure out that the experimenters were allowing rather wide latitude for procedure in their "scientific tests."

But Eisenbud, leaping to the bait the "gismo" supplied, was quick to proclaim that though Serios *liked* to use the paper tube, he often *did not*, merely holding his hand there instead. When two photographers—Charles Reynolds and David Eisendrath—and Persi Diaconis, a prominent conjuring authority at Stanford University, went to Denver

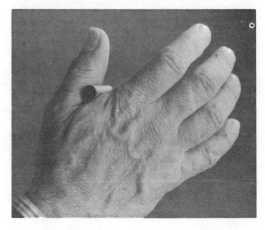

The Serios gimmick as it is held before the lens of a Polaroid camera. It can be concealed by surrounding it with a larger paper tube. The device is secretly and easily disposed of later.

to see the super-psychic in action, they got the same old runaround. After one attempt, Serios quickly placed his hand in his pocket. Diaconis reached for it, trying to intercept the "gismo" before it could be emptied. Eisenbud threw himself between the two men and objected to this action, apparently forgetting that he had invited the three there to observe and that he was now interfering with that observation. A moment later, Serios produced the then-empty paper tube from his pocket for examination. A bit late.

Observers are invited to observe, but are blocked when they look too closely. . . .

Diaconis notes that at one point Dr. Eisenbud had asked of the observers, "If he's only genuine 10 percent of the time, isn't that enough for you guys?" No, it's not. For that 10 percent is well within the noise level of your very loose "experiments," doctor. In fact, a much higher percentage would still be within those very generous limits, given the expert observations of Reynolds, Eisendrath, and Diaconis. But we

When a photographer for *Technology Review* at the Massachusetts Institute of Technology developed a roll of film from his own camera, this was one of the photos. A chair is visible in the photo, superimposed over a shot of the author's hand as it was held against the lens. As can be seen from the in-focus building, the camera was set for "infinite" focus for this shot, which was taken under the same conditions as the famous "psychic photographs" of Ted Serios. Technology Review

will admit that if the experiments had been done with good security and at least a brave attempt at proper control of the subject, 10 percent would be impressive. As it is, no one is impressed or satisfied.

Life chose not to say a word about the Reynolds-Eisendrath-Diaconis investigation, which had shown that the experiments they observed, contrary to what had been said by Eisenbud in his book, were "without adequate control over the essential materials" and revealed "irreparable methodological flaws in all phases of the experiments." *Life* was well aware of both the use of the giveaway "gismo" and the definitive report of the three competent observers, but in order to make a convincing case it ignored the contradictory evidence. When I questioned the magazine's staff about these omissions I was told that "an earlier draft of his [Welch's] story included mention of the 'gismo' struck out of the final version, as Serios does not *always* use it." True. But a murderer does not kill *every* person he meets either. And what of the Reynolds-Eisendrath-Diaconis exposé? Nary a word from *Life* in response.

Eisenbud, demonstrating perfectly the irrationality of his kind, issued a challenge to me following the NBC "Today" show on which we had appeared with Serios and TV personality Hugh Downs. It was his inane idea that I submit to a preposterous set of controls—this after it had become quite plain to all investigators that his Trilby had been allowed to operate under the loosest and most incredible circumstances. I was to allow myself to be searched—including "a thorough inspection of body orifices"—and then "stripped, clad in a monkey suit, and sealed in a steel-walled, lead-lined, soundproof, windowless chamber." I had to be drunk as well. Then, I was to produce pictures. Why? Because Ted Serios operated under those conditions, said Eisenbud. Oh, yeah? When Reynolds, Eisendrath, and Diaconis were there, doctor, the security was so bad that not only was Serios allowed to wander in and out of the room, but Diaconis was able to switch a whole batch of film *right under your nose*, and you never even knew it! And I have all three witnesses (sober, and not in monkey suits).

If this great investigator and peerless observer required Serios to perform under the conditions he outlined for me, why didn't he mention it earlier? I refer the curious to the *Journal of the American Society for Psychical Research (JASPR)*. In that publication Eisenbud wrote thousands of words about his experiments with Serios, referring many times to tests wherein sealed rooms were used, lead glass was employed, and the camera was kept isolated from Serios. I would like to know where in these accounts is mentioned a test of the kind he claims to have performed. It simply does not exist. Also nonexistent are the powers of Serios and the objectivity of those who investigated him.

Dr. Eisenbud is at his best when he writes for the parapsychology journals. There he can throw around terminology that obfuscates the basic facts beautifully. In the July 1967 issue of the *JASPR*, Eisenbud and his associates damn themselves with their own pens. Here they discuss the "gismo" and mention that without it Serios obtains results "no different from the results he gets with its use." They then proceed to describe a "target" attempt in March 1965 in which Serios achieved wonderful things. All six "associates" suggested targets, and Dr. Johann R. Marx suggested a World War I aircraft. Serios and Dr. Marx had spent much time discussing early aircraft, a subject of great interest to both men, and I am not surprised to discover that Serios came along that evening, knowing that Marx would be there, equipped with an appropriately prepared gimmick for the occasion. Eisenbud carefully points out that Serios, during that session, sometimes used the gimmick and sometimes did not, and produced five prints, all bearing pictures of the same general object—part of a vintage plane.

Early in the *JASPR* piece Eisenbud compounds his naïveté by saying of the "gismo" that "indeed, no other reason [than to aid in concentration] for its existence or use has yet been discovered." If Eisenbud had looked at his data carefully, as I did, he'd have seen that a use just might suggest itself, because Serios produced pictures *only* on trial numbers 15, 20, 22, 26, and 33—*the only five during which he used the "gismo."*

To this day, so I'm told, Eisenbud believes that a bellboy from Chicago could imprint pictures on film by miraculous means. His ego simply does not permit him to realize that he was duped, and he will carry his delusions with him to the grave. Perhaps Dr. Börje Löfgren, writing in the *Journal of the American Psychoanalytic Association*, had it right when he described Eisenbud and other parapsychology enthusiasts as "decaying minds" with "thinking defects and disturbed relations to reality." At the very least, it seems that Dr. Eisenbud is not rowing with both oars in the water.

Statistician Persi Diaconis, whom I have known for many years (since his early interest in conjuring), is in a particularly strong position from which to judge the value of parapsychological claims. His knowledge of sleight of hand and mentalism is second to none, and I do not make that statement lightly. Persi is capable of miracles with a deck of cards that would put to shame many a professional magician, and his awareness of the psychological subtleties of the conjurer equip him perfectly for such investigations. Unhappily for the art, Mr. Diaconis long ago chose a more serious profession and today is involved in heady statistical problems. His help as a consultant has greatly assisted my work, and though he has withdrawn from active participation in the CSICOP, he contributes to our efforts when he can spare the time.

A recent paper of his, published in *Science*, the journal of the American Association for the Advancement of Science, stirred up quite a few para-scientists who were castigated in the article. Diaconis correctly pointed out that "modern parapsychological research *is* important . . . [but] poorly designed, badly run, and inappropriately analyzed experiments seem to be an even greater obstacle in the field than subject cheating. . . . There always seem to be many loopholes and loose ends. The same mistakes are made again and again." It stands to reason that if either subject cheating or bad experimental procedure can damn the work of a parapsychologist, then a combination of both these elements double-damns it.

Diaconis has long been examining parapsychological work, not as a passive observer but as an involved investigator. In addition to having been one of the experts called in to examine the Serios-Eisenbud episode, he has been close to the work of Charles Tart, prominent parapsychologist. The case of "B.D.," a card-trick artist who fooled the paranormalists, fell apart under Diaconis's examination.

But of course, there are always examples of these wonders that he cannot get access to, because of the secrecy that often surrounds them, the unwillingness of the investigators to reveal important details of the experiments, or simply the barriers of time and distance. "I have certainly read and been told about events that I cannot explain," says Diaconis. I must of course admit the same thing. I also very much agree with his judgment in another statement he has made: "I have been able to have direct experience with more than a dozen experiments and detailed second-hand knowledge about perhaps twenty more. In every case the details of what actually transpired prevent the experiment from being considered seriously as evidence for paranormal phenomena."

There exists in modern physics a very awkward, far-out, and seemingly egghead concept that will be quite difficult for me to make clear. Reduced to simple terms by means of an analogy, it conveys a startling idea. Suppose that you remove both kings from a chess set. One is black, the other white. You seal each in identical boxes and mix the boxes. You now have no idea which is which. You mail one away to a remote location and return home to contemplate the remaining box. Now get ready—here comes the hard part.

You cannot tell, at this moment, the color of the absent chess king. Mathematically speaking, it is evident that it has exactly a fifty-fifty chance of being either black or white, whichever you choose. If you open the remaining box, you immediately know for sure what the color of the absent king has been all along—correct? Wrong, according to this concept. It maintains that until you open the box that has been retained, the absent box contains *neither the black nor the white king*, but a king that is "half black and half white," so to speak! Opening the box you have causes the other king to *be* the opposite color.

Perhaps you are hoping that the above is a typographical mix-up or the writing of a lunatic, but it illustrates in simplified form what modern physicists tell us actually *does* happen in particle physics—*on a subatomic level only*.

A small digression. We have all learned something about Newtonian physics—falling apples and simple formulas to calculate the behavior of objects influenced by gravity. Then came that troublesome man Albert Einstein, who confused everything with his Theory of Relativity, which was said to be much better than what Newton told us. But that is a judgment subject to interpretation. For example, falling apples are well and accurately handled by Newton's formulas. Einstein adds nothing at all to such calculations. But when we consider the movements and behavior of very large bodies (stars, galaxies), very small bodies such as electrons, or objects moving at very high speeds, Newton fails miserably and Einstein steps forward to supply the tools. It is all a matter of scale, with our ordinary workaday world served by one set of rules and more exotic worlds by another. The laws that Einstein introduced to physics were not operating on the scale that Newton handled; the variables are there but amount to insignificant quantities.

By the same token, we cannot assume that conclusions reached in Einsteinian physics can be applied to answer questions about falling Newtonian apples. That is just what has been done by the "paraphysicists" in their rush to develop a theory to explain what they mistakenly think they have proved to exist; in their world, observations are not respectable without an accompanying theory to explain them.

One of the outstanding authorities in quantum mechanics—the system of mathematically accounting for actions and values on atomic and subatomic levels in terms of tiny "packets" or discrete "quanta" amounts—is enraged at the paraphysicists for this misuse of a perfectly sound theoretical construction. He is John Archibald Wheeler, a former director of the American Association for the Advancement of Science, former president of the American Physical Society, and presently director of the Center for Theoretical Physics and professor of physics at the University of Texas at Austin. And he is very familiar with what has become known as the "Problem of Measurement" and its abuse.

To return to our chess pieces: What holds true in the world of electrons does not govern the world of chess and apples. For example, it is possible to create a pair of photons ("packets" of light) that we know must have opposite directions of vibration, one vertically and the other horizontally. They will split off, traveling in different directions. Discovering the direction of vibration of either photon is a simple process. It is passed through a measuring device, and the direction of vibration is determined. But the photon is altered—sometimes annihilated—by the measurement process. We have had to interfere with the system in order to observe or measure it. However, as soon as we have determined its direction of vibration, we immediately know the direction of vibration of the other, remote photon—which we have *not* measured or interfered with. What it boils down to is that in order to measure on this level, we have to substantially interfere with the thing being measured. The oddity is that we have also measured the other half of the set—and without interfering with it!

I am reminded of a gag I once pulled on Mike Douglas, the TV personality. I was speaking about counterfeit money and asked him to allow me to show him a test to determine if a twenty-dollar bill was fake or not. He offered one for that purpose, and I crumpled it into a ball, switching it simultaneously with another made of nitrocellulose, which ignites easily and leaves no ash. I touched a match to what he believed was his money, and it flashed out of existence. "That," I assured him, "was a *real* bill. Counterfeits won't do that." His expression was priceless, and I had certainly demonstrated the rule that has become known as the Heisenberg Principle—that the act of measuring something interferes with the phenomenon.

Our photon example, a phenomenon known as the Einstein-Podolsky-Rosen Paradox, seems to show that information can be instantaneously transmitted from one photon to the other photon light-years distant. This has delighted the paraphysicists. One such, Dr. Evan Harris Walker, has made the jump into madness by postulating that the secret of it all is the consciousness of the human being doing the observing. But part of his problem, to the dismay of John Wheeler, is that he has misinterpreted the language in which the matter is stated. In physics, "observing" is synonymous with "measuring"; Walker has assumed that a human observer must perform the measuring operation and thus interfere with the thing measured. What is really meant is that a device or other foreign influence—it need not be a human being, and the "consciousness" inherent in that term—interferes with the observed event in the process of measuring it. On the basis of this misunderstanding, the paraphysicists have been sprinting down yet another stretch of the Yellow Brick Road.

In referring to Walker's opinions on this subject, Professor R. A. McConnell, another toiler in the psi vineyard, has employed a term I may not use in this book. Dr. David Bohm, of Birkbeck College, London, has similar feelings about Walker's knowledge of quantum mechanics and its application to psi theory. But Walker became the golden boy of paraphysics with his quantum mechanics theory of psi—until Dr. Wheeler decided to set the record straight.

In January 1979, at a session on "Science and Consciousness" during a conference of the American Association for the Advancement of Science (AAAS) in Houston, Dr. Wheeler discovered to his chagrin that he was a scheduled speaker on a panel that included some parapsychologists, Harold Puthoff and Charles Honorton among them. He made it clear that if he had known this would be the case he'd have withdrawn from the panel. He described the notions of the parapsychologists as "absolutely crazy ideas put forward with the aim of establishing a link between quantum mechanics and parapsychology—as if there were any such thing as 'parapsychology.' " In no uncertain terms he complained that the AAAS had made an error in admitting the parapsychologists as affiliates, and that they had used that affiliation to lend an air of legitimacy to their claims. He was quite correct in this, for one Albert

Moseley, a philosopher at the Mount Vernon Square Campus of the University of the District of Columbia, in a letter to *The Humanist*, called that magazine's exposé of parapsychology "appalling" and said that "the acceptance of the Parapsychological Association as an affiliate of the American Association for the Advancement of Science grants a credibility to research in the area that your articles seem purposely to ignore."

Dr. Wheeler, referring to the decade that had passed since the AAAS admitted the parapsychologists, asked a simple question: "[Has] this field of investigation . . . produced any 'battle-tested' result?" His overall conclusion, in view of the skimpy findings obtained and exaggerated into great significance by the para-scientists, was simply "Where there's smoke, there's smoke." Dr. Wheeler called on the AAAS to oust the Parapsychological Association from its ranks. It is interesting to note that even the AAAS had found it difficult to categorize this ugly child in admitting it as an affiliate. It was the only group listed under the heading "General Category."

On the basis of their spurious quantum mechanics theory of psi, the parapsychologists have clamored loudly for the skeptics to recognize that quantum physics—with the Heisenberg Principle, the Einstein-Podolsky-Rosen Paradox, and other recently popular points of discussion—has given credence to their claims that skeptical attitudes and skeptical observers can inhibit psychic happenings, and that at last there is faster-than-light transfer of information. The thrust of these claims is that only very modern aspects of science, and not the old fuddy-duddy cause-and-effect kind, can be used to validate parapsychology. And they have sought to use John Wheeler as proof of this contention. One paraphysicist, encountering Wheeler at a conference in Europe, threw his arms around him and announced his great pleasure on hearing that Wheeler had at last accepted the paranormal. Indignant, Wheeler categorically denied this absurd assumption before a meeting of the AAAS:

"Henceforth, let us absolve consciousness from the charge of magic. Let us recognize it as a rational part of the biochemical-electronic machinery of the world. Let us not invoke either "consciousness" or "observer" as prerequisite for what in quantum physics we call the elementary act of observation." In other words, the *observer* must not be confused with the *measuring instrument.* The fact that some phenomenon has been recorded as an image on photographic film or as a pulse on magnetic tape satisfies the criteria of physics, and a human being observing the performance of a "psychic" or recording physical effects in connection with such a performance has no more influence than a simple instrument doing the same thing. The skeptic's inhibiting effect on supernatural powers is thus relegated to its proper domain. It is a mere fantasy.

In concluding his speech to the AAAS, Dr. Wheeler urged all

present to "continue to insist on the centuries-long tradition of science, in which we exclude all mysticism and insist on the rule of reason. And let no one use the Einstein-Podolsky-Rosen experiment to claim that information can be transmitted faster than light, or to postulate any so-called 'quantum-interconnectedness' between separate consciousness. Both are baseless. Both are mysticism. Both are moonshine."

Recently, while attending a film of some acrobatics performed by a group of Indonesian martial arts devotees, I expressed my doubts about the "mystical" claims made. I was accosted by a ragged gentleman who started shouting "Heisenberg" in my face. He was trying to get across the idea that I, as an observer, was interfering with the demonstration because of my skeptical attitude. How this could have been true, since I was watching a *film* of the miracles, I could not comprehend. I merely corrected him by insisting that the Heisenberg Principle be applied only on an atomic or subatomic level. He paled a bit, for I was not supposed to know about such things, but then rallied and countered that he was speaking of the *"Psychological* Heisenberg Principle"! How easily basic discoveries of real science are adopted by pseudoscience and metamorphosed along the way! The trick in this case was using the principle on a scale it was not intended for, then switching it to another discipline, and finally renaming and misapplying it. *Voilà!*

Despite the many falling heads in the parapsychology hierarchy, until recently it was difficult for this skeptic to handle the problem presented by the work done in the 1940s by Dr. S. G. Soal in England. Soal reported that he had discovered a powerful psychic, Basil Shackleton, and the half-million tests that were run on him seemed to prove conclusively that he had genuine ESP powers. It appeared to be an airtight case, and Soal's death a few years ago sealed the matter from further investigation, especially since he had reported his original data "lost" on a train. It was a case of choosing either to believe him or to reject his claims. And until recently one had to believe him, it seemed, or call all the investigators liars.

Soal used a table of logarithms to compile a list of numbers from 1 to 5 in random order. He chose the eighth digit from every hundredth logarithm, subtracting 5 when it was between 6 and zero—not by any means a perfect system, but relatively good enough. He would sit with his list and try to transmit each image (represented by a digit) to Shackleton. Shackleton's reply was given orally and written down before witnesses.

Professor G. E. Hutchinson of Yale declared the system "the most carefully conducted investigations of the kind ever to have been made." Professor R. A. McConnell of the University of Pittsburgh said of one of Soal's published works, "As a report to scientists, this is the most important book on parapsychology since . . . 1940. . . . If scientists will read it carefully, the 'ESP controversy' will be ended." C. D. Broad, the philosopher, said that the work was "outstanding. . . . The precautions taken to prevent deliberate fraud [were] absolutely watertight." Even parapsychologist J. B. Rhine gave glowing approval of Soal's design and results. These results *were* truly fantastic—on the order of billions to one against mere chance. The accolades continued to come in from all corners of the globe. Referring to some of Soal's work, Sir Cyril Burt, the grand old man of British science, said, "It must, I think, be agreed that the Soal experiments are unrivalled in the whole corpus of psychological research." Sir Cyril was recently discovered to have faked extensive data himself in research on heredity and even to have invented witnesses and authorities for his reports. A prominent parapsychologist, Professor Beloff of the University of Edinburgh, called Soal's reports "The most impressive evidence we have for the reality of ESP." Of late, he has not repeated that opinion.

Not long after all this acclaim, it began to appear that there might have been some hanky-panky at work. An observer reported that she had seen Soal altering some 1's into 4's and 5's—his 1's were written very short and therefore were easily altered to produce the desired figures. When notified, Soal decided it was not "important enough" to report officially. But in 1973, when Christopher Scott and P. Haskell investigated, the case for Soal's deception was very strong. There were too few 1's and too many 4's and 5's in the target numbers. Many of the 4's and 5's in the list turned out to be "hits" in Shackleton's tests. Apparently, when the target was a 1, and the subject called out "four," it was simple and tempting for Soal to "correct" the 1 to a 4. But— and it is a huge "but"—even with these digits accounted for, the results of the tests were far better than mere chance would have them, and so the tests, though shadowed, stood as the best example ever of ESP proof.

In *Proceedings of the Society for Psychical Research*, Betty Markwick, a statistician, revealed early in 1979 the damning facts about Soal that had not been suspected. Aside from changing a few digits when the opportunity arose, it seems he also cleverly managed another simple ruse. Markwick found—after much labor—the places in the logarithm tables where Soal had chosen his digits. Not only had he gotten unforgivably lazy and repeated some series on the lists without properly arriving at them; he also had left *spaces* in his target list every few digits, into which he inserted "winning" target digits as the tests were conducted. No one had thought to observe him, and in fact they could not, since according to the rules his list was supposed to be secret until presented for checking. But the evidence was there, for the "E.D.s" (extra digits) that had been discovered were "hits" that agreed with Shackleton's guesses. Suddenly, there was no longer any mystery about where these results had come from.

Soal was down and out for good, and the last bigshot in the business was discredited. But it remained to J. G. Pratt, a parapsychologist at the University of Virginia Medical Center, to provide the most astonishing bit of rationalization in defense of Soal that has ever been heard in this field—a field long famous for its Catch-22s and superb alibis. A'though Pratt admitted that he "must put all of this work aside marked to go to the dump heap," he could not refrain from the ingrained tendency to excuse the obvious peccadilloes of his former colleague. The work of Miss Markwick, said Pratt,

> does not provide an unambiguous interpretation . . . that would, for example, justify our concluding that Soal consciously cheated in his research. . . . I am the person who suggested that Soal might have become his own subject on some occasions when preparing the lists of random numbers on the record sheets before the sittings were held. This explanation would require that he used precognition when inserting digits into the columns of numbers he was copying down, unconsciously choosing numbers that would score hits on the calls the subject would make later. For me, this "experimenter psi" explanation makes more sense, psychologically, than saying that Soal consciously falsified for his own records.

What Professor Pratt is trying to tell us, folks, is that S. G. Soal had powers of precognition that allowed him to unconsciously predict the numbers that Shackleton was going to call the next day, and that he unconsciously inserted these predicted numbers into the list! Pratt adds that "we cannot sit in judgement of Soal regarding his behaviour, motives and character."

Oh, yes, we can. And we did. Guilty as charged.

As Walter Levy, Targ and Puthoff, Soal, and other "biggies" among the para-scientists began to crumble one by one, journalists found it more difficult to find heroes to extol. Michael Brown, writing in the magazine *Atlantic Monthly* in 1978, found only one exciting person left in the cast—a scientist from the Mind Science Foundation in San Antonio, Texas, named Helmut Schmidt. It seemed that his experiments were the only ones being done in a properly controlled fashion, and his results seemed to be promising. He was working with highly sophisticated hardware and basic goals. The only problems were that (1) his experiments had not been monitored by outside observers, (2) the experiments had not been properly replicated, and (3) at least one set of results was so bizarre in its implications that even battle-scarred parascientists were loath to discuss the conclusions, especially since they depended entirely upon the quantum mechanics theory of psi that had been refuted by John Wheeler.

I met Schmidt at a meeting of the American Physical Society (APS) in New York. He is an Ichabod Crane type, very much the scientist in his demeanor, properly baggy and charmingly vague. I liked him instantly and consider him to be honest. But I believe him to be a naïve man who has embraced the basic tenet of the paranormal: Any absolute contradiction is evidence of profundity. He spoke at the meeting, calling his talk "Is There a PK Effect?" Happily, it was a question and not a conclusion.

Schmidt spoke of experiments in which a random generator, operating on several levels of randomness at high speed, was used to perform as an electronic "coin-flipper," producing a "head" or a "tail" (or a "yes"-"no," "red"-"green," "plus"-"minus") signal randomly. Subjects were asked to try to influence the generator to produce, for example, more "heads" than "tails"—and it seemed they were able to.

Certain mathematical procedures are involved in such experiments. If you were to flip a fair coin repeatedly and get a result at variance with the half-and-half "heads"-"tails" ratio, you would have to apply simple statistical rules to this outcome to find out if it were significant beyond chance. In essence, 100 tosses must produce 60 "heads" to be deemed significantly beyond chance. That's 10 percent above expectation. But in 50,000 flips, a margin of only 224 "heads" (.45 percent) more than the 50-percent figure is just as significant, and in a million throws 0.1 percent would be acclaimed. Of course, we are assuming perfectly fair tosses and recording methods.

In Dr. Schmidt's experiments, all results were automatically recorded and total, immediate feedback was given to the subject, who thus knew at all times how he or she was doing. The number of experimental "runs" was decided upon in advance. At first, he reported, he got no results, because, he said, he just didn't believe hard enough. What he did notice were small, almost-obscured, negative results when he used ordinary subjects. Then he began testing gifted persons, and the results were heavily negative. But he had allowed for that, he said, since he was in the habit of running a set of preliminary tests to find out if a particular subject on the day of the experiment tended to get negative or positive results, and that tendency would then be decided as the object of that test.

"I have other experiments," said Schmidt, "that did not work out."

How many, we were not told. The number of successes that resulted from the "good" experiments looked very small indeed. Professor Beloff of the University of Edinburgh had tried the same experiment with a random generator and had found nothing.

In the question-and-answer period following Schmidt's talk, the persistent problem of "optional stopping" came up. Briefly stated, if the subject is allowed to stop whenever he or she wants, there is no value to the experiment, since the subject can stop or be stopped when ahead, and the total result is a win, regardless of what would have happened had the test continued. For this reason, the experiment must have an announced number of trials determined firmly in advance, as was done. But optional stopping can also be optional continuing. It's the same problem. If results don't look too good—and remember that Schmidt's subjects had immediate feedback, telling them if they were ahead or not—it is easy to throw in another few dozen trials to see if we can get ahead before stopping.

Schmidt said he ran as many as 4 million "flips" of the generator in a test run to see if it was doing a proper job of fifty-fifty distribution. The machine seemed to be just fine—right on the mark. However, during the experiments, he said, the "flips" ran a small fraction either side of the midpoint line, as if a paranormal force were operating! But, as already mentioned, short runs tend to show greater deviance. Certainly the test run should have been of the same magnitude as the experimental run. As for the normal results of the very long test run, any tendency of the machine to produce a periodic bias in favor of either "heads" or "tails" would be effectively smoothed out. This assumes, of course, that fifty-fifty distribution is the only feature that the 4 million "flips" are used to test.

Also suspect was the practice of running a test series in advance to determine which way (positive or negative) the subject tended to lean that day, for if the machinery had any bias lasting a few thousand "flips," this would simply be testing for that bias, and following that with an official run that would only tend to *exhibit* that bias! The APS audience received assurances, however, that other random generators were periodically substituted during the tests. This seemed like starting a trip in a leaky balloon and carrying lots of repair materials, rather than taking off in a sound vehicle to begin with.

The bothersome thread that wound through all of Dr. Schmidt's talk was that basic defects were accounted for or excused by means of what seemed to be after-the-fact adjustments. When the experimental results showed nothing more than the law of averages, it was because "no enthusiasm" was applied. Negative results were reevaluated as positive ones after certain statistical ceremonies were carried out. There were aspects of the procedure that came to light only after close questioning. The telling moment of the evening came when Dr. Ray Hyman, whose investigations of parapsychological testing procedures have been extensive, asserted that Dr. Schmidt was using the science of statistics far beyond its normal limits and extracting from it much more than was justified by the exhibited results. There seemed to be considerable agreement on this point among the APS members present.

In his reply, Dr. Schmidt seemed to have thought of some means of getting around these objections. But I was most interested in another flaw. I asked him why he had not mentioned the most startling of all his observations, the one that stood out more than any other result ever claimed in the field.

This wonder had already been written and theorized about. It seems that in one experiment Dr. Schmidt set his random generator to work recording a number of "flips" on tape. No person observed the pattern, and no one produced a "readout" (printed record) of the session. The next day, the subject was given the task of influencing the generator, not knowing that the machine was not operating in the usual manner at that moment but running the tape of the night before instead. Bear in mind that the usual job of the subject was to try to psychically influence the machine as it generated the signals; here, the subject was presumed to be able to *go back in time and influence the generator as it existed the night before* when it turned out its tape! Since the Paradox of the chess pieces maintains that the absent king figure is neither black nor white until an observer enters the situation, it follows that the machine's signal is neither "heads" nor "tails" until the will of the subject makes it one or the other! Only when the subject is present and concentrating on the generator will the "consciousness" so beloved of Walker exert its influence, you see.

This is rough going for anyone unfamiliar with the intricacies of this kind of thinking. I'm not at all accustomed to it, and I'm naïve enough to think that a chess piece in a box is really a certain color whether I look or not. Because of this stubborn rationality I am cursed with, a typical ignorant question occurred to me. I asked Dr. Schmidt to suppose that a paper readout of the tape had been prepared immediately after it had been produced by the generator, unseen by human eyes. I asked him to further suppose that it had been mailed off to some inaccessible and primitive part of the world like Middletown, New Jersey, before the test commenced. When the experiment was ended, would the readout match the tape, or would only the tape agree with the observed experiment? His answer was obscure, and I did not follow it. I had hoped to ask for results if it were supposed that 250 copies of the tape (unobserved, of course) had been prepared; would all 251 tapes have been changed miraculously to agree with the observed results? If so, what a prodigious amount of work for the performer—going back in time without being aware of it, and changing all those tapes. Imagine taking a photograph of the readout (without looking!) and checking to see if the undeveloped latent image on the emulsion is also changed. The mind reels in astonishment when one considers the possibilities.

Why had Dr. Schmidt not mentioned these wonders in his lecture? He replied that the matter about which I expressed curiosity was far too complicated to go into in the short time he had. That was probably quite true. But I note that John Wheeler had—only a few days before—delivered his blast at the paraphysicists who had attempted to apply quantum mechanics to their madness, and Schmidt perhaps thought it prudent to avoid getting *that* dragon stirred up again at that moment.

As a result of the Schmidt lecture, the American Physical Society began making noises about conducting definitive tests of the Schmidt claims, beginning with sending Dr. Ray Hyman to San Antonio to observe a series of tests. But here we have a problem. If the observer interferes with the observed phenomenon, would not any failure be attributed to Hyman? And would not any success be similarly credited? Chance results—anathema to parapsychological experiments—might also put in an appearance. What to do?*

At lunch the next day, following a spirited press conference, I asked Dr. Schmidt just what he would do if his claims were proved to be faulty and his results erroneous. He paused for a moment, then looked me straight in the eye. He would not welcome such a turn of events, he said, but he certainly would accept it. I was gratified to hear this, suspecting as I do that this man has slipped into the same rut in which all parapsychologists seem to find themselves: They read into negative or minimal results much more significance than is warranted. Nevertheless, my first impression and present conviction concerning Dr. Helmut Schmidt is that he is an honest man, and I see no reason to summon the tumbrels.

---

* In the more than four years that have passed since Hyman was invited to observe the procedures, Schmidt reports that he has done *no further experiments* of this kind. Surprisingly, in light of the apparently startling nature of these tests.

12

Gods with Feats of Clay

Everyone has some hype going for them . . . can you
prove that it ever did anybody any harm?
—Tony Curtis, actor,
commenting on Uri Geller
and other "psychics"

The subject of religion hardly belongs in this book, but certain aspects must be included. The very nature of religion dictates that it need not offer or claim *scientific* proof of its teachings. (*Philosophical proof is another matter.*) Occasionally some sect or other ventures to produce scientific proof, and this makes it a legitimate target for questions that probe such claims. Some religions have used outright deception in the same way that less respectable individuals and groups have done. These are part of our examination, and quite properly so.

One battle that rages hot is the struggle between the creationists— who thump their Bibles in support of the idea that God created each species independently and instantaneously, then planted fossil bones in the earth to test our faith—and the evolutionists, who preach Darwinism and the evolution of species. There are TV evangelists who give their viewers what seems to be good science, and who would fail a simple school test if they took one.

Jack Van Impe, a TV evangelist who perspires and preaches his version of science regularly to millions of believers, recently gave us an Easter message that reflected his ignorance of science. He referred to the preposterous "Jupiter Effect" so beloved of some nuts, which is supposed to cause wonderful catastrophies in 1982. The Earth should be a mess at the end of this claimed alignment of the planets, and I can hardly wait to see the show. Said Jack, "The Earth will be seven times hotter." Codswallop. The term has no meaning. "Seven" is a number, Jack. If you take the normal temperature to be 70 degrees Fahrenheit, that makes the new reading 490 degrees Fahrenheit. If you're in Europe or Canada, that same temperature is 21 degrees Celsius, giving the other folks a break with 148 degrees C, which is equal to only 298 degrees F.

But, says Jack, the Bible tells us that one of Ezekiel's visions of spaceships was "the color of beryl." This is green. Aha, says this great thinker, isn't it amazing that beryllium (he conveniently or through ignorance pronounced it "beryl-ilium") is used to make alloys for space satellites? The bible sure has the facts, folks! As if to underscore that conclusion, Jack Van Impe assures us that "we're reading the same truths in the *Reader's Digest.*" Well, that convinces *me.*

When naïve individuals cling to a charismatic idea that "bombs out," one would think that the idea would be thenceforth rejected and that the sucker would smarten up. Not necessarily. A chap named William Miller, back in the nineteenth century, predicted for his faithful followers (by means of much arithmetic) that between March 21, 1843, and March 21, 1844, the End of the World would come. His adherents gathered atop mountains to await this important event as the deadline approached. It failed to arrive, and Miller took another look at his calculations. Seems he had dropped a few fractions, and the new date was given as October 22, 1844. Again the dummies gathered expectantly, and when the prediction again fizzled on them, a few abandoned the group. But not all. Today, more than 135 years after the fiasco, the Millerites are still with us, preaching the End and warning of doom. But now they are known as the Seventh-Day Adventist Church or the Advent Christian Church and by a few other names. Nothing succeeds like failure.

Although America must take the blame for having invented the "religion" known as spiritualism, it is in England that it still flourishes most strongly. In the United States there are several centers where this brainchild of the famous Fox sisters is the main industry—Ephrata, Pennsylvania; numerous towns in Florida; Camp Chesterfield; and, of course, California are the leading centers now—but in the United Kingdom every village has its local practitioner, and newspapers are jammed with advertisements extolling the specialties of the various mediums who officiate daily at table-tippings and message-readings. Whether you seek a séance that features "voices in unknown tongues" or one that promises "trumpet communication," you are sure to find your particular need satisfied somewhere.

I try to attend as many séances as I can, wherever I travel. Often I find it difficult to gain admission, since I am recognized. The Devil is not welcome at the wedding. When I manage to blend in with the others, I see exactly the same methods being used to deceive the faithful in every country. Two of the most common gimmicks are the stalwarts of the trade: table-tipping and billet-reading. A brief discussion of these procedures will serve to illustrate just how simple yet devious the methods of operation can be.

The Fox sisters—daughters of an otherwise normal rural family of Hydeville, New York—discovered in childhood how easily raps and thumps might be produced secretly and ascribed to discarnate beings. From toe raps on the footboard of their bed, they graduated to tables, around which the faithful sat. Any noise at all, a creak or a tremor, was considered a communication from Summerland (their cute terminology for heaven). But when the table began tilting about, then rising from the floor, spiritualism was at last airborne. And nothing could keep it down.

There are various degrees of this miracle, and the description of the actual event, as usual, always rises a degree or two, never lowers. In its simplest manifestation, a light table such as the common folding card table tilts upward on two legs while four persons sit around it, hands pressed on the surface with palms down. Often the outer digits of the hands so placed are touching to establish "control" (a word freely thrown about in this business), assuring everyone that no chicanery is possible. This is like tightening the cork on a bottle with a hole in the bottom. Explanations of the table-tipping trick are obvious.

When NBC-TV (before this network totally committed itself to

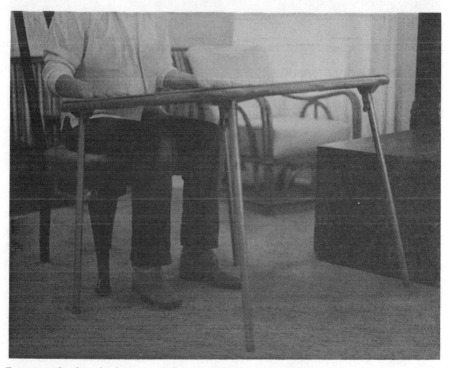

Pressing the hands down and drawing them toward the body causes the table's two far legs to lift off the floor.

Pressing the hands firmly on the tabletop and pushing to the left causes the two right-hand legs to rise.

supporting such matters) called on me back in the early 1960s to oversee a table-tipping conducted in the apartment home of Mrs. Nandor Fodor, widow of the prolific writer on poltergeists and other wonders, the planned filming went down the drain after I was able to establish the *modus operandi* for this activity. In this case, the mediums were a woman and her teenage son, whose method was to sit opposite one another while the table cavorted. Immediately complaints were raised about my "negative presence," so I offered to leave the séance after telling the NBC-TV crew how to set up proper conditions. The performer was required to sit against the wall, with hands flat on the table and elbows pressing two pieces of cardboard against the wall. Any attempt to creep the hands forward for a horizontal pull to tilt the table would cause the cardboard pieces to drop. They did, several times, and the experiment was called off.

Such simple, direct tests are easily designed by anyone. But they inhibit psychic phenomena for some strange reason. . . .

The second stage of table-tipping involves actual "levitation" and was a feature of the famous Eusapia Palladino, an Italian medium who visited the United States and was finally exposed—though not in the opinion of the believers—by experts who troubled to open their eyes and declare the truth. She used a variety of methods, to judge from the reports, but one standby involved the use of her foot and one hand in what has come to be known as "The Human Clamp." It takes a fair amount of strength and some weaseling about, but both required qualities were available to her in full.

The edge of the sole of the shoe is placed under the tip of the table leg. These table legs are often equipped with a rubber "bumper" that raises the wood from its contact with the floor a distance about equal to the thickness of the leather sole. Thus the insertion of the shoe is quite easy. If no bumper is present the maneuver can still be done by jogging the table up momentarily onto the small shelf of the sole. Next, one hand is placed directly above the table leg used. By pressing down hard with the hand and raising the foot, the performer

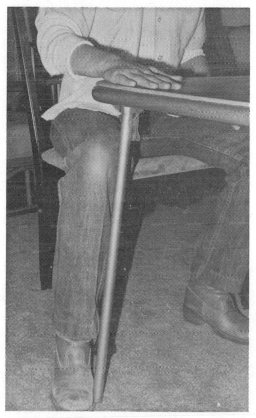

The edge of the shoe is inserted under the tip of the leg of this light card table, the hand is pressed down hard, and the foot is lifted. The result is that the table rises straight up, with all four legs off the floor.

can cause the table to rise *straight up*, all four legs off the floor, for a short distance. If it then slips off the shoe and crashes to the floor, the effect is just as good as when a slow descent is made. And there are no gadgets to get rid of, no wires or hooks at all. The performer is "clean" and may be searched before and after the levitation.

The art of billet-reading, another standby of the spiritualists, is done in full light and using the simplest of ruses. Because it is so simple it is quite deceptive. The method used simply does not occur to the observer, who is looking for something very sophisticated.

In 1960 I was invited by author William Lindsay Gresham to attend a meeting at Camp Silver Bell in Ephrata, Pennsylvania, a spiritualist stronghold from which Bill had gotten a report of visitors' mail having been opened at the hotel adjacent to the church. We were accompanied by Stewart Robb, a well-known writer and believer in psychic phenomena, to whom we were determined to demonstrate the truth about what he had always believed to be the genuine ability of mediums.

We tried to participate in some of the specialized séances, noting at some establishments a large board with chalked-in miracles such as "slate messages," spirits communicating in Egyptian (ancient, of course), and varieties of table-tipping and thumping about. But we were unknown to the very severe-looking guardians of these events and could not pass inspection. We settled for the regular all-welcome message reading offered in the main church. At the door we were asked to write on an ordinary file card a statement about something personal, then were told to place it in an envelope and tuck the flap inside. We were then to write our names on the outside and deposit the envelope in a huge basket. We all did so.

After much "Rock of Ages" singing, the main business was begun. (Oh, I almost forgot. A collection was taken to defray costs. A rather important and never-neglected aspect of all such religious activities.) An insipid little man came out on the platform, walked to the lectern bearing the basket of envelopes, and summarized what we had been asked to do. We learned, too late, that we were supposed to have written only our initials on the envelope, and the card was to have had on it a personal question that needed an answer. Having fouled up the procedure, we felt like idiots. But—and this is the important point—*we wrongly assumed* that everyone else had done the thing right—that the other envelopes bore only initials and questions.

To prove to Stewart the method of deception practiced at this gathering, we had prepared him and his envelope. The flap had been slightly moistened and stuck to the card inside, and his envelope had been sharply folded. That way, we could see plainly if his envelope came up in the sequence. We sat and awaited that possibility. The operator began by glancing at the first envelope, reading the initials, and holding the envelope above his head. He babbled on about ghosties and other bump-in-the-night things, finally getting down to the apparent contents of the envelope and giving an innocuous reply to the question inside apparently without having seen it. He then opened the envelope to check the contents, nodded in a satisfied way, and discarded it. On to the next.

The method is known as One-Ahead. The performer came out there knowing the contents of *one* of the envelopes in advance. That envelope had been put at the very bottom of the basket. In picking up a new envelope, he had deliberately misread the initials, calling out those on the discarded envelope. All had assumed that he held that one in his hand at that moment. Actually the one he waved about was entirely strange to him. The reading he gave included divining the entire name from merely the initials, but he only *seemed* to be doing this, because others had done the same as we, *writing their entire names* on the envelope front. They were following the same instructions we'd received. Then, using the *statement* he had peeked at in advance, he turned it into a question. Opening the envelope he held as if to check the value and truth of his answer served to give him another message and name, which he would apply to the next strange envelope he held up over his head.

But as the medium picked up a *folded* envelope, Stewart sat up and took notice. A long rambling message followed, one that had nothing to do with Stewart's statement, and the initials he had called were not Stewart's. Yet the envelope he held seemed to be his, a supposition that was verified as the performer opened the envelope—supposedly to check his answer—and the flap audibly tore away from the card he removed from inside. It was no surprise when the next envelope he picked up was announced to bear the initials S.R.

The development of the message was interesting. The performer immediately "got an impression" of a child, a boy, name beginning with P—Peter, known fondly as Petey in both this life and now in the hereafter. With him, continued the man, were Jimmy and Annie and Bobby. Were any of these names familiar? Yes, answered Stewart, he once knew a Bobby. The message reading ended, and the performer opened the envelope he held. Much nodding and smiling followed, as if the man derived great satisfaction from the information given him by the spirits.

The message that had been written was, "Petey is in spirit. I hope he is with his friends." Petey, unknown to both performer and his ghost friends, had been a parakeet who expired the day before. The other names given by the man were names that almost *had* to hit somewhere. There was little mystery to the reading Stewart had received.

The usual process in a One-Ahead session is to provide only a dozen or so readings, then invite those whose messages have not been used to attend a private séance, arranged through the front desk. After having seen "proof" of the miracles promised, many would be willing to arrange for an expensive private reading. And the envelopes bearing full names and statements would be great ammunition in these subsequent encounters. These operators use everything but the squeal of the victim.

Bear in mind that this is only one (though the most widely used) of the billet-reading methods. Whole books have been written on the subject and the multitude of techniques available. There are two elements in it: First, to determine what is written on the paper without it being evident that this has been done. Second, to develop this information in a clever manner that implies knowledge of more than what was written. At Camp Silver Bell we saw some performers who were pretty poor compared to others I have encountered. A real pro would not have touched a folded envelope under any circumstances.

In 1976 Lamarr Keene, a spirit medium who had bilked thousands of Florida residents out of their fortunes, decided to give it up. He confessed all to the IRS and to readers of his book, *The Psychic Mafia.* In 1977 I interviewed him and discovered that he knew little about the more subtle methods of chicanery. He explained to me that he didn't *need* to know much. Anything he did would serve to convince the faithful, he said. They fell for the most transparent ruses, many of which were thought up on the spur of the moment, and he and his fellow charlatans laughed themselves silly, at the end of an easy day's work, as they recounted how simple it had been. Keene's book caused a storm in spiritualist circles. Threatened by phone and letter, he moved from place to place to avoid his former friends in the business, who told him they were out to get him. He went into the import trade, changed his name, and hoped to settle down. But his book was not wrongly named. One night, as he emerged from his shop, a car pulled up and shots roared out. Lamarr Keene fell to the pavement, hit in the midsection. As of this writing he is recovering after long hospitalization. His "friends" had attempted to make good their threat.

One voice that was almost silenced by different means is that of Paulette Cooper, a free-lance writer. In 1971 she wrote *The Scandal of Scientology*, a book critical of this cult, founded by L. Ron Hubbard. The book was almost immediately withdrawn by the publisher when the Scientologists sued her for fifteen million in damages. Remaining copies were destroyed, and the Church of Scientology set out on a project code-named "Operation PC Freak Out" to discredit and harass Ms. Cooper. In return for her determination to speak out, she has suffered ever since. She was robbed, threatened with a gun, and vilified in letters sent to her neighbors saying that she was a sexual deviant with venereal disease. As a capper, she says she was framed on the charge of making bomb threats against the church—a federal offense—and came very close to being locked up. Her efforts to defend herself cost her more than $32,000. Then, suddenly, there was a turnabout, as a fresh element was introduced into the case.

Federal warrants fell on the Scientologists like rain when they were discovered rifling the files of government officials who were looking into their affairs. As a result, in October 1979, eight Scientologists were convicted of conspiracy in federal court. The defendants, including the new head of the church, were sentenced to prison. Information about "Operation PC Freak Out" also was discovered, and Cooper made her own trip to the bar of justice with a $40-million suit against her oppressors.

Hubbard, anxious to protect the flimsy foundation upon which he had constructed his quasi-religious, quasi-scientific cult, was quite direct about what means might be used to wage war. He issued a "Policy Letter" (copies of which leaked out) specifying that lawsuits should be used as a weapon against enemies—known to the Scientologists as "SPs" ("suppressive persons")—not with any hope of winning the lawsuits but for the purpose of breaking the SPs financially. Scientology, with its claimed 4 million membership (the actual number is probably about 50,000) has wealth amounting to untold millions in cash and property and is far better able to withstand a lengthy legal battle than its opponents.

Another charming aspect of this "religion" is a directive that announced the policy of "fair game." Under this operating principle, any persons who drop out of the church may be "sued, tricked, lied to or destroyed" by any means. A beautiful thought, don't you think?

In late 1979 a Toronto newspaper reporter was looking through the Scientology files seized by the U.S. government and made available in Washington. These were the records upon which the successful federal case was based. The newsman came upon a sheaf of documents headed (in true science fiction–comic book style) "Guardian Programme Order 1074." It concerned a confidential order issued in England to "WW" (worldwide) offices of the Scientology church and called "Programme: HUMANIST HUMILIATION." This was a plan to handle "terminatedly" the Committee for the Scientific Investigation of Claims of the Paranormal and *The Skeptical Inquirer*, the official journal of the CSICOP.

Recipients were cautioned in this semiliterate document that "Security must be maintained so that there is no come back [sic]." The idea was to create the impression that the CSICOP was supported by the U.S. Central Intelligence Agency. Thus, the Scientologists reasoned, the public would believe that the CIA was attempting to monopolize psi research and keep it ultra-secret. From the Scientologists' point of view, discrediting the CSICOP was essential, since the Hubbard nonsense is dependent on a belief in the paranormal.

Another angle of Order 1074 was to convince the leaders of major religions that the CSICOP was out to get them too. This was to be done by circulating bogus letters on CIA letterheads. Although the whole fairy tale seems to have failed to get off the ground, several fake letters were sent out on duplicated CSICOP letterheads, but they were pretty obvious forgeries that fooled no one.

Exposure of the many zany "programmes" described in the seized files of the group wiped out the whole James Bond operation, and the Scientologists stood exposed for just what they are.

It will take some time, but I think that Paulette Cooper will see the Scientology colossus topple. In Paris, in 1978, Hubbard was convicted *in absentia* of illegally soliciting funds, heavily fined, and sentenced to a prison term. In England, a group of Scientologists was denied entry into the country to hold a convention because according to British laws their cult did not qualify as a religion. Michael Meisner, at one time the fifth highest official among Scientologists in the United States, reported that the church put him under house arrest, gagged and handcuffed him, and tried its version of brainwashing on him—they call it "auditing." His defection, of course, now makes him "fair game" under Scientology rules. Nice bunch of folks.

In late 1978 the world was shocked by a horror that as a fictional plot would have been rejected by the most charitable editor of fantasy fiction as too preposterous to be considered. Who would believe that nearly a thousand adult human beings would stand by while others murdered their children and close friends and then would voluntarily drink grape-flavored Kool-Aid that they knew had been mixed with cyanide? Yet on the instructions of an egomaniac who called himself both a minister and a god—and was believed—the inhabitants of a failed utopia called Jonestown in Guyana, South America, did just that. The quesion Why? has been echoing about ever since.

"Reverend" Jim Jones was as charismatic a leader as any who ever swayed reason. Despite his farcical philosophy, he managed to convince a considerable number of California's populace that he had a direct pipeline to the gods and to salvation. With the kind of sleight of hand

and sleight of mind that characterizes such charlatans, he "proved" that he could raise the dead—he performed the "miracle" forty-seven times in his church—and showed his followers that he was able to cure cancer and other afflictions by removing masses of organic junk from their bodies. After his death, cult members came forward to testify that, after threats from Jones, they had agreed to fake death and then stage instant resurrections. The surgery was even simpler than that still being performed by the "psychic surgeons" of Brazil and the Philippines. Jones merely reached beneath the clothes of the intimidated faithful and pulled out chicken gizzards and other material, according to witnesses. Those who did not see through the tricks were convinced; those among his loyal followers who *did* recognize a trick when they saw one forgave this good man for the small deception because it was necessary to sell his point.

Because the effects of Jones's ministry seemed so beneficial, and because he used his ministry politically, prominent public figures sent him letters and affidavits of approval and appointed him to important positions. The "miracles" he performed were a bit of fun, after all; who would be hurt by a few conjuring tricks in the name of charity? The abattoir of Jonestown was a grim answer to that naïveté.

Consider, for a moment, the following information: A man who preaches love and tolerance is recognized by political and civic leaders as a man of God. He runs a wealthy and growing church. He can show his power to raise the dead and cure fatal illnesses, and no one denies his abilities. He creates and promotes interest in a community in another country wherein followers will be safe from the evils of pollution and prejudice. He teaches them methods of self-defense, warns them against "outsiders," and is obeyed and believed in all he does. Would it not be logical to follow this man wherever he leads? Such is the thinking of idealistic, lost souls who are easily deceived by appearances.

Some perhaps reasoned: If he were a fake he would not have had the support he displayed and the endorsements he advertised. Those who might have been misrepresented in his claims surely would object, wouldn't they? His tricks—if he had any—would surely have been exposed immediately, don't you think? Yes, that is what *should* have happened. But *no one spoke up and denounced Jones* early in the game— or at *any* point prior to the mass murder/suicides of November 18, 1978. U.S. Congressman Leo Ryan, certainly a hero among heroes, was one of the very few who bothered to get up on his feet and bitch about it. Ryan, who flew to the jungle settlement to investigate rumors of strange goings-on there, got his face blown off for his trouble. To thank a man like that is impossible—except by following his example and yelling loudly when another Jones comes along. The face and name will be different, but the methodology will have the same old smell. And there are others even now scrambling to replace Jones.

Aside from the failure of the knowledgeable to blow the whistle, the main reason people follow a Jones is that they abandon critical judgment on the assumption that their leader is infallible. Consider the Unification Church of the "Reverend" Sun Myung Moon. He tells his fanatical followers that a "New Messiah" is coming and that he will be a Korean male born this century. Moon is a Korean male. He was born in this century. He says that this "Third Adam" will become the father of a "Perfect Family" that will redeem mankind. Moon, who has had several marriages, is certainly a father—seven times over. When asked uncomfortable questions, Moon replies to his disciples— who may be seen in the streets of New York City begging money—"I am your brain." Obviously, the busloads of young people who are daily carted off to posts throughout Manhattan (from the church's headquarters at the former Hotel New Yorker) to solicit funds for the millennium believe this statement and are happy with it. *Would they, too, drink cyanide if Moon commanded them to?*

Synanon is an organization whose leader is presently accused of attempted murder with a venomous snake. *Would its members drink poison if told to do so?* L. Ron Hubbard, a science-fiction writer, told a select audience years ago that the secret of success is to find out what people need and sell it to them. He then went to the typewriter and invented the pseudo-science known as Dianetics. This segued into a supposed religion, with all the protection that implies, called Scientology. To his adherents, Hubbard is infallible too. The federal court case against him has already told us of the devotion Hubbard inspires. *Is it enough to drive the believers to sip cyanide?*

The Children of God, Eckankar, and Transcendental Meditation sects are run by leaders who have obtained fanatical followings as a result of philosophical claptrap and/or other flummery. Miracles are claimed, and scapegoats are drummed up. And few speak out. *When is the next poison party to be held?*

In 1977, during the annual meeting of the Committee for the Scientific Investigation of Claims of the Paranormal, a question was asked at the press conference. A reporter wanted to know what damage belief in the paranormal could do. Was it not just a harmless, if somewhat nutty, pursuit? Our answer was that such irrationalities lead to victims' losing their sanity, their money, and sometimes their health and lives. In response to that comment, the *Washington Star* trotted out its finest editorial style to treat the CSICOP as if it were a group of old ladies who had scolded once too often. The newspaper remarked:

> Nothing is funnier than the misapplication of a rigorous
> discipline to tasks disproportionately trivial. It is overkill. It is
> classic gnat-killing by sledgehammer. It is the machine-gunning
> of butterflies . . . the line between sense and nonsense is not,
> we think, so stark as these earnest vigilantes of science make it
> out to be, nor the dangers of mass popular delusion so menacing.
> . . . What has happened to their funny-bones?

I do not know who wrote that, but he must know that it infuriated
more than one member of the CSICOP. That writer never saw the
distraught faces of parents whose children were caught up in some stupid
cult that promises miracles. He never faced a man whose life savings
had gone down the drain because a curse had to be lifted. He never
held the hand of a woman at a dark séance who expected her loved
one to come back to her as promised by a swindler who fed on her
belief in nonsense. "Nothing is funnier . . ."? Tell that to the academics
who lost their credibility by accepting the nonsense about telepathy
that came out of the Stanford Research Institute. "The machine-gunning
of butterflies"? Explain that to those who spent their time and money
trying to float in the air because a guru said they could. Are the "dangers
of mass popular delusion" not "so menacing"? Mister, go dig up one
of the 950 corpses of those who died in Guyana and shout in its face
that Reverend Jim Jones was not dangerous. "What has happened to
their funny-bones?" That deserves an answer. Our collective sense of
humor has been dulled by the grief, frustration, and anger that comes
of preaching in the wilderness. The *Star*, apparently, would like that
wilderness to continue to be empty of rational forces.

I hope they enjoyed their big laugh.

13

Put Up or Shut Up

Nothing ever becomes real until it is experienced.
—John Keats

During a radio panel discussion back in 1964, I was challenged by a parapsychologist to "put your money where your mouth is," and I responded by offering to pay the sum of $10,000 to any person who demonstrates a paranormal power under satisfactory observational conditions. I have carried around with me ever since a check in that amount, immediately awardable to a successful applicant. In response to that challenge, over 650 persons have applied as claimants. Only 54 (as of this writing) ever made it past the preliminaries, and none of them ever got a nickel.

The offer is still open, and will be during my lifetime. It is stipulated in my will that if the amount is still unclaimed and available upon my death, the same offer will be made by my estate in perpetuity. The money was never safer.

The realm of the paranormal being the strange never-never world it is, the parapsychologists are now having at me because the offer has been made, not because I failed to make it! Now I am called a cheap showman who depends on theatrics to impress the public. You can't win. The nutties are so used to having it both ways that they expect it in all things. They say they'll die—and also live. When an ESP test succeeds, it proves their case; when it fails, it is called a "negative success" and also proves their case. They want scientific investigation—and then they say it's too "artificial." They complain that I won't put up my money—and call it cheap theatrics when I do.

Mind you, I decided from the beginning—when I began to get calls from a contender in Oregon asking for air fare for a flight to New York so that he could show me a few tricks—that I was not about to invest any "up front" money in the matter. Such persons must pay their own way, and do it at my convenience. But I have never refused an applicant, and never will if the offer is made seriously. Here, for those who may be interested, is my latest formal offer:

This statement outlines the general rules covering James Randi's offer concerning psychic claims. Since claims will vary greatly, specific rules will be formulated for each individual claimant. However, *all claimants* must agree to the rules set forth here, before *any* agreement is entered into. Claimants will declare their agreement by sending a letter so stating to Mr. Randi. All correspondence must include a stamped, self-addressed envelope, due to the large amount of mail exchanged on this subject. Thank you.

I will pay the sum of $10,000 (U.S.) to any person who can demonstrate *any* paranormal ability under satisfactory observing conditions. Such a demonstration must be performed under these rules and limitations:

(1) Claimant must state in advance just what powers or abilities will be demonstrated, the limits of the proposed demonstration (so far as time, location and other variables are concerned) and what will constitute a positive or a negative result.

(2) Only the actual performance of the announced nature and scope will be acceptable, done within the agreed limits.

(3) Claimant agrees that all data, photographic materials, videotape or film records and/or other material obtained, may be used by Mr. Randi in any way he chooses.

(4) Where a judging procedure is needed, such procedure will be decided upon in advance after the claim is stated. All such decisions will be arrived at by Mr. Randi and the claimant, to their mutual satisfaction, in advance of any further participation.

(5) Mr. Randi may ask that a claimant perform before an appointed representative, rather than before him, if distance and time dictate that procedure. Such performance is only for purposes of determining whether claimant is likely to be able to perform as promised.

(6) Mr. Randi will not undertake to pay for any expenses involved on the part of the claimant, such as transportation, accommodation, etc.

(7) Claimant surrenders any and all rights to legal action against Mr. Randi or any other participating agency or person, so far as may be legally done under present statutes, in regard to injury, accident, or any other damage of a physical or emotional nature, or financial or professional loss of any other kind.

(8) In the event that the claimant is successful under the agreed terms and conditions, Mr. Randi's check for the amount of $10,000 (U.S.) shall be *immediately* paid to that claimant, in full settlement.

(9) Copies of this document are available to any person who sends a stamped, self-addressed envelope to Mr. Randi requesting it.

(10) This offer is made by Mr. Randi personally, and not on behalf of any other agency or organization, though others may be involved in the examination of claims submitted.

(11) This offer is open to any and all persons in any part of the world, regardless of sex, race, educational background, etc., and will continue until the prize is awarded.

(12) CLAIMANT MUST AGREE UPON WHAT WILL CONSTITUTE A CONCLUSION THAT HE/SHE DOES *NOT* POSSESS THE CLAIMED ABILITY OR POWERS. This will be a major consideration in accepting or rejecting claimants.

NOTARIZED: Signed
State of New Jersey
Jane V. N. Conger   JAMES RANDI

County of Monmouth
Signed before me this 18th of June, 1981

Just who has shown up in the last fifteen years to claim this handsome sum? Only two types: those who honestly believe they have the claimed powers, and those who are outright fakes. The first group far outnumbers the second, I have found. The fakes are unwilling, if they're smart, to accept my offer.

There is one rather cute angle that the second class has adopted when accepting my offer. It is to refuse ahead of time to accept the money if the test is passed—not that anyone has ever even come close to passing it. When the contestants enter the arena proving pureness of motive by surrendering all claims to the $10,000, the mantle of saint-hood seems to fall upon them. But I don't much believe in saints, so I'm not impressed at all. I'm just a bit warier.

For example, Jean-Pierre Girard, in France, and Suzie Cottrell, in the United States—both claiming to be psychics but demonstrating simple sleight-of-hand tricks when examined—refused the reward in advance, should they be successful. In both cases I was told by their entourages that such crass things as a monetary reward would provide "negative atmosphere" and inhibit their performance. Strangely, as soon as the conditions were proper for observation, neither person could perform, try as they might.

To relate all the cases that I have examined would be beyond the scope of this book. I am not writing *Paradise Lost*. But I will spend some pages detailing a few cases typical of the general run of attempts that have been made to get rich at my expense. In some, it was quite a pedestrian attempt that followed predictable patterns; in others, the approach was novel and clever. We will begin with one of the latter, which took place in Buffalo, New York, in 1978.

Suzie Cottrell is a rather pretty twenty-year-old blonde from Meade, Kansas. Some months before she came to my serious attention, and that of the Committee for the Scientific Investigation of Claims of the Paranormal, she had appeared on the "Tonight Show" on NBC-TV, performing a card trick and apparently fooling the show's star,

Johnny Carson, who has had a reputation as a magician since his early days in the entertainment business. Carson had told me previously that he was not about to allow anyone who claimed paranormal powers on the show unless that person would submit to controls. One such, Mark Stone, had approached the staff of the Carson show asserting that what he demonstrated was the real thing. That night, Carson wiped him out by suggesting a simple change in the conditions of the trick, and Stone failed. Johnny told me that Stone's manager had insisted that he be presented as the real thing, and that he was willing to be put to the test. He was.

It was not too difficult to see why Carson had been fooled by Suzie. He's a sharp and observant man, but a pretty twenty-year-old farm girl was too much for him when she performed a rather obscure card trick that Carson was unlikely to be familiar with. Besides, I have heard a story concerning one Jimmy Grippo, a highly skilled card worker in Las Vegas who is said to have touted Cottrell to Carson and to have provided a demonstration of her talents for Johnny in advance of the NBC appearance. Suddenly, everyone is mum about this story, and Grippo is denying having anything to do with pretty Suzie. One wonders. . . .

It turned out to be Suzie's father who had contacted the CSICOP,

Suzie Cottrell. Buffalo Evening News

asking that his daughter be carefully tested. It was also specified that my own offer of $10,000 must not even be mentioned, to avoid imparting a crass commercial flavor to the procedure. After some negotiations, the date of March 16, 1978, was agreed upon, and Paul Kurtz, Chairman of the CSICOP, gave Martin Gardner and me responsibility for designing and controlling the procedure. We prepared a testing area by installing a videotape camera and outlining with white tape the exact area to be covered by the camera. This was to be the limited test area in which all action had to take place. Should Suzie's hands or any of the cards wander out of the test area, the experiment was to stop immediately and return to "ground zero," all materials being confiscated and held for examination. We had a good number of decks of cards, all labeled and fresh. And, most important of all, we were going into the fray with a definitive statement that had been read and understood and agreed to by Suzie Cottrell and her group.

A word about that last circumstance would be proper at this point. In my thirty-five years of looking into these matters, I have found that the most common reason for failure to come to any firm conclusion in such testing procedures is the lack of a firm understanding of the conditions and parameters from the beginning. Thus I insist that the subject must know in advance exactly what is expected, must agree in advance that conditions are satisfactory for the demonstration of whatever miracle is to be shown, must know exactly what will be accepted as proof, and finally must agree to abide by the decisions reached under these conditions. This way, second-guessing and weak rationalizations for failures are not acceptable.

We told Suzie that from the moment she entered the test room she would be under video surveillance, and she agreed to that. We asked if all was well—the "vibrations," the weather, the time of day, and so on—and she agreed that things were just dandy. She'd had a press conference in which she mentioned how nervous she was, and we wanted to eliminate that alibi as a reason for any failure that might be noted. But she assured us of her excellent state of mind, and we were all ready to go. After Suzie and her dad signed the agreement, we entered the test room.

A TV camera was perched on a tripod, its lens fixed on the marked-off table. Unfortunately an ABC-TV camera crew was there as well, and in spite of my admonitions not to block our camera setup they did so repeatedly, but fortunately not at any moment of import. The subsequent story was not used by ABC in a documentary they were preparing about the paranormal. The reason for this was not made clear, but I think that since Suzie failed utterly it was the kind of thing they call a "non-story." If she had been in any way successful, however, I suspect it would have been a prime-time special. That's the way it is in this business: The successes are glorified and the far more numerous failures and exposures are discarded.

A reel-to-reel videotape machine sat on the large table, off to one side. Psychologists Irving Biederman and Jim Pomerantz from the State University of New York at Buffalo were there, since we needed their careful observations and recordkeeping for future analysis of what we were about to see. Martin and I sat behind the chair in which Suzie would be seated, each to one side about five feet away. Several other people from the university were there to act as a subject pool for Suzie to choose from.

We questioned Suzie about her abilities. She said that she could name all the cards in a face-down deck "some of the time." We expressed dissatisfaction with the vagueness of this estimate, and she then estimated her success rate to be forty-eight out of fifty-two, on the average. Concerning several other feats that had been attributed to her in the newspapers, and which she mentioned in interviews, she gave similar estimates of success rates. But one demonstration, the stunt on the Carson show, was the one she said was her best. She was "almost invariably" successful with that one.

Briefly, the routine in question consists of her predicting, in writing, which card will be selected by someone else from a spread-out, face-down deck. In addition, the deck used is a new, shuffled deck not supplied by her. The choice is quite free, the prediction is written down well in advance, clearly and boldly, and the paper is retained by another person, not Suzie.

What you have just read is what the popular press has seen fit to use as a description of the Cottrell routine. It is quite correct—as far as it goes. As the reader will discover, there are a few "twists" involved that make it far less than convincing as a psychic marvel.

But back to the lab: While the videotape machine near her remained at the ready but not running, Suzie was told that she would be allowed to perform her special routine without any controls. But she also was made to understand that this would not be part of the test, only a warm-up. She agreed, but not until her father was ushered out of the room. He made her nervous, Suzie told us; the father averred that this was usually the case and that he was accustomed to being put out of the room when Suzie worked. There was a bit of chuckling at this comment, but Martin and I exchanged glances. Something was becoming rather evident; her method was a bit clearer.

We gave her a deck of cards. She noted that it was "plastic-covered" stock and said she didn't much like working with that kind of card. Immediately, I offered to withdraw the deck and give her a standard

Bicycle Poker deck, but she decided to use the one originally provided. It was important, you see, not to allow her any later excuse for failure. Even a deck of cards she did not feel comfortable with could have provided adequate excuse (in terms of the usual parapsychological negative-vibrations reasoning) for failure.

She shuffled and cut the deck many, many times, commenting at one point with a cute smile that she was "not very good at this sort of thing." Martin and I did not smile, recognizing a put-on at first flush, and Suzie dropped the inept act from then on. She fussed endlessly with the cards until the moment of truth came. Suzie then asked for a piece of paper, wrote something on it, and continued. Martin and I observed the necessary moves being made, then watched as she suddenly slapped the deck flat on the table and began spreading the cards wildly about with both hands in a circular fashion, rearranging them repeatedly and patting them into seemingly random patterns. She pushed them into various configurations while she spoke, asking that her subject, a young woman she'd chosen to sit opposite her at the table, reach into the spread and select "any five cards." As each card was slipped out of the spread, Suzie rearranged them somewhat, seemingly at random. At one point, however, she stopped doing this and backed away from the table.

The subject had five cards face down before her. Suzie then eliminated some until one was singled out (more about that later) and announced it was the required card. In the four times she performed for us, she was right three times! Odds of this being done are a whopping 1 in 36,000—assuming, that is, that no trickery is being used.

But the trickery was quite obvious to Martin and me. The routine was one that is well known to card magicians and has been in print and available to the public for many years. Suzie's fussing with the cards was quite haphazard until, at one point, she gathered the pack and straightened it out. At that time—the "moment of truth"—she glimpsed the top card as it fell into place. This was the card she then wrote upon the piece of paper as the one that would be chosen. Further shuffling become more orderly, and each shuffle and cut retained the top card in place. Suddenly the deck was slammed on the tabletop and a rapid spreading commenced, with the curious circular motion. But, we noted, the top card almost immediately was pushed off to one side, close to Suzie and near her arm, which would cover it during the fussing about. She would then press her thumb to the card and slide it about a bit, then drop it off again in a different position but always accessible.

Finally, Suzie introduced the chosen card into the main mass of cards, arranging it all by patting and pushing so that the one important card lay in a position where it was most likely to be chosen. Then the selection process began. If the card was not chosen right away, additional patting served to push it into a spot immediately within reach of the subject.

After all, she had five chances in fifty-two of having the required card chosen. Furthermore, most of the cards were in motion or under her reach, and so kept out of contention. But even with the correct card among the five selected ones, how was she able to force the final selection of that one from the five?

Here is where the demonstration really fell apart. Suzie used almost *any* means to arrive at the correct one-out-of-the-five, and seldom the same means. Suppose the desired card was in the fourth position. She would say, for example, "Name any two numbers between 1 and 5." If the answer was "1 and 3," she would brightly suggest that 1 plus 3 equals 4. A winner! Or, if the numbers given were 1 and 2, she would promptly eliminate card numbers 1 and 2 and narrow it down to the remaining three cards, telling the victim to choose "another number" and cashing in if the number named was 4. Otherwise she would continue to play around until only the desired card was left. Or she could turn a 2 into a 4 by counting from the opposite end of the row of cards. The variations are many, and I'm sure Miss Cottrell knows them all.

On the Carson show, seeing the ace of spades on the bottom of the deck as Ed McMahon shuffled it, Suzie asked *four* people at the table to select cards. She saw McMahon take the correct card, and then, with her back turned, asked them to choose "the highest card" in anyone's hand. Of course, it turned out to be the ace of spades in McMahon's hand! How can we be so certain of that? Because in this day of home video recorders several people taped the performance, and the ace of spades even showed up on the bottom of the deck for the home viewers. Also, viewers saw Suzie kneeling down at the table to get a better peek.

Which brings us to a point that certainly must be troubling the astute reader who has been following the protocol and implementation thereof in this account. I said that Suzie had agreed to being recorded on videotape from the moment she entered the test room, but I then referred to the video recorder as "ready but not running" *after* we had entered the room. True, *that* machine was not running, but *in the next room* the actual machine of record *was* running, and it recorded all Suzie's "informal," uncontrolled tests in great detail, unknown to her! Thus, she had made no great effort to hide her methods, figuring we were falling for the trick.

Later, of course, we were able to verify our observations very easily— able to see her peek at the top card, to observe the false cuts and

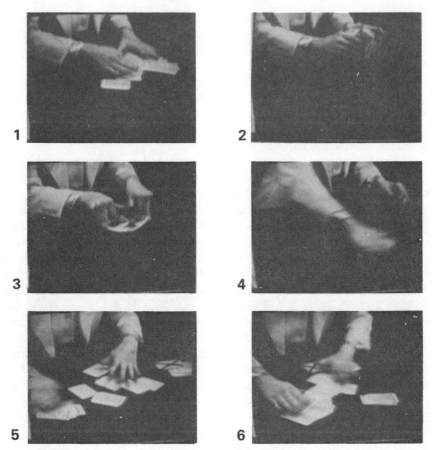

These photos were prepared from videotape (made without her knowledge) of Suzie Cottrell performing her card trick. (1) Cottrell haphazardly spreads the cards, face down, to "mix" them. (2) The cards are gathered together and straightened out. In the process, the card faces are turned toward her and the fingers of her right hand slide the top card (marked with an X) up so that she can peek at it. From this point on, she carefully keeps track of the top card, the Three of Hearts. The spreading of the deck that took place in the first frame shown necessitated that the cards be handled in this way, and thus the movements required for the "top peek" seem perfectly innocent. (3) She riffle-shuffles the cards, making sure that the top card stays on top. Several similar shuffles follow. (4) In a sudden move, she leans forward and spreads the deck. (5) Immediately, a small group of cards *from the top* is pushed to one side. (6) The left hand draws back the top group while the right hand pushes others forward and around in an arc. (7) After much spreading and

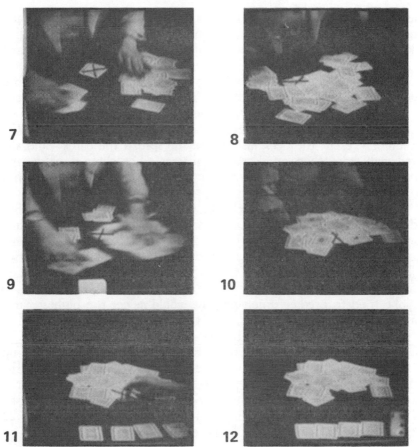

circling of the cards, the top card is still close to her, under control. It gets nudged from time to time but remains identified. (8) She stops a moment, the top card still within reach. (9) The cards go into motion again, and the left thumb, which is most often used to control and move the critical card, takes hold of it again and pushes it forward. (10) After the cards have been patted and pushed into position, the top card ends up somewhat inside and partly underneath the mass of cards. It is in an ideal position to be selected by the spectator. (The cards marked "O" and "X" are the cards that are about to be selected.) (11) Five cards are selected by the spectator. The fifth one is the former top card, and it is placed in position number five. The spectator is then asked to name any two numbers from 1 to 5. Those named are 1 and 4. "Good," says the performer. "That makes five. Turn over the fifth card." (12) The card is turned over and turns out to be the card predicted by the performer.

false shuffles, and to note the final manipulation of the crucial card. Frank Garcia, the renowned expert on card techniques and gambling trickery, has seen this tape, and certifies that Martin Gardner's and my observations are correct.

Well, Suzie Cottrell, not realizing that we had the cat in the bag already, agreed that it was time for us to get down to serious business. We started the dummy videotape machine, and Suzie tried her trick several more times. Now, however, there was a slight change in the procedure. We cut the deck just before she spread the cards—and she scored *zero* from then on. For your interest, her chances of getting zero cards right in another set of four attempts was 92.5 percent in a fair test.

In another test, Suzie asked that two different subjects draw five cards each from the deck and compare their hands to see if they had "corresponding" cards—that is, to see if one had a card with the same number and color as the other (Jack of hearts/Jack of diamonds, two of clubs/two of spades, etc.). In this experiment, which she herself suggested, she scored zero.

She tried to predict which persons would select the highest cards in a simple dealing of the pack. She tried 80 times—again, her idea, not ours, but strictly controlled by us—she failed 80 times.

In another test, in 104 attempts to predict cards to be turned up she fell somewhat short of her estimated 92.3 percent success rate; she scored zero. A following set of 40 predictions failed 100 percent. In a series designed to test her ability to determine the suit of a card by psychic means—an ability she had claimed—her success rate was 22 percent, though 25 percent would be expected by chance. And so on and on.

In a press interview later, Suzie complained that I had been "setting up mental blocks." Actually, though I had offered to leave the room—and the building—if she wished, she had declined my offer. It was a poor excuse for her failure, but an expected one, brought out of the bottomless bag of excuses with which these folks trot about the country.

But there are two things I have not yet revealed. First, in the document that Suzie Cottrell signed before beginning the tests were a number of statements that she agreed to explicitly. She certified that she had not in the past used any form of trickery, that she would not on this occasion use any deception, and that she would not feel compelled by the pressure of the situation to resort to any such methods. Yet she performed, in magician's parlance, the top-peek, false three-way cuts, top-retaining shuffles, and the Schulein force, followed by multiple-choice forces! There's not a great deal left in the lexicon of the cardsharp!

Second, there came a pause in the middle of the testing procedure when Suzie asked for a break. I had been shuffling a deck for her to use, and I placed it on the table, within camera range of course, to await her return to the room. When she reentered she saw the videotape reels not moving and sat at the table while the hubbub went on around her. On the videotape we see her hands casually pick up the deck. She blatantly looks at the top card, then replaces the deck in position. Then in a loud voice she announces that she is ready. You bet she was, and until I reached forward at the last moment to cut the cards before she resumed the tests, she was anticipating imminent success.

Suzie Cottrell does tricks with cards. The methods are standard conjurer's methods and not in any way psychic miracles. Her intentions are appealing: She says she wants to develop her powers to help autistic children, wants no money, and has no interest in becoming a professional psychic. After the encounter in Buffalo she need not specify the last intention. It seems fairly obvious, on the basis of certain aspects of the examination, that her father is unaware of the trickery and believes Suzie has genuine powers.

As she left the session in tears, Suzie Cottrell turned to one of the psychologists who had controlled the tests. "I'm going to forget what you did to me today," she cried, "and if you ever have any autistic children I'll help them all I can, in spite of what you've done!" Martin and I turned away in dismay. Later, Irving Biederman, the psychologist, summed it up for the press this way: "On the basis of the tests, one cannot discriminate between Suzie Cottrell and a fraud." Amen.

The Cottrell case reminds me of the Olle Jonsson matter. His public knows him better as Olof (or Olaf) Jonsson. It was Jonsson who so spectacularly achieved "psi-missing" in U.S. astronaut Edgar Mitchell's outer-space test. "Psi-missing" is a process by which parapsychologists excuse any spectacular failure by pointing out that it is statistically remarkable to have the performer achieve *very poor* results. Jonsson was one of three persons (the others were never named) who attempted to receive Mitchell's brain waves from outer space during the Apollo 14 space flight. Mitchell announced that the results obtained were "three thousand to one" against chance but neglected to tell us at the time that Jonsson had *failed* so badly that the chances of his doing so poorly were three thousand to one! Jonsson was well tested, however, by Benjamin Burack of Roosevelt University, Chicago, in 1971. Professor Burack reports that the "psychic" failed repeatedly and finally declared that he was "not feeling well" and terminated the tests. He then continued informally *under no control* and was successful. His illness was suddenly forgotten; it seemed to be present only when he was under control. Burack's fifty years of experience in designing experiments—*and his*

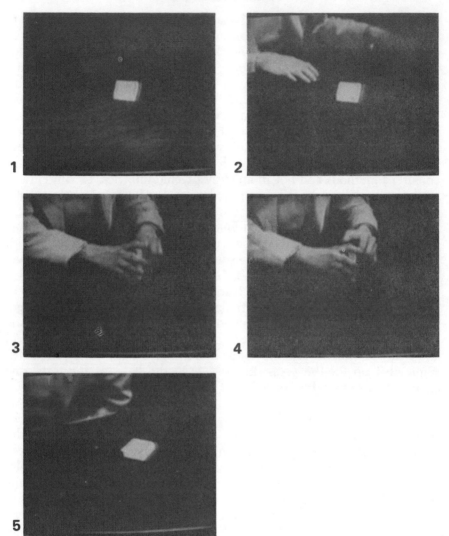

(1) The deck of cards is left on the table, having been shuffled by one of the experimenters. (2) After a five-minute recess, Cottrell returns and sits at the table. The spectators are still milling about, paying little attention to her. She needs to know what the top card is. (3) She picks up the deck and casually squares it on the table with the face of the deck within her view. (4) She places the left index finger against the top card and lifts it slightly so that it is visible to her. She has now performed the "peek." (5) She replaces the deck face down on the table and, leaning back, announces that she is ready to resume the experiments. (However, since protocol was in effect, the deck was simply cut by one of the experimenters and she failed the test.)

knowledge of conjuring techniques—had effectively dampened the results. The similarity between Jonsson and Cottrell is evident when we examine the kinds of tests to which each was subjected. Their tests were done with playing cards and were quite similar in nature. Similar effects were attempted, and with equally disastrous results—except in one case, wherein Jonsson called Edgar Mitchell by telephone (so much more dependable than ESP) and performed card-guessing with him that way. Jonsson reported a four-out-of-ten success rate where only two out of ten would be expected. But in this test Jonsson was (1) the "psychic," (2) the experimenter, (3) the scorer, and (4) the reporter! That is undoubtedly a winning combination.

Even the *Parapsychological Review* of Dr. J. B. Rhine, after reporting in 1949 that Jonsson had been demonstrating phenomenal success in tests, followed up in 1950 with the statement that he had been playing all these roles himself. The journal said that investigators of these claims "had in the main only small samples and uncontrolled demonstrations."

In many demonstrations of this sort, Professor Burack found that if a warm-up run was successful the "psychic" wanted to continue, and these results were counted. If it was not a success the preliminary run was dismissed and the "real" test commenced. In spite of all this— and the fact that runs were not announced in advance, so that "optional stopping" could further aid the desired results—Jonsson was a failure.

Later reports of these tests performed with Burack revealed another favorite gimmick. A result (that of the Mitchell phone call, a totally uncontrolled test) was quoted by Jonsson as "six out of ten." Actually, it had been four out of ten. A little hyperbole slips in, as we see, but never to depress the results; only to fluff them up a bit.

When we examine the only definitive tests known to have been done with Olof Jonsson, we find, not unexpectedly, that he cannot perform. Informal, uncontrolled tests, on the other hand, yield spectacular results. The conclusion is obvious.

In January 1978, CSICOP Chairman Paul Kurtz and I appeared on the TV program "Point Blank," hosted by Warner Troyer in Canada. We were to debate with Dr. Howard Eisenberg, author of the book *Inner Spaces*, which dealt with the paranormal, and with Geraldine Smith, a well-known Toronto "psychic." The latter claimed powers of psychometry, the supposed ability to divine facts by handling objects. Numerous newspaper accounts had praised her abilities, and I was prepared to test them.

Geraldine was rarin' to go. She'd been accompanied by several members of her family to the studio, and they had glared me nearly to death. After the usual preliminaries, during which the host made his skepticism about these claims very clear, we settled down to business. There were a number of spoons sealed up in an envelope by the host, and the host's wristwatch. In a mysterious bag of mine was a concealed artifact, and sundry articles chosen by the host for some testing. He decided to try a silver chain bracelet first.

HOST: Tell me something about the owner of that [handing her a Medic Alert bracelet].

SMITH: Okay.

HOST: A little bracelet. Other than the fact that they need a Medic Alert bracelet . . .

SMITH: [laughs] Okay. First of all, I'm getting a very strong gold. Now one thing I should let everybody know is, I also work with what is called "auras," and I've tuned myself into picking up vibrations, colors, from the article that the person has worn—had for some time. Now, first color is gold, and that is an extremely sensitive color. It's also, of course, allergy color, too. It's the color of super, super, super nervousness. This person I'm feeling physically—upper-, lower-back-area problems. I'm also seeing some upper-stomach-area things going on. Do you know this person?

HOST: Uh-huh.

SMITH: Personally?

HOST: Uh-huh.

SMITH: All right, there's something in this area here [points to chest]. You see, as soon as I pick up an article I will physically feel different areas that perhaps have been affected by the person. Feeling this area [indicates chest], feeling this area [indicates forehead]—headaches, eyestrain, something like that. Upper- and lower-back areas. It's also the intuitive color. I would also . . . I'd have to say that the person who owns it is extremely intuitive, probably clairsentient, which is very clear on the gut-feeling-type areas. I'm seeing—there's a separation around this person. Are they in this area now? Because I see them, like, not here.

HOST: Physically not here?

SMITH: Physically not here. No.

HOST: Uh-huh. Well!

SMITH: Which—which would make me wonder if the person is [laughs] either dead or if there's been some very, very bad health problems with them, because I'm just *really* feeling sluggish myself. Interesting. I'm seeing the month of January here—which is now—but there would have to be something strong with the person with January as well.

HOST: Okay. What color is *my* aura?

SMITH: You've got blue, you've got gold, you've got green.

HOST: What do those things *mean?* What's an aura?

SMITH: An aura is—I perceive it as a color. A color energy vibration that surrounds the person's body. It tells me mental, physical, spiritual . . . uh . . . general personality. Green is the color of the communicator. Anybody in the communications area has to have green in their aura. In other words, in any area. . . .

HOST: So you can tell me that without looking, huh?

SMITH: Yeah. In other words—yeah. In other words, you've got to have good communication in all areas. The one thing I would emphasize very strongly right now is that the green is a little bit blocked in the mental area of your aura, so that means you have been very frustrated in the area of communication on a personal level. It's almost as if you've been talking to the wall. I'm seeing a lot of [laughs] a lot of vibration there. And it's more in a personal area rather than in, you know, a work . . . business situation.

HOST: Okay. . . .

The host, who had been very careful not to tip his hand, following my instructions to him before the program, was the owner of that Medic Alert bracelet. He had not tried to conceal the fact; he merely picked it up from a small table to hand it to the "psychic." She assumed that it belonged to another person and gave her "reading" on that assumption. Note that she did not tell us the age, sex, or relationship of this mythical person. She tried to pump the host by asking whether he knew the person and whether the person was physically there or not. Warner carefully gave answers. Yes, he knew the person. And he answered her question about the whereabouts with another question. I'm proud of him.

Jumping the gun, she guessed the person was absent, and then covered all bases with a classic generalization/cop-out: "which would make me wonder if the person is either dead or if there's been some very, very bad health problems." Note that she was only "made to wonder," not *know*, and that this phrase implies a question that might prompt an answer but in this case failed to do so.

The host was neither dead nor absent. His back, he assured her, was excellent, nothing was wrong in the chest area, and when she tried to add a neck-upper shoulder area quickly to the reading as he revealed his good state of health, he denied that as well. As he outlined his good physical condition she mumbled an encouraging "excellent . . . fine" to cover the fact that she was dead wrong. He was neither nervous nor allergic, he continued, and had no stomach problems. Headaches and eyestrain, he assured her, did not bother him either.

But I must report that our host tumbled for one of the commoner tricks of such readings. You see, the victim is allowed and encouraged to read more into the recitation than is actually there. Smith had said, "I'm seeing the month of January here" and during his denial of the accuracy of her reading he admitted that she *had* determined that his birthday was in January! But she had said nothing about a birthday, particularly *his* birthday, since she didn't even know the bracelet belonged to him! When confronted with all this evidence, Ms. Smith explained, "The thing is that, to me, in a reading, means quick removal from a situation, which means either leaving this place, leaving the country— quick removal." Perhaps she was expressing her own desires of the moment; it certainly didn't make any sense to me. Looking at Paul Kurtz and me, she tried another tack. "Understand, I can totally see what the two of you are saying. The thing that I take a little bit further down the line is—my readings, as much as many things, can be applied to many people. Aren't there a lot of similarities in life? [There was a short, stunned pause here as we all tried to fathom what she could possibly be trying to say.] You know, we get married or we don't, we're male or we're female, we have children or we don't."

Dear reader, I leave it with you.

After this first confrontation Ms. Smith was a bit subdued but smiled bravely. She had yet to be tested with an object that I had brought along specifically for the purpose. This item was something I had owned for some time, and I knew its complete history. For a psychometry reading it was excellent material. I will reverse the usual procedure by telling you in advance all about the object and then give you her entire word-for-word reading of it. You will then be in the position I was in, and be able to do your own analysis of her accuracy.

The object was a small bisque-fired ceramic, black in color and of Peruvian origin. It measured seven inches in length and was in the form of a bird, with a spout at the top. It was a fake—a replica of a genuine Mochica grave object and had been made by a friend in Lima who is Peruvian by birth but Chinese by ancestry. He is a short man, five feet six or so, heavy, straight black hair, twenty-eight years of age, with totally Chinese features to all appearances. He is single, or was at the time the reading was made. He speaks only Spanish. His business is making accurate replicas of original Peruvian art and repairing ceramics. He gave the ceramic to me because it had broken, and I repaired it myself when I returned to the United States. I have a large collection of similar pieces, both genuine originals and good replicas. I had brought this one with me to the broadcast to avoid breaking a valuable original and to get around the tendency of "psychics" to expound on nonexistent people long extinct who they can safely claim to have been associated with such an article.

Geraldine Smith took a deep breath and began her reading of this article, while I sat there carefully, unblinking.

SMITH: Okay. The first thing that—actually I'm very quickly being taken over maps, and I'm tuning in very strongly to Mexico, United States—general area there. I'm seeing three *very* strong personalities, two females and a male, and I'll describe them all for you. First of all, the man I'm seeing is approximately five foot eight, five foot nine. To me, that's short for a male. Very deep brown hair, but receding at the temples. Glasses, quite thick. Obviously very bad eyes, because the focus I'm seeing is very, very strong. I'm seeing kind of a round-neck shirt. It's not the type you have on now. I guess it would be more along the line that he is wearing [she pointed at two of us]. Then I'm going to the two ladies. Oh, I didn't give you an age on the man. He would have to be forty-five to fifty. Something like that. The ladies I'm seeing— one would be . . . hmmm . . . five foot. Very short. Four-nine, five foot. The other lady is quite a bit taller. One is very, very, very heavyset, and shortish, curlyish hair, but fluffy. And the other one, the shorter one, is just—well, there's nothing really big about her. I'm seeing these three people very much in connection with this. Do you recognize them at all?

RANDI: Now you're asking me something. You're supposed to be *telling* me.

SMITH: I mean, *do* you recognize them?

RANDI: Do you now want the history of the object? Is the reading finished?

Some observations about the above are obvious. She took a guess at an Indian origin, but missed. It could have been North American Indian or Mexican to the uninitiated, but it was not. She threw in three people for a "try-on," and I'm still trying to fit in the two women, but can't. The man's eyesight is excellent; he does not wear glasses. As for height, she's great on that, and the fellow does wear turtleneck sweaters frequently. His hair is very definitely *not* receding; quite the contrary. The age she gave him was at least seventeen years off the mark.

You should know two other things about this test. First, I told Geraldine Smith very clearly that this was not to be considered a formal test. My reasons should be obvious: It was quite possible for her to have looked into my background and discovered my interest in Peruvian archaeology, and she could easily have visited a museum and prepared herself to come up with the origin of the object. Second, she agreed to consider a formal test administered by the CSICOP, to be conducted regardless of the outcome of this demonstration. We have not heard from her since.

The Fall 1978 issue of *The Skeptical Inquirer* contained an excellent analysis by Dr. Ronald Schwartz of some similar readings by "psychic" Peter Hurkos. This man has a reputation—of his own invention—for being a crime sleuth who is constantly "consulted by police" who need his assistance to find killers. Here is a typical performance:

HURKOS: I see an operation.
SUBJECT: (no response)
HURKOS: Long time ago.
SUBJECT: No. We have been very lucky.

Hurkos does not say that *the subject* had an operation. He says that he "sees" an operation. Thus *any* operation will fill the bill. Notice also how Hurkos "extends the domain" of his first guess with "Long time ago." If there had been a recent operation, he'd have refrained from this modification. As it is, he is pretty safe. He uses this ploy of "an operation" in almost every session. Most people have had or will have some kind of medical operation. Having failed to get a positive response, Hurkos now makes the subject look like an incompetent who cannot remember the incident:

HURKOS: (somewhat angrily) Think! When you were a little girl. I see worried parents, and doctor, and scurrying about.
SUBJECT: (no response)
HURKOS: (confidently) Long time ago.
SUBJECT: (yielding) I cannot remember for certain. Maybe you are right. I'm not sure.

As Dr. Schwartz pointed out, Hurkos appears confident and "knowing"; the subject appears to be perverse and obstinate. Schwartz also noted a common gimmick Hurkos employs. He tries to establish how many are in the family. Numbers are always impressive:

HURKOS: One, two, three, four, five—I see five in the family.
SUBJECT: That's right. There are four of us and Uncle Raymond, who often stays with us.

This same tactic was used on one of Johnny Carson's "Tonight Show" programs that I recorded years back. But it went somewhat differently:

HURKOS: I see four people. Maybe five.
SUBJECT: No, there are only three of us in the house.
HURKOS: No, there are four I see. . . .
SUBJECT: Oh, my brother. He hasn't been with us for a long time now. There are only three of us now.

HURKOS: But there *is* your brother. Yes, it is your brother. And what about the "dook"?

SUBJECT: The *what?*

HURKOS: The *dook.* The *dook!* I see a dook in the house.

SUBJECT: I don't know. Oh, you mean a *dog?* [laughter]

HURKOS: Yes, yes, a *dook!* What about the dook?

SUBJECT: We don't have a dog.

HURKOS: But you used to have a dook, *didn't* you?

SUBJECT: No, never. At least not while *I've* been there.

HURKOS: Not while you were there. Aha! I see! [applause]

In spite of a big loser, Hurkos comes out ahead anyway! Schwartz, too, noted the "dook" gimmick. In a telephone conversation Hurkos says, "I see a dook." Responds the listener, "Why, that's amazing! Our dog is right here in the room with me!" Consider, as Schwartz does, that "dook" can be interpreted as duke, dock, doc, duck, or dog, depending upon the listener's expectation. The listener is free to interpret the word however he or she wishes to—and certainly will.

Another Hurkos ruse is the name Anna or Ann. In an exchange recorded by Professor Benjamin Burack, Hurkos, speaking with dwarf actor Michael Dunn, revealed that Dunn had "suffered much" in his early life. Not an astonishing guess at all. Then the "psychic" astounded everyone by announcing that the name Mike meant something to the actor. Dunn sourly noted that it should—it was his first name. Hurriedly glossing over this dumb pronouncement, Hurkos tried another name: Anna. Dunn answered that he knew several Annas and added that one was his grandmother. A big hit! Says Hurkos, "This one is dead, right?" Considering Dunn's age, and the fact that his reference to his grandmother was in the past tense, it is hardly a surprise that Hurkos guessed right. Another Ann(a) shows up in Schwartz's article:

HURKOS: Who is Ann? (Note that there is no identification of Ann, just a question.)

SUBJECT: Ann? I have an aunt. My aunt's name is Ann.

HURKOS: Yes. She has trouble with her legs, too. Left leg.

SUBJECT: Could be!

The name Ann(a) is just different enough to be safe. The name Bill or Mary would be too obvious. Therefore Hurkos leans on finding an Ann(a) everywhere. Mind you, if the subject just quoted had failed to come up with one, Hurkos would have argued *ad nauseum*, throwing in Annie, Anastasia, and every variation possible, trying to bully an admission that *somewhere* there was a person who would fit, however badly. Failing that, he'd have brushed it off as unimportant and surged ahead.

I will not trouble my reader with much more—and there is *much* more—about the Smith-Hurkos guessing game, but I think I should make several other observations about the Hurkos saga before leaving it. Professor Burack, having followed the Hurkos story quite closely, notes that there are a few examples of rather serious discrepancies between what Hurkos would have us believe and the actual truth. Hurkos claims that he has "met twice" with Dr. J. B. Rhine (then associated with Duke University). But Rhine's *Parapsychological Bulletin* (1960) denies this, adding, "Television, radio and newspapers have been giving widespread publicity in recent months to claims of unusual clairvoyant powers of the Dutchman, Peter Hurkos. One statement was that Hurkos has been at Duke University and had given ESP performances with 100 percent success. . . . Hurkos has *not* been investigated at the Duke laboratory and is not known to have given any such performances as those claimed in any university laboratory. An invitation was extended to Hurkos by the Duke laboratory."

Peter Hurkos has survived (though he has assumed a very low profile recently) in spite of the almost uninterrupted series of failures for which he has become famous. He has wrongly identified a number of persons as murderers, and when he has been right the people were already in custody. He claims to have identified the famous Boston Strangler. He did not. A few days after Hurkos's Boston Strangler consultation had been completed, the Federal Bureau of Investigation arrested a man who had claimed to be one of its agents. In his car was discovered a collection of police badges and an assortment of pistols and rifles. The paraphernalia seemed ideal equipment for putting up the front necessary to obtain information about police matters. He was put on trial on charges of impersonating a federal agent, found guilty, and fined $1,000. The man was Pieter Van der Hurk, otherwise known as Peter Hurkos.

The baseball and football predictions offered by Hurkos have been pretty bad. He "found" a fabulous gold mine in Colorado which never produced the wealth he predicted, and when the promoter ran off with Hurkos's wife the Dutch "psychic" took another swallow. In 1950, he concocted a story about having been rushed to England by Scotland Yard in utmost secrecy to help them find the stolen Stone of Scone, which Scottish nationalists had swiped from Westminster Abbey. Hurkos claimed to have been responsible for recovering it. He was not, and the Yard officially denied all connection with him. He still has not reversed himself on his declaration that Adolf Hitler is alive. Wrong. Henry Belk, heir to the Belk department stores, was a great fan and supported Hurkos. Then the "psychic" steered him into a disastrous uranium venture, advised that two of his stores would do well, and told him not to worry about his missing daughter. The stores failed, the uranium fizzled, and the girl was found drowned. Even Charles Tart, the California parapsychologist, tested Hurkos officially in a laboratory and was unable to find any psychic powers. If Tart can't find such powers, they *certainly* aren't there! *Yet Hurkos claims his powers are "87.5 percent accurate"!*

There is at least *one* prediction that a good predicter should be able to come up with, and Peter Hurkos has even failed to do that. He prophesied that he would die on November 17, 1961. Today, nineteen years later, Hurkos is still alive and making bad predictions. But Dr. A. Puharich, who gave us Arigo the Psychic Surgeon and Uri Geller, and who believes in *all* wonders from UFOs to mind-reading horses, has referred to Peter Hurkos as one of "the greatest telepathic talents of modern times," so how can we doubt it? In the face of superior judgment, we must simply discard the awkward facts.

In April 1978 I received a letter from a Rosemary DeWitt, representing "Research Associates, a private research group." The letter informed me that I was about to have my $10,000 snatched away due to a demonstration of "a paranormal talent impossible to replicate." I was assured of the group's integrity by the statement that "as scientists with research backgrounds ourselves, we employ the most advanced scientific techniques known to us in our methodology."

I replied immediately and heard nothing until August. I sent Ms. DeWitt a preliminary test by mail, since her claim seemed to lend itself to such treatment. She had described to me her ability to "dowse" a map to locate ancient ruins and artifacts, whether the map was marked with coordinates or not. I agreed that such a talent was indeed eligible for my award and told her that I would carefully prepare a map of an area that I knew to have such relics. She was free to mark upon it the spots she thought were important, and return it.

To this end I drew a map (with the aid of Earth Resources Transmission Satellite space mapping photos) of an area that I frequently visit. That Ms. DeWitt might be aware of this fact was not very important, since it was only a preliminary test. However, in preparing the map, which was called "map A," I made sure that it lacked any indication of orientation and scale. Chances of her being able to locate this part of the globe were remote indeed.

Very soon I had a reply. I quote a part of that letter so that my reader may see how diffuse and indeterminate such replies can be. It is quite typical of the genre:

> The location of at least two archaeological sites seemed to be what you were asking for, although I believe there are more.

> You didn't ask for anything else, or even a totality of the sites, so I'm not including any other information at this time.
>
> There are three areas I find to be generally promising archaeologically speaking. Apparently there are several more within these approximate confines which may yield additional material. My information suggests there are sites in the area you mapped that are as yet unknown. It will be most interesting to me to learn from your feedback just how much of this is "real" as we perceive reality on the physical plane we inhabit.

Note the generalities and vague statements in this reply. I did not ask for any specific number of locations; I merely asked Ms. DeWitt to "work on this sample." She suggests I asked for "at least two" and adds that she "believes" there are "more." This covers the possibility that there are others she missed and yet does not say that there *are* more, just that she *believes* there might be. Also, she tells me that she is "not including any other information at this time." This provides the opportunity of adding more later, yet does not say that there *is* more.

The areas marked are "generally promising." But she has marked only *two* areas on the map; she said she found *three!* Thus she leaves an unspecified location hanging in the air, perhaps to be defined when she knows where she *should* have indicated another site. Next, she says there are "apparently several more" inside these "approximate" confines which "may" yield more. All just vague possibilities—an attempt to give elasticity to her limited findings. And she says that her "information suggests" there are additional sites "yet unknown." So, if what she's chosen is wrong, it's only because these are not yet known to be the wonders she has determined they are.

An interesting further assumption on her part is mentioned. She says, "It will be most interesting . . . to learn from your feedback." I was not about to provide *any* feedback in any form. She was to "do her thing" as she pleased; I would not demand anything or offer anything except the basic raw materials for the test. Also, Ms. DeWitt provides herself with a possible escape route with her statement that she wants to learn "how much of this is 'real' as we perceive reality." In other words, if she is totally wrong according to the logic of the real world, she can invent some obscure universe in which errors turn out to have validity due to new and wonderful rules. It is a hedge often employed by "psychics," who frequently warn us not to think of these wonders in ordinary terms. She is putting us on notice, just in case.

Following this semantic *tour de force*, with its multiple evasions and well-worn rationalizations for possible failures, I prepared a further test of her abilities, since a peek at the results had shown that for all her heavy efforts to determine points of interest, Ms. DeWitt had chosen two spots in a well-explored jungle area that held no known ancient ruins. Ms. DeWitt had claimed that she did best with prominent, obvious, above-ground ruins, and such structures did indeed exist in the mapped area she was given. In fact, I had chosen an area containing structures that are probably the most impressive and well-known ruins in the western hemisphere, and certainly among the most famous and prominent in the world. But let us continue with the test.

On September 19, 1978, I visited Washington, D.C., and arranged to meet with Ms. DeWitt in the company of Philip Klass and Robert Sheaffer, both members of the CSICOP. We were equipped with tape recorder and camera, and I had prepared a new map, "map B," for this next test. For the first time I saw the device Ms. DeWitt used in her determinations. It was a simple brass tube about six inches long, with a piece of coat-hanger wire bent to form nearly a right angle and inserted into the tube.

When Ms. DeWitt brought the device near a "hot" portion of the map it would begin to swing. It also answered queries with a spin one way for "yes" and the opposite way for "no." Klass took some time exposures of the device in operation, and these clearly revealed her method. Ms. DeWitt was simply—and perhaps unconsciously—giving the thing a bit of a swing, which caused a rapid spin with very little energy input due to the balanced nature of the device. Any inclination from the vertical caused a movement.

But the method of getting a spin going was not the most important aspect of the phenomenon. The crucial question was, *Did it work?* First, she chose to make another attempt with "map A." She spun her rod mightily, creating quite a breeze, while we watched. I stood looking over her shoulder, but unknown to her I was *not* watching the map but staring at the rod instead. This was to prevent any unconscious cueing on my part, since I was the only one there who knew the nature of the map.

Ms. DeWitt determined *seven more* possible sites on "map A"; there were now *nine* places marked on this map. I made no comment at all, accepting what she marked and having it signed and dated by the witnesses. I then gave her the new map, "map B." She worked on that one, expressing a great deal of uncertainty about all the decisions she made. There was "perhaps" a spot here, but maybe not. This or that area looked "promising" but not positive. "How about this?" was frequently asked of the dowsing rod, and tentative marks were made on the map. Four spots were determined this time, and Ms. DeWitt rested.

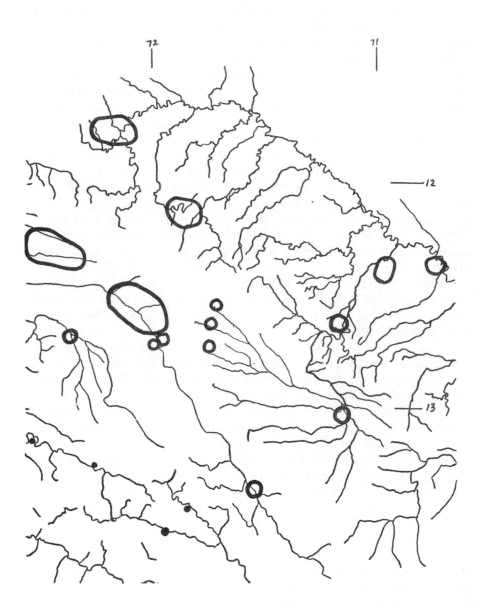

One of the maps on which dowser Rosemary DeWitt attempted to mark the locations of artifacts, sight unseen. The circled areas are DeWitt's guesses; the dots designate the actual sites.

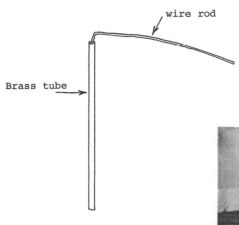

wire rod

Brass tube

The dowsing device used by Rosemary DeWitt. It is held upright as shown, and the rod spins around as a result of a slight, circular motion of the hand.

Rosemary DeWitt marks "map B" while the dowsing device whirls away in her left hand. The action of the rotor was "stopped" in this photograph by the short exposure. Philip Klass

The dowsing device is stationary in this two-second exposure. There is no motion of the tube. Philip Klass

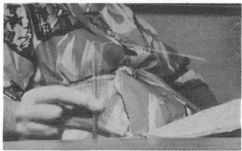

The rotor has begun to spin rapidly, and obvious movement of the hand and tube is seen in this two-second exposure. Philip Klass

We learned a bit about her background. She told us that she worked at three different colleges in the Washington area, teaching a "smorgasbord" of noncredit courses dealing with paranormal subjects. It sounded very much like the kind of adult education classes that today are being taken seriously all over the United States—the astrology, psychokinesis, healing, etc., classes that otherwise sober administrators allow to be taught by self-proclaimed experts with no real credentials. Ms. DeWitt's claim to be a scientist was based on a master's degree she had earned in library science, and "Research Associates"—which I was unable to find in any listings—she described as a private group she formed to provide to employers people she had trained as "psychics." It was all rather nebulous. And, reported Ms. DeWitt, she had lost her job with a library in Charles County, Maryland, "because [I] am a psychic."

In her courses, she said, she tried to teach "biofeedback alpha-level retraining of the self-image" to her students, and she had been trying to get this accepted as part of the federal Law Enforcement Assistance Administration procedure, without success. She designed the system, she said, by "psychic guidance."

Shortly after the September meeting in Washington I sent Rosemary DeWitt a third map, designated "number 3," this time with the coordinates plainly marked upon it. Since she had failed completely with the first two maps, I was interested to see if she would suddenly be able to find the sites of ruins on a map she could identify. If she were to fail here as she had on the unmarked maps, it would at least indicate that she was honest—that she had not referred to any other maps to determine the locations of ancient ruins.

I had no answer from her for almost three months. Finally, during a meeting in Washington early in December, I contacted Ms. DeWitt and she agreed to visit me and some other CSICOP members to tell us her findings concerning the third map. Dr. Ray Hyman was present, along with Robert Sheaffer and Michael Hutchinson. The latter had recently done a definitive test of a Japanese "psychic photographer" in England and wanted to see what miracle-workers we could come up with.

In less than fifteen minutes we discovered the truth. Rosemary began by telling me that she "felt" we were in Peru, in the area of Machu Picchu, site of the ancient Inca city. She said she also felt that all three maps were similar! She scolded me for having denied in the previous meeting that the mapped area was Machu Picchu and claimed that, since I had misled her, she had been correct in getting an impression of a "P" and in assuming that this meant Panama rather than Peru. This was a total fabrication. Every word said during the previous meeting had been recorded, and neither Peru nor Machu Picchu had been mentioned. Nor was a "P" brought up. In fact, never had there been any attempt, in our meetings or in written accounts, to even vaguely identify any location.

Ms. DeWitt set about her rod-spinning and immediately went to the right area of the map. But then she faltered, vacillating between two adjacent rivers and finally settling upon *the wrong one*. The proof was now in, and the verdict obvious. Rosemary DeWitt had failed the tests.

In summary, DeWitt identified *fifteen* different spots on three different versions of *the same map*, for in each case she had been looking at *the same archaeologically rich area of Peru*, an area with which I am very familiar. She not only failed to identify *any* spot twice in three different attempts but also missed the most significant sites of all— Cuzco, Machu Picchu, Pisac, Urubamba, and many others in that area. She instead came up with locations in deep jungle and other uninhabitable spots with no ruins or artifacts whatsoever. Yet she had told us that she did best with exposed, above-ground ruins—a strong feature of the Cuzco and Machu Picchu ruins. Only when she was supplied with the coordinates could she even guess that the mapped area was in South America, and her claim that she didn't have a globe of the world (and thus could not have determined the location) is a weak excuse indeed. In short, when she was correct *at all* it was only when she was told what area of the world the map represented.

Surely the case is proved. Perhaps Rosemary DeWitt really believes she has psychic powers. Certainly she was not able to prove it. And if her other claimed successes are based upon evidence as flimsy as that presented to us, we may dismiss her pretensions altogether.

My two-year stint on all-night radio at station WOR in New York brought me in contact with many interesting people. As our tired but happy group broke up early one Saturday morning, a panel guest took me aside and told me of a matter in which I might be of use. The man, a psychiatrist, informed me of a series of experiments being performed quietly at a laboratory of the New York State Department of Mental Hygiene. A young girl from a small town in Massachusetts who seemed to be able to see while blindfolded was being tested there, and two of the young graduate students at work on the project had requested my guest to ask me to visit the lab. Like my guest, both were convinced that the girl was cheating, but they could not figure out the trick.

The psychiatrist had already suggested to the project director that I be consulted but had been told that there was no need for my services.

Hearing this, I decided that I would at all costs attend the tests to be held a few hours from then, and my informant and I worked out a method whereby I would be able to do just that.

We had breakfast nearby, then went to the laboratory. An open locker in the basement offered a white jacket that looked quite official, and thus garbed and carrying my own large clipboard and a formidable array of pens, I slipped into the lab unnoticed. A few persons there eyed me warily but decided not to question my presence. A bearded man looks proper in such a place, especially with his glasses on his forehead, an affectation I adopted to look as if I was at ease in the surroundings. One of the graduate students recognized me and almost blew the whole episode right away, but I spoke with him and his fellow sufferers to prevent this. I learned from them that they were anxious to be relieved of the job so that they could move on to more important work. I agreed with their sentiments, and together we pursued the quarry.

Linda Anderson was her name, and she was fifteen. According to her parents, she had discovered her "powers" while in church. She said that while reading a prayer book she realized that she was seeing right through it to the floor. Since it had happened in church, it couldn't be all bad, and her father, Arthur, had brought her to the attention of these men of science, who had devised experiments—all but the right ones—to test her ability to see through blindfolds.

The blindfold she used was one she had brought with her. This was allowed by the experimenters in the lab, for they had thoroughly examined it. And besides, Linda preferred her own blindfold, and worked much better while using it than when wearing others. By such means do mice make fools of men. Her favorite blindfold consisted of a pair of aviator goggles painted black on the inside, with rubber sponge all around the edges. It was held on with heavy elastic. All present had tried on the mask, and they could not see while wearing it. But, I was convinced, Linda *could.*

Seated in a chair under good room light, Linda was able to read that morning's *New York Times* while blindfolded. She held the newspaper well to the left side of her body. Occasionally an experimenter would cover the left or right eye area with a slip of paper. When the left eye area was covered in this way, it did not inhibit her reading at all. When the right eye area was covered, she read on for a few words, then stopped or began making errors. I noted that on one attempt she was not reading the text at all a few seconds after the paper was slipped into place over the right eye area, but was *inventing* the copy. No one but me seemed to have been checking to see! When I called attention to this, Linda threw back her head, said she was tired, and asked for a break.

At about this time my identity became known. Although there was some objection, most of those present agreed to let me stay. Linda had been successful up to that point and did not seem to mind, though she fixed me with an unblindfolded eye.

During the break, I pointed out something of interest to those present. Linda's face had been photographed from several different angles against a squared background. The photos looked for all the world like large mug shots and had been made for the purpose of studying and mapping various areas of her face. You see, it was believed that she was "seeing" with a portion of her facial skin near her nose. They were almost right.

The profile photo emphasized something unusual about Linda's features. She had a short, concave nose that gave her an ability few possess. If my reader will perform a small experiment, it will be seen what I mean. Close your left eye and look to the left with your right eye. You will probably be looking right into your nose. But Linda Anderson was looking *over* her nose when she did the same thing! After a little investigation, her method became obvious. On the left side of the right half of the goggles, between the right lens and its sponge trimming, was a small crack. Linda, holding the newspaper on her left side, was able to read the newsprint through this hole *with her right eye!* Thus, covering the left eye did nothing at all to inhibit her vision.

Time for another reader experiment, please. Begin reading a newspaper aloud. Have someone suddenly place a piece of blank paper over the part being read, and continue "reading" as long as you can. You'll be surprised to find that you will know as many as four or five words that follow the last word you read. The reason is that most persons "scan" ahead a bit when reading out loud, and it is this advance information that you are recalling. Linda must have discovered this fact with great delight. It accounted for her ability to briefly continue reading when the area around her right eye was covered.

After the break, another test was started, but this time I asked if I might apply the blindfold, and I was permitted to do so. I affixed the same blindfold to Linda, and added a few bits of black tape to the obvious separations near her nose. She required a short settling-in period before she started each test, and we sat there waiting. Linda asked for some chewing gum, which was always kept on hand "to make her comfortable," I was told. I knew the real reason for it, but wanted my colleagues (dare I say that?) to notice it. She began chewing the gum rather savagely, contorting her face grotesquely until the tape loosened at the edges. Then she announced she was ready—but I wasn't.

I suggested to her that she should not chew gum, because her movements had dislodged the tape. She apologized, but not, I thought, without a slight gritting of teeth. We attempted to reapply the tape, but Linda wanted to be excused for a moment. When she returned and sat down to suffer my attentions again, I noted that she had layered on some makeup. I pointed out that the tape would not stick to the makeup and held up a moistened tissue. "Let's wash it off," I offered. Linda objected, saying that soapy water gave her acne. "Then we needn't worry," I countered, attacking her cheeks with the tissue, "because this is witch hazel." I could not resist using the word. The devil made me do it.

At last properly blindfolded, Linda sat there in silence. She yawned a great deal and brought her fingers up to her face, but each time there seemed to be a break in the seal, I replaced it. It was a little like continually picking the scab off a wound, and Linda got very angry with me. She asked to speak with her father alone. We left her and the father together for a few minutes, and while we waited outside I offered a confident prediction that the tape would again be loose when we returned. Sure enough, it was, and the father told us that Linda felt uncomfortable when blindfolded this way.

We began the final chapter in the drama. I offered to remove the blindfold altogether, but she objected, saying she needed total darkness for her powers to work. I assured her that I would supply that for her, and I meant it. I cut from a piece of black cloth tape two ellipses just big enough to cover her eye orbits and put them in place. If tears could have seeped through the tape, Linda would have drowned us. She was unable to see with this most minimal of all blindfolds. The area of her face that the scientists thought she was using to "see" with was well exposed, so she had no excuse.

In a very disturbed state, and obviously wishing to get *something* out of the session, she demanded to return to the previous blindfold. I agreed, and even said that I would not put the annoying tape on the edges! She was ecstatic, and the white-coated figures around me thought I was mad. But I had an ace to play from my sleeve. After the blindfold was in place, I simply stuck to the bridge of her nose a small "wing" of tape that she apparently was unaware of, and no matter how hard she screwed up her face, she could not see. She was now looking at the tape as most of us look at the side of our noses, and the game was up.

But I insisted on a *coup de grâce*. We had already asked Linda several times if her eyes were shut under the blindfold when she was reading. She had insisted that she shut her eyes tightly. I wanted to prove that this was not so; we needed a way to see her open eye as she read the newspaper. To this end, I carefully told one of the men exactly what to do. He lay on the floor and looked upward, the newspaper blocking his view of Linda's face. I held the newspaper, and removed the tape "wing" I had applied. Linda was now able to read. I told her to do so, and as she began I snatched the newspaper away. The man on the floor rose to his feet. "I saw her eye," he said, "and it was open."

One more thing remained to be done. The staff and I returned to an anteroom where the tape recorder was set up. Into the mike were read the final results of the day's testing. As we were at this, the door opened and an elderly man who I later learned was the project director burst into the room and denounced one and all for bringing a magician into the lab. He disassociated himself from the tests and left. In a report published later in *Science* magazine, researcher Joseph Zubin told of the termination of the tests. The report ended with a brief and ungrateful remark. "It was found useful," it said, "to have a professional magician present." "Useful"? Yes; "necessary" would have been a better word.

If she expected to find another naïve researcher in Professor James A. Coleman of American International College, Linda Anderson was in for another surprise. At a press meeting arranged in Auburn, Massachusetts, Coleman offered Linda one hundred dollars if she could convince a panel that she could see supernormally. One member of the panel was Sidney Radner, a man who had long experience with magic and who I was sure would not be fooled. I was also present but had been brought in unseen because it was thought that Linda would bolt if she knew I was there.

A reporter for the *Boston Record American* was able to see in much the same way Linda had been able to, using the same blindfold. The mask having provoked controversy, Professor Coleman suggested that Linda merely close her eyes and not peek. Linda demurred, but finally agreed that Coleman could put tape over her eyes. As I had previously discovered, her makeup was heavy and the tape would not hold. It was finally secured in place after some of the makeup was cleared away, and as chinks began to develop Coleman blocked them with zinc oxide ointment, a clever method, since the material was quite opaque and stayed in place well. Although Linda was able to read a few words whenever a chink developed, she was struck blind, as planned, when repairs were made.

There were complaints about the "pressure" of the tape. There were long periods of nothing happening, then Linda reading a few words of the text, Coleman applying a dab of ointment, and more long waits. It was a fiasco, and Coleman held on to his money. Mr. Radner was not easy on Miss Anderson. He said her performance should be considered a variety act—nothing more. There were grumblings all around.

Finally, Coleman asked Linda's father if he would like to comment on the tests that had been done in New York. The father said that he could not, since the results had not yet been decided. Although he was unaware of it, the verdict on the New York tests had long been in. I was called upon to comment on the tests, which I did, to the consternation of the performers.

Linda Anderson, after one more failure, faded from public view. She had provided police with a description of the whereabouts of, one Kenneth Mason, a five-year-old boy from Lowell, Massachusetts, who had been missing for four months. Linda had said that the boy would be found in a house, not in the local river, as expected. Shortly after her Auburn failure, she was proved wrong when Mason turned up on the banks of the Merrimack River. He was drowned.

I must tell you of a strange comment concerning the Anderson case that continued to ring in my ears for some time. As I left the press meeting in Auburn, I encountered a subdued Linda, her parents, and a young man who said he was a close friend of hers. The boyfriend came up to me and seized me by the lapels. Tears streaming down his face, he looked me in the eye and asked, "Why did you do this, Mr. Randi? Don't you believe in God?"

I have seldom been stuck for an answer. This time, I was.

Early in June 1977, I visited the Paris laboratories of France's fifth largest private company, Péchiney Ugine Kuhlmann, a metals and chemicals firm specializing in aluminum production. I had accepted an invitation to view recordings of tests that had been performed under the direction of Dr. Charles Crussard, a scientist who heads the entire Péchiney lab complex and supervises its three thousand research personnel. Crussard had become enthralled with the tricks of one Jean-Pierre Girard, a pharmaceutical salesman from Paris. Girard had begun some years previously, as an amateur magician, to "set up" scientists in France to show that they could be easily fooled à la Geller. And Crussard had fallen for it all. The only problem was that Girard, obviously enjoying the notoriety that resulted from his efforts, decided to abandon his original plan to expose the trickery and instead become a "psychic" himself. (An embarrassing relic of his former status appears in one of the official listings of the French magic associations, which tells us that Girard specializes in the Geller type of trickery.)

Dr. Crussard agreed to supply me with copies of all the films and tapes of tests that I and my colleague, Alexis Vallejo, viewed. What we watched was appalling. Although most of the footage did not show the preparation, identification, or selection of the metal bars used in the experiments, those segments that *did* show the complete procedure revealed that Girard employed the simplest of sleight-of-hand tricks to accomplish his "miracles" for the cameras. A heated argument ensued between Crussard and me, with Crussard denying that any cheating had taken place, and I insisting that careful observation would prove the contrary. We ran one section of film several times, and Crussard, after making measurements on the screen, finally agreed that perhaps I had a valid point. Vallejo and I did not attempt to point out much of the subsequent conjuring; it was too obvious.

At one place in a taped sequence, Crussard asserted that Girard had achieved an "impossible effect." Two "strain gauges" had been attached, 90 degrees apart, to the sides of a cylindrical, aluminum-alloy bar about 2 centimeters in diameter and 25 centimeters long. Viewing the chart record, we saw that Girard had caused strain effects to show up first on one gauge, then on the other. This meant that the direction of his "paranormal" force changed 90 degrees while he held the bar in one hand. Crussard was absolutely convinced that this effect could not be accomplished by trickery.

We had already exposed one of Girard's methods to Crussard. It consisted of holding the bar in one hand—*after* it had been secretly bent while out of sight—and then rotating it 90 degrees between fingers and thumb to bring the bend into view. Girard's secret bending had not been very cleverly performed; it had been done while his back was turned to the camera. By measuring thumb-to-fingertip distances on the screen, Vallejo and I easily proved that the rotation had taken place. Girard's method was not only visible, it was measurable.

Now we applied the same reasoning to this problem. Crussard showed me the original bar, with the sensors attached. I conclusively demonstrated to him exactly how the same maneuver would enable Girard to rotate the bar and produce the signals on the two sensors just as shown by the record. Crussard agreed it was possible but denied Girard had done this.

I reminded him that I had been promised copies of the tapes and films we had been shown so that the CSICOP could view them. He promised me that I would be given them, and Vallejo and I departed for Grenoble, where we were to meet Girard in person.

Shortly before I went to the Péchiney lab in Voreppe, near Grenoble, I received a phone call from Crussard, who astonished me by announcing that he had remeasured the films and tapes and had reversed his earlier decision. Now, no trickery was visible to him, nor to his assistant, who agreed with these new findings. Further, said Crussard, the entire encounter had been a test of *me*, and I had failed to pass. He said it had been *staged* to catch me, and that I had been found out. I told him I did not believe this, but he assured me that it was of little importance, since the experiments we had seen in the films and tapes were "not really scientific tests anyway" and that I would surely see the proof when I saw Girard that evening. But those films and tapes had been represented to us in Paris as scientific documents, not mere amusements, and Crussard had insisted that we were seeing proof of the claims he made for Girard. Vallejo and I decided to wait until that evening, however, rather than argue with Crussard over the phone. A "live" demonstration was, after all, much to be preferred.

In the company of Dr. David Davies and Dr. Christopher Evans, a CSICOP member, who had come from England to observe these tests, I viewed several more tapes and much data concerning Girard. None of us gave much credence to the extensive instrumentation that had been applied by the Péchiney scientists to Girard, since evidence concerning surveillance and security precautions was not given, nor were such procedures evident in the data at hand. We sat down to design the protocol for that evening's tests.

The rules were simple. All test bars—supplied by Péchiney in the sizes usually used in the many previous tests of Girard—were to be marked with broad colored stripes running from one end to the other, so that any rotation would be obvious. All bars were coded and sealed up so that Girard would have no chance to handle them and would not know which ones would be used. We drew up standards for testing the bars in advance for straightness. We would insist that all tests be done before a video camera, with the carefully delineated test area included at all times within the camera view, the bar offered "on camera," and all handling done in full view of the camera.

These simple rules were agreed to in advance by Girard and the two Péchiney scientists, Bouvaist and Dubost. They admitted that it was the first time they had followed such rules, though we were not told why this was so. Such precautions seemed to us to be minimal; we even wished to apply more stringent procedures if and when Girard passed these tests. After all, this was a man funded by huge amounts of money to prove a fantastic claim. Prodigious investments of personnel had been made as well, though under the French system, in which all workers tend to agree with the boss, I did not expect to find any difference of opinion expressed by lesser luminaries than Crussard. I was quite correct in this assumption. Not one of the dozens of personnel we met expressed any disagreement with his determination to prove paranormality in Girard, and he issued firm instructions to them that were followed slavishly.

One edict from on high was that Vallejo must not be present at the tests. The suspicion was that he might act as my confederate, Crussard apparently having lost track of who was being tested. Since Mr. Vallejo has seen dozens of spoon-benders of all sorts, he was not very interested anyway and gladly substituted a tour of Grenoble for a boring lab session of watching silly people try to do silly things. Along with my other colleagues, I was committed to watching the dreadful drama and determined to see it through.

We three had no idea of the softening-up process that was about to be set in motion. Looking back on it, it is inconceivable to me that Bouvaist and Dubost were unaware of the bizarre nature of the preferred conditions under which Girard had insisted he be allowed to work. They were conditions carefully designed to put observers at the worst possible disadvantage, and it was all we could do to avoid being incapacitated as competent experimenters.

At about eight thirty that evening, we were picked up at our hotel and offered aperitifs, which I declined. I seldom drink, and I was not about to become befuddled. My sensitivity to alcohol is extreme, and in France, where dining without wine is barbarous, I have always been at a disadvantage. The restaurant that we visited was kept open especially late for our party, and in an upstairs dining room, waited on by the proprietor himself, we supped sumptuously at the considerable expense of Péchiney. Girard, ensconced at the head of the table, ordered vast amounts of cognac and wine, and saw to it that everyone's glass was filled. The meal itself I cannot describe adequately. The specialty of the house was a boiled chicken dish that contained mostly intoxicating substances; a fowl never was complimented with finer attention, or greater saturation in wine. In spite of my avoidance of the alcohol that many others were accepting, I was in danger of losing my objectivity, and when the dessert—a *bombe* liberally flavored with rum—arrived, I drew the line.

I noticed that Davies and Evans were quite careful about their intake too. Dr. Evans, known for his appreciation of good food and drink, remarked afterward that one of his greatest regrets was that he had to pass up so much fine beverage. His sacrifice was duly noted.

Two members of the party were introduced as magicians. One was an angular gentleman who drove me crazy with an affected cigarette holder that seemed to be constantly pointing in my face. He was André Sanlaville, an entrepreneur who makes his living somewhat on the fringes of the conjuring profession, promoting various festivals and conventions. The other was known as Ranky, a small, rotund man who has thrown in his lot, for whatever reason, with Girard. Both have seen Girard work many times, and both have declared him the real thing. I do not think they lie; I think they merely do not see very well. These two experts were as liberal with the intoxicants as most of the rest of the party, and the results were to show up later.

It was now approaching midnight, and Davies, Evans, and I were anxious to get started before conditions deteriorated into a real bacchanal. We were supposed to be there for a scientific experiment, and it was looking less like one every minute. Finally we were packed into cars and went not to a laboratory but to the apartment of Dr. Bouvaist, where we found a videotape setup ready. There was, of course, an ample supply of cognac as well. Girard seems to function well in such an atmosphere.

A word about Girard as we settled into this drama. He is, it appears, in his early thirties, a small man, well knit, quick and lively, dressed in fashionable velvets and a huge velvet bow tie. Altogether a show-business personality, and quite conscious of his reputation, he had refused my $10,000 offer through Crussard, and I had been admonished that even the mention of the reward might be enough to inhibit the results of the test. I played along with this notion. Also, I suspected that Girard had already been at work before our meeting, and it turned out I was right. In conversation the next day with Alexis Vallejo (you will remember that he had been banished), he told me that on the afternoon before the tests he had been staying at the apartment of one of the investigating scientists and had been invited by an unknown gentleman to hike into the hills nearby to hunt for mushrooms. Alexis had welcomed the diversion but wondered about the obsessive curiosity of his companion concerning me and my personal life. Since communication was difficult due to language barriers, and Vallejo was not about to divulge more than polite conversation might require, the mysterious questioner came away with little information. Vallejo was astonished to discover later that his companion had been Girard.

We must understand the status of both Davies and Evans in this matter. David Davies, editor of the science journal *Nature*, brought Evans with him as a referee. The year before, Crussard had submitted to *Nature* a report that told of 116 bending feats performed by Girard. It was admitted that "in some cases the experiment was confused and a trick may have been possible. But we never saw any tricks." An experiment involving a stainless-steel bar was performed in a closed—but not sealed—tube, said Crussard. The repertoire of feats read more like a theatrical bill than a series of scientific experiments, but Crussard's reputation as a metallurgist made Davies take him more seriously than he might have otherwise. I was reminded of his dilemma with parapsychologists Russell Targ and Harold Puthoff and *their* vague "scientific" paper, which *Nature* did publish.

Evans, in the company of Davies, had already met Girard and had seen some bending done. He had claimed no expertise and merely reported that he had witnessed something he could not explain but that he thought should be seen by a conjurer.

All of us agreed that the conditions imposed by Crussard had been inadequate, to say the least. The metal samples in particular had not been well controlled, and Girard had even been invited to take bars home with him to practice with, thus making it possible to substitute an already bent bar on his return. The taped and filmed tests we had seen always showed a great number of bars strewn about the table rather than just the one in use at the time. But this, remember, was *the way Girard liked to work*. Again, we found that the mouse was running the experiment.

Davies and Evans, in their first contact with Girard, had made no attempt to control anything. The method was to allow things to happen *comme d'habitude*—without interference. This way, the defects, if any, would show up. They showed up. And our efforts that afternoon had assured us that the new conditions Girard would face were adequate to prevent any deception, but in no way would they inhibit any genuine powers from operating. Davies and I wrote out in detail the simple rules, and Evans was put in charge of the box containing the samples to be used. We were prepared.

What followed was a comic opera. Girard stroked himself into a froth trying to produce a bend. At one point a tray of glasses was upset in the kitchen with much breakage. Many eyes turned toward the noise, but three pairs never left the test. Ranky, peerless observer that he was, succumbed to good wine and food and several times snored so loudly that we had to wake him up. Sanlaville never took his eyes off the experiment—except to cross the room to refill his glass, to light up another in an endless chain of noxious cigarettes, to chat with Ranky when he was awake between naps, and to doze off serenely a few times himself. If these were the standards they had previously used to put Girard to the test, it was little wonder they were bamboozled. As for Davies, Evans, and me, our eyes were falling out with exhaustion. Girard was as fresh as when he had started, and as he ebulliently stroked away we noted several times that his enthusiasm included a move we knew was quite sufficient to put the proper kind of pressure on the sample. We would interrupt the process at that point to replace the sample with a fresh one.

That afternoon Chris Evans had inadvertently ruined one sample. It was a bar marked "999," and we discovered that it was 99.9 percent pure aluminum. Tiny amounts of other metals in an aluminum mix produce astonishingly different qualities, but the almost-pure metal is also surprising. Chris had put a very small amount of pressure on the thick bar and it had bent so easily that he was amazed. We thus learned that almost-pure aluminum is *very* easily bent with very little pressure, and we wondered how many times Girard had been successful using this same material. We had already seen a quite hard and heavy bar he'd bent in an earlier experiment, but we also knew the conditions under which he had performed in previous tests, so there was little mystery about that.

Girard failed to produce any results at all over a period of three and a half hours when tested by competent and careful observers. (The latter did not include the two French magicians present. If a fireball like Gérard Majax had been there, we'd have had better representation from that quarter.) Our conclusion concerning Girard was totally negative, and so was the judgment of others who tested Girard within a few weeks of our confrontation with the great "psychic."

Dr. Yves Farge, with two assistants and the conjurer Klingsor, met with Girard for tests at the Centre National de la Recherche Scientifique, where Farge serves as director. They insisted on the same methods and rules that Davies, Evans, and I had worked out previously. Predictably, Girard produced nothing. I had met at length with Farge well before the tests and had briefed him about precautions, though I hardly think he needed any help. He was a tough nut to crack—just the kind of control that Girard needed and should have had from the first.

Gérard Majax was called in by Farge to design the second part of the test, in which Girard was supposed to move objects by psychokinesis, as advertised. He failed utterly in two lengthy tests. Although he had been carefully informed in great detail beforehand about the nature of the tests—a precaution that we always insist upon to prevent complaints of unusual or difficult conditions—he nonetheless beefed that things hadn't been to his liking. Crussard, of course, chimed in, saying that in *his* tests conditions were not that tight (yes, Charles, we are well aware of that) and that Farge had agreed to "work according to not-too-tight protocols." Right, but not too loose either.

The Péchiney bunch even called in Bernard Dreyfus, Research Director of the Nuclear Study Center in Grenoble, and pushed him into serving on an examining committee on short notice. He was annoyed at being ill-prepared for all this, and he recognized the desperation of the Péchiney team. Again nothing happened, and Girard was caught at the end of the test, *after it was officially terminated,* putting enough pressure on a bar to cause a minuscule bend of about four thousandths of an inch.

Dreyfus—determined that there would no longer be any cries from the parapsychologists of France that their colleagues in real science would not look at their results—put Girard through a set of tests (using the rules Davies, Evans, and I had established) in September 1977 that really cooked his *pâté de foie gras* once and for all. Girard strove mightily, but except for the now-expected marginal result accomplished *after the tests were concluded*, again nothing showed up to revolutionize science. Dreyfus, for good measure, also tested a kid named Steven North, whom John Hasted had introduced to him as a surefire miracle-worker. Steven, too, bit the dust before the steady gaze of Bernard Dreyfus.

Jean-Pierre Girard as he tried to perform his tricks in the lab of Professor Bernard Dreyfus. Magnetic needles were balanced on pivots, and he was to cause them to turn without using magnetic materials. La Recherche

Marcel Blanc, writing for the journal *New Scientist*, reported on Girard at length. He also said that Crussard had spent long hours trying to talk him into accepting his results in spite of the evidence against it all. Dreyfus, Blanc noted, had accepted the challenge and confronted the claims; he had not ignored the issue as if it was beneath the dignity of real science. Charles Crussard, said Blanc, "likes comparing himself to a new Copernicus or, as he told me, to Newton. At any rate, he cannot say, after the recent series of experiments, that he has been treated like Galileo."

Events moved swiftly. Girard withdrew a lawsuit against Jean-Pascal Huvé. He had taken legal action after Huvé wrote an article in which he said that Girard had admitted to him in person that it was all a scheme to prove that scientists can be deceived easily. Girard had to pay the costs. Crussard, not about to admit anything, maintained that though Girard does sometimes cheat, he still has psychic power. He also said that "Randi [has] it too, but refused to acknowledge the fact, and . . . used it to inhibit Girard's power." Again it's a case of "I'm so smart that if I can't see the trick, it's not a trick."

We had rejected the excessive instrumentation and the very delicate measurements previously applied to Girard's performance, since films and tapes had shown the protocol to be very relaxed and not sufficient to the task. Instead, scientifically correct, simple, direct tests of a claimed miracle-worker had been used. Girard failed. Then why did he try at all? He had professed total disinterest in my offer of $10,000 for one simple demonstration of a paranormal nature. I find this difficult to believe. However, he was very much interested in having my endorsement and that of the CSICOP. He got neither, since he is a common conjurer who must establish *his* conditions—understandably—to perform.

After my return to the United States, I received letters from Crussard announcing that Péchiney no longer felt bound by its promise to supply me—in return for my participation in the Girard tests—with the videotape and film material I had viewed. It was reminiscent of the situation at Stanford Research Institute, where thousands of feet of film and videotape, used to record experiments there, hold the solution to the tricks. But we may never see these well-guarded records that announce the New Age of Miracles. They are far too secret for ordinary mortals to view.

Piero Angela is a TV journalist who works for the Italian Radio and Television service (RAI). When he produced in 1978 a series of five one-hour special programs about his investigations of the paranormal, he brought down upon his head a hail of threats, denials, and complaints that he found hard to believe. Individuals and groups both within and outside Italy, dependent on the lack of definitive investigation of their claims, felt very strongly his interference with their comfortable situation, and both he and RAI were assaulted with telegrams and letters demanding that he withdraw his statements, which had blasted the parapsychologists and the whole psi industry. Angela would not, and as if to reaffirm his findings he published an account of his investigations, *Viaggio nel mondo del paranormale (A Journey into the World of the Paranormal)*, subtitled *An Investigation into Parapsychology*. The objections redoubled.

I first met Piero Angela via telephone. He had arrived in the United States to visit various centers of psi work and called to ask my advice concerning individuals he might question. I suggested, of course, the crown princes of psi, Russell Targ and Harold Puthoff. Charles Honorton of Maimonides Hospital, with his Viewmaster-slide dream telepathy game, was included for variety, and Charles Tart of Learning-to-Use-ESP fame was suggested for light entertainment. One now-prominent investigator, Helmut Schmidt, was at that time a mystery to me, but was on the list as well. I warned Angela that if his experience was anything like mine, he would extract very little from these funambulists unless they were convinced that he was a believer. A few weeks later, when he called me from California to tell me that they seemed unable to answer simple questions without heroic, evasive declarations and hedging, I suggested that he consult Ray Hyman, Martin Gardner, and me to get a firmer grip on his slippery subject. He did just that, and the result was his devastating series on RAI in Italy.

If Piero had not been the excellent journalist that he is, he could have easily accepted the honeyed words offered him by the semantic wizards of psi. A favorable story would go down easily back home, and a negative one would be hard to make acceptable. But Angela was accustomed to flying in the face of convention. He was determined to get at the facts and bypass the fancies. The series, as eventually aired, was a powerful indictment of parapsychologists, the literature of the subject, and the shameless acceptance of such claptrap by the media. And, I dare say, this excursion into pseudo-science brought an enormous change in the life and career of Piero Angela.

Early in 1979 Piero invited me to Italy again (I had been there the year before to be filmed for the TV series) to respond to more than forty wonder-workers who had taken me up on my offer of $10,000 to anyone able to perform just one genuine paranormal feat. As the weeks went by between my acceptance and my departure for Italy in March, the challengers dropped out one by one. This was partly owing to my conditions that they had to agree in advance that the presence of a skeptical observer such as myself would not inhibit the results and that they had to allow me to use any data obtained during the tests. Some of these folks believed that they could get me to agree (as Uri Geller had with many of *his* investigators) not to reveal the results if they failed. By the time I arrived in Rome to meet the performers, only ten were left.

Accompanied by a colleague, William Rodriguez, I went into conference with Piero Angela. RAI was covering the event, and made two special Sunday programs from the film they shot. The aspirants came from all over Italy, divided, as usual, into two distinct groups: those who mistakenly believed they had genuine powers and those who were out-and-out fakes. The latter group was small and confined to the table-tippers. Here are the stars of our drama:

Mrs. Antonetta Petrignani, who produces "spirit pictures" with a Polaroid camera.

Professor Giuseppe Festa, a mummifier of fruits and meat. He holds the sample between his hands to "irradiate" it.

Mr. M. Salvatori, specializing in projecting dream images into the nighttime thoughts of his subjects.

Mrs. Catarina Zarica, a table-tipper and table-knocker, assisted by her husband.

Mrs. Clara Del Re, a table-tipper, assisted by her husband and daughter.

Mr. Fontana, Professor Borga, Mr. Stanziola, and Mr. Senatore, all water-dowsers; some able to find metals as well.

Mr. Jacovino, a key-bender and watch-stopper (who failed to show up at the last moment).

Thus there were nine ready-and-willing contestants scheduled to perform, and various claims were involved.

My thirty-five years of experience in this field dictated that certain necessary steps be taken. Such performers are consistent in one thing above all: They offer rationalizations and convoluted excuses of the most outrageous sort when a test fails. To thwart these alibis, I insisted that a long questionnaire be answered first, so that we understood one another. I will discuss the challengers in turn, detailing the main features and problems of each case.

First, Mrs. Petrignani from Milan. This little lady, I must say at the outset, impressed us all as one who was honestly deceived by her inability to take good pictures. This became sadly evident to me when I examined a huge stack of several hundred Polaroid photos she brought with her and listened to her interpretations of what she saw therein. One of them showed—to her eyes, at least—a man crouching on a plank with a rock beneath it. I could see nothing but a blur of gray and white against a black background. As she sorted through the prints, I put that one aside for later use in a test I had in mind. Mrs. Petrignani had taken these photos with an electric-eye Polaroid camera, using square-format, black-and-white film. She habitually pressed the shutter release with the camera pointed at her face under poor lighting conditions. At first she was steady and composed. She pressed the shutter release slowly, allowing the automatic shutter to make the correct exposure. But as she continued and went "into trance," she shook and wobbled about, pushing the shutter release violently and jerkily. She did not allow the automatic feature to operate, and all pictures came out black with slight gray smears. The time of development, normally 10 seconds, went to as much as 35 seconds. The result was that the first photos were almost sharp, in spite of the fact that she held the camera about 20 inches away when the focus was set for 39 inches (one meter). Subsequent shots, taken as close as 8 inches away, and while moving, produced the smears that she interpreted as "psychic."

Mrs. Antonetta Petrignani concentrates on taking another fuzzy picture.

During my examination of her results, I turned the man-on-a-plank shot 180 degrees and submitted it to her again as if I'd selected it from among the unsorted photos. This time, viewing it upside down, she said she saw part of an old building and a dog in the photo. Further examination showed that of her twelve most successful shots of "psychic" scenes, six were viewed upside down, two had been turned 90 degrees to the left, two others had been rotated 90 degrees to the right, and two were right side up. Psychic power knows no direction. . . .

The results of our test were interesting. When the studio was well lighted, all her photos were reasonably sharp. The automatic feature of the Polaroid system gave sufficient exposure in spite of the short shutter release. When the light was diminished to much lower levels, smears appeared, but all were attributable to out-of-focus facial features or to bad development resulting from pulling the film too quickly from the camera. One thing I must say: At least Mrs. Petrignani followed instructions and wiped the rollers clean inside the camera before taking the photos. No "contamination bars" were visible, which was not the case with other "psychic photographers" I have examined.

Mrs. Petrignani admitted that she could never tell what result she would get and that recognizable images were only "sometimes" obtained.

She made no claims about the strange results she got, and she was willing to listen to reason if I offered a probable explanation. She listened, seemed to accept my analysis, and retired from the scene gracefully. She didn't even ask about the $10,000.

But Professor Giuseppe Festa was feisty. As proof of his healing power, he claimed to be able to mummify foods with radiation emanating from his hands. The test was easily set up, and the questionnaire was most revealing. Had he ever tried the test with the samples wrapped in plastic? No. Had he tried controlled tests with some samples treated and some not? No. Were hamburger, chicken, and veal satisfactory for

Professor Giuseppe Festa, who claimed to be able to mummify food as proof of his healing touch.

the tests? Yes. How many times had he done this before? About four or five times (?!). Rate of success? One hundred percent!

The Festa tests lasted nine days. This was because the samples had to be allowed to mature—and mature they did—for at least three days. The rules specified that we would conduct three tests, and two out of the three had to be wins in order for me to surrender the $10,000 prize. I began to worry when I noticed Professor Festa staring at expensive electronic equipment in a store window on the first day of the tests. The hamburger was divided into ten portions, and each was packed into a plastic dish, numbered on the bottom. From a hat, Festa chose a number and held the corresponding sample between his hands for ten minutes, then returned it to the tray. The samples were shuffled about so that no one knew which was the treated one, after which the tray was taken by another party to be locked up safely. Three days later we met to view the results.

A judge was asked a simple question: Had any of the samples been mummified, and if so, which one(s)? The answer was no. All were in advanced states of putrefaction, which was quite evident from the smell. Festa asked if the samples might be kept longer, and I agreed, noting that he had specified seventy-two hours, and that further retention of the samples was to be considered outside the limits of the testing procedure. Next we tried chicken, which Festa claimed he had handled with great success. In fact, he had shown us samples of chicken, a pear, and an orange that he had "mummified" in his home. The chicken was like glass, the pear was shriveled and black, and the orange was hard, shrunken, and desiccated. Questioning revealed that Festa had placed these samples in the open air with a breeze blowing. In my opinion, they had merely been dried quickly, in the same fashion that American Indians prepared pemmican, without smoking or other preserving processes. In fact, I have before me at this moment an orange that my cat knocked under the furniture months ago. It is in every respect identical to Festa's orange, having naturally dried out.

After the test with the chicken breasts failed as well (with much more dramatic olfactory manifestations!), Festa announced that he was not satisfied with the test procedure, claiming that the nine untreated samples had affected the one treated sample by their proximity. In a third test, this time with veal, all samples were separated but kept under similar conditions of humidity, temperature, and so on. Again mummification failed to take place. Festa went on at length about inhibiting factors, but he was washed up as a psychic.

I believe that Professor Festa really thinks he has these powers. The fact that he had never been subjected to a controlled test before was significant. A perfectly ordinary phenomenon had become, to him, a miracle. After all, if the news in some quarters is full of ordinary persons with supernormal powers, why should the principal of a high school not be endowed with similar ability? I trust that his powers of reasoning are not transmitted to his pupils either in quality or degree.

Mr. Salvatori was next in the tumbrel. It was his claim that if he projected a "target" to a subject at night, that target would enter the dream(s) of the subject. He needed to know the subject first by meeting him or her, and had to have a photo of the subject to transmit with. He said we were free to choose the subject, and we prepared a list of twenty different targets to choose from. The list contained such items as chickens, an execution, Paris, digging the garden, walking a dog, walking on the moon, and Christmas. Salvatori was shown the numbered

Festa's evidence: a dried orange, chicken breast, and a pear—all psychically "healed," he claimed.

list of the targets, and he chose from the inescapable hat a number from one to twenty. He was the only one who knew the number and thus the target, and he signed the numbered slip, mixed it among the others in an envelope, sealed the envelope, and put it into the hands of a security person along with the list. The subject had been photographed and chatted with *before* this process, then whisked away to dream.

The following day, sure that Salvatori had not contacted the dreamer, we presented the list of targets to the subject. He was to determine if there was a target there that defined or suggested strongly his dream(s) of the previous night. There were three such tests, and in all three the subject failed to find *even one* listed target that matched a dream. But there was an angle in this case that very much interested me. First, conversations with Salvatori revealed that it was his habit to invent his own target for transfer to the subject. This gave him a "preferred-target" advantage, since we found that he tended to choose the themes—such as flying or falling—that would most likely occur in a subject's dreams. Second, we found that Mr. Salvatori always asked the subjects to describe their dreams before telling them the target, leading them in the direction of the target and accepting any vague, peripheral connection as evidence of success. Knowing all this, I allowed Salvatori to discuss his subjects' dreams with them only *after* they had examined the list and arrived at a conclusion. True to expectations, he tried to match up *anything* in the dreams to the chosen targets. In the first case, when "an execution" had been the chosen target, the subject had dreamed of receiving a phone call from the wife of a man who had been murdered. To Salvatori, that was a success.

The Salvatori case is a good example of a performer not knowing what a double-blind controlled test is, and of his trying to fit facts to

Mr. Salvatori, projector of dreams via telepathy. He lost, 3 to 0.

a theory. It's an old and tired story. Salvatori had told us, in the questionnaire, that he was satisfied with the target selection and the subjects, that he usually selected his own targets "any way," that he had never tried a controlled test like this before, and that his power worked over any distance. He also claimed that "a psychologist" had tested him and validated his ability, but when we pressed him for the name of the man, Salvatori told us that the investigator would not want to get involved. Mr. Salvatori retired from competition, and the next contender stepped forward.

Catarina Zarica, a rather spare and mysterious lady, told us that the spirits would manifest themselves when she and her husband placed their hands on a table. But, she said, she required a three-legged table. We scouted Rome for such an item, and shopkeepers thought us a bit strange when we turned down perfectly good tables because they had four legs. Finally, we had to order a special table made to Zarica's specifications. Meanwhile, we went ahead with Mrs. Clara Del Re and her fellow table-thumpers.

We had been assured in advance that Mrs. Del Re was "very religious." If so, I would like to know how her religious philosophy accommodates such shenanigans. Her husband, who spoke good English (my Italian is confined to *E pericoloso sporgersi*), had a long conversation with me in which he promised that a table would "walk over to you" during the séance. We shook hands on that, and I agreed that I would be appropriately impressed—$10,000 worth—with such an occurrence.

The Del Re family bombed out. They sat around the table (mom, dad, and daughter) seemingly forever, and it would not move. We lowered the lights. Still no action. The crucifix and rosary were moved about the table, and family members changed positions. Nothing. They admitted defeat but promised that later that night, during an *informal* demonstration, wonders would blossom. I could hardly wait, especially since it was quite obvious to me why no miracles had been seen. A discussion of a few fundamentals of physics is required to explain my precautions.

There are two basic methods of table-tipping. If a portion of the

Mrs. Clara Del Re, table-tipper. Under conditions that precluded cheating, she and her family failed to move the table.

table that is outside the possible fulcrum position is pressed down, the opposite side will rise. In Diagram 1, applying pressure in direction D with the hands at the position marked by the stars will cause the table to tilt upward in direction R, the legs at F acting as a fulcrum. Thus the sitter at point S1 is the instigator, while S2, S3, and S4 can be quite innocent, though S3 has to cooperate by applying *very* little pressure on that side. The second contributor to table motion is a move that consists of placing the hands down firmly at the position of the two arrows and *drawing* the table in direction H, horizontally. The result is the same, F acting as the fulcrum and the table tilting upward in direction R. Pressing *down* within the area delineated by the broken lines, however, will not produce any table motion; only horizontal pulling will do this when the hands are in this area. To eliminate any movement of the table by either of these means, first insist that the hands be kept within the area bordered by the four broken lines, with no part of the palm or any finger allowed to contact the table outside that

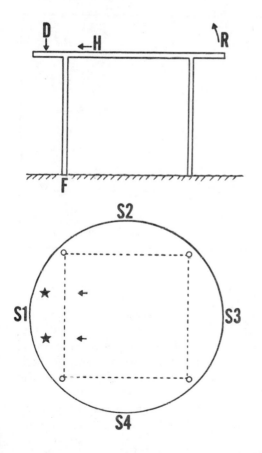

Diagram 1. Downward pressure at D and drawing the table in direction H cause the table to tilt upward at R.

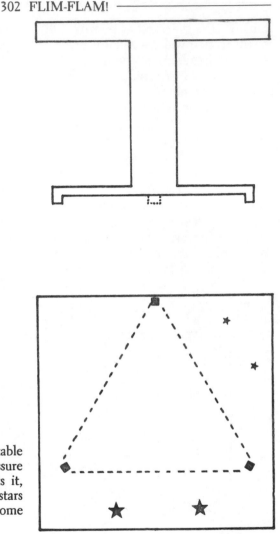

Diagram 2. The special table made for the Zaricas. Pressure at the large stars easily tilts it, and pressure at the small stars also causes a tilt, but with some difficulty.

area, and with all arms held off the table. Then place two sheets of waxed paper, one atop the other, beneath the hands of the "psychic" performer. You will have the results that we observed with the Del Res and with the Zaricas. The table cannot move in any way. Horizontal pulling only makes the hands slip on the paper, and pressing down is of no use. (We are not taking into account the possibility of using the feet or legs in this discussion.)

Michael Faraday, the famous inventor, devised a way of proving this by placing a board on ball bearings atop the table. The medium had to place his hands on this board. The table stayed put, though the board moved around a lot.

The Zarica team, despite the fact that we had made the table to their specifications, was unable to move it. This table, represented by Diagram 2, weighed about sixty-five pounds and gave enormous advantages to the performers. Again, pressing at the spots marked by the large stars would tilt the table easily. Even pressing at the position indicated by the smaller stars would produce a good tilt, though much more pressure is necessary. One of the TV crew, pulling within the "dead" triangular area, was able to tilt the table slightly, though he had to stand to do it. It is evident that the pressing technique is much easier if the tilter is seated high, and though we supplied chairs of standard height to Catarina and her husband, they asked for another six inches of height in the form of cushions to sit on. Even with this advantage, the table stayed put.

The Zaricas complained that the table was too heavy. But, we reminded them, they had told us that at home they used a table of these dimensions regularly—and it weighed 220 pounds! Aha, countered Mr. Zarica, to the evident satisfaction of Catarina, but *this* table had a triangle drawn in white on the top, and that, as everyone knew, was the sign of the devil and inhibited the effect. The offending triangle was erased, but the Zaricas felt they'd had enough and flew into individual tantrums, alleging negative vibrations everywhere and a general lack of sincerity.

We had been promised great results that evening under informal, subdued-light conditions with no cameras. I carefully informed all present that I would not tolerate their claiming that they had been successful if that evening, under uncontrolled conditions, the table cavorted. They were not pleased but were forced to agree.

With the camera crew packed up for the night, I was invited to sit at a regular round table. The Zaricas sat side by side, and the Del Res and I completed the circle of six. Almost as soon as we sat down, the games started. The table began scooting about, obviously pushed by Mr. Zarica, whose efforts were not resisted by the others. The illustrations will show how the movement was evident. After Mr. Zarica had pushed the table around for a while, with his hands pressed tightly to the surface, he announced that all should contact the table only very lightly and called attention to the fact that now only his fingertips were in contact. But Mrs. Zarica, responding to the cue, now pressed her hands down hard and took over the action. I was surprised to note that she made one very careless and obvious error. Most of the time we had to stand, since the table was zipping about, and I could see that just before the table began to move because of her efforts, *she*

Mr. and Mrs. Zarica examine the made-to-order table suspiciously.

began to step in the direction it was about to move! Thus I not only always knew which way the "spirits" were about to toss the table, I could also plainly see who was moving it. Their sitters must be pretty dense to believe this act.

When we settled down to serious business, after transferring our

The Zarica séance. Note that when cameras were present the Zaricas touched the table lightly. The result was that nothing happened.

The Zaricas and another sitter are unable to move the table with their hands inside the "safe" area.

efforts to the special Zarica Table—to no avail whatsoever—I suggested some test questions. I offered to indicate the truth or falsity of answers that they said my dead grandmother could give me. To obviate any claims that I was simply denying the truth of the answers, I'd prepared the answers in written form and had the document sticking out of my shirt pocket. The "psychics" claimed they definitely had contacted the proper spirit, and I began the questions. The answers were given by raps of the table: one rap for "yes," two for "no." Here are the questions and answers:

Q: Was her husband's name George?
A: No.
Q: Was it Nicolai?
A: No.
Q: Was it Walter?
A: Yes.

I gave no feedback during this exchange, refusing to indicate whether the answers were right or wrong until the test was over. In fact, the answers were 100 percent wrong. You see, my grandfather's name was George Nicolai Zwinge; the table had answered all three questions incorrectly. I asked the names of my grandmother's daughters, with the same results. It was then suggested that they could tell me

Mrs. Catarina Zarica, table-tipper. She and others took turns
pushing the furniture around.

something for which we could have immediate verification. Perhaps something in my passport? Well, we were staying at the same hotel where
this séance had been arranged, and much of my passport information
was recorded there. But one thing in my passport I knew had not been
recorded, and that was a name written in the back. On the chance
that my passport had been filched from my room for examination, I
sent my colleague Rodriguez for it, and when he arrived with it safely
in hand, I asked the others to give me the name, which, I told them,
had six letters.

The table began thumping mightily, once for each letter of the
alphabet, but since the Italian alphabet is lacking some letters of the
English alphabet, we had to count thumps and translate it two different
ways. Neither way made any sense. One gave us Itpbmt, the other
Ivrbov. Neither even approaches Marvin, the name in the passport.
Nor do I think I will ever meet Mr. Itpbmt. . . .

William Rodriguez, who had previously been excluded from the
séances for having a "frivolous" attitude (who could blame him, seeing
grown people pushing a table around?), observed something that was
beyond my line of sight. It happened while the table-thumping was
being accomplished by little Mrs. Zarica, who was pressing the tabletop
at the appropriate spot and drawing horizontally at the same time. Properly done, this combination of maneuvers produces a very satisfactory
lift of the opposite side of the table. But with all those hands atop
the table, and the great effort required, Rodriquez noted that every
time the table tilted, *her feet came off the floor!* It was the unavoidable
consequence of having to push like crazy to make the tilt, and Newton's
Third Law was demonstrated. If the table had been tilted that way by
any other means, her feet would have tended to push down, never up.

Mysteries remain, however. What part did the Del Res play in the drama? It was clear that Mr. Del Re assisted the table as it scooted around the floor, but he remained passive, as did the others, when the table thumped out its errors. Were the others in on the imposture? Undoubtedly they were familiar with these methods, so one can assume they were well aware of what was going on. But there is another distinct possibility. In such a group, each individual knows that he fakes the thing *when he is the operator.* Might he not suspect that when he is *not* pushing the table about or tilting it up, it is happening by genuine psychic means? How many husbands have convinced their wives that the wives have psychic powers just by performing the physical work themselves? One wonders. Certainly, the Zaricas had their act together. One took over from the other on a signal, and neither doubted the reason for the perambulations. But as for the others—I just don't know who knows what. I tend to think they are all mountebanks.

The Del Res took their defeat gracefully, though not without considerable alibi-ing as they packed up to leave. The Zaricas, due to return on the following day to tackle the Zarica Table once more, returned instead to Palermo and fired off a few telegrams crying "foul!" and claiming a victory. When I notified them that I had caught them cheating, they informed me that they denied my expertise and did not accept my opinion. Tough, kids. You failed on a grand scale. No Kewpie doll.

I was left with weighty matters to consider, however. Mrs. Del Re had informed me that her contact with Grandma elicited this information: I was born in New Jersey. Wrong; I was born in Canada. There was one toy, unidentified otherwise, to which I was particularly attached in my childhood. Who knows? A not uncommon circumstance, but I cannot remember. In my business, I was warned, there is a colleague whom I must not trust. A poor and very general attempt at psychic revelation, but if they considered *themselves* colleagues of mine, they were 100 percent right. I am personally ambitious, I was told. So was Brutus, but he was honorable. Finally, Grandma is angry with me. Not unlikely, though it is I who should be miffed at Grandma for fluffing all those simple questions. And now that I think of it, the table never "walked over to me" as promised, and we had shaken hands on that.

Five down, four to go. While all this nonsense was going on, with spoiled hamburger, faulty dreamers, and unstable tables everywhere, a small crew of men were at work thirty miles outside Rome in a little town called Formello. In accordance with careful plans I had drawn, they were building a network of plastic pipes that we would be using to test the water-dowsers who still clamored for the $10,000 prize. They arrived at the hotel, submitted themselves to our questionnaires, and settled down to await being summoned to the field of battle. They occupied their time by describing their wonderful accomplishments to one another, with appropriate gestures and, I'm sure, some exaggeration.

But all was not well at the site. The first engineer wanted 3 million lire to do the job, and I had to turn him down and change the pipe chart. Piero Angela's assistant obtained another man, who turned out to be an idiot. The 10-by-10-meter plot he laid out was a rhombus, and all had to be revised again. By the time the thing was ready, three days had passed and the dowsers' noses and divining rods were all twitching. On the appointed day I was awakened at 4 A.M. by peals of thunder and a hailstorm that stirred all Rome. By the afternoon we had gathered our wits enough to assemble the four aspirants in Formello, and there was time to test one of them. The problem was that he had to be shipped out of town right after the test so that he could not inform the others of the layout in the slightest detail. No results were to be announced until all the papers were ready and evaluated, so the findings would not be available until the next day.

Since these tests were, to my knowledge, the first really proper testing of dowsing claims, I will describe the procedure in some detail. Of primary importance to the long-range results, of course, was the removal of all possible Catch-22 conditions that might be employed after the tests to excuse failure. To that end, the questionnaire was extra-carefully designed to assure that everything was understood and accounted for in advance. The conditions were:

1. In a 10-by-10-meter area, pipes 3 centimeters in diameter have been buried at a depth of 50 centimeters.
2. There are three different paths of three different lengths available, one to be chosen at random for each test.
3. Three tests will be performed with each person, and the same path may be used more than once, since the choice is random.
4. The chosen path may enter at any point on any side of the square and exit at any point on any side of the square.
5. First, the dowser must scan the area for any natural water or other distractions (metal or other objects) and mark these "natural" places.
6. Any secondary distractions will be outlined on the ground visibly.
7. Second, the dowser must demonstrate, on an exposed water pipe, while the water is running, that the dowsing reaction is present.
8. The dowser will determine the path of the flowing water in the pipe being used, and this path will be marked on the ground.

9. The dowser will place from ten to one hundred pegs in the ground along the path he traces.
10. To be counted, a peg must be placed within 10 centimeters of the center of the pipe being traced.
11. Two thirds of the pegs put in the ground in each of the three tests for each dowser must be placed within the limits specified by condition 10 for that test to be considered a success.
12. Placement of each peg will be transferred to a scale chart by the surveyor to the satisfaction of the dowser, who will sign this chart along with Mr. Randi, the lawyer, and other witnesses.
13. No results will be announced until all tests are finished and the location of the pipes is revealed.
14. After a dowser has performed, he will be isolated from those yet to be tested.
15. Two out of three of the tests must be successful (as in condition 11) for the dowser to have passed the testing procedure.
16. If a dowser passes the test (conditions 11 and 15), the check for $10,000, which has been deposited with the lawyer, will be awarded to him. If no dowser is successful, the check will be returned to Mr. Randi.
17. If the test is failed, no further claim may be made against Mr. Randi.

A few additional points were added after consultation with the dowsers. I specified that no single pipe crossed itself, though it might cross others. Only one pipe would have water in it at any particular time. Pipes outside the square would not run along the side within 50 centimeters of the edge. With these additions, everyone was satisfied.

Next, the engineers' statement was read to all:

1. There are three paths, laid according to James Randi's instructions on the engineering plan.
2. Valves A,A control flow in pipe path A.
   Valves B,B control flow in pipe path B.
   Valves C,C control flow in pipe path C.
3. When both valves on any path are opened, water flows at a rate of at least five liters per second.
4. I have not communicated any information about this plan to anyone except those directly involved in construction.

Finally, a list of questions for the dowsers:

1. Are you a professional, semiprofessional, or amateur dowser?
2. To what do you attribute your power?

3. Have you read and understood the list of conditions?
4. Are these conditions satisfactory?
5. Do you feel able to perform today?
6. Have you ever done a test so carefully controlled?
7. Have you read and understood the engineer's statement?
8. Is the water flow sufficient for your abilities?
9. Do you agree that this test will determine the validity of your powers?

The last question was struck out by all the dowsers—a fortunate choice for them, as we shall see.

Just before each dowser started the tests, he was asked (1) what he felt his rate of success would be (all answered either "99 percent" or "100 percent") and (2) what he would conclude if he was, for example, 90 degrees out of line with the actual water flow (all answered that this was an impossibility).

Following each set of tests, the dowsers were asked (1) how successful they thought they had been (three answered "100 percent" and one had not completed the test) and (2) if they thought they had won the $10,000 (the same three answered very affirmatively).

With this sort of preparation, I felt that the results would help to explain just why so many otherwise intelligent people think they have the power to find hidden substances with sticks. All probable "outs" had been covered, and the outcome might well convince even the dowsers themselves that their performances were combinations of a peculiar "instrumentation" and poor standards of validation.

The instruments used need to be discussed and evaluated. The most common tool, particularly in the United States, is the forked stick. When the stick is grasped properly and moderate pressure is exerted to further spread the "fork," a state of unbalance is quickly approached. Without effort on the part of the user, the "pointer" *must* go either up or down to relieve the pressure applied, though such movement is kept under control by small adjustments in the position of the wrist. The strong tendency of the pointer to move seems to be independent of the will of the user, and the impression is given that some external force is acting on the rod. I have seen such a stick whip up and strike a dowser, breaking his glasses. My reader should try it and experience the phenomenon.

We often hear that the bark on the green stick that is used will peel away under the force. That is true. Green sticks with slippery bark (willow is ideal) make the best dowsing sticks, since they are harder to control, and the bark often breaks loose. In fact, the stick sometimes flies out of the hands, so sudden is the whipping motion of the pointer.

Construction of the site is begun. The inlets will be on the right, the outlets on the left.

The inlets before they were covered. From top left, counterclockwise, they are A, B, and C.

Paths B and C cross each other, but water runs through only one pipe at a time.

The outlets into the reservoir are tested before the pipes are covered.

The outlets as the dowsers saw them.

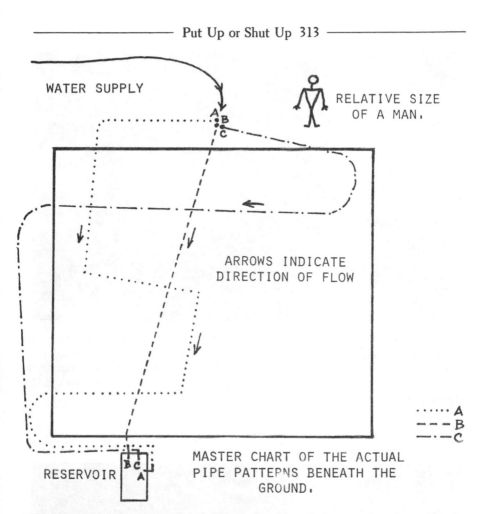

WATER SUPPLY

RELATIVE SIZE
OF A MAN.

ARROWS INDICATE
DIRECTION OF FLOW

······ A
– – – B
—·— C

RESERVOIR

MASTER CHART OF THE ACTUAL
PIPE PATTERNS BENEATH THE
GROUND.

The completed layout of the dowsing site. The plot was reduced to an area of nine by ten meters due to last-minute problems at the site.

The water-pipe network is covered and the dirt is leveled.

The traditional (in the United States) dowsing rod. A forked stick, held as shown, is put under stress as the heels of the hands are turned toward the body. When this is done, it is quite difficult to keep the rod horizontal, and *any* shift of the grip or twist of the wrist will cause a deflection upward or downward.

A slight turn of the wrists has caused the rod to move downward, and the hand positions have changed to retain a grip on the stick.

The rod has jumped all the way down. The upward and downward whipping of the rod as it responds to very slight changes in tension and direction of strain is involuntarily controlled by the user.

All this has nothing to do with any mysterious force; we are dealing with a physical system under tension and in a state of delicate equilibrium. Why does the stick point when the dowser believes he is over water? Because it is easy to tilt either wrist *very* slightly to make the stick move, and if the dowser knows where the water is *supposed* to be, or has made a guess about where it is, he can easily and unconsciously guide the stick.

I have heard of some dowsers who claim 100-percent success in their attempts to find water and of others who claim only 90 percent. The sad fact is that dowsers are no better at finding water than anyone else. Drill a well almost anywhere in an area where water is geologically possible, and you will find it. Dowsers have the strange notion that water travels in underground rivers, and they will happily trace these hidden torrents for you. But geologists know otherwise. Bob Huguley, a geologist who works for the Planning Board of Monmouth County, New Jersey, doesn't know of one dowser in the area who has ever been successful. He also estimates that less than 1 percent of the earth's underground water actually flows beneath the surface. That small fraction is confined to areas rich in limestone (known as "karst" country) and the resulting caves, where real underground streams can occur. Underground flow can also occur in porous material, but that flow amounts to only a few feet or a few miles in a year. Most water that is obtained by means of wells and so forth is in pools and reservoirs underground. It does not flow.

The reason dowsers consider themselves successful is easy to discover. When the dowser's customer digs and finds water, the dowser attributes this success to his detection of the right spot. No one ever bothers to drill nearby and discover the same source. Like so many other self-deluded "psychics," they simply choose to believe.

The test I devised did not allow the performers to excuse any failure easily. They had shown that they could detect the flowing water in the pipe—when they knew where it was. They had determined what they thought were the locations of naturally existing water under the ground and could make allowances for it; thus they could not claim interference after failure. And after the test they would know, definitely and easily, just where the water *was*. In addition, we had determined the minimum flow they needed (one required at least five liters per second) and we supplied more than twice the minimum, fed by gravity.

After unbelievable problems with the pumping system, we photographed and mapped the scene with great accuracy and got everything down on paper, attested to and witnessed thoroughly. The shuttle bus sped off to town to bring the first contestant to the scene.

Mr. Fontana had come from Pisa. He had told us that he had the ability to detect ordinary water traveling in pipes under the streets, but not sewage water ("not enough magnetism"), and that he dowsed maps for oil with "100-percent success." Further questioning revealed that he had *never checked* any of his oil findings! But he was happy to show us a huge world atlas he carried about, and he traced for us a massive, underground *river of oil* extending all the way from Greenland through England, France, and Italy and Sicily, ending in Tunisia. The folks at that end, said Fontana, were robbing Italy of oil by draining it off. I kept my doubts to myself.

Please note that the dowsers' claims and theories mentioned here are typical of the breed all over the world. They are not especially bizarre, as such notions go in this most widespread of all delusions. I have heard more farfetched theories frequently.

Fontana checked the area for existing natural water, then tested his dowsing device over the exposed pipe. He determined that two underground streams crossed each other on the site, and we marked them for his reference. He thought they would not interfere with the test. Using a straight willow rod, as Stanziola would do later on, he found

what he believed to be the entry point of the flowing pipe and started
in. Then he changed to a pendulum. The accompanying map shows
where he walked and plotted, compared to where the water actually
was. And it shows why I feared for my prize money as this first contestant
proceeded.

Fontana had drawn path C for his first test. He started off at the
position opposite the inlet faucets and zipped across the plot, waving
his pendulum wildly and pointing out spots where pegs should be placed.
On this first try he came surprisingly close to path B, though it was
empty during that run. In fact, some of his pegs were within the limits
of the test, if applied to path B. As I saw this, I feared that perhaps
the plan of the pipes had gotten out (I did not know which path had
been chosen) and that I'd been had. But I trusted that the dowsers
were basically honest, and under no circumstances would I renege on
my offer. I had committed myself and would stand by the agreement,
whether cheating was going on or not.

Mr. Fontana was a direct and uncomplicated man. He had assumed
that the pipes entered on one side and exited on the other. He was
almost right. I'd put in one simple pipeline, path B, to demonstrate
that even a direct, straight flow was not detectable by the dowsers
That was amply shown by the rest of the contest.

Mr. Fontana (his name means "fountain") wiggles a pendulum while following
nonexistent underground water.

It happened that path B was the third of Fontana's tests. He decided that this was a repeat of the first one (which was actually path C) and terminated his efforts. Thus in one test, his third, he got a very small score. It was quite far from winning, and had in no way demonstrated any dowsing ability, but Fontana was the best of the four dowsers we tested.

We were now ready for the flamboyant Professor Borga from Trento. He had carried on at great length about vast destructive rivers he had discovered beneath Florence, responsible, he told us, for the flooding of that city. He wanted to tap into these rivers and divert the water

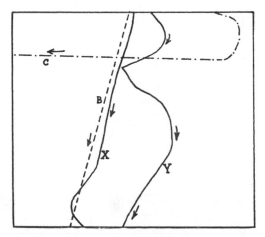

Fontana traversed the vertical line X in his attempt to follow path C (the horizontal path at the top), then the line Y in another attempt to locate C. He decided not to make a third try, saying we could use his first attempt (X) as his third guess. Thus his first and third guesses actually paralleled path B—the direct line between the valve and the reservoir!

from the art treasures. Borga claimed he could detect "almost any flow" of water and said he was also sensitive to oil. However, when he buzzed about trying to find the natural water in the plot, he found nothing. (We wondered what had happened to the two underground torrents Fontana had detected.)

Borga used two hinged, stiff sticks that whirled about in his hands, raising calluses at the lower edge of his hands along the little fingers and palms. From a straight-up position, the hinge went down and away from his body, arced in toward him, then moved toward his face and away and outward to repeat its circular motion. Occasionally it would stop and reverse its direction. Pressing the arms together while holding this device produces the tension characteristic of the forked stick or Fontana's flexible stick. The system is unstable; any small change in wrist position or tension causes the gadget to rotate. Such small impetuses are easily and involuntarily introduced to the device by the dowser.

The professor's sticks whirled about like an amusement park attraction. He stepped around the plot like a pinstriped crane in mating season, uttering short commands to the assistant, who inserted pegs for him, and laughed and mumbled to himself, obviously delighted by visions of wealth and fame. It is interesting that, in the third test, Borga provided proof of the idiocy of such beliefs and established beyond doubt that dowsing is all in the imagination of the performer. The five-thousand liters in the truck supplying the water at that moment ran out. As Borga headed toward the finish, the engineer signaled to me to look at the reservoir, and I saw that the water had ceased flowing. I cautioned him to say nothing, and Borga continued. The sound of the pump was such that he could not tell the flow had ceased. After Borga had proceeded a bit farther, we told him that the water was "running out." Immediately his sticks began slowing down and he cried out to us to notice that his powers had detected this fact.

Actually, this was the most important moment of the entire dowsing experiment. Borga had been certain (he said he was 100 percent certain) that he had plotted the three paths. His sticks reacted very strongly, and he even "adjusted" one of his attempts, moving the sticks as little as an inch or so to ensure accuracy. But Borga was detecting *nothing*. There were no pipes there, water-filled or not. And—most important— he had continued to detect water, in the wrong place and direction, even after the flow had ceased! I felt no guilt in not having told him that the water had run out, since he had already failed the test spectacularly.

Borga retired, after making a statement to the TV cameras in which he expressed his confidence in the results. Next up was Stanziola, a

Zero hour. Mr. Borga begins his attempt. The inlet area is on the left; the starting position is marked by the striped pole.

Borga hot on the trail.

Borga's unusual dowsing rods: two stiff sticks, hinged with a pin. The apparatus allegedly whirls around when water is detected.

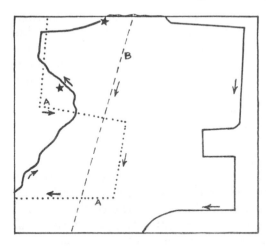

Borga's three attempts were far off the mark. He traced the pattern on the right as path B (dashed line), then traced it again as path A (dotted line). He then followed a course indicated by the solid line on the left in an attempt to trace path A again. The section of Borga's course between the stars was traversed by the dowser after the water in path A had ceased flowing; Borga continued, not knowing this.

young man who turned out to be a pupil of Borga. His attempt was to be short-lived. After finding a natural stream he said was running across the plot, he stepped over to the exposed pipe to detect the running water, placing his foot upon it and glancing toward the outlet, which he could not see from where he was. His dowsing stick refused to dip,

The surveyor plots the position of the pegs that were placed by Professor Borga. Although Borga adjusted these pegs carefully, shifting them as little as two centimeters for "fine tuning," he was fully eight feet from the nearest water.

and he asserted that no water was flowing. It was my opinion that Stanziola thought we were deceiving him by not running water in the pipe, since he could not feel any vibration in the part he stood on. (Because the feed was by gravity, the pipes did not vibrate at all. This was essential, since it might have been possible to detect the path this way, even through the earth cover.) We turned up the flow until it was a torrent, and still Stanziola detected nothing. The decision was that he could not compete, and he was officially disqualified.

However, I offered informally to test him by asking him to re-find the natural stream while blindfolded. He could not refuse such a test, and though only two of the points he chose came within three feet of the original path he'd traced, he claimed peripheral effects, and we did one last test in which he was moved around the plot at random and asked whether he was over the natural water or not. Of the four times he *was* in position, he called "no" twice, and of the four times he was not, he called "yes" twice. At least he was consistent.

Senatore came next and proved to be the most dramatic of all the performers. He used a piece of cane, broken almost in two at the center to provide a flexible joint. The device was similar to Borga's, but when Senatore operated it we stood back. It continually flew out of his hands; once it hit the cameraman, and it was replaced five times after breaking. He threw his head back and frowned mightily, stomping around the area and adjusting the pegs minutely. It had been decided that Senatore could use only one test rather than three to decide the matter, since darkness was approaching quickly, and he agreed completely to this additional and necessary rule in writing. His one attempt was hopelessly inaccurate. Need I add that he declared before the cameras that he had been 100 percent successful?

Piero and I drove off, leaving the pipes in place in case anyone wanted to check the layout, though we believed correctly that the dowsers would accept the sworn affidavits of the engineers, the surveyors, and the lawyer as to the position of the pipes and all the other pertinent details. We had been scrupulously honest with them about the affidavits and the conditions, and we found they had reciprocated. Piero was concerned that revealing to Professor Borga that he had failed would destroy him, since he had carried on at such great length about his flawless record and imminent success. But I assured Piero that he, as well as the others, would bounce back easily. Fanatics are not easily discouraged by facts or the truth. As we drove to the restaurant where the denouement was due, the three dowsers (Fontana had left to return home, delegating Borga to represent him) were talking to one another, trying to rationalize the discrepancies in their results.

After arriving at the appointed place, along with the dowsers and

Mr. Stanziola, using a flexible willow wand, looks for "natural" water.

all the officials, it dawned on me what a strange situation this was. Angela, Rodriguez, and I were embarrassed, not the dowsers. I shook off the feeling and resolved to tell it like it was. We presented the concealed plan of the pipes to the assembly and watched the expressions on their faces. There was a short silence. Then Borga spoke for the group, settling back in his chair. "We are lost," he said.

But two minutes later he launched into a long tirade about everything from sunspots to geomagnetic variables, though nothing he said in any way excused the dreadful failure that was evident. We had supplied generous quantities of wine as a preliminary to the meal and as a general anesthetic for the occasion, hoping that when the food arrived Borga would be silenced. No luck. He continued on through mouthfuls of scaloppine and pasta.

All the dowsers who were tested had failed. The two who "found" natural water disagreed spectacularly, and those who found no water disagreed too. All had had positive dowsing reactions and were certain

Mr. Senatore, using his twisted piece of cane, concentrates mightily—and "bombs out."

they were correct, but actually they had detected nothing at all. All had considerable reputations as successful dowsers, yet all asserted that this was the first time they had undergone a test that was controlled and could be checked thoroughly for correctness! Only a method similar to the one I designed could settle the matter once and for all. Their first and only proper tests had proved the subjects did not have the ability to dowse. Yet I am quite sure that these people *still* claim they are dowsers. Incredible? Yes, but typical.

Before we leave the subject, it is well to report that one Michele Giovannelli of Genoa, author of various books on parapsychology that he believes make him an ally of mine, offered to perform endless wonders for me if I would meet a long list of *his* conditions for the tests. He wanted, among other things, to have a group of specialized scientists and clergymen present, and some impossible circumstances he insisted were essential. Mr. Giovannelli was answered several times. I told him that when I put up *my* money, *I* make the rules. He responded by claiming my prize money by default. This behavior makes no sense by normal standards, but in paranormal terms it is quite logical. Piero Angela

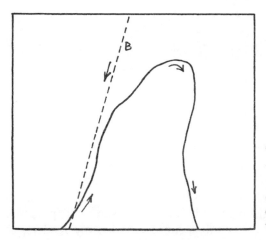

The path traced by Senatore. He was able to make only one attempt due to lack of time. He crossed the actual water path only once, and was going the wrong way.

warned me not to say anything about this man, since he would use it in some way out of context. Well, let him try this: Michele Giovannelli has offered to do the usual nutty run of demonstrations that are the stock-in-trade of the "psychics." If he can do so, let him stop talking and get on with it. He says, for example, that he can tell me the color of a book just by feeling its surface. Okay, Michele, do it to a statistically significant degree, and I'll hand you the check for $10,000. But—and this goes for the dozens of other "psychics" who have been filling my files with endless correspondence and no action—*get on with it.* I have put my money where my mouth is. You can ask no more.

The challenge is clear: Put up or shut up.

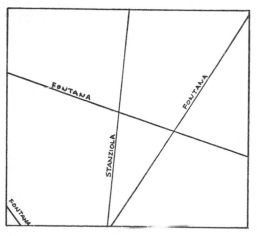

Only two dowsers, Fontana and Stanziola, decided there was any "natural" water on the site. Thus they disagree with the other two, who said there was no such water there. As seen in this diagram, Fontana and Stanziola even disagreed with each other about where this water was.

Epilogue

The tumbrels now stand empty but ready for another trip to the square. Candidates seem to be in endless supply. As for my readers, of whatever opinion they may be, my writing of this book was dictated by a feeling that I *had* to tell what is here revealed. I believe every word of it to be true and you have read what I believe to be adequate proof. Parapsychology is a farce and a delusion, along with other claims of wonders and powers that assail us every day of our lives. Knowing what I do, and holding the opinions that I do, has not made this world any the less exciting and wonderful and challenging for me, nor should it for you. On the contrary, to know that you are an individual not put here for some mysterious reason by some supernatural means, and that you are not protected by unknown powers or beings; to know that you are a product of millions of experiments in the evolutionary process and not the result of a seed thrown on this planet by extraterrestrials—that, to me, is *very* exciting. I am a responsible member of a race that reached out into space and walked on the moon, folks! In a small way I also walked there, and so did *you*. And I'm thrilled about it!

Throw away the Tarot deck and ignore the astrology column. They are products offered you by charlatans who think you are not the marvelous, capable, independent being you are.

Nonsense has reigned too long as Emperor of the Mind. Take a good look. The Emperor has no clothes!

Appendix

Hollywood has the Oscar, television performers their Emmy, and the recording industry the Grammy. I felt that it was only fair to create a suitable award for the billion-dollar business that has earned its fair share of the world's income. Parapsychology is the respectable front of the fortune-tellers, gypsies, quacks, pseudoscientists, and charlatans who labor to produce miracles and hide behind this foggiest of all philosophies. Therefore I present my personal annual award, known as the Uri (in honor of a former "psychic" superstar whom you may remember) and given in four categories on the first of April each year.

The categories are:

1. To the Scientist who says or does the silliest thing relating to parapsychology in the preceding twelve months.
2. To the Funding Organization that supports the most useless parapsychological study during the year.
3. To the Media outlet that reports as fact the most outrageous paranormal claim.
4. To the "Psychic" performer who fools the greatest number of people with the least effort in that twelve-month period.

Such periodicals as *Fate* magazine do not qualify for category 3, since it is conceivable that their editors actually *believe* what they print and so cannot be held responsible. However, *Fate* may come in for honorable mention as a result of a particularly imaginative conception.

The trophy consists of a stainless-steel spoon bent in a pleasing curve (paranormally, of course) and supported by a base of plastic. Please note that the base is flimsy and quite transparent.

I am personally responsible for the nomination of the candidates. The sealed envelopes are read by me, while blindfolded, at the official announcement ceremony on April 1. Any baseless claims are rationalized in approved parapsychological fashion, and the results will be published

The annual "Uri Award" in parapsychology.

immediately without being checked in any way. Winners are notified telepathically and are allowed to predict their victory in advance.

It is about time that parapsychology is recognized for what it is. The Uri Award is a step in this direction.

Winners for 1979 were:

• Professor William Tiller, of Stanford University, who said that, even though the evidence for psychic events was very shaky and originated with persons of doubtful credibility, it should be taken seriously *because there is so much of it.*

• The McDonnell Foundation, who gave $500,000 to Washington University, St. Louis, to study spoon-bending children.

• Prentice-Hall and American International Pictures, for *The Amityville Horror,* labeled "A True Story."

• Philip Jordan, who was hired by Tioga County (New York) Public Defender R. L. Miller to assist in choosing jurors by viewing their "auras."

Winners for 1980 were:

• Isaac Bashevis Singer, for declaring belief in demons.
• The Millennium Foundation, who gave $1 million to parapsycho-
logical research. (In 1982, the award was withdrawn when the foundation
decided, instead, to invest the million in a "psychically discovered oil site.
It was dry.)
• The "That's Incredible" TV show, for declaring a simple magic
trick, since admitted as such by the performer, James Hydrick, to be
the real thing.
• Dorothy Allison, the housewife/psychic who was called to
Atlanta, Georgia, to solve a string of murders. She failed to do anything but "showboat" around town, giving the police *42 different
names* for the murderer, and was sent home.

Winners for 1981 were:

• Charles Tart, parapsychologist, for discovering that the further in
the future events are, the more difficult it is to predict them.
• The Pentagon, for spending $6 million on a project to determine if
burning a photo of a Soviet missile would destroy it.
• TV station KNBC, Los Angeles, for accepting the Tamara Rand
hoax as the real goods without troubling to check it.
• Tamara Rand, who claimed she had predicted an assassination
attempt on President Ronald Reagan months before the event; she actually did it 24 hours *after*.

Selected Bibliography

I have compiled this bibliography with a view to acquainting the reader with what I consider to be some of the more blatant examples of promotion of the paranormal, and also with skeptical analyses of alleged supernatural phenomena.

PERIODICALS

Pro-paranormal

Fate. Curtis Fuller, ed. 500 Hyacinth Place, Highland Park, Illinois 60035. $10/year.

Anti-paranormal

The Skeptical Inquirer. Journal of the Committee for the Scientific Investigation of Claims of the Paranormal, Box 229, Buffalo, New York 14215-0229. $20/year.

BOOKS

Pro-paranormal

Cayce, E. V., and H. L. Cayce. *The Outer Limits of Edgar Cayce's Power.* New York: Harper & Row, 1971.

Doyle, Arthur Conan. *The Coming of the Fairies.* London: Hodder & Stoughton, 1921. Reprint. New York: Weiser, 1975.

Eisenbud, Jule. *The World of Ted Serios.* New York: William Morrow & Co., 1967.

Fuller, John G. *Arigo: Surgeon of the Rusty Knife.* New York: Thomas Y. Crowell Company, 1974. London: Hart-Davis, MacGibbon, 1975.

Gardner, Edward L. *Fairies.* London: Theosophical Publishing House, 1945.

Geller, Uri. *My Story.* New York: Praeger, 1975.

Krippner, Stanley, and A. Villoldo. *The Realms of Healing.* Millbrae, Calif.: Celestial Arts, 1976.

Panati, C., ed. *The Geller Papers.* Boston: Houghton Mifflin Company, 1976.

Puharich, A. *Uri.* New York: Doubleday, Anchor Press, 1974.

Taylor, John. *Superminds.* New York: Warner Books, 1975.

Thommen, George. *Is This Your Day?* New York: Crown Publishers, 1964.

Vandenberg, Philipp. *The Curse of the Pharaohs.* New York: J. B. Lippincott Company, 1975.

Wilson, Colin. *The Geller Phenomenon.* London: Aldus Books, 1976.

Anti-paranormal

Angela, Piero. *Viaggio nel Mondo del Paranormale.* Rome: Aldo Garzanti Editore, 1978.

Barrett, Stephen, and Gilda Knight, eds. *The Health Robbers.* Philadelphia: G. F. Stickley Co., 1976.

Bok, Bart, and L. Jerome. *Objections to Astrology.* Buffalo: Prometheus Books, 1975.

Christopher, Milbourne. *ESP, Seers & Psychics.* New York: Thomas Y. Crowell Company, 1970.

———. *Mediums, Mystics & the Occult.* New York: Thomas Y. Crowell Company, 1975.

Cohen, Daniel. *The New Believers.* New York: M. Evans & Co., 1975.

Condon, E., et al. *Scientific Study of UFO's.* New York: Bantam Books, 1969.

Crosby, Jan. *Sannheten om Uri Geller.* Osol: Bjornsen & Schram, 1974.

Dingwall, E. J., and Harry Price. *Revelations of a Spirit Medium.* London: Kegan Paul, 1925.

Evans, Bergen. *The Natural History of Nonsense.* New York: Alfred A. Knopf, 1946.

———. *The Spoor of Spooks and Other Nonsense.* New York: Alfred A. Knopf, 1954.

Evans, Dr. Christopher. *Cults of Unreason.* London: George G. Harrap & Co., 1973.

Fair, Charles. *The New Nonsense.* New York: Simon & Schuster, 1974.

Gardner, Martin. *Fads & Fallacies in the Name of Science.* New York: Dover Publications, 1957.

———. *Science: Good, Bad and Bogus.* Buffalo: Prometheus Books, 1981.

Goldsmith, D., ed. *Scientists Confront Velikovsky.* New York: W. W. Norton & Co., 1977.

Hansel, C. E. M. *ESP: A Scientific Evaluation.* New York: Charles Scribner's Sons, 1966. 2d ed., rev. Buffalo: Prometheus Books, 1980.

Houdini, Harry. *A Magician Among the Spirits.* 1924. Reprint. New York: Arno Press, 1972.

Jerome, L. *Astrology Disproved.* Buffalo: Prometheus Books, 1977.

Kammann, R., and D. Marks. *The Psychology of the Psychic.* Buffalo: Prometheus Books, 1980.

Keene, M. Lamar. *The Psychic Mafia.* New York: St. Martin's Press, 1976.

Klass, Philip. *UFO's Explained.* New York: Random House, Vintage Books, 1974.

Kovoor, Dr. Abraham. *Begone Godmen!* Bombay: Jaico Publishing House, 1976.

Kusche, L. *The Bermuda Triangle Mystery—Solved.* New York: Warner Books, 1975.

MacDougall, Curtis D. *Hoaxes.* New York: Dover Publications, 1958.

Mackay, Charles, LL.D. *Extraordinary Popular Delusions and the Madness of Crowds.* London: 1841. Reprints. Wells, Vermont: Fraser Publishing Co., 1963. New York: Farrar, Straus & Giroux, 1970.

Majax, Gérard. *Le Grand Bluff.* Paris: Fernand Nathan, 1978.

Menzel, D., and E. Taves. *The UFO Enigma.* New York: Doubleday, 1977.

Mulholland, John. *Beware Familiar Spirits.* New York: Charles Scribner's Sons, 1938.

Nolen, William A., M.D. *Healing: A Doctor in Search of a Miracle.* New York: Random House, 1974.

Perera, Ramos. *Uri Geller—Al Descubierto.* Madrid: Sedmay Ediciones, 1975.

Proskauer, Julien. *The Dead Do Not Talk.* New York: Harper Bros., 1946.

Randi, James. *The Magic of Uri Geller.* New York: Random House, Ballantine Books, 1975.

Rawcliffe, D. *Illusions & Delusions of the Supernatural and the Occult.* New York: Dover Publications, 1959.

Ridpath, Ian. *Messages from the Stars.* New York: Harper & Row, 1978.

Sagan, Carl. *Broca's Brain.* New York: Random House, 1979.

———. *The Cosmic Connection.* New York: Doubleday, 1973.

———. *The Dragons of Eden.* New York: Random House, 1977.

———. and Thorton Page. *UFO's: A Scientific Debate.* New York: W. W. Norton & Company, 1972.

Seabrook, W. *Doctor Wood.* New York: Harcourt, Brace & Co., 1941.

Sklar, Dusty. *Gods & Beasts.* New York: Thomas Y. Crowell Company, 1977.

Smith, Richard F. *Prelude to Science.* New York: Charles Scribner's Sons, 1975.

Standen, A. *Forget Your Sun Sign.* Baton Rouge, Louisiana: Legacy Publishing Co., 1979.

Story, Ronald. *The Space-Gods Revealed.* New York: Harper & Row, 1976.

Taylor, John. *Science and the Supernatural.* New York: E. P. Dutton, 1980.

Thiering, B., and E. Castel, eds. *Some Trust in Chariots.* New York: Popular Library, 1975.

Vogt, E. Z., and Ray Hyman. *Water Witching, U.S.A.* Chicago: University of Chicago Press, 1959 and 1979.

Ward, Philip. *Common Fallacies.* Cambridge, England: Oleander Press, 1978.

White, Peter. *The Past Is Human.* New York: Taplinger Publishing Co., 1974.

Wilhelm, John L. *The Search for Superman.* New York: Simon & Schuster, Pocket Books, 1976.

Index

(Numbers in *italics* denote illustrations)

335